A Cultural History of Dress and Fashion
General Editor: Susan Vincent

Volume 1
A Cultural History of Dress and Fashion in Antiquity
Edited by Mary Harlow

Volume 2
A Cultural History of Dress and Fashion in the Medieval Age
Edited by Sarah-Grace Heller

Volume 3
A Cultural History of Dress and Fashion in the Renaissance
Edited by Elizabeth Currie

Volume 4
A Cultural History of Dress and Fashion in the Age of Enlightenment
Edited by Peter McNeil

Volume 5
A Cultural History of Dress and Fashion in the Age of Empire
Edited by Denise Amy Baxter

Volume 6
A Cultural History of Dress and Fashion in the Modern Age
Edited by Alexandra Palmer

A CULTURAL HISTORY OF DRESS AND FASHION

VOLUME 6

A CULTURAL HISTORY OF DRESS AND FASHION

IN THE MODERN AGE

Edited by Alexandra Palmer

Bloomsbury Academic
An imprint of Bloomsbury Publishing Plc

B L O O M S B U R Y
LONDON · OXFORD · NEW YORK · NEW DELHI · SYDNEY

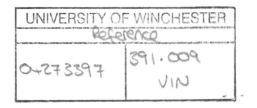

Bloomsbury Academic

An imprint of Bloomsbury Publishing Plc

50 Bedford Square	1385 Broadway
London	New York
WC1B 3DP	NY 10018
UK	USA

www.bloomsbury.com

BLOOMSBURY and the Diana logo are trademarks of Bloomsbury Publishing Plc

First published 2017

© Bloomsbury Publishing, 2017

Alexandra Palmer has asserted her right under the Copyright, Designs and Patents Act, 1988, to be identified as Editor of this work.

British Library Cataloguing-in-Publication Data

A catalogue record for this book is available from the British Library.

ISBN: HB: 978-0-8578-5602-9
         HB set: 978-1-4725-5749-0

Library of Congress Cataloging-in-Publication Data

A catalog record for this book is available from the Library of Congress.

Cover design: Sharon Mah
Detail of zipper vest by Maison Margiela, 1998.
Gift of Ms. Marlene Mock. Photo: Royal Ontario Museum © ROM,
with the permission of Maison Margiela © Maison Margiela

Typeset by RefineCatch Limited, Bungay, Suffolk
Printed and bound in Great Britain

CONTENTS

List of Illustrations   ix

Introduction   1
Alexandra Palmer

1   Textiles   21
Susan Ward

2   Production and Distribution   43
Véronique Pouillard

3   The Body   63
Adam Geczy and Vicki Karaminas

4   Belief   85
Susan J. Palmer and Paul Gareau

5   Gender and Sexuality   107
Annamari Vänskä

6   Status   131
Jane Tynan

7   Ethnicity   151
Simona Segre Reinach

8   Visual Representations   171
Rachael Barron-Duncan

9   Literary Representations   191
Irene Gammel and Karen Mulhallen

Notes   211
Bibliography   235
Notes on Contributors   255
Index   259

LIST OF ILLUSTRATIONS

INTRODUCTION

0.1 Two-piece woman's day suit (wool crepe tabby, 1 percent nylon), designed by Azzedine Alaïa, France (Paris), F/W 2003–4.   3

0.2 Cotton knit T- shirt as high fashion by Maison Margiela, sold with how to wear instructions, c. 2000.   4

0.3 *Robe de minute*, Paul Poiret, 1911.   6

0.4 1972 fashion illustration by Antonio Lopez, of Charles James' spiral wrap around "taxi" dress that was sold at Best & Co. 1933–4.   7

0.5 In 1964 the monokini, a topless bathing suit, was designed by American, Rudi Gernreich.   8

0.6 Jean Paul Gaultier's T-shirt and dress screened on nylon net with Jean Fouquet's *Virgin and Child Surrounded by Angels*, produced by Fuzzi Spa, Italy, 1994.   10

0.7 Model Iman, designer Calvin Klein, and socialite Nan Kempner, both in trousers, attending *Fete de Famille II* AIDS Benefit, on October 1, 1987, New York City.   12

0.8 Lowri-Ann Richards pregnant in the summer of 1995 wearing Vivienne Westwood toga dress (F/W 1982–3) at her farm in Wales.   13

0.9 Woman's jacket and asymmetrical over-vest worn by poet Karen Mulhallen, of wool twill, cotton tabby and twill, horsehair interlinings and linings, Comme des Garçons, 1999.   16

0.10 Digitally printed *Imperial Watersleeve* gown by Vivienne Tam, Fall 2011 collection. The design references Qing court costume.   17

0.11 IZ Adaptive leather jacket designed for ease of dressing when using a wheelchair (2014).   20

CHAPTER 1

1.1 Loose-fitting suits of wool or silk jersey were a trademark of Paris couturier Gabrielle "Coco" Chanel, seen here wearing a geometrically patterned example from the mid-1920s.   25

1.2 The introduction of Lastex inspired the development of glamorous novelty fabrics for swimwear, such as the glossy stretch satin worn by Hollywood film star Esther Williams in a publicity photograph, 1944.   26

1.3   This 1954 dinner ensemble by Paris couturier Christian Dior, made of
      crush-resistant nylon and rayon velvet, exemplifies the highly structured
      silhouette of the 1950s.   29

1.4   This 1966 mini-dress and jacket by couturier André Courrèges shows his
      innovative use of dense, heavy fabrics and topstitching to emphasize
      the structure and clean lines of his garments.   32

1.5   Numerous designers experimented with vinyl (PVC) and other
      "space age" materials during the 1960s. This 1969 ensemble of
      wool and quilted PVC was designed by couturier Pierre Cardin.   33

1.6   Flowing jersey knit was a staple fabric of the 1970s for both day
      and evening wear. The fabric for this 1974 gown by American
      designer Chester Weinberg was made of DuPont's Qiana nylon.   35

1.7   The unstructured wool and linen suits popularized by Italian
      design Giorgio Armani in the 1970s and 1980s played an important
      role in the revival of natural fibers in fashion.   38

1.8   The permanently pleated, heat-set polyester garments created by
      Japanese designer Issey Miyake, such as this "flying saucer" dress from
      1994, challenged traditional distinctions between textile and garment.   40

CHAPTER 2

2.1   French stylist Paul Poiret's models at the seaside, in the fashion
      magazine *La Gazette du bon ton*, 1920.   44

2.2   *At the Milliner's*, painting by Edgar Degas (1882–before 1905).   46

2.3   Edward Steichen photograph of evening dresses by Madeleine Vionnet
      for *Vogue*, 1930.   48

2.4   Lace dress with large shoulder bow by Hattie Carnegie, January 1934.   50

2.5   1959–60 toile (muslin) coat by Castillo for Jeanne Lanvin, Paris sold to
      an American manufacturer for copying.   53

2.6   Four pairs of fashion and work wear jeans for men and women, made by
      Canadian manufacturer's J.P. Hammill & Son, and Wrangler, c. 1960–75.   57

2.7   Paul Shakespeare in 1972 wearing a suit by John Warden, for manufacturer
      Bagatelle purchased in the Canadian boutique, Le Château.   58

2.8   A model presents a creation by Japanese designer Rei Kawakubo
      for Comme des Garçons during the Spring/Summer 2012
      ready-to-wear collection show, October 1, 2011, Paris.   60

CHAPTER 3

3.1   Gabrielle Chanel. Evening dress. Black silk satin and ecru alençon
      lace, c. 1926.   66

3.2 Leni Riefenstahl. Naked discus thrower in Classical pose, scene from
Leni Riefenstahl's film *Olympia*, part 1: "Festival of the Peoples," 1936. 68

3.3 Olympische Spiele 1936 in Berlin-Turnerin, Bild aus Riefenstahls
Olympia-Film. 69

3.4 Christian Dior evening dress of machine lace, chiffon tape, tulle, 1957.
Anne Fogarty silk jacquard taffeta evening dress, c. 1954. 71

3.5 Cary Grant—Schauspieler, GB/USA in "Nur meiner Frau zuliebe." 73

3.6 Cary Grant (born Alexander Archibald Leach), with Randolph
Scott (front) in their house in Santa Monica. 74

3.7 André Courrèges. Mini-dress. Light gray wool, c. 1968. 76

3.8 Trimfit pantyhose. Blue nylon pantyhose in cardboard packaging. 1967–8. 77

3.9 Diane Von Furstenberg. Wrap dress. Multicolour printed acrylic knit. 1973. 79

3.10 Jean Paul Gaultier. Dress. Orange shirred velvet, 1984. 82

CHAPTER 4

4.1 Noble Drew Ali's Moorish Science Temple Conclave, Chicago, 1928. 87

4.2 African Rastafarian, c. 1990. 88

4.3 Crowning of his holiness the Messiah Hamsah Manarah in Castellane,
France, on March 1, 1991. 90

4.4 The King Messiah in the Mandarom Shambhasalem Monastery,
Castellane, France on March 1, 1991. 90

4.5 Portrait of Yahweh leader Yahweh ben Yahweh, December 1986. 92

4.6 Uriel, cosmic visionary and co-founder of the Unarius Educational
Foundation, in the Flame Room, 1980s. 94

4.7 Doukhobor nude protest, January 1, 1930. 100

4.8 Raël, the leader of Raëlian sect ready to perform human cloning experiment
at a press conference in Tokyo, Japan, April 4, 2002. 103

4.9 GoTopless, a group associated with Raëians help a protest against
not getting a permit to be topless on Ashbridges Beach, Toronto, 2011. 104

CHAPTER 5

5.1 Actress Ina Claire wearing a herringbone tweed skirt and jumper by
Chanel, *Vogue*, 1924. 109

5.2 Man's two-piece wool leisure suit with knickerbockers, c. 1920, as worn
by the Prince of Wales (left) and the Duke of York (right). 110

5.3 Young woman on a bicycle, wearing a three-piece Aquascutum trouser
suit, October 1939. 112

5.4   French fashion designer Christian Dior arranging one of his evening
      dresses. Paris, mid 1950s.   114

5.5   A man wearing a smoking jacket from Christian Dior's collection
      at the Dior Men's Boutique in Paris, 1955.   116

5.6   Models wearing clothes by Mary Quant at the Carlton Hotel,
      August 15, 1967.   118

5.7   Transvestite superstar Jackie Curtis photographed in 1970, the
      year Curtis began filming *Women in Revolt*.   120

5.8   Sid Vicious, Vivienne Westwood, and punks in audience at a
      Sex Pistols gig, November 15, 1976.   121

5.9   Jean Paul Gaultier. Man skirt, Paris, c. 1987.   123

5.10 A New York billboard displaying Kate Moss for Calvin Klein, shot by
      photographer Steven Meisel.   125

5.11 The new millennium has seen the rise of children's high fashion.
      All the major brands have their children's lines, New York, 2010.   127

5.12 Clothing does not only make gender, it makes the human. In 2010s,
      fashion's search for ever-new markets is going to our pets. Fashionable
      clothing for lap-dogs sold in a specialized boutique, Tokyo, 2014.   128

CHAPTER 6

6.1   The Royal Family watch the annual Trooping the Colour ceremony
      at Horse Guards Parade, London, June 13, 2015.   132

6.2   A fashion show at Centrum Warenhaus department store at
      Alexanderplatz in East Berlin, April 1974.   133

6.3   American feminist, journalist, and political activist, Gloria Steinem
      (left) with art collector Ethel Scull and feminist writer Betty Friedan
      (lower right) at a Women's Liberation meeting at the home of Ethel
      and Robert Scull, Easthampton, Long Island, New York, August 8, 1970. 135

6.4   The pinstripe suit is emblematic of upper class power.   136

6.5   Fashion clearly identifies age and gender, 1940s.   138

6.6   A white-collar worker stands with a blue-collar worker at an office, c. 1940.   139

6.7   School uniforms worn by students at the Liceo Diurno Avenida
      Independencia (Chile) March 2008.   140

6.8   A foreign detainee is walked by two US Army MPs at Guantanamo
      Bay, Cuba, in March 2002.   141

6.9   Past and present members of the Irish Guard on parade in Whitehall,
      London, March 15, 1965.   142

6.10 Shop display window, East Berlin, Germany, c. 1960.   147

6.11 A group of punks in London, late 1970s.   149

CHAPTER 7

7.1 A model presents a hanbok, traditional Korean dress, during a fashion show in Hanoi, September 8, 2013.   152

7.2 A model walks the runway during the Stella Jean show as a part of Milan Fashion Week Womenswear Spring/Summer 2014.   155

7.3 *High Heels* Dutch Wax style printed cotton factory cloth for East African fashion market, 2005. CHA Textiles (Hong Kong) founded United Nigerian Textiles Ltd. (UNTL) in 1964 in Nigeria and has factories in Ghana.   157

7.4 A model presents a creation by Pakistani designer Sarah Gandapur during Bridal Couture Fashion Week in Karachi, June 2015.   159

7.5 A pair of young women in a crowd of hippies dance at an outdoor event, late 1960s or early 1970s.   162

7.6 An Indonesian Muslim woman fits a headscarf or hijab at Indonesia Moslem Fashion Expo, 2013.   164

7.7 *Deese* "goddess" sandal by John Galliano for Christian Dior Spring/Summer 2009, prêt-à-porter collection.   167

7.8 Model wearing a Krel Wear hijab during Miami Fashion Week Funkshion Fusion 2005, Florida.   169

7.9 An Indian woman combines her sari with a sweater in February 2015.   170

CHAPTER 8

8.1 Baron Adolph De Meyer. Elsie Ferguson in a Callot gown. *Vogue* [New York], February 1, 1921 p. 40.   173

8.2 Edward Steichen. Marion Morehouse wearing a dress by Chéruit and jewelry by Black, Starr and Frost. *Vogue* [New York], May 1, 1928, p. 64.   175

8.3 George Hoyningen-Huene. Models wearing dresses by Germaine Lecomte and Callot Soeurs. *Vogue* [New York], May 15, 1932, p. 48.   177

8.4 Horst. Mrs. Leo (Edwina) d'Erlanger wearing a dress by Alix. *Vogue* [New York], February 15, 1936, p. 43.   178

8.5 Martin Munkacsi. Lucile Brokaw. *Harper's Bazaar*, December 1933, pp. 46–7.   180

8.6 Jean Shrimpton in dress by Pierre Cardin, Paris, January 1970. Photograph by Richard Avedon © The Richard Avedon Foundation.   182

8.7 Helmet Newton. Verushka, Nice, 1975.   184

8.8 Bruce Weber. Tom Hintinhous for Calvin Klein, on a billboard in Times Square, New York City, October 1982.   185

8.9 Mario Sorrenti. Kate Moss for Calvin Klein on a bus panel, defaced, 1994.   187

8.10 Audience members use smartphones and cameras to photograph the
     Hervé Leger by Max Azria fashion show during Mercedes-Benz
     Fashion Week Spring 2015, New York. September 6, 2014.   188

CHAPTER 9

9.1 Design for a Poiret-style empire waist evening gown by Paris couturier
     Jeanne Paquin, 1911.   194

9.2 Claude McKay in Paris c. 1930, dapper and formal in a suit and
     dress coat, a testament to his sartorial versatility.   196

9.3 Recruitment poster for female land-workers during the First
     World War, showing the functional, masculine uniforms worn by
     the "land girls."   198

9.4 F. Scott Fitzgerald, an icon of jazz-age style, 1925.   199

9.5 Romaine Brooks's self-portrait, showing her signature top hat, 1923.   200

9.6 Dancer and choreographer Desiree Lubovska wearing a dress of
     georgette crepe decorated with bands of cock feathers in front,
     designed by Jean Patou, 1923.   202

9.7 Audrey Hepburn as Holly Golightly, in a promotional photograph
     for *Breakfast at Tiffany's*, 1960.   203

9.8 Sean Connery as James Bond in *Goldfinger*, 1964.   205

9.9 Dishevelled and rumpled, the notorious silver-screen movie star
     Frances Farmer smokes a cigarette, 1943.   208

9.10 Robert Mapplethorpe photograph of Patti Smith, 1975.   209

Introduction

ALEXANDRA PALMER

Fashion from the First World War to the present day is a cacophony of styles, looks, peoples, and technological wonders. It records an exponential expansion of markets and ways of manufacturing that continue centuries-old craft traditions and push new boundaries. Today, clothes are transformed into body wearables, wirelessly connected to us so that, in real time, they sense and adjust to our physical change in heart rate and body heat, and we transform into cyborgs. Fashion is mercurial. It annoys, supports, disappoints, saddens, and gladdens our lives in the day to day. The look or smell can evoke powerful memories and imaginings. Its importance is repeatedly highlighted in formal and informal social rites from birth to death. It embraces the symbols of art, taste, power, gender, and status.

A Cultural History of Dress and Fashion in the Modern Age maps key developments in fashion that make up a plurality of fashions. It collapses and brings together rich histories by viewing the subject as through a kaleidoscope. Each view is fractured, indicating more and more views that are limitless, because fashion has an intimate relationship to the artistic, physical, psychological, sociological, political, and technological, and is so intertwined that writing a "complete" history is impossible. This is what makes fashion history so interesting—and difficult—to study.

The complexity and fickleness of fashion has inspired many to try to harness this beast through rational analysis in order to understand what makes fashion tick, how it works, shifts, and why we care and participate. Looking at, talking, and writing about fashion has never been as discussed as it is today. The Internet and social media are filled with images, discussions, and opinions of fashion given by authoritative fashion professionals, independent writers, bloggers, and social media that constantly critiques "friends'" clothes, while dressing up and posting selfies is a form of entertainment and on-going self-fashioning.

Fashion history is now transformed from the illegitimate or ugly stepchild of university art history or history courses into fully-fledged under graduate and graduate programs. There is a burgeoning list of academic books and journals that specifically address fashion. Museums regularly mount large, attractive exhibitions that can even be profitable and are held in the main galleries.[1] Theories of fashion are old, but the numbers of writers theorizing and recording fashion has exploded in the late twentieth century. Traditionally, "serious" studies tended to be categorized by discipline and were the purview of professional males in academe. George Darwin, son of Charles, developed an evolutionary theory about the function of male dress related to mobility and self-protection, and pointed out the contrasting frivolity and "instability" of women's dress.[2] Flügel's theories of shifting erogenous zones were developed by Bergler's "independent clinical investigation" based on Freudian psychoanalysis to prove that clothes are a masculine invention thrust upon women to assuage "man's unconscious reassurance against his own repressed fears of woman's body."[3] He determined that there are "sartorially speaking—no 'tasteless' women, only neurotically inhibited ones," and went on to critique homosexual fashion creators who were women's "bitterest enemies" and responsible for the "fashion hoax" that addressed women's fears and punished them.[4]

The disciplines which fashion encompasses are wide and include art, design, economics, sociology, psychology, psychiatry and philosophy. Sarah Fee has mapped anthropologists "on-gain, off-again interest in dress and fashion" and also points out that their conclusions are influenced by the nationality and cultural biases of whom ever is doing the writing.[5] The study of fashion is eminently suitable for a multidisciplinary magpie approach that offers up new ideas and understandings. This is reflected in the work by leading scholars, and the essays in this volume. Drawing upon as many disciplines as needed helps to explain fashion in new ways, making for a more nuanced study. One of the interesting aspects about this project is that it has necessitated inviting scholars who do not usually focus on fashion to apply their insights to the field. Their frequently highlight ideas that are under-represented in fashion studies. This volume with its intertwined themes is a synopsis of fashion studies now.

But with all the rationalization, examination, and historification of fashion it is easy to forget that our original interest stems from personal engagement with it. The ephemeral aspects of fashion are hard to record—the sound, smell, and touch—and explains why James Laver's book, *Clothes,* was part of the Pleasures of Life Series. The significance of this volume is that it is a reminder of the complexity of the subject and examines why fashion gets under our skin, in both positive and negative ways.[6]

The modern age covers many key themes in which fashion plays an integral role in society. This includes the on-going debates about women's hemlines or whether trousers or skirts are appropriate for women or men. Along with this goes the transformation of the body and an increasing focus on athletics, youth and health that is connected to our understanding of gender, race, as well as the secularization of society at large, and the dynamics of the individual over groups. Jeans have completely transformed from their roots, as laborer's working dress, to a global, unisex uniform. Jeans are an integral garment in the democratization of fashion in terms of price and access and linked to the escalation of production, not only in the numbers of units produced, but also the speed of fashion itself and its circulation, that is more complex than it has ever been. Today we are witnessing a complete transformation of the fashion system that may even not be sustainable. The top down model is obsolete as it is fact that social media can trump corporate marketing. Looking at the past may prove to be useful for the present.

Susan Ward's insightful chapter on textiles reveals the gaps in the field. Astonishingly, textiles are often completely absent from many discussions of fashion (Figure 0.1). The focus is usually on the design, the genius of the creator, the fantastic presentation of it on the runway, how it sells, or how someone looks in the clothes. Even museum labels for fashion exhibitions tend to feature designer, date, nationality while the material is either ignored or included in the "tombstone," the section with donor credit and museum number, or else it is used as a finding aid to link label and object (i.e. red satin). Ward's essay provides an important corrective and demonstrates that frequently it is the textile and textile technology that either stimulates inventive fashion designs or makes the common or older styles that continue for years, *appear* to be new and of the season. Historically, textiles were the new fashion as styles changed slowly. Since the twentieth century, the pace of fashion change has escalated exponentially, making it hard to determine what is new. Even in 1913, a Torontonian remarked that the "dresses of the debutantes might easily have been 'hand-me-downs' from the coming-out of some older sister" if it were not that the materials were "obviously new."[7]

Textiles were instrumental in Chanel's extraordinary success, and it is questionable if we would know her name without the work of the textile designers and manufacturers in France, Switzerland, Italy, Scotland, and America. Her "come back," when she reopened

FIGURE 0.1: Two-piece woman's day suit (wool crepe tabby, 1 percent nylon), designed by Azzedine Alaïa, France (Paris), F/W 2003–4. Gift of Azzedine Alaïa. Photo: Royal Ontario Museum © ROM.

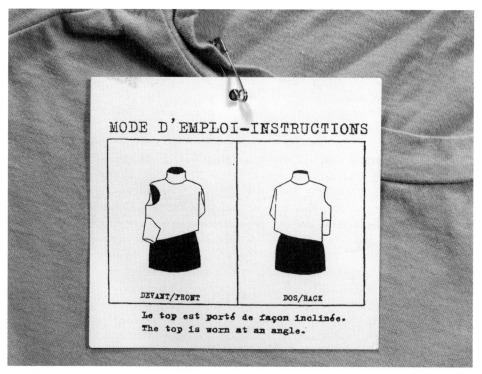

FIGURE 0.2: Cotton knit T- shirt as high fashion by Maison Margiela, sold with how to wear instructions, c. 2000. This acquisition was made possible by the generous support of the Louise Hawley Stone Charitable Trust. Photo: Royal Ontario Museum © ROM, with the permission of Maison Margiela © Maison Margiela.

the house in 1954, was secured with the clever use of innovative fibers, including nylon and later Lurex, and new weaves that ranged from nubby tweeds to complex knits. Chanel's little black dress (LBD) became a modern fashion Ford in the 1920s, and is still so today. It was named after the Model-T car that became an icon of mass production and capitalism. The same was also true of her relaxed suit with cardigan-style jacket and slim skirt. The LBD and the Chanel suit are two of the most copied fashions of the twentieth century. It can be argued that her success with these two styles was in fact because textile manufactures produced fabrics that were more modern than the actual fashion designs that were recycled again and again. It was the new weights, textures, colors, fiber, and weaving technologies and the incredible range in quality and price of the textiles, that made it possible for so many, world-wide, to profit from millions of spin-offs of Chanel styles at all price points.[8]

Ward discusses innovation but also regulations and trademarks that serve to create brands, control quality, and attract consumers. Copyrighting and protecting designs and brand is a recurring theme across this volume, as Véronique Pouillard also explains in the following chapter on production. Both touch on the significance of branding that is evidenced in the 1970s with cotton (Figure 0.2). Post-war man-made fibers were rejected in favor of the "natural" in fibers and colors. The success and renewal of the cotton industry was also linked to a renewed interest in the "natural" that was played out in physical fitness, body building, and the disco scene as is explained by Adam Geczy and Vicki Karaminas in their chapter on the body. Today the key issue is sustainability.

Innovation in textiles and cut was seminal to the "Japanese revolution" in the late 1970s and 1980s. Many of the authors in this volume discuss this fashion moment that changed the idea of the feminine and what constituted the modern. Miyake is central to this history and has collaborated with the leading textile engineers to push the boundaries of technology. Eiji Miyamoto for Miyake meddled with the binary possibilities of creating textile structures, by re-jigging the actual machines and coming up with new methods of weaving pattern. The resulting and alarming 1980s "deconstructed" "bag-lady"' fashions of Kawakubo and Yamamoto were adopted by the avant-garde. Its traces can be seen today in fast fashions. Nearly thirty years later, cheap clothes with unfinished seams and exterior details that previously would have been considered very shoddy goods, are marketed as synonyms for "cool" and "deconstructed."

Who controls the production and dissemination of fashion is the subject of Véronique Pouillard's chapter. In 2005, Vinken wrote that "the century of fashion is over: the very idea of Paris fashion is at an end—even an anti-fashion could not save it."[9] The Paris couture dress is a sign of high social status and elite conspicuous consumption, as Jane Tynan also points out, and is worn by celebrities, the newly rich, and a few left over aristocrats. Earlier in the century, couture was a requirement for the elite that served as a badge of entry to social functions.[10] Today, luxury brands are stronger, more centralized, and more diverse in products and distribution than ever. For instance, Christian Dior has flagship stores designed by leading architects that on the web-site show Dior-identified continents of Asia, Africa, Europe, Middle East, Oceania, and the Americas, as well as in locations that even ten years ago would seem more than unlikely—Russia, China, India and Kazakhstan. The global economy is fast and large, and fashion offers profits, authority, and diversity. The difficulty now is retaining any kind of exclusivity when access and price is, for so many, not an obstacle.

The initiative by Hedi Slimane for Yves Saint Laurent is a case in point. Slimane created an über-exclusive private line or club. The *New York Times* reported that it is for men and women, day and evening wear but only for "'friends of the house,' [and that] . . . Hedi Slimane decides these orders case by case." As the article notes, brands are making bespoke garments for celebrity clients part of their business so, "Why not make that official and call it what it is? Couture—just outside the official world of the French governing body." This is an interesting twist on exclusivity that seems to undermine the couture system by creating a higher, post-couture level. Slimane has created a new oligarchy where the designer has absolute control over clients and image. The only spokesmen for the brand are Slimane and Francesca Bellettini, the chief executive. The article concludes by asking: "Will positioning himself as the grand chieftain of deciding who gets to wear a YSL couture garment make Mr. Slimane, and his clothes, more attractive, or will it just make people mad?"[11]

Pouillard's discussion of the tangible (garments, production) and intangible (ideas, creativity, design) gets to the complexity of the fashion system. She maps out the diversification of the manufacturing and labor sector that today not only makes huge profits and losses but also continues the historical waste of materials and manpower, as the Shirtwaist Factory fire and Rana Plaza disasters so clearly bring home. Creativity is hard to measure and can be produced in different ways. For instance, new machines and systems can increase production and save time. But creativity can also be used to accelerate the time to make a garment, as in Paul Poiret's *Robe de Minute*, or for fast fashion. The time it takes to get dressed, or undressed, can also be measured, as Charles James did with his "taxi" dress with three closures, and cut in a spiral, making dressing and undressing simple when seated in a moving vehicle (Figures 0.3 and 0.4).

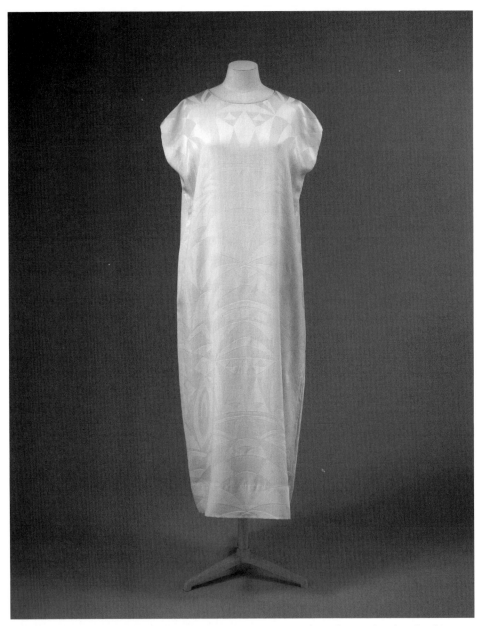

FIGURE 0.3: *Robe de Minute*, Paul Poiret, 1911. Hand-sewn figured satin, lined with silk chiffon. Photo: © Victoria and Albert Museum, London.

Pouillard outlines the complex and numerous types of organizations that control and create fashion systems and values, and questions who has control over what. Fashion ecosystems have now proliferated. The establishment of Paris, in the nineteenth century, as the epicenter for fashion has become destabilized as new fashion cities emerge with strengths in design and/or manufacturing so that now there are over 130 fashion weeks held around the world.

FIGURE 0.4: 1972 fashion illustration by Antonio Lopez, of Charles James' spiral wrap around "taxi" dress that was sold at Best & Co. 1933–4. Photo: Chicago History Museum/Getty Images.

Simona Serge Reinach's chapter on ethnicities offers more understanding of how the Western concept of fashion versus costume, or traditional dress emerged and underscores the significance of geography and location when discussing fashion. She raises discussions of race and whose body is being considered fashionable. The body is a mutable cultural construct that is linked to issues of labor, class, and status.

Adam Geczy and Vicki Karaminas engage us in the unobtainable metastable body, and point out there has "never been as much variation [in the body] as in the twentieth and twenty-first centuries" (p. 63) and that the body ideals are not gendered but for all sexes. The manipulation of the body with shaping structures, bodybuilding, diet, and surgery is integral to the creation and quixotic character of fashion, and part of the suspicion, fantasy, and allure associated with it. From the mature Edwardians, to the 1920s and 1960s androgyny, through to the present porno-body ideal, all are versions of a modern body. Today our bodies are also recorded as never before, on selfies and YouTube home-made videos that log the embarrassing and the ideal, a point taken up in Rachael Barron-Duncan's essay on representation.

Camouflaged or clothed bodies are as significant as the body naked, or partly dressed (Figure 0.5). What parts of the body are revealed and concealed, and how those parts are shaped or toned, constructs fashion. At different times different body parts are foregrounded and sometimes are contentious. The problem of women's legs is a recurring theme, whether accentuated by "masculine" trousers, or "feminine" loose harem-style *jupes culottes* of Poiret (taken from Middle Eastern chalwar), or hot pants, mini-skirts and Spandex leggings. Each example clearly identifies the fashion culture of the period, and all depend on context. This is highlighted by Lawrence Langer's comment that during the Cold War, Russians were obsessed with feet and shoes, and he pointed out that, "Moscow is the city where, if Marilyn Monroe should walk down the street with nothing on but shoes, people would stare at her feet"[12]

FIGURE 0.5: In 1964 the monokini, a topless bathing suit, was designed by American, Rudi Gernreich. Photo: Paul Schutzer/The LIFE Picture Collection/Getty Images.

The emphasis and look of the physical body changes with time and can signal rebellion, modernity, political action, social enfranchisement, or concern with health. The recreation of versions of the classical antique Greco-Roman body is pronounced in the modern age and the shifting sands of what is construed as "healthy," that includes the Aryan-Nordic ideal and the 1929 Men's Dress Reform Party. Geczy and Karaminas trace the history of the athletic body from its turn-of-the-century roots, through to the twenty-first century. They seize on key moments to explain, for instance, the post-war ideals of the tough, outdoorsman, the Marlboro Man, and the bachelor, characterized by Gary Cooper and later James Bond. These types are also discussed in terms of sexuality, representation, and literature later in this volume. The gym body has produced entire industries from clothing, equipment, classes, and dietary regimes to individual trainers and Internet programs, such as the *Yoga with Adriene* series. Reshaping the body is a continual science experiment, from hair to makeup, musculature, and creating new enhancements for both sexes. The phenomenal success of Spanx for men and women is a case in point.[13]

New scientific methods, including chemicals and surgery, have pushed how we measure gender, age and aging, and status, all issues that intersect with other chapters. The cult of the toned and youthful body has changed our understanding of young and old and fashion. *Vogue* now includes sections on women in their twenties, thirties, forties, fifties, sixties, seventies and up, that are promoted as stylish role models. This is also the case for older, gray-haired men, who are hot fashion models because of the age demographic of baby boomers. Today, Mick Jagger at seventy plus is still a sex symbol.

Advertisements and fashion designers have broadened the boundaries of who and what is fashionable in size including *zaftig* Sophie Dahl. But any fashion can be too much of a good thing and the thin body of the 1920s, 1960s, and the heroin chic of the 1990s was a backlash to the investment in the time and finances needed to acquire a muscular body. These super-thin bodies were made by natural youth, drugs, cigarettes, bulimia, sex, and partying. Even though *Vogue* announced in 2012 that it would not use photographs of models under the age of sixteen, or images of models that look as though they have eating disorders, the magazine and fashion industry perpetuates and relies upon the cult of young and thin, as Geczy and Karaminas explain in the discussion of the modern porn body.

Jean Paul Gaultier has perhaps been the most significant fashion designer to continually push the boundaries of what is the correct body size and issues of gender within the fashion industry by showing this collections on non-traditional models who are "normal" people, to make the point about fashion being for all—however you want it and whoever you are.[14] This is taken up by Annamari Vänskä in her section on gender and sexuality. Geczy and Karaminas bring us to the present writing that the body is now a "new masculine and feminine body ideal, one that does not equate beauty with biology and gender, rather the condition of . . . shifting possibilities" (p. 83) (Figure 0.6).

Fashion historian James Laver noted that, "moralists . . . have usually denounced clothes not because their wearers found no pleasure in them but because they found too much. Clothes . . . ministered to the lust of the eye, and the pride of life."[15] The morality of fashion is often defined by religious belief. At the end of the millennium, fashion designers looked to mainstream religions for design inspiration. Some of the borrowings were graphic, such as oversize bejeweled crosses, and examples abound from couture to T-shirts. Sometimes the "borrowings" were contentious as was Jean Paul Gaultier's *Rabbi Chic* Fall-Winter 1993 collection that raised opposition from the Hassidic community who regard their dress as a key component of their faith. At other times, it was interpreted

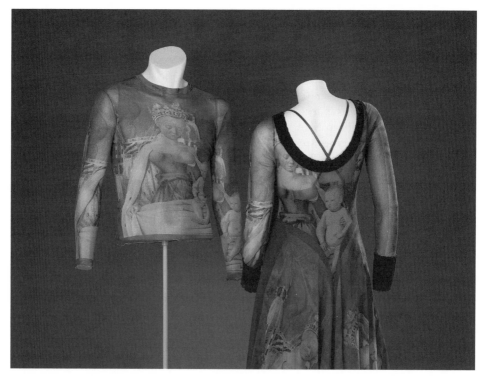

FIGURE 0.6: Jean Paul Gaultier's T-shirt and dress screened on nylon net with Jean Fouquet's *Virgin and Child Surrounded by Angels*, produced by Fuzzi Spa, Italy, 1994. Gifts of Christopher Estridge and Karen Mulhallen. Photo: Royal Ontario Museum © ROM.

as naughty and playful as John Galliano's couture pope ensemble in Dior's *haute couture* Fall-Winter 2000–1 collection.

But what Susan J. Palmer and Paul Gareau describe is how newly formed religions in the modern world harness fashion to further their beliefs and identity. They focus on examples of newly invented fashions created by New Religious Movements (NRMs) and analyze why their dress operates as "flash points" that gets under the skin of mainstream society. The described micro-societies in NRMs undermine and depopulate the mainstream religions that are found lacking for contemporary needs and thought. They are significant because, as with other "subcultural" groups such as of mods, punks, or hippies,[16] whose dress is well studied, they are, as S.J. Palmer and Gareau say, "almost parodies of the multicultural and multifaceted experiments in fashion found in twentieth century 'mainstream', secular society" (p. 86).

The NRM fashions are both traditional and eclectic. The classic symbols of religious paraphernalia include the crowns of Mandarom, or the wedding dresses employed by the Army of Mary, or the use of traditional nineteenth-century folk dress that is worn as a statement of Old World values by the Doukhobor. These spiritual symbols represent what Laver called the "Hierarchical Principal," an anthropological distinction of rank and authority through clothing. Tynan also describes this as a sign of status and a clear way for order within a church, or other groups as diverse as businessmen, prisoners, or punks. Explored is the quasi-monastic-Barbarella space age look of Raël and his Angels, who await brethren from outer space, who could also be mistaken for a Cosplay convention ensemble, or the too-flashy dress of the "pretender" Yaweh ben Yaweh ben Yahweh, whose frock coats could be worn by a Motown artist. Their clothes are suspect and used as evidence of the inaccuracy and falsity of their beliefs, because fashion is an easy and familiar target for discrediting people as incorrect, deviant, dirty, or unconventional—in whatever culture it is measured. The fashions are seen as code for threatening the majority. But, as Arnold writes, "Who is to say when . . . dress is 'suitable'?"[17] as the debate over the burkini illuminates.

Fashion is our second skin and this volume describes many ways and reasons for protecting, hiding, and showing it. One of fashion's central roles in the modern age is to disguise our daily decline, or maybe it is indeed one of its paramount duties. Bergler even suggests that women's fashion is an "improved skin."[18] Several authors in this book flag the importance of understanding naked. The problem of being naked, or in an "unnatural" state in a "civilized" society, relies upon the binary of naked and clothed.[19] If naked were a fashion it would not be remarkable, but it is because it denies fashions artifice and role of socio-cultural identification, as S.J. Palmer and Gareau point out.

In the case of the Doukhobors, their naked protest was due to the enforcement of laws that went against their beliefs. The public and press took notice because the majority is clothed. Naked is linked to the original sin in the Christian doctrine, but also seeing too much flesh, let alone all of it, was a moral affront, inappropriate and ugly: it was NOT fashion. The image of Doukhobors as vulnerable, nude people—not athletes or models— was a shocking contrast from seeing them in quaint nineteenth-century historically-located rural dress. Their nakedness is not that of Classical high art, it is not glorified and not mediated. It is far from the Greco-Roman ideal that Geczy and Karaminas describe as a nostalgic and moral ideal, but it is a political tool. The Doukhobors' tired and very middle age skin is all too human. Naked in this context is a reminder of our mortality and the very body that fashion seeks to hide, enhance, and glorify, and it is unsettling because it is a harsh fact of who and what we really are—mortal.

Just as fashion is a flash point for religions, so it is too for gender. Fashion is one of the most distinctive markers of gender and sexuality that is applied as soon as a child is born. As Annamari Vänskä describes, gender is socially constructed. Clothes disturb when they appear to blur the sexual and social roles and throw convention on edge. Thus, the modern 1920s flapper, who was the antithesis of the pre-First World War shapely Edwardian woman, was seen as an entirely new woman with revealed legs, flat chest, and short hair. She was physically mobile as Western women had never been before, and was thought to be more easily sexually available in her short dress. The same anxieties of promiscuity were raised in the 1960s with the adoption of the mini-skirt that came in tandem with the Pill.

This brings us back to another the contentious garment: trousers for women. In the late 1960s, New York socialite Nan Kempner, was refused entrance to La Côte Basque, an exclusive restaurant on West 55th Street, because she did not meet the dress code. She was wearing the latest couture fashion, an Yves Saint Laurent trouser suit. She circumvented the dress code by taking off the trousers, so her ensemble with long tunic jacket became a mini-skirt.[20] The mini-skirt that revealed legs to the crotch was acceptable while a much more body covering, but "threatening," masculine trouser was not. This scenario may seem ridiculous today, but it speaks volumes about society's understanding of women's place that crossed all levels of income, even the very rich and famous (Figure 0.7).

The inverse is men in skirts, the focus of an exhibition, *Bravehearts: Men in Skirts,* at the Metropolitan Museum of Art (MMA) in 2003, sponsored by Jean Paul Gaultier. It

FIGURE 0.7: Model Iman, designer Calvin Klein, and socialite Nan Kempner, both in trousers, attending *Fete de Famille II* AIDS Benefit, on October 1, 1987, New York City. Photo: Ron Galella/WireImage.

looked at designers and individuals who have appropriated the skirt "as a means of injecting novelty into male fashion, . . . transgressing moral and social codes, and . . . redefining ideal masculinities."[21] The exhibit title played upon the popular 1995 film, *Braveheart*, starring Hollywood-approved manly-man, Mel Gibson, along with a large cast of other actors as tough thirteenth-century Scots, all in kilts. However, perhaps the more interesting aspect was played out in real life with the 100 Men March by the Male Unbifurcated Garment Movement. They did not march far, a couple of blocks from the Guggenheim to the MMA, and attracted no hecklers. A reporter disparagingly wrote, "Consider the plight of the man who wears a skirt. Schoolchildren snicker as he passes. Construction workers give him grief. Perfect strangers assume the right to criticize his wardrobe. He might be fired. He might be beaten up. His wife might leave him for a man in slacks." However, despite the rather retro introduction to the article, the journalist was surprised that the march did not attract much attention, instead revealing that in 2004 men in skirts was not much of an issue in a large metropolis.[22]

Other aspects of male dress—jackets, tailoring with padded shoulders—were appropriate for wartime from the Second World War to Vietnam and became associated early on with dandy lesbians. Too "feminine" garments, that can include color and texture as Ward notes, were associated with homosexuals. But, as Vänskä writes, these stereotypes were constructed by sexologists in the interwar period, and that the male body is mirrored by the female body and both fluctuate between hard and soft. The post-First World War masculine fashion for soft and draped textures and relaxed designs such as sweaters and unstarched collars can be considered effeminate. It is a look that Mulhallen and Gammel identify in their discussion of *The Great Gatsby* [1925].

The fusion of fashion, street culture, and music is the culture of the time as Angela McRobbie has identified[23] (Figure 0.8). The "artificial" gender bending of the late 1970s

FIGURE 0.8: Lowri-Ann Richards pregnant in the summer of 1995 wearing Vivienne Westwood toga dress (F/W 1982–3) at her farm in Wales. Photo: courtesy of Lowri-Ann Richards.

and 1980s is seen in the stage and day clothes of David Bowie, Marc Bolan, and Boy George. The rebellious casual fashions of teenagers—jeans and T-shirts, and even leather jackets— that emerged in the 1950s was tied to the rise of rock 'n' roll. Michael Jackson, from the 1980s onwards, relied upon fashion to blur gender and racial lines. The significance of Madonna's book, *SEX*, and her Jean Paul Gaultier S&M corsets and lingerie worn in her 1990 *Blonde Ambition* tour are now legendary, so much so that new versions were made for her *MDNA* 2012 tour. The significance of these fashion movements are further discussed in the following chapter on status. Vänskä concludes with ideas about the "posthuman phase" where children and pets are interchangeable in diminutive ensembles. Designers, such as Alexander McQueen and the work of Iris van Herpen whose "textiles" are extruded plastics, are confusing the traditional boundaries of gender, sex, and clothes only for humans.

Power is status, as Jane Tynan explains, is inextricable from fashion and it is complex. Anything can be imbued with status as long as there is an approved common cultural understanding of the criteria. To understand this it is helpful to look at the classic iconic fashions from couture to jeans and uniforms, and Tynan discusses what kind of status is conveyed and examines structures of power related to these fashions. The power of fashion marks identity and conveys class, economic position, group identity, role, gender, and politics. Distinction in dress, even so-called subcultural style, is one of its central and potentially democratic functions, even though we speak of blue- and white-collar workers who are still clearly defined by dress. Tynan shows how jeans, originally a working man's dress for hard labor, have morphed into leisurewear and designer wear, as has workout clothing. Sneakers have their own complex culture and can be worn for high performance athletics, street wear, and dressing up.

Understanding the role of uniforms is a complex and intriguing labyrinth and Tynan's discussion shares many strands with other authors in this book. The power of a uniform clearly signals group affiliation and rank that can be positive or negative. Here the examination of Fascist and communist uniforms ties in with the body as highlighted earlier, and the politics of fashion are foregrounded. Tynan also looks at social groups according to age, including children's fashions that are less studied. As she points out, today children's wear is a large fashion market that is broken down by small age groups with specialty lines. A parent can even make purchases for the entire family within one stand-alone shop, such as the GAP. Previously, this was only possible in large department stores and entailed visits to individual departments on separate floors and areas. This highlights how the process and meaning of conspicuous consumption has changed over time.

In the twentieth century, the old hierarchical class system, based on birthright, broke down. There is now a fantastic diversity of possible fashions available due to the new incredible volumes of clothes and enormous price range. The dissemination of fashion in the post-war period is both top-down and bottom-up. Along with this came unprecedented access to fashion and the choice from a huge stylistic range, from couture-inspired to fast fashion, second-hand, vintage, and ethical fashion. Consumption has never been so easy and available due to modern systems of industrial transportation and now post-industrial Internet and drones. The "value" of fashion derives from communal social recognition of the fashion, whether it is the logo, textile, or cut. Fashion relies upon readily identifiable identities, and status is constructed in a myriad of ways including by style, brand affiliation, and profession— there are innumerable ways to define group identity, and fashion plays a central role.

Discussing the roots, concepts, and fictions of ethnicity in fashion, Simona Segre Reinach offers several important correctives when discussing modern fashion. A central difference is how clothes are made and worn. Western tailored fashions are considered more modern and "civilized" than draped clothing by Western colonialists. Draped clothing is not fixed and is remade each time it is worn. A length of cloth is versatile. It crosses cultures and genders. It can be a headscarf, shawl, a partial or whole body wrapper such as a sarong, lunghi, or sari. Western tailored clothing is fixed. It is made from cloth that is cut, reassembled, and sewn to be worn only one way. It is limiting as it is made to fit a certain body proportion if ready-to-wear, or an individual if couture or custom tailored. Simmel was specifically referring to Western tailored clothing when he explained that fashion is a civilizing force that marks our progress and improvement[24] (Figure 0.9).

Thus the colonial project has created Western "'fashion" versus "costume," or ethnic authentic regional dress. As Reich writes, this is a culturally constructed division between the West and the Rest in a search for cultural authenticity that singles us out from others. Clearly, dress in any culture is not fixed as change produces fashion yet the West has perpetuated a romantic orientalist fantasy of frozen ethnic fashions that are "authentic," by rejecting any attempt to understand difference. The important point is that meaning is dependent on context, and scholars need to be careful when identifying fashion strategies. For instance, there are many interpretations of the veil that can be seen as a sign of rejecting secular modernization or community and/or religious belonging, and it is both and more and specific. The colonial history of Western fashion and describes the East–West and North–South history, and differences. How this debate has been shaped is important in order to study contemporary fashion/s that is a mélange of all cultures. This can be seen in 1960s hippie fashions that borrowed "ethnic" garments from around the world, to the 1980s Japanese designers who showed in Paris. As Reich notes, the current global community of fashion is reflected in the culturally diverse students studying in fashion schools internationally.

Hybridity, or cultural appropriation, is an old language used to create modern fashion, but employing it can be contentious. Our histories and cultures are composed of continual cultural exchanges that continue to create new products and ideas (Figure 0.10). The potent, highly reflexive, and fickle fashion world treads a slippery slope of cultural appropriation that is highlighted by world politics. In New York, Miguel Adrover was hailed as a new design star presenting a global fashion fusion and even used second-hand materials. His Fall 2001–2 collection, *Meet East*, shown in February 2001, featured long Middle-Eastern kaftans, headscarves, and shawls on androgynous male and female models. It was "a full-fledged Middle Eastern collection . . . staged in an incense-drenched market-turned-tent, included everything from floor-length caftans and coats worn with turbans and chadors to blazers with harem pants and jodhpurs, layered printed tunics and jet-black robes."[25] One journalist said that the key to his success was "his ability to appropriate diverse cultural elements to create something utterly new. While most native New Yorkers develop early on a talent for deciphering stereotypes and social codes, Adrover knows that, sometimes, it is the foreigners who ultimately get it right."[26]

However, judgment of right and wrong is at the heart of fashion journalism and that Fall, his Spring 2002 collection, *Utopia* about an "ethnic journey," was shown a day before the Twin Towers attack on September 11th. This time his fashions were interpreted as "righteous dressing. His models came out mostly covered head to toe, in dull caftans and stern pantsuits, and while the workmanship was beautiful and obviously costly, the effect of such enforced modesty was deadly. He is right to express individuality, but to take his themes from countries where woman have few rights, whether in the Middle East or Latin America, squeaks of being earnest."[27] What Adrover intended was "an exploration of rustic ideals of Old Spain colliding with modern dress. As documented by the media, it

FIGURE 0.9: Woman's jacket and asymmetrical over-vest worn by poet Karen Mulhallen, of wool twill, cotton tabby and twill, horsehair interlinings and linings, Comme des Garçons, Japan, 1999. Gift of Karen Mulhallen. Photo: Royal Ontario Museum © ROM.

FIGURE 0.10: Digitally printed *Imperial Watersleeve* gown by Vivienne Tam, Fall 2011 collection references Qing court costume. Gift of Vivienne Tam. Photo: Royal Ontario Museum © ROM.

was a romantic take on Taliban culture—already topical anathema days before Americans were attacked on their own turf. It was bad timing," Adrover admits. "People got it confused. And I suffered for it. I was investigated by the CIA. I thought New York was about people coming together; suddenly, we all took ten steps back in our personal freedoms."[28] Soon after, Adrover lost his backing and left the fashion world. Thus Middle-Eastern styles and influences at one moment were exotic and attractive, and a few months later became politically charged, identified with terrorists and un-American. The language of cultural appropriation and exchange is fraught with political, racial, religious, and social entrapments as well as being a rich, and fruitful path for building global communities. Reich concludes, "authentic" fashion takes place in the present and has to be evaluated and understood as such, however complicated the exchanges.

The power of fashion magazines, visual representation and the presentation of fashion is examined by Rachel Barron-Duncan who traces technological advances and how photographers, magazines, advertisement, film, and video respond to new tools and create theatrical and hyper-real effects. The modern age shifts between the presentation of fashion as faithful, real life images that clearly document clothes, to images where the fashions themselves are unreadable in favor of capturing a mood, or dream of fashion that may not even include the product. The still portrayal of the body changed for one in movement that was a modern way suitable to show the concept of sportswear and active wear. The action shots of the 1960s became so classic that they are still emulated today. The trope of the modern, artistic photographer, captured in Antonioni's movie *Blow Up* (1966), also persists as a modern version of the artist as fashionable role model. The studio photographs of the 1960s conflated the portrait with fashion, and vice versa, creating a new fashion world and visual language. The power of photography to intimidate, glorify, document, and comment was brilliantly explored by Helmet Newton whose images elide with film as the viewer builds a story about the scene depicted that implies a before and after scenario.

The public face of fashion exploding onto billboards and moving on buses within cities has created a world of pervasive fashion marketing. Barron-Duncan's discussion of Calvin Klein's underwear ads by Bruce Weber, on the beautiful male body of the toned pole-vaulter, was astonishing at the time. This was not only because of the scale of the billboard in Times Square, but also because of the overt glorification of the male body in a public space, no longer sequestered as gay porn or a timid page in *GQ*. This theme is central to our age and is reiterated in the chapters on the body and gender. The acceleration and ease of digital photography and its distribution has transformed our visual world, and as Barron-Duncan says, has "de-centralized" us from the formal and former medium of print and film. The fashion show now is just as much about who is present as the clothes themselves. The selfie has become its own genre of photography along with its new accoutrement, the selfie-stick. Barron-Duncan concludes that the new focus is on the "fact of fashion, rather than its fiction" (p. 189).

The text of fiction and fashion in the modern age is also the subject of Irene Gammel and Karen Mulhallen's elegantly-written chapter on the significance of fashion in literature that captures the sensual importance of fashion that so evocatively conjures up character and mood. Gender, status, sexuality, image making, morality, consumption, textiles, and style are all interwoven in literature. This chapter reminds us of the ephemeral understanding of textiles, correct dress, class, and gender in fashion and etiquette.

Fashion is a marker of who you are—insider, outsider—and your place in society. It reinforces and betrays. Gammel and Mulhallen note that it exposed Gatsby, "the self-made man, as a social outsider in Daisy's world of old money" (p. 198). The significance of wearing black is brought out by Isherwood's Sally Bowles whose choice of black fashions denoted her as bohemian, and also described by Hemmingway who employed Chanel's LBD as the style of modernity and sexuality. Gammel and Mulhallen point out that to get fashion right is one thing, but to get it wrong sends another message. Thus Holly Golightly's irreverent and socially incorrect riding attire causes confusion. But a modern reader might not understand this. What Capote described could now be construed today as cool, grunge, original, and make her an "It" girl, but the point in the novel was not that at all, as Gammel and Mulhallen explain. Thus learning about context, history, manners, and social appearance is central to understanding fashion, as the authors point out, when reading older novels. Young historians need to be aware of these nuances.

The artistic, and deliberate use of fashion as a reflection of authenticity is explained by Patti Smith's original choice of the "backward look," in vintage dresses and her appreciation for patina. Smith's creative and irreverent use of second-hand male and female clothing was part of the bohemian circle she lived in and fashion plays an important part of her autobiography. The overlapping issues of gender, crossdressing, masculinity, and femininity are entangled, or can be overtly simple as explained in the discussion of James Bond. This can be read with Geczy's and Karaminas's examination of the post-war bachelor and the tough and rugged outdoorsman, and Vänskä's playboys. Gammel and Mulhallen continue by critiquing *American Psycho* (1991) that is a staggering litany of branded goods and dovetails with the discussion of the postmodern body and sexuality. Clearly, literature is a treasure-trove for fashion studies that is only beginning to be tapped, as fashion is central to describing public and private histories and our imaginings of the past, present, and future.

So what does the future of fashion hold and what are key areas for research and experimentation? Julia Twigg writes that age is a neglected social category and that what constitutes "old" varies across history and cultures.[29] The legal system is confusing and shifts on what constitutes adult and child, while the fashion market is constantly seeking new segmented markets. One group not embraced by the fashion industry is those who use wheelchairs due to injury, disease, and age. We live in a time with a huge population that is aging and whose fashion needs have not been addressed. Canadian designer Izzy Camilleri's, IZ Adaptive clothing, offers a corrective. The line has affordable and fashionable garments for a seated clientele and includes jeans, pants, shirts, and dresses, and extends to suits, wedding dresses, and leather jackets. The designs look conventional but are revolutionary in cut to accommodate a seated, not standing, L-shape body. The problems of sitting in traditional clothing have been addressed and Camilleri has removed ugly bunched fabric at the tummy, corrected the cut of pants so they don't ride down at the back, and made seated hemlines level. She has reduced these fashion problems by talking to users and then employing clever, non-traditional pattern making. These fashions are transformative and give power to the wearers who are at the margins of design and speaks to many of the issues discussed in this volume (Figure 0.11).

The perennial million-dollar question, "What is the next big fashion or trends of the future?" cannot be answered. As Langer wrote in 1959, "Prophecy is always dangerous, yet in the matter of the future of clothing we have a long past and a vivid present to aid us in arriving at our conclusions." He predicted that in the near future geriatric clothing with "bulging, sponge-rubber appurtenances" would be developed for extreme old age that would enable the elderly to literally bounce back from a fall. He also commented on

FIGURE 0.11: IZ Adaptive leather jacket designed for ease of dressing when using a wheelchair (2014). Photo: Izzy Camilleri/IZ Adaptive.

men's wear possibilities but then wrote, "But who dares to prophecy the trend of women's future fashion?"[30]

If we knew the answers we would not be writing and reading this book, but making billions. However, even if we still cannot predict the future, we do know, and this volume clearly underscores the fact, that fashion matters, that fashion is complex, powerful, and is here to stay because of its flexibility and portability. It is almost too easy to make a statement—dressed, undressed, and in between. Today, the key issues of ethical and practical sustainable fashion are increasingly being addressed and encompass the entire fashion cycle from production to distribution and consumption. Yet we are still very far from a fashion system with zero waste. How we manage our varied and racially-mixed bodies, and how we cope and understand age, and access healthcare that includes fashions that assist us, remains to be seen. The global age connects us to others but it also serves to disconnect and fragment us as so many groups and nations strive to clearly mark their identity through the powerful tool of fashion.

Studying fashion offers tremendous insights into where we are and what we think at any particular time and place. By understanding its complexity, society's biases and by looking in a three-way mirror and seeing multiple views, we can become more insightful into our world and better understand our place and differences with more curiosity, empathy, tolerance and pleasure.

CHAPTER ONE

Textiles

SUSAN WARD

The relationship between textiles and fashion in any era is complex, multi-layered, and constantly changing; this was particularly true during the twentieth century, which saw sweeping cultural, economic, and industrial changes worldwide. With this larger context in mind, this chapter discusses broad trends in textile manufacture and use for fashionable clothing worn during the twentieth century. Highlighted are the moments when trends changed direction, or new trends emerged. I draw on existing studies of the artistic, economic, technological, and cultural changes affecting the use of textiles in fashion.

As someone who grew up learning to sew garments and visiting fabric stores during the "fiber wars" of the 1970s, I have also taken a more pragmatic approach. For each period I have asked simple questions about the kinds of textiles available and the kinds of garments that were constructed. What were the most important new kinds of fibers, fabrics, and finishes? What new silhouettes or kinds of garments did those textiles make possible, and/or did they change existing styles? And from the garment/fashion point of view, what new silhouettes, approaches to using fabrics, or wardrobe needs were introduced? What kinds of textiles did those new styles require, and what textiles were developed in response?

The answers to these questions require an understanding of the ever-shifting interplay between design innovation and style leadership, scientific and technological innovation, and economic, lifestyle, and geopolitical developments. Addressed are questions of availability, of style, aesthetics, and performance—what textiles can do, and what they are asked to do, and how that changed over the century.

What emerges is often surprising. First, many of the familiar fashion milestones appear to be "missing" from this history. This is not because they were unimportant, but because they were not primarily about innovative textiles or textile use. For example, exaggerated shoulders were a near-universal feature of women's fashionable clothing from the mid-1930s through the 1940s, but the style was not associated with any particular kind of textile. This look could be, and was, easily achieved using traditional construction methods, in the fabrics already in use, from stiff woven wools to fluid rayon crepe. Second, developments across the century seem to tell two overarching stories. The proliferation of man-made fibers, the so-called "fiber revolution," transformed both the fiber and textile industries, as well as wardrobes worldwide. It set in motion processes and debates that continue into the twenty-first century. Coinciding with this revolution was the rise of knitwear and knitted textiles. The development of knitting, as Schoeser has noted, "has been responsible for the most striking and fundamental changes in textiles and clothing" over the last several centuries. Much of this change took place during the twentieth century, and an estimated one in five garments worn today is knitted or made of knit fabric.[1]

Fashion textile innovations and influences come from many sources, as the textile and fashion industries comprise a vast, interactive, and highly structured system. There are many ways in which "new" textiles and looks can be created and popularized. The fashion leadership of Paris *haute couturiers*, for example, depended upon textile manufacturers continually developing new designs, colors, structure, and texture. The manufacturers in turn relied upon well-developed networks of fiber manufacturers, spinners, dyers, and printers to produce new textile effects, and relied upon the couture designers to create garments that showed off their textiles to best advantage.[2] Although few consumers could afford the highly publicized, combined fashion-and-textile creations of the Paris couture, they were important trend-setters for both fashions and textiles. Similar dynamics between designers and manufacturers played out at all levels down the fashion chain, and continued as other style sources began to supplant the couture. The designers and companies mentioned in this discussion are exemplars; they were not the only innovators or important contributors at a particular time but were chosen because they exemplify a trend, or were particularly innovative in their use of textiles.

INTER-WAR: 1918–30s

The Rise of Man-made Fibers and Modern Textures

The years of the First World War brought tremendous changes to world economies and industries, and marked a turning point in the history of man-made fibers. Before the war, Germany was the leading producer of synthetic dyes. On March 1, 1915 the British instituted a blockade on German ports. World access to the best coal-tar dyes and other chemical products was cut off. As Field and Blaszczyk have discussed, the "dye crisis" that followed was especially disruptive to manufacturers in the United States, with its highly developed textile industry.[3] The dye shortage, along with wartime needs for products such as medicines and explosives, spurred on the rapid establishment of the American chemical industry, and laid the groundwork for the production of man-made fibers on an industrial scale.

Before the twentieth century, virtually all textiles were made of mechanically processed yarns from plant and animal fibers. The most commonly used natural fibers for clothing are cotton and linen, processed from plants; wool, cashmere, and other animal-hairs; and silk, obtained from the cocoons of silk worms. The term "man-made," or "artificial," is used to describe a fiber that is not found in nature, although some are chemically derived from natural materials. Such fibers are usually created using a chemical solution or liquid from which fibers or filaments can be drawn or spun.

The first successful man-made fibers were invented in the nineteenth century and were developed from cellulose, a natural polymer found in plant materials such as wood pulp. Called "cellulosic" or "semi-synthetic" fibers, they include viscose (also called viscose rayon, or simply rayon) and acetate (cellulose acetate), also marketed under the trade name "Celanese." Synthetic fibers, by contrast, are not derived from natural materials, but are made by building up (synthesizing) complex chemical structures from simpler chemicals. The first of these was nylon (also known as polyamide), introduced in 1938. Other synthetic fibers that have been important for fashion textiles include acrylic and polyester.[4]

Man-made fibers derived from cellulose were already the basis of successful industries in European countries before the war, but American manufacturers had been suspicious of them, and were highly successful in the production and use of cotton, wool and silk.

This situation changed rapidly after the war. In the early 1920s, the US chemical corporations that manufactured so-called "artificial silk" (renamed "rayon" in 1924) became major players in the American textile industry. Man-made fibers gained increasing acceptance through the 1920s, largely driven by the market research and promotional efforts of major fiber manufacturers such as E.I. du Pont de Nemours and Company (DuPont) in the US, and Courtaulds in the UK.[5] In the US, rayon and acetate had previously been used primarily as a cheaper substitute for silk in hosiery and knitted goods, or blended with natural fibers. The appearance of all-rayon fabrics toward the end of the decade paralleled the growing importance of the ready-to-wear industry; as rayon was roughly one third the price of silk in the late 1920s, such fabrics appealed to price-conscious US garment manufacturers, and greatly expanded the range of "silky" garments available in the mass market.[6]

The shift from custom-made and home-sewn garments to ready-to-wear brought major changes at all levels of the fashion and textile industries.[7] Textile manufacturers, who had previously marketed their fabrics directly to consumers and dressmakers, were now relying on clients in the garment industry, and were under constant pressure to bring down costs.[8] Keeping the price of clothing low became even more important after the stock market crash of 1929 ushered in the Great Depression, resulting in the collapse of the American silk industry along with many other textile and apparel manufacturers worldwide.

Textured fabrics of all kinds also assumed new importance in fashion in the inter-war years. The 1915 dye crisis stimulated interest in new textures as a substitute for color and prompted manufacturers to experiment with undyed raw and wild (tussah) silk, an irregular, inexpensive fiber that had rarely before been used for high-fashion fabrics.[9] The resulting rough-textured silk fabrics, known as "sport silks," were in tune with the more practical mood of wartime fashion, and were produced in great quantities during the war.[10] The French luxury textile firm of Rodier was a major source of innovation in textured fabrics from the 1910s to the 1930s. Rodier's "kasha," a pebbly textured cashmere blend introduced in 1914, was durable and resilient but also soft, warm, breathable, and wrinkle resistant. It quickly became an international success, and a staple of the company's line in the decades that followed.[11] Kasha was originally intended for sports clothes, but by the early 1920s it and other rough-textured Rodier fabrics were adapted for winter suits, afternoon and dinner dresses.[12] By the middle of the decade, Rodier was also a recognized leader in the production of woolens and wool-blend fabrics with modernist geometric patterns and novel color effects.[13]

Rodier's textured and patterned woolens, along with traditional rough-textured, woven wools such as British tweeds, became increasingly popular for tailored dresses, suits, and coats through the late 1920s and into the 1930s. As the cut of women's garments became more complex, designers worldwide used such textiles to draw attention to the cut and to create subtle visual effects; London designers in the 1930s were particularly skillful in their use of striped and plaid woolens.[14]

Garments—Knits, Sportswear, and Silhouette

An important textile turning point for fashion came just at the outset of the war, with the introduction of jersey knit as a high-fashion fabric. Previously, wool and/or cotton jersey had been used primarily for underwear. This fashion innovation is generally credited to French couturier Gabrielle "Coco" Chanel. In 1914, she used wool and silk jerseys, many of them manufactured by Rodier, to create unstructured women's suits and loose pull-over sweaters, said to be inspired by the sweaters worn by fishermen and male polo players.[15] Chanel's designs were practical, comfortable and elegant, and well suited to the uncluttered aesthetic of the war years and the growing importance in women's wardrobes of sports clothing and so-called "spectator" sportswear (Figure 1.1).

By 1917, the name of Chanel was well-known on both sides of the Atlantic, and jersey had become a "classic" fabric for day dresses and tailored garments.[16] Knit fabrics would go on to assume even greater importance in wardrobes over the next century. Chanel's introduction of a utilitarian, "special purpose" textile into the vocabulary of fashion design also set a pattern that would be repeated by other designers, with other fabrics, in the decades that followed.

In addition to clothing made from knitted yard goods, hand- and machine-knitted sweaters became more widely worn by both men and women during the 1920s and 1930s. Couturier Jean Patou did much to popularize this fashion and was famous for the knit V-neck sweaters, matching cardigans, and bathing suits in bold geometric patterns and stripes he designed beginning in 1924. They were quickly copied, especially in the US, and helped to establish high-fashion knitting as a mass-market industry. Patou was also one of the first to realize the new importance of sports clothes, opening a sportswear boutique called "Le Coin des Sports" in his couture house in 1925.[17] Knitted wool tank swimsuits were worn by both sexes, and a sizeable industry, led by the American firm Jantzen Knitting Mills, grew up to produce fashionable styles for the mass market. Twin sweater sets, consisting of a fitted, short-sleeved crew-neck sweater and matching long-sleeved cardigan, became fashionable in the mid-1930s, and were a standard item in women's wardrobes for the next thirty years.

Paris couturier Elsa Schiaparelli's first collections under her own name in 1927 included hand-knitted sweaters that quickly helped to establish her reputation. The most famous of these was a *trompe-l'oeil* bowknot design that was widely copied by American and Austrian manufacturers.[18] Knitwear designers also looked for function and fashion in the dress of those in rural occupations and the clothing worn by professional athletes. Men's V-neck wool sweaters and sweater vests in Fair Isle and argyle designs along with heavy rib-knit cardigans, derived from those of fishermen and farmers in the north of Britain, became very fashionable for sporting clothes and informal sportswear. Fashion also adopted the cotton piqué sports shirts that were popularized in the late 1920s by tennis stars, such as the Frenchman René Lacoste.

Another turning point in fashion textiles came in the late 1920s and early 1930s, when longer skirts and more fitted silhouettes came into fashion. The waistline of women's clothes returned to the natural waist, and the boyish figure was replaced by a return to feminine curves. The cut of women's clothing became more complex, sophisticated, and close to the body, with the aim of creating a sculpted, streamlined look. The cut of these new garments, as couturier Jacques Heim expressed it in 1931, was to serve as both structure and decoration, eliminating the need for fussy details.[19] The use of fabrics cut on the bias was pioneered by Paris couturier Madeleine Vionnet in the early 1920s. The bias cut became widespread in all kinds of garments, and the most fashionable fabrics were those with a fluid drape, such as crepe, chiffon, and "transparent" (or chiffon) velvet. Fine silk jersey, arranged in neoclassical drapes and fine pleats, was the specialty of her fellow couturier Alix (later known as Madame Grès). Evening-wear fabrics, in particular, emphasized surface texture, and contrasts between shiny and matte surfaces; crepe-backed satin, which combined the two, was a favorite fabric of Vionnet, and was often used with the face and back sides juxtaposed.[20]

FIGURE 1.1: Loose-fitting suits of wool or silk jersey were a trademark of Paris couturier Gabrielle "Coco" Chanel, seen here wearing a geometrically patterned example from the mid-1920s. Photo: Sasha/Getty Images.

Textile Innovations of the 1930s

To a great extent the fitted silhouette of the 1930s was made possible by an important man-made yarn called Lastex introduced by the US Rubber Company in 1931. This was an elastic yarn consisting of an extruded rubber core covered in cotton, rayon, silk, acetate, or wool. It could be used in both knitted and woven fabrics, and was quickly adopted for use in girdles and other undergarments. Sleek foundations made of stretch fabric with Lastex replaced bulkier boned corsets, and contributed to the success of body-hugging designs cut on the bias.

The introduction of elastic yarns revolutionized the swimwear industry, and spurred on the development of a wide variety of waterproof novelty fabrics. Since California swimwear manufacturers formed promotional alliances with Hollywood studios and stars, these innovations even included producing overtly glamorous fabrics such as waterproof stretch velvets, and the rayon acetate and Lastex "sea satin" fabric used in BVD swim suits (Figure 1.2).[21] This was a time when fiber science, textile technology and fashion worked hand in hand to produce true innovation.

FIGURE 1.2: The introduction of Lastex inspired the development of glamorous novelty fabrics for swimwear, such as the glossy stretch satin worn by Hollywood film star Esther Williams in a publicity photograph, 1944. Photo: Eric Carpenter/John Kobal Foundation/Getty Images.

During the 1930s and early 1940s, rayon crepes and other fluid plain-weaves, both printed and plain, became a staple fabric for mass-market women's dresses. For the first time, man-made fibers began to make their way into textiles used for high-fashion collections, where keeping costs low was not a concern. Schiaparelli favored fabrics with unusual textures for her couture designs and early on adopted newly developed novelty fabrics such as a boldly crinkled "treebark" rayon crepe, introduced in 1934, and the brittle, transparent "Rhodophane" fabric that was developed for her by the textile manufacturer Colcombet. She used it for a "glass cape" the same year; such innovative fabrics were key to her avant-garde image.[22]

Undoubtedly, the most important textile development was the invention of nylon, the first truly synthetic fiber, announced by DuPont in 1938.[23] The first nylon products available to consumers, nylon stockings, were an overnight success. The new stockings were sheer, durable, could be heat-set to shape for an improved fit, and were welcomed as a means of reducing America's dependence on silk imported from Japan. About three-quarters of a million pairs were sold the first day they went on sale in May 1940.[24] DuPont built on this success to become a world leader in synthetic fibers after the war.

THE 1940s & 1950s—FIBER AND LIFESTYLE REVOLUTIONS

Wartime 1939–45

Changes in the use of textiles during the years of the Second World War were related to issues of availability: fashion fabrics, as with all textiles and raw materials, were in short supply worldwide. Purchases of new clothing and fabrics were discouraged and rationed. Patriotic public relations campaigns encouraged women to "make do and mend." Governments passed regulations such as the Utility scheme in the UK, and order L-85 in the US, intended to reduce the amount of vital materials that could be used in garment manufacture by setting limits on the length and width of skirts and jackets, and banning superfluous details such as extra pleats and pocket flaps.[25] Under these restrictions women's fashions took on tailored, slim lines, and emphasized simplicity and practicality rather than fussy details that required more cloth.

In the United States and most European countries, wool, silk, leather, and newly-developed nylon were reserved for military and defense applications. For civilian clothing, the most common substitute fiber used was rayon, but other novel materials such as aralac, made from milk protein, were also put into production. Meanwhile, man-made fiber manufacturers continued to develop new fibers and processes to meet military wartime needs for such materials as rot-proof Saran mosquito netting that was required in the South Pacific, and rip-stop nylon for parachutes. As the war drew to a close, these manufacturers, including the American companies DuPont and Dow Chemical, also devoted considerable energy toward developing new post-war markets for their products, setting in motion a synthetic fiber boom that would transform the textile industry worldwide.

Post-war Industrial Developments

After the war, Europe and Asia struggled to rebuild their textile and garment industries, while dealing with persistent shortages of raw materials and investment capital.[26] In the US, where conditions were considerably better, manufacturers quickly moved to take advantage of the new possibilities offered by the man-made "Fiber Revolution"—a term already in use by 1948.[27] Over the following two decades, new trademarked fibers, yarns, processes, and finishes appeared so rapidly that even many in the garment and retail trades seem to have found it difficult to keep abreast of new developments.[28] Manufacturers of these new, unfamiliar synthetic fibers, and in particular DuPont, mounted comprehensive promotional plans designed to create demand and provide technical and sales support at every step in the selling chain, from the spinning, weaving and knitting mills to the purchaser/wearer of the finished garment.[29] Similar campaigns were particularly important in Western Europe, where poor-quality rayon fabrics produced during the war had built up considerable consumer resistance to synthetic textiles.[30]

In some cases, industry promotions, and customer acceptance, centered on the aesthetic qualities or fashionable appearance made possible by a new material. The synthetic metallic thread Lurex, introduced in 1946, was lightweight, inexpensive, and washable, making fabrics with gold or silver threads much more practical and widely available. DuPont also emphasized the stylish appearance of fabrics made with their fibers by enlisting leading French couturiers to include them in their collections (Figure 1.3).[31]

More often, however, the primary selling point of a fabric or finish was the "high performance" quality of the new textiles: the ways in which they out-performed existing textiles in resiliency, durability, comfort, resistance to wrinkling, and, above all, ease of care.[32] These qualities were highly desirable at the time when there were fewer household servants. More consumers were washing and caring for their own clothes and sought liberation from the traditional drudgery of wash day. DuPont's Orlon, for example, an acrylic fiber introduced in 1948, made it possible to produce women's sweaters (including the ubiquitous twin sets of the 1950s) that felt similar to wool but could be washed without shrinking, while Dacron, a polyester fiber introduced by DuPont in 1951, was elastic and highly resistant to wrinkles. Both fibers, alone or blended with other fibers, could be heat-set for dimensional stability and permanently creased or pleated.[33] Between the early 1950s and the mid-1960s, several different resin finishes were developed that would give similar "wash and wear" properties to cotton fabrics, and make possible "permanent press" cotton dress shirts and wool trousers.[34] Lycra (Spandex), DuPont's trademarked stretch fiber introduced in 1958, was another breakthrough that would go on to transform the performance, comfort and ease of care of traditional fabrics and garments.

Garments—"New Look" Formality and Post-war Sportswear

Concurrent with the "Fiber Revolution," two major style trends influenced the direction of fashion textiles postwar. The first was associated with the fashionable silhouette of tightly-fitted waists and broad flaring skirts that came into fashion with Christian Dior's "New Look" collection in 1947. By the early 1950s, women's dresses and suits were more highly structured than they had been before the war. To create the shapes, more formal and often crisp fabrics such as taffeta, faille, tulle, brocaded silks, and heavy satins returned to fashion and replaced the fluid crepes of the 1930s. Woolen fabrics used for tailored garments changed less dramatically, but took on more body and structure than their pre-war counterparts. Nylon, acetate, and other new synthetic fibers that were light in weight, strong and resilient, were ideally suited to the new silhouette that was often formed with easy-to-care-for petticoats (or "crinolines") of nylon net as the foundation.

FIGURE 1.3: This 1954 dinner ensemble by Paris couturier Christian Dior, made of crush-resistant nylon and rayon velvet, exemplifies the highly structured silhouette of the 1950s. Photo: Hagley Museum and Library.

Men's suits did not change dramatically during this period, but could now be made "wash and wear" in synthetic blends and all-synthetic fabrics.

The second major post-war trend in fashion textiles was associated with the popularity of sportswear, and in particular the comfortable, casual styles promoted by pioneering American ready-to-wear designers. Beginning in the 1930s, Claire McCardell championed knit jersey through the masterful, elegant swimwear, dresses, and separates she designed for the mass market. McCardell also made frequent use of utilitarian fabrics such as cotton gingham, and was credited with popularizing denim as a fashion fabric, much as Chanel had done with jersey forty years earlier. American designer Bonnie Cashin was known for her distinctive combinations of materials such as leather and wool tweed, and wool jersey trimmed with suede.[35] California's swimwear manufacturers, including Catalina and Cole of California, added other casual garments to their lines during this period, and the "California look" influenced leisure styles worldwide.[36] Knitwear designers and manufacturers, aided by improved post-war knitting machines, developed a wider variety of stitches and surface textures through the 1950s, along with new styles such as the first T-shirt dresses that in 1954 "revolutionized the industry"; by 1967 an estimated ten million of them had been sold.[37]

The innovative work of Italian designers and ready-to-wear manufacturers also came to international prominence in the 1950s, thanks to American aid provided through the Marshall Plan to speed post-war reconstruction, and the interest of American retailers and journalists. Italian resort clothes and knitwear strongly influenced the development of sportswear fashion.[38] The most famous Italian sportswear designer, Emilio Pucci, introduced capri pants of cotton and silk shantung in the early 1950s, followed in 1960 by stretch versions in "Emilioform" (a mix of silk shantung and the texturized elastic yarn Helanca). These styles were widely copied at all price levels. In 1959, he introduced casual, versatile, and easy-to-pack printed dresses and pullover tops of fine silk jersey. These became status symbols associated with the international jet-set, and an iconic style of the 1960s and 1970s.[39]

The sportswear trend was also very influential on men's wear. Informal sports shirts that were worn without a tie were revolutionary, and assumed greater importance in wardrobes after the Second World War. They were made of softer and more varied fabrics than traditional men's shirts, and brought new color into men's wardrobes. Glossy printed rayon, for example, was the preferred fabric for short-sleeved aloha shirts, a Hawaiian style brought to the mainland US by returning servicemen after the war. By the mid-1950s, knitted sports shirts and pullover sweaters, some inspired by Italian styles, were increasingly replacing woven shirts for informal wear.[40] Sport coats, usually of a highly-textured fabric such as wool tweed or cotton corduroy, and worn with non-matching trousers, emerged as a popular alternative to the suit during the 1950s, and brought the sportswear concept of mix-and-match separates into men's professional wardrobes. Toward the end of the decade, some men began to wear their sport coats with turtleneck sweaters rather than standard men's shirts, a look that remains popular to the present day.

The expanding market for sportswear also encouraged traditional American manufacturers of work wear, such as Pendleton Woolen Mills and Levi Strauss & Co., to expand and create new lines of fashionable separates of wool plaid and denim, for both men and women.[41]

THE 1960s & 1970s

Garments—Structure and Knits, Blue Jeans and Leisure Suits

In the 1960s, the traditionally "top-down" fashion system, in which new ideas originated from acknowledged style leaders such as Paris couturiers and percolated down to the mass market, began to break down, and the fashion market became more diverse and fragmented. The rise of street and boutique clothing, specifically designed by and for the youth market, was a new development; another was the related adoption of blue jeans as a nearly universal fashion later in the decade. Throughout the 1960s and 1970s, as fashion and its sources became ever more diverse and global, innovations came from many directions and followed each other in close succession. Still, several distinct, albeit simultaneous, trends in fashion's use of textiles occurred.

In the late 1950s, an important fashion direction emerged following the introduction of so-called chemise, or "sack," dresses in 1957, when women's dresses and tailored suits began to assume more structured, architectural forms that stood away from the body.[42] This trend was exemplified by couturier Cristóbal Balenciaga's highly influential semi-fitted suits, over-blouse or tunic dresses, and voluminous gowns and coats. Balenciaga's designs depended on the weight and shape-holding qualities of the fabrics for their success. Many of his most iconic designs were made of silk gazar, a firm, tightly-woven fabric incorporating high-twist yarns for added resiliency, created in 1958 by the Swiss manufacturer Abraham.[43] By the early 1960s, similar pared-down boxy suits and structured dresses entered mainstream fashion, along with the more substantial fabrics—both traditional and newly developed—that were necessary to produce them. This fashion was a particularly clear example of the close link between the cut and shape of fashionable garments and the composition and structure of fashion textiles, and of the often symbiotic relationship between the fashion and textile industries.

The trend toward structure was strengthened in the mid-1960s by couturiers André Courrèges and Pierre Cardin, who in 1964 presented clean-lined, futuristic space age collections that came to epitomize the mod style embraced by 1960s youth culture. Courrèges, who had worked for many years as a cutter for Balenciaga, showed radical, simple mini-dresses and jackets in heavy, interlined wool gabardine and whipcord, a dense twill weave. The thickness of the required fabric was further emphasized with top-stitching at seams and pockets, a detail that was widely imitated (Figure 1.4).[44]

Couture garments were made with fabrics layered together by hand but similar effects could be achieved using a dense, double-sided fabric that also rose to prominence at this time: double knit. Wool double knits were first introduced by Italian manufacturers for the luxury trade in the 1950s. By the early 1960s, double knits were being made worldwide and in a variety of synthetic fibers, and were commonly used for ready-to-wear suits in the US.[45] A variety of other fabrics suitable for structured garments were popular throughout the decade, including metallic brocaded fabrics, heavy tweed and mohair suitings, heavily-textured Crimplene (a "crimped" polyester manufactured in the UK by ICI), and bulky synthetic knits; some of these were backed with a layer of urethane foam to give them more body.[46]

The space race also sparked interest in overtly synthetic futuristic materials, such as vinyl, plastics, mylar, and polyurethane (Figure 1.5). In 1968, Pierre Cardin introduced a special vacuum-formed high-relief fabric called "Cardine," probably developed in collaboration with the Union Carbide Corporation.[47] British designer Mary Quant and American Rudi Gernreich both made extensive use of vinyl (PVC) and clear plastic for dresses and rainwear beginning in the early 1960s; PVC became a signature fabric for Quant following her "wet look" collection in 1964.[48] Other novelty metallic, coated, and laminated fabrics, along with brightly colored and obviously synthetic fun fur, were popular throughout the decade. French designer Paco Rabanne dispensed with textiles

FIGURE 1.4: This 1966 mini-dress and jacket by couturier André Courrèges shows his innovative use of dense, heavy fabrics and topstitching to emphasize the structure and clean lines of his garments. Photo: Reporters Associes/Gamma-Rapho via Getty Images.

FIGURE 1.5: Numerous designers experimented with vinyl (PVC) and other "space age" materials during the 1960s. This 1969 ensemble of wool and quilted PVC was designed by couturier Pierre Cardin. Photo: Photo: Evening Standard/Getty Images.

altogether for some of his early collections, making dresses out of chain mail, or linked metal and plastic disks. Perhaps the ultimate in novelty fashion was reached during the 1966–8 fad for disposable paper dresses; the "paper" was usually a non-woven mixture of wood pulp and cotton fibers, but disposable garments were also made in a silver foil material used for insulating space suits, and in a DuPont plastic, Tyvek.[49]

Another trend that continued through the 1960s and 1970s was steady growth in the importance of knitted garments and fabrics. Younger women in looser-fitting 1960s clothing gave up wearing girdles and garter belts, and thigh-high stockings were replaced with stretch tights (or pantyhose) that entirely enveloped the legs. This allowed for the introduction of the mini-skirt, as the gap between the garters and the stocking tops vanished. Colorful, textured tights, along with other all-in-one knitted stretch garments such as bodysuits, leotards, and body stockings (or catsuits), became an integral part of the "mod" look of designers such as Cardin, Quant, and Courrèges. Rudi Gernreich, a former dancer who first became known for the unstructured wool jersey swimwear he designed in the 1950s, continued as a knitwear innovator through the 1960s and 1970s, designing collections in geometrically patterned, heavy wool knit fabrics for the American manufacturer Harmon Knitwear. These often featured ensembles with multiple matching parts (e.g, top, skirt, and stockings), for an effect he called the "total look."[50] He was also one of the first modern designers to make extensive use of matte stretch jersey (silk, later nylon), a fabric which would become ubiquitous in the 1970s.

At the end of the 1960s and through the mid-1970s, knitwear became more fitted with layered styles that nostalgically recalled the knitwear of the 1920s and 1930s. This trend was exemplified by the colorful, close-fitting and densely patterned knit dresses and ensembles by Italian designers Ottavio and Rosita (Tai) Missoni. They received worldwide attention after their first Paris showing.[51] Jersey knit fabrics became a staple fabric of the 1970s, used for day dresses, separates, and evening wear (Figure 1.6). The famous jersey wrap dress was introduced by Diane von Fürstenberg in 1976, and Halston became famous for his minimal flowing jersey evening dresses.

Knits became more body-conscious, as successive fads for jogging, tennis, disco dancing, and aerobic exercise served to expand markets and fashionable venues for attractive stretch active wear.[52] By 1979, jogging and warm-up suits in velour and terry cloth were being adopted as informal street wear. The following year American designer Norma Kamali showed an influential collection of high-end day and evening wear using grey, white, or black cotton fleece, more commonly called sweatshirt material. Previously fleece had only been worn by male athletes for training and warming up. Kamali carried fitness fashion onto the street and into offices and chic restaurants.

Meanwhile, following on the youth fashions of the early 1960s, an eclectic range of counterculture fashions developed in reaction to conventional mass-market styles. Cotton denim jeans, which had been popular among teenagers since the 1940s, exploded in popularity through the 1960s, and by the end of the decade the combination of jeans and cotton T-shirts had become a global youth fashion. The universal adoption of jeans inspired Finnish designer Annika Rimala in 1967 to design the unisex and all-ages "tasaraita," an even stripe, cotton T-shirt for Marimekko. It is a design classic that is still in production today.[53] By the early 1970s, jeans were no longer exclusively worn by youth.[54] The first expensive "designer" jeans, made of dark, unfaded denim, and cut for a skin-tight fit, appeared later in the decade; jeans such as those designed by Calvin Klein did not use a new kind of denim, but represented a new way of finishing, branding, and marketing denim as a luxury product. By contrast, traditional jeans were not considered

FIGURE 1.6: Flowing jersey knit was a staple fabric of the 1970s for both day and evening wear. The fabric for this 1974 gown by American designer Chester Weinberg was made of DuPont's Qiana nylon. Photo: Hagley Museum and Library.

fashionable until they had been "broken in" and fitted the wearer's body by wear and shrinkage, and the most desired look was a well-worn patina attained through years of wear. In response, "stonewashed" jeans were introduced in the late 1970s, and were the first garments to be sold with a built-in patina of "wear," created by tumbling the finished garment with pumice.[55]

Men's wear underwent dramatic changes during the 1960s and 1970s, as the range of fashion options expanded for men. Early in the 1960s, Pierre Cardin introduced radically simple, collarless jackets that were widely publicized after being worn by the Beatles, and he was credited with introducing the similarly clean-lined Nehru jacket. Cardin's "Cosmocorps" collections of the 1960s featured minimal, uniform-like tunic outfits for both men and women. Like his other jackets, these were accessorized with rib-knit turtlenecks instead of shirts, a style which became more popular throughout the decade.[56] In addition, a greater variety of fabrics previously associated with women's evening wear, including cut velvet and metallic brocade, made their way into menswear during the so-called "Peacock Revolution" that started in London boutiques such as Granny Takes A Trip in the mid-1960s.[57] Lycra and other synthetic fibers were also increasingly used for close-fitting men's casual wear.[58] In the mid-1970s, this trend culminated in the short-lived fashion for "leisure suits," casual suits with shirt-like jackets that were made in fabrics ranging from cotton denim to polyester double knit, and in colors such as soft powder blues, quite unlike those seen in woolen suits. These were worn not just by the young, but also by middle aged men who were fashion conscious.[59]

Textiles—Space Age Synthetics, Stretch, and the Natural Fiber Revival

Through the 1960s, textile manufacturers continued to introduce new man-made fibers and finishes, including the novel "space age" materials mentioned previously, and to seek new markets for their existing products. DuPont's Lycra (also known as Spandex, or elastane) fiber, introduced in 1959, greatly expanded the potential for stretch textiles, which had previously depended on elastic yarns made by wrapping a rubber core (such as Lastex). Lycra, a lightweight, resilient fiber much more elastic than rubber, had originally been developed with the intention of improving women's girdles, but through the 1960s it introduced the quality of stretch into men's and women's garments of all kinds.[60] Lycra revolutionized the swimwear industry as Lastex had thirty years previously, and inspired comfortable, lightweight undergarments such as Rudi Gernreich's "No-Bra" of 1964, a bra without form, structure, padding or bones.[61] In the 1970s, Lycra's improved elasticity was also central to the aerobics- and disco-inspired active wear fashions discussed earlier. Another notable innovative branded fiber was Qiana, a silk-like form of nylon that was widely used for both knitted and woven fabrics. This was introduced by DuPont in 1968, and fabrics made from it were extensively promoted to the home sewing market.[62]

The 1970s also marked the arrival of Ultrasuede, the first successful fabric made from microfibers, that arguably marked both the end of the post-war "fiber revolution" and the beginning of the new high-tech synthetics industry that would emerge in the 1980s. Ultrasuede was introduced by the Japanese company Toray Industries in 1971, and was considered a breakthrough "fabric of the future," combining the easy-care qualities of synthetic fibers with a luxurious surface and (unlike the majority of synthetics on the market at the time) the ability to "breathe." It was an expensive, luxury fabric at first because of the complex manufacturing processes needed to produce it, and became a status symbol after designer Halston used it for a highly successful shirt dress he designed in 1972.[63]

By the early 1970s, a reaction had set in against man-made textiles, in part due to the sheer quantity of synthetics being manufactured. Between 1950 and 1966, the synthetic fibers' share of the world textile fiber market doubled, and the production of man-made fibers continued to rise eightfold between 1966 and 1976.[64] It was also because a fashion for all things "natural" grew out of 1960s counterculture. By the late 1970s, polyester double knit had become a symbol of artificiality and bad taste, and was considered out of date by the young.[65] Other important influences were the growing environmental movement, which focused new attention on water pollution problems and other negative environmental impacts associated with the textile industry.[66] Finally, the 1973 energy crisis made the manufacture of petroleum-based synthetic fibers more expensive, therefore lessening their appeal for clothing manufacturers.

The rediscovery of natural fibers was also assisted by coordinated efforts on the part of natural fiber producers to save their besieged industries. In 1964, the International Wool Secretariat launched the Woolmark symbol as a quality-assurance mark for products made of 100 percent pure new wool.[67] In 1960, cotton accounted for 78 percent of the textile products sold at retail in the US, but it reached a low of 34 percent in 1975. By 1970, virtually the only all-cotton articles available in the US market were blue jeans, T-shirts, and bath towels, prompting American cotton growers to found a promotional organization called Cotton Incorporated, to address cotton's declining market share. In 1973, this organization launched the Seal of Cotton® symbol, as part of a comprehensive plan to boost industrial innovation and build consumer demand.[68] These quality-assurance symbols appeared in a wide range of advertising campaigns and cross promotions as a direct (and timely) challenge to the competitive brands and trademarked fiber names that had long been promoted by chemical companies.

1980s—PRESENT

Textiles and Garments—Natural Fibers, Techno Textiles, and Sustainability

Since the 1980s, the fashion and textile industries have become ever more fragmented, diverse, and global, with seemingly contradictory trends often at work simultaneously. The pace of innovation and global communication has accelerated dramatically, and it has become difficult to single out specific influential designers or textile developments. The use of new and experimental fabrics in high fashion was once exceptional, but it is now nearly universal, as collaborations between textile and fashion designers have become much more common. Many recent developments in fashion textile history can nevertheless be seen as following three interrelated trends: the revival of natural fibers and fabrics; the development of high-performance "techno textiles"; and the birth of the concept of "sustainable" fashion.

By the beginning of the 1980s, the trend toward natural fibers in fashion was well under way; new "durable press" finishes had been developed for 100 percent cotton dress shirts, and cotton sheets were successfully reintroduced to the American market.[69] In an era of conspicuous consumption, expensive, high-maintenance wools and linens became the new status fabrics, with natural/synthetic blends as a less-expensive alternative. In fashion, a key figure behind this transformation was Italian designer Giorgio Armani, who in the late 1970s introduced unstructured jackets in luxurious natural-fiber fabrics that brought an entirely new look to menswear[70] (Figure 1.7).

Other prominent designers, including British designer Laura Ashley and Americans Ralph Lauren and Calvin Klein, used traditional natural-fiber fabrics such as printed cotton and nubby wool tweed to create fashions inspired by a nostalgic view of the past,

FIGURE 1.7: The unstructured wool and linen suits popularized by Italian design Giorgio Armani in the 1970s and 1980s played an important role in the revival of natural fibers in fashion. Photo: Erin Combs/Toronto Star via Getty Images.

and (as with denim and designer jeans) marketed them as luxury textiles in highly successful advertising campaigns.[71] The association of natural-fiber clothing and fabrics with old-money, upper class life was further reinforced in the US with the 1980 publication of Lisa Birnbaum's tongue-in-cheek *The Official Preppy Handbook*.[72]

Meanwhile, despite the general distaste for synthetics, Lycra leotards and leggings gained increasing acceptance in the early 1980s, as the aerobic exercise craze reached new heights. The actress Jane Fonda was a key figure in popularizing this "look," through her best-selling workout books and videos.[73] Skin-tight Lycra was concurrently re-launched as a high-fashion fabric by French designer Azzedine Alaïa, who showed his first ready-to-wear collection in 1981. Alaïa created his intricately constructed garments by draping directly onto the body, often manipulating and stitching together bands of heavy rayon jersey to hug the wearer's figure like soft armor.[74] Through the 1980s, active sportswear made of Lycra stretch fabrics, such as leotards and bicycle shorts, continued to be worn as everyday fashion and to inspire fashion designers; by the 1990s, knit stretch fabric backed with neoprene, commonly used for insulation in wetsuits, was also being used in the men's and women's fashion collections of French designer Jean Paul Gaultier, among others.[75] During this period, the traditional rules about specific functions for garments and textiles broke down, and the fabrics used for day, night, work, leisure, and exercise wear all became interchangeable. Designers now felt free to choose whatever textiles would best express their aesthetic and design intentions, and crossing such boundaries often inspired fashion innovation.

A new and highly-influential approach to the development of fashion textiles emerged from Japan in the early 1980s, when the work of fashion designers such as Issey Miyake, Yohji Yamamoto, and Rei Kawakubo first came to international attention. The Japanese designs involved close collaboration between designers, textile engineers, and inventors, and freely combined traditional craft techniques, such as hand weaving and dying, with the latest synthetic fibers, and modern manufacturing technologies such as heat-setting and needle punching. This is exemplified by the work of textile designers Junichi Arai and Reiko Sudo, who founded the textile company Nuno Corporation in 1984. Nuno designers experiment with new materials and processes that are often borrowed from other industries. They combine materials, construction, and finishes in imaginative and unexpected ways, and work directly with fashion designers to create unique textiles that are often the starting point of a garment's design.[76] In the 1980s, these designers did much to overturn negative assumptions about synthetic fibers, and reintroduced them to the West as high-status artistic textiles.[77]

Japanese designers also produced pioneering collections that challenged Western distinctions between textiles and garments, and integrated the processes of design and manufacturing. For Issey Miyake's *Pleats Please* line, developed with textile designer Makiko Minagawa and introduced in 1993, pattern pieces are cut three times larger than the intended size, in a polyester knit fabric. The finished, assembled garments are then put through a pleating machine, which, owing to the heat and thermoplastic properties of polyester, sets the pleats and "shrinks" the garments to a wearable size. The resulting garments are permanently pleated, easy to store and care for, and fit a wide variety of body shapes and sizes because the pleats expand and contract like elastic. Like traditional Japanese kimono, they only take on three-dimensional form when worn. The Miyake studio often experiments with cutting and folding the garments before pleating to produce more dramatic transformations[78] (Figure 1.8).

FIGURE 1.8: The permanently pleated, heat-set polyester garments created by Japanese designer Issey Miyake, such as this "flying saucer" dress from 1994, challenged traditional distinctions between textile and garment. Photo: Niall McInerney.

Miyake's revolutionary *A-POC* (*A Piece of Cloth*) line, first shown in 1999, is manufactured by a "single form creation process," in which a computer-controlled knitting machine constructs a continuous tube of knit fabric from which the finished garments can be cut in multiple ways, according to the wearer's preference.[79]

Inspired in part by developments in Japan, the traditional dichotomy between natural and synthetic fibers continued to break down in the late 1980s, when a new generation of high-tech man-made fibers, or "techno textiles," began to appear upon the fashion scene. In the past, synthetic fibers and new fabric technologies destined for apparel had for the most part been developed as inexpensive or better-performing replacements for existing (natural) materials, or as disposable novelties, such as the perishable "space age" fabrics of the 1960s. Beginning in the 1980s, more emphasis was placed on developing fibers and textiles with entirely new, "un-natural" aesthetic or functional properties.[80]

Many of the new materials, such as Gore-Tex, Polartec polyester fleece, and the insulation Thinsulate, were developed for specialized applications such as competitive sports or winter mountaineering, but these "high-performance" textiles and materials soon entered fashion and everyday wardrobes. The new concept of "performance" referred to how the textiles performed while worn; this marked a change from the 1950s and 1960s, when "performance" had referred to how well a garment washed, and how easy it was to care for. New high-performance microfibers, valued for their aesthetic qualities as well as their potential to improve the comfort and versatility of conventional fabrics, also began to be adapted for fashion use in the 1990s, and to be blended with other synthetic and natural fibers. For example, water-repellant microfiber fabrics with a soft surface recalling Ultrasuede are now commonly used for fashion outerwear.[81]

The most important new development that has paralleled advances in natural and high-tech textiles since the 1980s is the issue of ecological impact and sustainability. Since the 1970s, when environmentalists primarily focused on waste generated during the textile manufacturing process, thinking has expanded to include the entire lifespan of a textile, from fiber creation to ultimate disposal.[82] In the face of the modern growth of inexpensive, poorly-made and disposable "fast fashion," increasing numbers of manufacturers, designers, and consumers are formulating strategies to create "sustainable fashion."[83]

One approach has been to educate consumers about the environmental impact of their clothing by creating ecological brands and certification labels to attach to garments, akin to the Woolmark symbol of the 1960s. The Oeko-Tex Association, an international union of textile research and testing institutions, has established prominent examples of this, with the "Oeko-tex Standard 100" label established in 1992, and the "STeP" (Sustainable Textile Production) certification introduced in 2013.[84] Other approaches have focused on production methods that produce less pollution, or that reuse industrial and post-consumer waste, such as Synchilla, a polyester fleece made from recycled plastic soda bottles introduced by American company Malden Mills (now known as Polartec) in 1993. More recently, Polartec has worked with manufacturers and retailers including Patagonia to collect used fleece garments and fabric scraps, and recycle those into new fleece garments.[85] And finally, research has focused on the development of new textiles made from regenerated natural materials, the descendants of rayon and acetate. Lyocell fibers, including Tencel, for example, are made from wood pulp, like rayon, but their manufacturing processes use non-toxic solvents and produce no hazardous waste, and the final products are biodegradable.[86]

CONCLUSION

Over the course of the twentieth century, numerous transformations have taken place in the kinds of textiles used for fashion, in conjunction with the development of new fibers and methods of textile manufacture. The range of fashion textiles greatly expanded beyond the primarily woven, natural-fiber fabrics worn by most people before the First World War. Many of these transformations were driven by innovation in man-made fibers and the dramatic growth of the world's chemical industries; the course and speed of this growth was in large part set in motion by two world wars. Other transformations, such as the shift from woven to knitted fabrics and the near-universal adoption of cotton denim jeans, resulted from the interaction of trends in lifestyles, attitudes, and economics, and the manner in which particular designers and manufacturers were able to influence and respond to those trends.

Considering the use of these textiles in fashion provides an instructive lens through which to view and begin to understand both the century's fashions, and the cultural context in which they developed. Such consideration also leads to the conclusion that during the twentieth century the development of new materials by the chemical and textile industries, and the adoption of "non-fashion" textiles into the fashion vocabulary, made textiles one of the primary drivers of fashion innovation.

CHAPTER TWO

Production and Distribution

VERONIQUE POUILLARD

Fashion leadership and design direction shifted from a luxury base to a mass phenomenon over the course of the twentieth century.[1] Fashion was both imitation and differentiation. At the start of the century, the social duality of fashion, as a marker of imitation and of distinction, remained. The trickle-down model of emulation, whereby fashion trends were initiated by the elites, then imitated down the social ladder by less affluent social groups, caused the elite to relinquish trends as they became too popular. But this was replaced by a multi-directional emulation as launching trends were no longer limited to the upper class, and trendsetters now originated from various backgrounds and geographic centers.

The processes of globalization and of democratization of fashions are subjected to change over time. Over the course of the century, fashion went from a hierarchical system centered in Paris, to a worldwide industry of many capitals and centers producing fashions for all, at all price points.[2] Fashion capitals are essential creative ecosystems, and post war they multiplied and diversified. Paris is now no longer the center for women's fashions and London for men's wear, as Milan, Mumbai, Tokyo, and Antwerp have all developed their own infrastructures where fashion design and production flourishes.[3] Fashion is mass manufactured for all, but this has not made the social phenomenon of distinction vanish overnight. The contrast between high-end goods and seemingly fashionable, but cheap knock-offs sold in a backroom of Canal Street in downtown New York is noticeable.[4] In the globalized world, fashion production and distribution have more diverse patterns than ever before.

The history of fashion centers on two major dilemmas pertaining to production and distribution. The first concerns the economic and social context of the material production of fashion. The second examines the tensions around the dissemination of fashion—who produces, buys, and copies it? Fashion is both material—the garment—and immaterial—the design idea. The intangible part of the industry has powerful consequences on the tangible production of fashion. Demand for new styles puts pressure on the manufacturers for flexible specialization.[5] Both material and immaterial dimensions of fashion are intertwined in the history of the twentieth century fashion industry, and underline the tensions inherent in the democratization and mass production of fashion (Figure 2.1).

In the nineteenth century, Paris was the acknowledged world capital of women's fashion design and production, while London was recognized as the leader for men's wear. European cities were ahead of those in North America in terms of design, but from the beginning of the twentieth century the US developed production capabilities and New York became the most advanced capital for the industrial production of garments.[6]

Fashions made by famous couture houses were emulated up and down the social and economic ladder. International buyers visited the fashion centers bi-annually to purchase

FIGURE 2.1: French stylist Paul Poiret's models at the seaside, in the fashion magazine *La Gazette du bon ton*, 1920. Photo: Photo12/UIG via Getty Images.

designs, and find inspiration in the latest materials, then sold the designs in original forms, the couture model, or manufactured imitations by the thousand. Women adopted the latest fashions according to their income and the same design could be worn by the less wealthy strata of society. The changes in the democratization of fashion are unevenly timed in the Western world, and the United States was quicker and more flexible than others in manufacturing ready-to-wear clothing.[7] The cycles of creativity in men's fashions were more slow and subtle than in women's wear, but underwent the same increased speed of production and variety in prices and range of styles.

RETAIL DISTRIBUTION

Textile expert Morris De Camp Crawford noted that in the 1910s most dresses in the US were made in the home. The century was marked by the shift from home-sewing to ready-to-wear and mail order. The working classes and lower middle classes made clothes at home from commercial dressmaking patterns that were widely distributed through magazines. Catalogs and mail-order garments helped to increase and disseminate new designs. For mass consumers, domestic production dominated their wardrobes. More affluent consumers had clothes made to order and measured by seamstresses who often worked as a one-person business or small enterprise. By the 1940s there was concern that American women would never sew again—even if, at that time, 25 percent of the dress fabrics were still sold over the counter, proving that many women still sewed either for economy or leisure.[8]

The roots of the shift toward ready-to-wear can be traced to nineteenth century novelty shops and department stores.[9] Rather than having to make separate visits to multiple businesses and traders, the new department store offered one-stop shopping, as it held a seemingly infinite variety of choices. Fabric departments allowed clients to reproduce patterns for themselves or to buy the appropriate material to bring to a seamstress. Department stores created a new territory where social classes mingled. The meeting of salesmen and women with the clientele resulted in increasingly blurred sexual and social boundaries creating a new consumer culture in the urban landscape.[10]

PARIS COUTURE AND ITS ECOSYSTEM

While the department store was influential in distributing fashions that became a mass cultural phenomena, the creation of the most fashionable garment designs was still controlled by a few Paris couturiers representing a small elite, or local high-end fashion designers who set up salons based on Paris models. *Haute couture* houses were laboratories for women's fashion, characterized by creativity, prestige, and their location in Paris.[11] The structure of the *haute couture* houses was largely inherited from the nineteenth century. Most often the enterprise took the name of the head designer, while an administrative director managed the business in his shadow. The symbiosis between the two was delicate, as creativity in the *haute couture* was an expensive process.

Fabric played an important role in the creativity of new designs. In France, textile production was concentrated in regional provinces. Silks from Lyons, ribbons from Saint-Etienne, woolens from Roubaix and Tourcoing, lace from Calais were high-quality materials that served as primary influence to the couturiers.[12] The French mills also created exclusive fabrics made to answer precise demands from couturiers. In turn, a new couture design that was sold and reproduced in higher numbers on world markets meant that the fabric design would also sell in greater numbers. The textile manufacturers showed their products to the couturiers before they started working on their collections to be sure of future sales. Manufacturers delivered the order to their couture clients on consignment, which meant that couturiers settled their accounts four times a year, and only paid for the textiles they had used. This arrangement favored experimentation for the couturiers but was difficult for the textile producers. In return, fabric firms considered the advertisement provided by *haute couture* to be considerable.[13]

COUTURE ATELIERS AND WORKERS

Haute couture ateliers were where creative designers experimented with new forms and materials. Creativity was difficult to rationalize, and could result in losses of material and many working hours before obtaining a final prototype. Fashion therefore developed as a creative tension between the design staff and the economic management of the enterprise. In Paris, the presence of an important pool of workers, both qualified—pattern-makers, seamstresses, and tailors—and unskilled—basters, sewers and helpers—nurtured innovation. The unskilled could provide extra workers when they were needed in the high season. The skilled craftsmen provided specializations like embroidery, flower making, feathers, and niche expertises that made an incredible range of specialty work available to the *grands couturiers*. By the late 1920s, some of these enterprises, such as Lucien Lelong and Coco Chanel, employed several thousand employees (Figure 2.2).[14]

The creative process varied between the houses reflecting their diverse backgrounds and training. Lanvin and Vionnet were immersed in every stage of the design, from the making up and creation of prototypes to the final line. Lanvin even established dyeing factories in Nanterre in order to create her colors, such as her signature blue that is said to have been inspired by Fra Angelico, her Velasquez green, and a rose Polignac, an homage to her daughter.[15] Vionnet did not sew but draped her prototypes on a smaller scale wooden mannequin. Chanel and Lelong worked along different methods, and their roles were closer to that of an artistic director. They gave instructions to a team of *modélistes* who then proposed how to make up their ideas. *Haute couture* garments were individualized, and required handwork and sewing machines for basic seams. Lanvin even cleverly and beautifully applied machine embroidery to decorate large expanses of fabric.[16]

FIGURE 2.2: *At the Milliner's*, painting by Edgar Degas (1882–before 1905). The Paris fashion industry benefited from an important reservoir of workforce for all fashion-related skills. This created a unique ecosystem whose style hegemony lasted until the mid-twentieth century. Photo: Fine Art Images/Heritage Images/Getty Images.

The 1920s marked the success of new couturiers whose enterprises were characterized by a familial model of capitalism, which means that there were few shareholders, and board members were usually united by family ties, as at Lanvin.[17] Most of the financial capital of *haute couture* houses was in French hands.[18] In 1929, journalist Georges Le Fèvre evaluated the costs of production to six million of French francs yearly for a large *haute couture* house. Of these six million, a collection of 300 designs cost two million, and was produced twice a year. The remaining two million were allocated to the day-to-day costs of the *haute couture* house, among which the most important post was the textiles and furs stocks.[19]

Couturiers innovated to try to respond to the paradox of the fashion industry: how to advertise fashions and protect new designs at the same time? *Haute couture* had started to serialize their production since Charles Frederick Worth, the acknowledged founder of *haute couture*.[20] In the first years of the twentieth century, *haute couture* houses experimented with making specific designs for manufacturing industries and department stores, albeit in limited numbers. Couturiers developed lines of tie-in products, for instance, Paul Poiret launched the Parfums de Rosine in 1911, and soon diversified to interior design with Ateliers Martine.[21]

Couture houses offered perks to their employees, to ensure the fidelity of their highly skilled workforce. Lelong had a canteen that fed hundreds of workers every day; at Vionnet, employees had access to medical and dental services, and to a nursery for their children, a consideration for female workers offered by a female employer.[22] Yet such paternalistic measures did not entirely compensate for the hardships of the trade. Couture was a seasonal industry, and one major difficulty was the irregularity of work. In times of the presentation of the collections and of deliveries, workers were pressed to complete orders, often overtime.

LEGAL ISSUES AND THE PROBLEM OF COPYRIGHT

Since the nineteenth century, fake Paris models (fashions) were made in France as well as in foreign markets.[23] Central Europe, around Vienna and Berlin, was an important producer of copies and fashion media, especially in the form of publications offering Paris fashion prints and patterns for reproduction. Paris had created a hierarchy of access for professional buyers based on who spent the most money. This meant that American buyers were the first allowed in to the *haute couture* houses to see and buy the collections, and thus were usually the first to reproduce copies of the latest designs. In New York workrooms, teams of workers reproduced Paris designs and models for the gigantic American markets.

The status of Paris as a fashion laboratory resulted from the fact that Paris designs were tried and tested. The designs initiated there had a chance to please the customer from an aesthetic point of view and, therefore, to sell. The desire to manage the risk inherent in the manufacturing of fashions that might not sell led to the development of professional fashion forecasting experts. New Yorkers were the first to create trend consulting and forecasting offices and brought the trends to manufacturers and department stores.[24] Experts, among whom the most prominent were Tobé Coller Davis and Amos Parrish, paved the way for today's trend forecasting offices like Li Edelkoort's.[25] Tobé and Parrish sold subscriptions to their trend reports and gave seminars that retailers could attend for a fee. Their services were tailored to the international markets, but they were quite expensive. It is therefore not surprising that fashion buyers, especially the ones working for lower-priced lines, attempted to reduce their design costs. A common strategy for buyers was to team up and share the use of a purchased model between several manufacturers.

The absence of a system of royalties and of an internationally unified legal protection of fashion design raised difficulties for couturiers wanting to secure the intellectual property of their work. This had been a problem since the nineteenth century but, in the 1910s, couturiers Callot Soeurs and Paul Poiret became more active and tried to fight the unwanted copying of their creations. A little bit later, in the early 1920s, Madeleine Vionnet joined in the legal battles against fashion piracy (Figure 2.3).[26]

Various countries, including France and the US, set up systems of design registration to prove and protect the intellectual property of design by way of anteriority research. According to this system, the person registering the design owned intellectual property on it for a variable amount of time.[27] Registration could be enforced within the framework of a law protecting copyright or protecting applied arts (*dessins et modèles* in France), but in the US, it remained a business practice that never was made law. In the US, despite

FIGURE 2.3: Edward Steichen photograph of evening dresses by Madeleine Vionnet for *Vogue*, 1930. Vionnet was one of the most revered designers by American buyers, and she was also one of the most copied. Photo: Edward Steichen/Condé Nast via Getty Images.

the numerous bills discussed in Congress, the copyright law did not include the protection of fashion design. It is still the case today. Other systems of protection existed. The trademark law could, when enforced, protect the brand or logo, but was of no avail to protect creativity in the design of original garments and accessories. The design patent law was too cumbersome and slow to apply properly to fashion.[28] The same issues continue in the most recently-developed fashion markets, especially in Asian countries.[29]

NEW YORK AND THE DEVELOPMENT OF MASS PRODUCTION

During the early twentieth century, ready-to-wear reached a new phase of prosperity and maturity in the US. Research on the conditions of development of technology clusters, such as Silicon Valley, has opened up discussion as to why some environments are more conducive to success than others.[30] Why do fashion hubs and capitals develop in some places and not in others? For example, in the inter-war period, why did New York develop as the fashion center of the US rather than Los Angeles? The geography of the fashion industry is linked to industry, workers, and factories.[31] Los Angeles and Hollywood studios were the center of a different important creative activity, where theatrical movie costume making was led by talents such as Adrian and Edith Head, who were also recognized for their own creative fashion lines. In 1938, Edith Head became the chief costume design of the Paramount Studios, the first woman to occupy such a position.[32] Hollywood attracted French couturiers such as Lucien Lelong and Gabrielle Chanel who both visited and developed collaborations to design costumes for the movie studios. But the practical imperatives of on-screen appearance and theatricality proved a challenging constraint to the French designers. Los Angeles developed as the second center of style in America. Californian designers were particularly skilled at developing sportswear and highly wearable lines. Designers include Louella Ballerino, who started in the wholesale dress business before she set up her own line, and former dancer Rudi Gernreich who would become famous for launching the monokini in the post-war period.[33]

New York had its own higher-end designers, like Hattie Carnegie, Elizabeth Hawes, Claire McCardell, and Nettie Rosenstein. Born Henrietta Kanengeiser in Vienna in 1889, Carnegie set up her first shop in New York with business partner Rose Roth in 1909 under the name Carnegie, Ladies' Hatter. Carnegie bought out her partner in the 1910s. In 1923, she opened a boutique on 49th Street where she sold seasonally renewed collections of Vionnet, Chanel, and other Paris couturiers. Carnegie understood the necessity to capitalize on her brand name but also to diversify to other price ranges. Her *Spectator Sports* lines retailed down to $16.50 in the late 1920s. An established brand name in the US, Carnegie built her reputation for well-made clothes of good standard (Figure 2.4).[34]

The specificity of the New York fashion industry was that it produced affordable fashions for the masses. Good quality factory-made clothes brought important changes in the life of workers. In 1900, the treadle machine operated by the foot was in use by 64.8 percent of the garment industry, and by 1911 only by 20 percent as electric machines took over. Ready-to-wear was a revolution of the labor force, rather than a technical one. Sewing machines in workshops were more specialized and faster than at home, but the technology was fundamentally the same. What changed was the standardization of labor. The diversity of quality and prices in the garment industry relied on a large labor force. The rhythms of work, the quality of the materials used, and the conditions of labor created diverse working environments.[35]

The Manhattan garment district produced 80 percent of the clothing for the US domestic market. The industry was divided into two groups: the tailored, or cloak and suit industry, and the draped, or dress industry. The 1920s shift dress was the chief product of the American garment industry at the time.[36] What distinguished the different

FIGURE 2.4: Lace dress with large shoulder bow by Hattie Carnegie, January 1934. This dress was designed by the New York-based entrepreneur, who also sold couture imports and reproductions of Paris fashions. Photo: Edward Steichen, with the permission of Getty Images.

prices of dresses that were virtually the same style was the quality of fabric, the numbers produced, and the time spent in the various operations of the production of the design. Dress manufacturers were categorized according to the price of the garments, yet production steps were identical. The design was made up by a sample maker, then a drafted pattern was graded in multiple sizes. The pattern was laid out efficiently on layers of cloth to conserve materials and lower costs. The cut parts corresponding to one dress model, were then assembled in "bundles." Errand boys ran the bundles to operators, mostly women paid on a piecework basis, who made up the dress by machine. The assembled dresses were then sent to the finishing department, where women sewed on the buttons, hooks, and eyes, and performed other hand operations. The dresses were then pressed, ready to be delivered to the merchant.[37]

The work was, most often, divided between "jobbers" and "contractors." Jobbers decided on styles and bought the primary materials. Some had their own employees who cut the fabric, others subcontracted cutting. Then, the jobbers distributed the work to contractors, who were organized in small units of production, who assembled the garments: on average workshops had twenty-five employees.[38] Subcontracting—when an industrialist delegated all or part of his production to workshops owned by a third party—was at the core of the problems in labor conditions.[39] The jobbers tended to play out the competition among contractors to bring down their costs. The lack of direct control of the workshops and the pressure for cheaper production resulted in reduced wages, and stress for the workers.[40] Nancy Green, in her detailed study comparing the history of garment manufacturing in New York and in Paris, shows how this fluctuated over the twentieth century, and concludes that positive developments in the conditions of production were no guarantee of stability.[41]

PRODUCTION ACCIDENTS AND ETHICAL DILEMMAS

In America, especially in New York, the workforce was relatively well organized, with a high number of unionized workers. The Triangle Shirtwaist Factory fire in March 1911, in which 146 New York City garment workers died, played a political, social, and symbolic role in the labor management negotiations, and decisive efforts toward better work conditions. Regulations were further strengthened by the legislature of the State of New York. Adequate control organizations verified their enforcement on the workshop floor. The New York garment workers were the best paid in the world during the inter-war period, but the industry remained sensitive to variations in the economy, and the securing of decent labor conditions remained the subject of tensions between workers and firms, especially in lower-grade manufacturing.[42]

During the course of the twentieth century, manufacturers trying to lower their costs relocated their production, first from the big centers to the periphery, where workers were less likely to be unionized in high numbers, and then overseas. From the 1960s onwards, Western multinationals relocated extensive parts of their production to Asia, leading to numerous developing economies that have been named the "T-shirt phase" by journalist Adam Davidson.[43] This has led to a new phase of increased specialization of workers. The T-shirt phase raises important ethical and social problems, among which the most pressing are child labor, the right to a living wage, and hazardous conditions in manufacturing. Consumers and non-governmental organizations concerned about the contemporary problems in labor conditions have, in the twenty-first century, reawakened debates that we can trace back to nineteenth-century consumer advocacy movements.[44] Asian countries are first in line because Asia today exports 58.4 percent of the world's clothing and textiles. However, the International Labour Organization conventions are not binding, and therefore are insufficient to ensure the protection of workers' rights. The problem of surveillance of the subcontractors remains, in an industry where middlemen attempt to cut down the costs of production.[45] Garment manufacturers are, more than ever, facing the need to address fast-changing styles. Subcontracting is a system where the large numbers of small workshops compete for orders, which results in pressure on workers' wages and overhead costs. The structural problems inherent in the garment industry that we have seen in the inter-war Western world resurface in the post-war emerging markets. The collapse of the Rana Plaza, a building for clothing workshops in Savar, a suburb of Dacca, Bangladesh killed 1,129 garment workers in spring 2013. The building had been constructed using a substandard concrete that did not meet building codes. The lack of production standards, the difficulty to enforce codes, and to obtain a rigorous surveillance at all levels of production and government remains a challenge for fast fashion industries.[46]

The ethical dilemmas raised by clothing and textile production are not easily solved. Researchers have underlined that boycotting the production of the countries where such violations occur is not necessarily the best strategy, as ultimately it is the underpaid workers, not the employers, who are the most hurt. The countries that remain outside of the T-shirt phase also meet economic difficulties, maybe even greater, for missing opportunities in the local creation of employment, and later hoping to catch up with phases of increased workers' specialization.[47]

DESIGN EXCLUSIVITY

But let us go back to the inter-war period to understand design exclusivity. Buyers flew to Paris two to four times a year to see the *haute couture* collections, and find inspiration. International fashion buyers were not all copyists. Couturiers, manufacturers, and retailers like New York's Hattie Carnegie were keen to acquire Paris originals in the most open and legal way. They could be based in the United States, in Canada, in South America, and in Europe, and considered their role to be privileged intermediaries between the couture salon and their local markets. They paid a one-time fee for a legal reproduction right. They received their purchase with an instruction sheet complete with textile samples, buttons, zippers, buckles, ribbons, or any other piece of material necessary to reproduce the garment true to the original (Figure 2.5).[48]

Fashion buyers working for higher-end shops and quality manufacturers were keen to maintain Paris couturiers' control over the dissemination of *haute couture*, in order to secure the prestige of couture. For fashion industrialists, one difficulty was to make selections from among all the new *haute couture* original designs. They looked for what would become a success or, as Green has noted "to run the interface between supply and demand."[49] This uncertainty resulted in what the New York Garment District entrepreneurs called "design risk." Mass manufacturers used to say that they "gambled" on the new designs. American garment manufacturers made around 75 percent of their profits on 5 to 10 percent of their models.[50]

PROFESSIONAL ORGANIZATIONS

The fashion system has many sectors and the professionalization lends it its authority. Sociologist Yuniya Kawamura uses the word "ecosystems" to describe fashion entrepreneurial landscapes. The notion echoes Roland Barthes' *système de la mode*, that the French scholar used to develop the study of the language of fashion, including its institutional tenets.[51] The concept of ecosystems goes further, it underlines that fashion

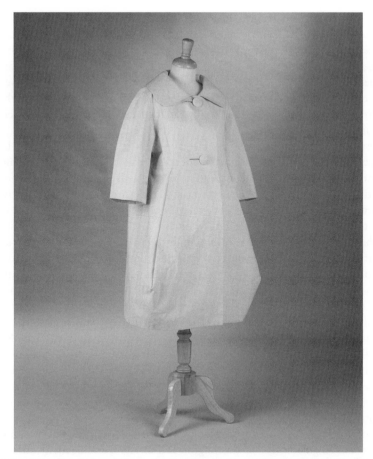

FIGURE 2.5: 1959–60 toile (muslin) coat by Castillo for Jeanne Lanvin, Paris sold to an American manufacturer for copying. Gift of Eaton's of Canada. Photo: Royal Ontario Museum © ROM.

creativity does not rest with isolated designers, but that fashions can only develop where a whole structure offers the right soil in which the industry can grow. Fashion creativity needs media, a thriving artistic and cultural scene from museums to avant-garde, the right economic support, skilled artisans, and flexible suppliers. The notion of ecosystems helps to explain that fashion developed at the crossroads of material and immaterial skills.

Business associations and employers' syndicates occupy a place that is important both professionally and economically.[52] The most prestigious of all trade associations is the *Fédération Française de la Couture du Prêt-à-Porter des Couturiers et des Créateurs de Mode*, that since 1973 has headed the *Chambre Syndicale de la Couture Parisienne*, the *Chambre Syndicale de la Mode Masculine*, and the *Chambre Syndicale du Prêt-à-Porter des Couturiers et des Créateurs de Mode*, also founded in 1973. The French syndicate gathered together branches of the industry that had been represented by separate associations during most of the twentieth century. The origin of the *Fédération* was the *Chambre Syndicale de la Couture Parisienne*, founded in 1868.

The *Chambre Syndicale de la Couture Parisienne* was reorganized in 1911 at a time when *haute couture* firms wanted to mark their separation from French manufacturers. It developed as an organization geared toward maintaining exclusivity of limited designs.

French manufacturers and department stores were not allowed in to see or buy from the *haute couture* shows until 1944. The *Chambre Syndicale* helped member couturiers with the organizing of work, preparing the calendar of the shows, registering buyers and journalists, and protecting creativity. The houses of Worth, Vionnet, Lelong, and Lanvin were at the forefront of syndical activity during the inter-war period.[53] Today, the *Chambre Syndicale* counts ancient couture houses and new, promising talents, among whom were, in 2015, Serkan Cura, Zuhair Murad, Yiqing Yin, and also the recently reawakened house of Schiaparelli.[54]

The power of the fashion professionals gave birth to new organizations. In 1928, a group of women in the fashion, beauty, and media industries founded the Fashion Group in New York as a division of the National Retail Dry Goods Association, with the intention of promoting the interests of women in the fashion industry, that was a business dominated by male manufactures, designers, and retailers who relied upon a workforce of women to promote and sell women's wear to women. The Fashion Group encouraged the professionalization of the American fashion industry at large and developed as a powerful media platform. Their first meeting of seventeen women was informally held at a New York tearoom. All the founding members were high-profile talents. Among them were journalists Virginia Pope of the *New York Times*, fashion editors for the press, Edna Wolman Chase of US *Vogue*, Carmel Snow who was then at *Harper's Bazaar*, and Julia Coburn of the *Ladies' Home Journal*. The Fashion Group was a gathering place for emerging home-grown American fashion designers: sportswear pioneer Claire McCardell, milliner Lilly Daché,[55] Hollywood designer Edith Head, and ready-to-wear expert Adele Simpson. High-profile retailers were represented by Dorothy Shaver, who would become the president of department store Lord and Taylor—the first woman to reach this position in America.[56] Elizabeth Arden and Helena Rubinstein were members in their capacity of beauty entrepreneurs. Fashion forecaster Tobé was also part of this founding meeting.[57] Besides the New York Group, a first regional group was founded in Cleveland in 1932, followed by Los Angeles in 1935, Washington DC in 1940, among many other American chapters. In 1956, Paris was the first chapter of the Fashion Group founded abroad.[58] Today, the association still exists, and counts 6,000 members.[59]

Professional associations such as these in the fashion industry played a fundamental role in the production and the distribution of fashions. Where the *Chambre Syndicale de la Couture Parisienne* sought to create ideal conditions for *haute couture* to thrive, the New York-founded Fashion Group intensely pursued media expertise and women's career development.

FASHIONING THE SECOND WORLD WAR

In 1939, the Phoney War reopened the question of the future of the French fashion industries. Couturiers mobilized for the war were rapidly sent back home and reopened their firms. Lucien Lelong, who was president of the *Chambre Syndicale de la Couture Parisienne*, encouraged his peers to pursue business as usual. The partial Occupation of France in spring 1940 cut Paris off from most its external markets. The future of Paris couture seemed uncertain. In many countries, people had to suffer shortages of raw materials, including textiles and fibers, that were needed for the war effort. Authorities in warring or Occupied countries set up policies that aimed to rationalize and limit the consumption of clothing, and to economize on materials. Practices including recycling and an ethos of "make do and mend" came back to the forefront of consumption.[60]

Few couturiers left Paris and production continued. Schiaparelli left for the US, but her Paris boutique remained opened during the war. Chanel closed, allegedly because the strained relations she had had with her workers during the great strikes in the mid-1930s discouraged her to carry on. As president of the *Chambre Syndicale de la Couture* Lucien Lelong was vested with the direction of the Couture Group (*Groupement de la Couture*) of the *Comité d'Organisation de la Branche des Industries de Création*, a division in the corporatist organization of the French economy set up by the German occupying forces. The participation of Lelong in the *Déjeuners de la Table Ronde*, hosted by the ultra-collaborationist networks underlines the ambiguity and the difficulty of his role during the Occupation.[61] His wartime activity has been the subject of debates: did he collaborate with the enemy, or act responsibly to keep a maximum of French employees at work and avoid them being deported for obligatory work in Germany? It is important to consider the question of accommodation within a comparative historical framework. When looking at other countries, we see that the fashion industry could often provide a means to survive in extreme conditions, especially for women on the home front.[62] American fashion expert M.D.C. Crawford, although fiercely opposed to Nazism, underlined the responsible and reasonable leadership of Lelong during the war.[63]

A major change decided in 1944, and enacted in 1947, was that the *haute couture* house members of the *Chambre Syndicale de la Couture Parisienne* opened their presentations to French ready-to-wear manufacturers, ending a policy of exclusion that had lasted more than three decades. It was now possible for French manufacturers to see *haute couture* like any other international buyer, even if they were the last allowed to see the collections. This paved the way for the emergence of French ready to wear industry.[64]

POST-WAR FRANCE

The question on everyone's lips at the end of the war was, could Paris re-establish its pre-war position as the center for fashion design? A young designer, Christian Dior, who had apprenticed at Lelong, embodied the renewal of Paris fashion. In the summer of 1946, Dior met textile industrialist Marcel Boussac, who offered him a job as head designer of an old Paris *haute couture* firm, Philippe et Gaston. Dior replied that he would rather have his own new enterprise. Boussac agreed and supported the new house with considerable financial backing. The young designer obtained the expertise of some of Boussac's managers. Dior presented his "New Look" with great success to the international press and buyers in spring 1947. His aesthetic, featuring wide skirts and wasp-waisted jackets, was a total break from the narrow cuts that had prevailed under rationing regimes. Or so consumers thought, as wasp-waisted silhouettes had been experimented with in the last years before Second World War.[65] The designer predicted that consumers needed to forget about the war and this was reflected in his designs. Yet, when Dior presented his renewed hourglass silhouettes, he met some opposition, notably from American consumers who were still subjected to post-war rationing and were shocked by such an excessive use of fabric.

Dior created recurring aesthetic revolutions throughout the 1950s by launching new silhouettes each season described by a letter, A, H, or Y line, or a word such as "Envol." International buyers and manufacturers again bought Paris couture originals as well as producing replicas at various price points geared to a clientele eager to follow, once again, the latest Paris designs.[66]

The house of Dior developed a policy of international expansion and inaugurated new management systems including brand licensing, followed suit by French couturiers Jacques Fath, Pierre Balmain, and Pierre Cardin, although none of them had financial backing as substantial as Dior's.[67] Dior developed new branches and lines produced in New York (1948) and London (1952) in order to keep control of the process of the reproduction of his own designs that directly catered to specific markets. The house brokered exclusive agreements with retailers in Cuba, Canada, Mexico, and Venezuela in the early 1950s.[68] We find similar strategies in the development of English fashion entrepreneur Norman Hartnell, as well as other designers.[69]

THE 1960s REVOLUTION

The US had become the leader in the area of media expertise and ready-to-wear manufacturing. Fashion professionals predicted trends and packaged them in books (*cahiers de tendances*) that were then sold to those engaged in the fashion industry. New French stylists such as Maïmé Arnodin, Denise Fayolle, and Françoise Vincent-Ricard differentiated themselves from the older generation of consultants by designing lines of clothing directly for the department stores and retailers, just as Ghislaine de Polignac did for Galeries Lafayette.[70] Fashion democratized with the notion of "beautiful for all" (*beau pour tous*).[71] French ready-to-wear designers such as Daniel Hechter, Elie Jacobson, Emmanuelle Khanh, Michèle Rosier, and Sonia Rykiel, flourished.[72]

Concurrently, Paris *haute couture* faced growing difficulties as the cost of overheads soared and the number of firms declined. Couturiers emulated the entrepreneurial model initiated by Christian Dior and founded their own ready-to-wear lines, with varying successful returns on investment.[73] Licensed and branded perfume and cosmetic lines proved to be the best strategy to ensure *haute couture*'s economic viability, but this led to a glut of licensing contracts bearing an *haute couture* brand, with the result that, by the late 1970s, the image of the designer or house became degraded. Some victims of excess licensing strategies needed years to restore their brand image.[74]

Other European centers emerged as competition for France. Italy became an important fashion and industrial design center offering high-end handwork, strong designs at prices that were below French styles. By the late 1950s, Italy had developed a strong knitwear market. In this context, new fashion capitals flourished, sometimes several competing in one country. For example, in Italy pre-existing industrial and cultural heritage made Florence, Rome, and Milan all potential fashion capitals. After a couple of decades of amicable competition, Milan came to the fore as one of the world's fashion capitals.[75] London also became known as a source for fashion. After wartime restrictions and difficult post-war reconstruction, fashion developed symbiotically with popular culture and subcultures. It was no longer designed from the top down with a handful of key designers or countries as the sole design source; furthermore, the revolution extended to how fashion was sold and to whom. The baby boomers created the fashions they wanted to wear.[76]

But it was New York that claimed the status of a fashion capital for ready-to-wear. New York workers were to a large extent unionized, which maintained comparatively high costs of production in the New York garment district. Manufacturers producing the cheaper lines or wanting to keep their overhead costs down could rely upon two strategies. One was to relocate overseas; the other, to employ new immigrants, who were often less skilled but also not unionized. New workers, Jews, Italians, Dominicans, Puerto Ricans, and Chinese followed in waves of immigration that sustained the New York garment industry. The old methods of batch production and flexible specialization were used but the pace of fashion quickened.[77] Production time accelerated to address a need for faster, immediate fashions that were in high demand among young consumers (Figure 2.6).

The top-down transmission of fashion was replaced by a system of emulation originating from multiple directions. The 1960s boutique emerged as a locus for new methods of retail and a new commercial culture to sell new fashions designed by youth and sold to youth. In London, Mary Quant, Ossie Clark, and the emporium Biba run by designer Barbara Hulanicki were among the pioneers of these new stores with fashions that catered to a young generation earning their own income and interested in pop music, clubbing, cosmetics. Mary Quant opened her first Chelsea boutique named Bazaar (1955) with £10,000 in capital and made dresses using Butterick sewing patterns. Her clothes achieved democratization of fashion and class subversion, as in her own words: "There was a time when clothes were a sure sign of a woman's social position and income group. Not now. Snobbery has gone out of fashion, and in our shops you will find duchesses jostling with typists to buy the same dress."[78] London boutiques changed the existing model of retail by eliminating store counters and staff uniforms thus subverting clearly defined roles and separation between the client and the retailer. Owners and clients alike shared the same tastes and cultural references which were now interchangeable.[79] The London boutique was emulated around the world (Figure 2.7).

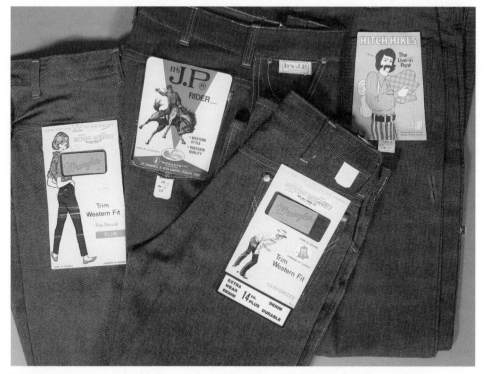

FIGURE 2.6: Four pairs of fashion and work wear jeans for men and women, made by Canadian manufacturer's J.P. Hammill & Son, and Wrangler, c. 1960–75. Gift of Robert Watson. Photo: Royal Ontario Museum © ROM.

FIGURE 2.7: Paul Shakespeare in 1972 wearing a suit by John Warden, for manufacturer Bagatelle purchased in the Canadian boutique, Le Château. Gift of Paul and Julie Shakespeare. Photo: Royal Ontario Museum © ROM.

By the 1960s, the material production component in the fashion industry globalized. A growing part of the textile and garment production of the West relocated towards developing countries, where labor wages were cheaper and work conditions more flexible. This phenomenon aimed production for mass markets at lower costs and had a considerable impact on the Western manufacturing industry. In addition, Europe had to meet the challenge and sizeable expense of replacing its ageing industrial equipment that was left over from the prewar period.[80]

TOWARD TODAY'S FASHION STRUCTURES

New centers of creativity multiplied with the emergence of new fashion capitals that developed with the encouragement of their governments and, increasingly, within the context of the European integration, of regions whose various levels of authorities perceived in fashion a reservoir to the promotion of creativity, industry, and tourism. The idea was that old European textile centers that had lost manufacturing to developing countries could reawaken by producing design creativity and added value. Governments mobilized to promote such projects, like the Belgian government did in the 1980s to promote the national designers. New fashion capitals would supersede the old industrial regions. Manufacturing relocated overseas, but Europe could still produce value in design, media, marketing, and retail. After shutting down most factory production, the West would now reconvert its creative strengths in the immaterial aspects of the fashion industry.

After 1989, the accession of former Eastern bloc countries to Western markets opened new possibilities of expansion in terms of production, distribution, and development of new fashion centers.[81] Countries from the ex-Eastern bloc have sought to develop their fashion industries and to adopt the recurrent features of fashion ecosystems, encouraging the development of their own fashion capitals and fashion weeks, seeking to emulate the Western structures of the industry, for instance in the city of Kyiv in Ukraine.[82] On one hand, the fast-growing fortunes of Russia, India, and China opened new markets to the developments of global brands into which luxury groups were quick to venture. On the other hand, the rise of Asia as the world's manufacturing workshop poses the question of whether or when will Asian countries be the center of activity in fashion design.[83] Already the Japanese creators of the 1980s have developed a durable renewal by re-shaping clothing drawing on traditional Japanese techniques and norms fused with Western tailoring construction, along with a deep perception of the *Zeitgeist*. Kenzo Takada, Hanae Mori, Rei Kawakubo, Yohji Yamamoto, and a generation after them have used Paris as the promotional platform for their creativity, because it still holds a privileged position for the legitimization of new creators and their brand (Figure 2.8).[84] The so-called Japanese revolution paved the way for the stylists of fashion deconstruction, especially the Belgians, with the Antwerp Six and Martin Margiela.[85]

The remapping of fashion creativity has, during the last three decades, been reflected in the geography of fashion schools, among which the Antwerp Academy of Fine Arts, La Cambre in Brussels, and Central Saint Martins in London count among the most prestigious programs, attracting talents from all over the world. *Haute couture* had, since its inception with the symbolic figure of Charles Frederick Worth, always cultivated cosmopolitan roots. Yet in the later twentieth century, fashion may have become more cosmopolitan than ever before, as witnessed by the hiring of Karl Lagerfeld in 1983 as the head designer for the house of Chanel, John Galliano at Givenchy (1995–6), Dior (1996–2011), and Maison Margiela (2014–), Alexander McQueen at Givenchy (1996–2001).[86]

FIGURE 2.8: A model presents a creation by Japanese designer Rei Kawakubo for Comme des Garçons during the Spring/Summer 2012 ready-to-wear collection show, October 1, 2011, Paris. Photo: François Guillot /AFP/Getty Images.

In more recent times, the dynamism of Asian groups as different as Shanghai Tang and Fast Retail (home to Uniqlo and Comptoir des Cotonniers) has demonstrated important capabilities in reinventing strategies and in answering consumers' demands.[87] European companies have broken the global borders with giants like Swedish H&M, Spanish Zara, and the Dutch C&A. The Zara method of vertical integration, and small variations, embody a unique historical phenomenon of affordable fashions that have developed into a consumption culture of fast fashion.[88] In the last couple of decades, this culture has been subject to debates pertaining to the environmental and social costs of the production of fast fashion.[89]

In such a context of mass production and mass consumption, the question of the ethics of fashion has come back in full force in the last decade.[90] The imperative for companies to increase profits, raise production and cut costs is a vicious cycle, with the fashion industry as a key player. How low and fast can production go? Will the consumer keep supporting fast fashion? Is the fashion system out of date? How do we forge a new path into the mid-twenty-first century? Many questions remain unanswered, for example the power of the consumers and the impact of their feedback that has found new platforms on blogs and social networks.[91] What is the sustainability of the fashion industry? How low can we go? For consumers, how much is too much? And for the future of economies, can we re-shore some of the fashion industries in the West? All these pressing and important questions are critical to the future of fashion production.

CHAPTER THREE

The Body

ADAM GECZY AND VICKI KARAMINAS

The idea of a metastable bodily ideal reads like an oxymoron. Within a Western framework, mention of the ideal body evokes stereotypical images of Greek statues: for men, sculpted statuesque musculature, and for women an uninterrupted smooth surface where the proportions are all in harmonic balance what has become known as the "Hellenic ideal." Correspondingly, the ideal body supports "classic" dress, such that to be a "good clothes horse" is to have proportions that do not distort the overall flow of the garment. While there has always been some variation in what constitutes the ideal body, there has arguably never been so much variation as in the twentieth and twenty-first centuries.

The plump corseted female body of the Victorian and Edwardian period in the nineteenth and early twentieth century was replaced in the 1920s with the "flapper" look, also known as the "boyene."[1] Women with tall, waist-less boyish silhouettes dominated fashionable literary and artistic circles and often wore their hair styled in a "bob" or "pageboy," complete with cigarette and monocle. By the 1950s, the ideal feminine body was replaced with the full figured look that was enhanced by popular fashion. Women often wore a "twin set," comprising a tight matching woolen cardigan and sweater that was designed to enhance breast size and narrow the waist. French designer Christian Dior's "New Look," launched in spring 1947, accentuated the waist, the volume of the hips, and emphasized the bust. By the 1960s, the plump feminine body made popular by Hollywood icons such as Marilyn Monroe and Jayne Mansfield was replaced by the thin waif look of British fashion model Twiggy. Named the "It Girl" of the 1960s, Twiggy's large eyes, long false eyelashes, and short hair coupled with a new androgynous dress style became an ideal look of beauty in Western popular culture that was a 1920s inspired revival. In the 1980s, whilst the thin androgynous look persisted, there was also an emphasis on health and fitness, and toned muscular bodies became prized. It was the era that saw the rise of the supermodel, Naomi Campbell, Claudia Schiffer, and Cindy Crawford, for instance. Media representations depicted ideal bodies as tall and slender; by the 1990s, the slender look had been replaced by the thin "malnourished" look known as heroin chic, and was made popular by Calvin Klein's advertising campaign for his underwear, jeans, and unisex perfume CK One. The thin waif body of the 1990s was soon replaced with a new ideal of a fit and muscular body, bodies that could be "perfected" through the use of cosmetic enhancement surgery.

Shifts in body ideals are not only regulated for women. Masculine ideals have also shifted across periods from the slim Victorian and Edwardian silhouette to the muscular shaped body of the 1950s and 1960s, epitomized by Hollywood icons James Dean, Marlon Brando, and the French actor Alain Delon, and made popular through magazines such as *Playboy* and *Hustler*. The über masculine male portrayed in the Marlboro man cigarette advertisement campaigns in the 1970s and 1980s depicted the ideal man as hirsute, rugged, and in the company of other men or alone in the wild. Ideal masculinity was represented as synonymous with nature and untamed. The 1980s gave rise to the commercialization of masculinity that was made popular by the "New Male" and the increase of dedicated male retail outlets and style magazines such as *Arena*. The metrosexual of the 1990s gave way to the gender blur of the new millennium, where ideal masculinities and femininities were paraded on the catwalk by the likes of transgender models Isis King, Andre (Andreja) Pejic and Casey Legler, a woman who models menswear. This chapter will examine the way in which the ideal fashionable body has morphed over time in the twentieth and twenty-first centuries and will argue that bodies are culturally inscribed with historical, and political meanings that shift. Like identities, bodies are not fixed, but are impacted by culturally inscribed mores.

THE IDEAL BODY

In the early part of the twentieth century, the ideal woman's body was represented as tall and slender with voluptuous bust and wide hips, a mature look that was achieved by corsetry that significantly pinched and pulled the waist, often resulting in fainting from lack of oxygen. The American illustrator Charles Dana Gibson (1867–1944) created a feminine ideal that incorporated the beauty standards of the time known as the Gibson Girl who was portrayed as fashionable as well as physically active. She was depicted as belonging to upper class society, well mannered, assertive, and independent, and she wore hair in the prevailing styles of the day, either in a *pompadour*, a *bouffant*, or raised into a *chignon* with curls spilling onto her shoulders. At about 1910, a new type of younger female dress became popular that represented the new bodily ideal. Attention was drawn away from the hips and the waist to toned down lines and narrow hips. The Paris couturier Paul Poiret was influential in proposing the transition from the grandiose and cumbersome Edwardian fashions to more versatile, relaxed clothing. Together with his wife and muse, Denise Boulet, Poiret designed clothing in classical and Orientalist styles. In his memoir he claims that he combated the burdensome influence of the eighteenth century with simplification and an emphasis on color.[2] Poiret gave himself full credit for liberating woman's bodies from bustles and corsets, although this was also in operation in the designs of Vionnet, Callot Soeurs, Margaine-Lacroix, and Fortuny, who were the leading exponents of the new early century craze for the English tea gown.[3] The flowing, narrow torso was topped with a scarf, or scarf-like hat, more or less turban-like, and commonly accented with jeweled or feathered aigrettes. Poiret's Spring 1911 collection was an Oriental feast: exotic fabrics, turbans, aigrettes, and the "*jupe-culotte*," and harem pants, which became his signatures. The *jupe-culotte*, otherwise known as *jupe-sultane* or *jupe-pantalon*, the more studied, elegant counterpart to bloomers, was sometimes pleated and gathered for maximal effect of billowing expansion and contraction. Their close resemblance to the dress reform and the sportswear bloomer meant they did not pass in Parisian society without a hiccup.

This was grounded in several points of reference. One was the allusion to the harem, the sexual overtones emphasized by the physical cleft between the legs. The separation of the legs also meant that women could sit and stand astride which seemed to imply to society an assertion of their strength (despite the convenient disavowal of the strength needed to endure childbirth). As opposed to the corseted Edwardian woman with her bustle and S-shaped silhouette, her small hands and feet as illustrated in large numbers of fashion periodicals, the harem-panted woman was the robust and matronly woman who had endured childbirth and who had taken command of her body.

Moreover, harem pants were recommended as informal clothing, but were also associated with radical bloomers and garments that were worn by reactionary women who supported liberation and suffrage. Bloomers and harem pants confounded the sartorial line between the sexes—rhetoric of sexual inversion was rife at this time—and the women's movement could be interpreted (although Poiret was definitely no feminist) as sanctioned in the illustrious halls of *haute couture*. No doubt such fears caused the inelegance of the silhouette to be decried. To others, as Valerie Steele notes, the "harem pants" were identified as lewd because the erotic and exotic were indissolubly united. By accentuating the leg they were scandalous.[4]

One contemporary couturier who was against the wearing of harem pants was Poiret's female rival, Jeanne Paquin. It may not have been out of the reservations that have just been described, but more to announce her difference from her competition, and simply out of personal preferences of taste. Paquin decried the ugly line of the pants, which caused the silhouette to slump rather than taper at the bottom. The culture wars of Orientalist appropriation in fashion and dress have their own intricately fascinating and convoluted histories, which had more than a physically liberating effect, stretching to the prospect of imaginary new horizons.[5]

Poiret helped to lay the platform for the main modern pioneers of easy lines and subtle after the First World War. Yet the mobile, athletic, and sleekly restive body advanced by both Patou and Chanel would soon jostle the languishing body of the Orient. In the mid-1920s, Jean Patou was easily the most famous and influential designer of his time. Not only did he play a large part in integrating the fashion model in the fashion industry, but he opened up the range of women's clothing. He violated the binary between formal and informal wear, with his shop *Le Coin de Sports* ("sport's corner"), where he introduced sport, play, and physical activity as concepts within fashion. In 1925, the same year as he opened his store, Patou created what was, arguably, the first unisex fragrance, *Le Sien* ("his/hers"), a concept and its marketing that has enjoyed a particular resurgence in the last three decades. The message from the "sport" concept is that the garment—and/or the fragrance—is characterized by a certain lack of encumbrance to allow for a level of exertion exceeding that of everyday social and work activity. What is striking about the entry of fragrances into this field, and of garments like jeans and collared shirts into contemporary fashion lines, is that "sport" reigns as much, if not more, as an idea than in terms of testable utility. But it was sport, whether as a physical activity or mere allusion, that was the arena by which women entered into modern public life. Accompanying his fragrance Patou announced that "Sport is the territory where men and women are equal."[6]

Changing ideas about health and boldly ideals were in flux in the two decades before the Second World War. One group that campaigned for changes in public health, hygiene, and dress was the Men's Dress Reform Party, an offshoot of the eugenics movement, which was established in 1929. The main platform of the party was hygienic dress codes and believing that men's clothes were too tight and unhygienic, favoring Bermuda shorts or the Scottish kilt. They argued that modern industrial conditions favored shorts and loose underwear in light, washable fabrics for hygienic purposes. Sandals were preferred to shoes and hats were only worn for protection against the rain and sun.[7]

The slim and maneuverable women's body of the 1920s flapper found its optimal sartorial counterpart in the little black dress, which, although ushered in by Patou, is more closely associated with Chanel. Patou's greatest rival, Gabrielle "Coco" Chanel was an unrivalled imitator. She, too, favored austere styles of dress, and was known for her short hair, considered a masculine style (Figure 3.1).

FIGURE 3.1: Gabrielle Chanel. Evening dress. Black silk satin and ecru alençon lace, c. 1926. Gift of Mrs Georges Gudefin. © The Museum at FIT, New York.

Chanel made sure that she was at the center of the equation where simplicity equaled elegance. Her designs emphasized a woman's boyish and slim silhouette with the emphasis on subtlety, not exaggeration. In 1931, during her visit to the United States, Chanel observed the processes of mass production. "The boyish flapper style of the 1920s," writes Patricia Campbell Warner, "gave way to a new silhouette—dresses with longer skirts and body-hugging slim shapes—that mimicked New York's newest skyscrapers, the Chrysler Building and the Empire State Building."[8] Understandably, the mass production of the little black dress found its parallels with Fordist production, also calling to mind his famous dictum, "any colour, so long as it's black" (Figure 3.1).[9]

For Chanel, the little black dress was the optimal sartorial alibi to the kinds of narratives used to drive advertisements. These were narratives that revolved around lifestyle, health, leisure—all allies to "sport"—and wealth. According to Warner, fashion in the United States in the 1930s was influenced by two major developments, clothing that was designed for sports that later became sportswear and the new body ideals that was connected to the thin, svelte sporting look creating by Hollywood films that depicted new fashion ideals.[10] The new black dress was based on the "less is more" modernist schema in one very important rhetorical respect, and that was that one was supposedly so confident of one's wealth that one did not have to show it. It was also reflective of a woman of action and agency as opposed to a woman as decorative object, or connubial chattel. This being the case, the little black dress was also a convenient vehicle for those who in fact didn't have so much, but who were not in a much easier position to play the part if those that did. It was manufactured at all price points.

THE DEPRESSION AND THE SECOND WORLD WAR

The social aftermath of the First World War was devastating, having dramatically reduced the male population as men went off to fight in the war. By 1920, almost every person in Europe and the United States of America had some knowledge of death as a result of the war or had witnessed it first hand.[11] The effects of warfare were so grisly that when forms of escapism such as the cinema emerged it helped to hide the horrors of starvation, homelessness, and death brought about by the war.

The kind of social and economic camouflage that an item like the little black dress afforded became an indispensable commodity after 1929 during the Great Depression, a time that swiftly demolished fortunes and made others. In the United States, the constitutional ban on the consumption and sale of alcoholic beverages, known as Prohibition, came into force in 1920 and was finally lifted in 1933. The Depression cut short the brief experiment in fashion and leisure that had reached carnivalesque proportions in the "roaring twenties," and was epitomized in Christopher Isherwood's novel, *Goodbye to Berlin* (1939). The relative austerity of dress that began at this time was conducive to the economic austerity of next decade. The image of the body at this time is best seen in advertising, through the documentary photography of artists such as Walker Evans, and from literature. In the novels of William Faulkner and John Steinbeck we are introduced to numerous examples of sinuously thin or alternatively voluptuous bodies. With the exception of a privileged few, dress was reduced to a set of expedients; the body makes the best of its circumstances.

FACISM, FASHION, AND THE IDEAL ARYAN LOOK

The rise of fascism in Europe witnessed a Hellenist revival, caused in no small part by societies driven by extreme financial pressures, and was manufactured and imposed for logical, but unfortunate reasons. When Adolf Hitler assumed power he envisioned establishing a German empire to rival that of Rome, and employed the heroic Greco-Roman revivalism as the inevitable choice. Through the examples of the three totalitarian regimes of the same period—Russia, Italy and Germany—we can observe a specific and common denominator of bodily beauty expressed in Classical Greco-Roman form and made to reflect the ideals of life (Figure 3.2).

These were highly realist and kept to gender stereotypes and clichés, in which women had good-sized breasts and men were muscular and capable of labor and war. In *Fashion*

FIGURE 3.2: Leni Riefenstahl. Naked discus thrower in Classical pose, scene from Leni Riefenstahl's film *Olympia*, part 1: "Festival of the Peoples," 1936. Photo: ullstein bild/ullstein bild via Getty Images.

FIGURE 3.3: Olympische Spiele 1936 in Berlin-Turnerin, Bild aus Riefentstahls Olympia-Film.
Photo: ullstein bild/ullstein bild via Getty Images.

at the Time of Fascism, Mario Lupano and Alesandra Vaccari note the way in which
Fascism influenced modernism and fashion. Control, rationality, and order are very
important parts of totalitarian regimes and these aspects are also prevalent in fashion,
dreams, and ambitions, new beginnings during this epoch.[12]

An attempt to define the ideal body by the Nazi Third Reich began as early as 1933,
when it was proposed that the female image would coincide with Nationalist Socialist
ideology—a "true German look" that women should embrace. It was a look that supported
the image of "Aryan-Nordic" beauty that was natural, strong, tanned, healthy and fertile
(Figure 3.3).

This look called for women to return to their pre-emancipation role of mother
and housewife. The use of make-up, hair dyeing, and foreign (especially French) fashion
and beauty brands were condemned and considered decadent and unhealthy vices.
The propagandist Elizabeth Bosch argued that red lips and painted cheeks suited
the "Oriental or Southern woman, but such artificial means only falsified the true
beauty and femininity of the German woman."[13] Magazines ran articles that gave
advice on make up techniques that reflected an emphasis on "natural or healthy"
beauty, fertility, and physical fitness; guidelines were published to illustrate the ideal
eyebrows, lips, skin, eyes, and cheek bones that women could accomplish. One
advertisement read:

Do you really think that I naturally look so fresh? You are mistaken! I, also, am often fatigued and then look pale and tired. But I always have two unfailing helpers in hand with which I can look instantaneously look fresh and youthful again, and these are Khasana cheek colour and Khasana lipstick. Surely you don't even notice that I have used these beauty aids. And that is the main thing, we do not want to be called paintings.[14]

Any representational distortions of the ideal Aryan-Nordic body that were not depicted as Greco-Roman were viewed as degenerate. Whilst avant-garde artists were trounced out of Germany after the Nazis seized power in 1933, artists of enviable skill produced sculptures and paintings of unconvincing, but perfect Classical bodies. Nazi social engineers, psychologists, and bureaucrats undertook physiognomics, the pseudo-science that studied facial characteristics to assign capacities of intellect and character.[15]

In Italy, Benito Mussolini had similar ambitions for his own empire when in 1927 he began building what was intended to be named the Foro Mussolini (Mussolini Forum). But following the war and the Axis defeat by the Allies, it was mercifully renamed the Foro Italico (Italian Forum). Completed in its first incarnation in 1937, all around the stadium are large, strongly homoerotic statues of naked or semi-naked men symbolizing various sports. According to Lupano and Vaccari, the Italian fascists were obsessed with measuring bodies. They introduced standard garment sizing, plastic surgery increased, and there was an upsurge in exercise and a strong awareness of ideal body types. This was in part an attempt to master the body and build the "perfect" humanity that the fascist had in mind.[16] Interestingly, Eugenia Paulicelli notes that the role of fashion in the Italian nationalist consciousness was particularly visible in the years of the fascist regime. Women's bodies in particular were manipulated in fashion magazines to boost national pride and identity by constantly referencing the Renaissance. "The Renaissance," Paulicelli writes, "is idealized as the epoch in which Italy seem to have exported its style and taste to the most powerful courts in Europe."[17] By aesthetic default, Mussolini was ushering in a new epoch commensurate with the Renaissance, itself a Classical revival based on a Greco-Roman ideal.

POST-WAR BODIES: SHIRTING IDEALS

Economic prosperity after the Second World War caused a dramatic realignment of society with a huge middle class. While Europe and North American were still run with a heavily industrialized economy, by the 1960s, domestic life was irrevocably altered with the availability and affordability of domestic appliances to solve tasks that had previously required lower class manual labor. The numerous devices from electric irons to washing machines suggested a more harmonious home life, affording greater opportunities for leisure time. But the increase of appliances and devices reduced the servant labor force and raised the expectations of what a single "housewife" ought to do.[18] Men returned from the war with the promise of work and the continuation of a public life, and women who had worked during the war were pushed back into the household and the domestic interior. The call to repopulate after the end of the war resulted in the "baby boom." The ideal female body of this time was not athletic so much as fecund and graceful. Going to the gym was not yet a fashionable way of using one's leisure time, but this was the time when being seen in states of leisure—carnivals, dance halls—was in vogue.

It was during this period that Cristóbal Balenciaga designed the "square coat" with sleeves cut in a single piece with the yoke. Balenciaga favored fluid lines that allowed him to alter the shape of women's bodies by raising the waistline, unlike Christian Dior who preferred the curvy hour-glass shape that he promoted in 1947 with the creation of his "New Look" (Figure 3.4).

FIGURE 3.4: Christian Dior evening dress of machine lace, chiffon tape, tulle, 1957. Gift of Nancy White. Anne Fogarty silk jacquard taffeta evening dress, c. 1954. Gift of Mrs William Messer. Photo: The Museum at FIT, New York.

In the *Feminine Ideal*, Marianne Thesander writes that Christian Dior wanted to return to elegant femininity, "a welcome trend after the clothes rationing, poverty and rather masculine lifestyle that women had been subjected to during the war."[19] The "New Look" promoted the traditional hour-glass shape of femininity that was nostalgic and harkened back to the Hellenic body ideal as represented by the Aphrodite of Milos, also known as the Venus de Milo, the Greek goddess of love and beauty. The sculpture, believed to be the work of Alexandros of Antioch, represents woman as a "natural" earth goddess and nurturing mother. Dior's new fashion look extenuated the breasts and hips and narrowed the waist, a style that was not natural and could only be achieved through corsetry and brasserie. Many styles of corsets and high waist girdles were available during the 1950s which, with the help of darts or spiral boning, created a slender waist that helped to sexually erotize and enhance parts of women's bodies. Hollywood film stars Marilyn Monroe and Jayne Mansfield, the sex symbols of the 1950s, all flaunted their feminine attributes by wearing tight sweaters and pencil skirts, and became fashion icons of a generation.

The post-war economic prosperity in the manufacturing and production industries resulted in an increase of living standards, leisure time, and spending. The process of suburbanization and economic boom in the United States created a greater division between genders as women were encouraged into the interior and the domestic space of the home, whilst men were encouraged to spend more time outdoors fishing, hiking, mountaineering, and generally spending their leisure time in the company of other men. For men of this period, the muscular body of Fascismo-Hellenism, if it can be called that, was eschewed in favor of slimness. The movie stars of this time, from William Holden to Cary Grant to Jimmy Stewart, were of no strikingly muscular build, but rather held themselves well in suits (Figure 3.5).

This was the lean American body that bespoke cocktails, business travel, and financial prosperity. To be too brawny or show too much flesh was to associate with the underclasses (Robert Mitchum in *Cape Fear*, 1962) or those who performed labor. Clothed civility had taken over naked force; conversation meant as much as action; future aspiration replaced nostalgia for (or justification from) antiquity. Men's bodies were represented in fashion magazines as slim, toned and well defined, dressed in paired down suits, slim ties, and sweaters (Figure 3.6).

According to Hancock and Karaminas, there were two types of discourses of masculinity in circulation during this time in popular culture, the fashionably narcissistic man embodied in the slim and affluent bachelor, and the traditional man depicted as the tough and rugged man of the outdoors with an active sexual appetite.

Conceived in 1955, "Marlboro Man", the figure used in tobacco advertising campaign for Marlboro cigarettes, often depicted a rugged cowboy, or a group of cowboy's wearing singlet's, plaid western style shirts and blue denim jeans, mustering wild horses or shearing sheep in a mythical Marlboro country. Set against a mythical landscape of natural wilderness, the Marlboro man embodied the virtues of traditional hegemonic masculinity of mateship, musculature and virility. Marlboro country was 'a man's country', a constructed imaginary place where men worked hard on the land and bonded with other men and their horses.[20]

Men's adventure magazines such as *True* and *Cavalier* provided a space where men were able to escape the domestic sphere. These magazines provided pictorials and articles on how to be an outdoor man by exploring exotic locations around the world through

FIGURE 3.5: Cary Grant—Schauspieler, GB/USA in "Nur meiner Frau zuliebe." Photo: ullstein bild/ullstein bild via Getty Images.

adventure sports like hunting wildlife and big game. These magazines provided a model for rebellion against the confines of domesticity and strong family values that was dominant during this time. The changing patterns of consumption and its associations with ideals of hedonism was cemented with the 1953 launch of *Playboy* published by Hugh Hefner. The American men's lifestyle magazine appealed to a new type of masculinity that emerged from the white middle class—the carefree bachelor. The bachelor represented a new form of male liberation from domestic ideology. In Hugh Hefner's words, the bachelor was "sophisticated, intelligent, urban—a young man-about-town, who enjoys good gracious living."[21] Epitomized on screen by stars like Frank Sinatra (*The Tender Trap*, 1955), Gary Cooper (*Love in the Afternoon*, 1957), Rock Hudson (*Pillow Talk*, 1958), Tony Curtis (*Some Like it Hot*, 1959), and Cary Grant (*An Affair to Remember*, 1959), the "bachelor playboy was more than a romantic male role in movie comedies," argues Steven Cohan.

> Interpreted with suspicion on account of his refusal to embrace the package of privileges and responsibilities that marriage was supposed to offer the male for his reigned-in sexuality, the bachelor cut an ambiguous figure; he was at once a lady killer and a woman hater, a party animal and a lonely guy . . . located on the margins of domestic ideology and central to its perpetuation.[22]

Slim and sophisticated, with tailored trousers, open-necked shirt, and loafers, the playboy bachelor offered an ideal version of heterosexual masculinity that was based on leisure

FIGURE 3.6: Cary Grant (born Alexander Archibald Leach), with Randolph Scott (front) in their house in Santa Monica. Photo: ullstein bild/ullstein bild via Getty Images, the Museum at FIT.

and consumption. "The playboy is a connoisseur, an expert on jazz, clothes food, design and culture, and he surrounds himself with things that proclaim his confident masculinity as well as his impeccable taste."[23]

At the same time, the emerging post-war youth culture clearly distanced themselves from their parent's generation by their taste in clothes, music, and pastimes. Teenage girls

enjoyed slumber or pajama parties, going to the drive-in cinema, and hanging out at the
soda shop or the ice cream parlor. Boys were rebellious, provocative, and at times violent
toward the generational conflicts that they were experiencing and turned for inspiration to
film idols such as James Dean in *Rebel Without a Cause* (1955) and *The Wild One* (1953)
starring Marlon Brando. Dressed in blue jeans, motorcycle boots, and white T-shirts with
a packet of cigarettes tucked under the sleeve or one hanging carelessly from their lips,
Dean and Brando became poster boys for a generation of young teenage men who felt lost
and disenfranchised by traditional middle class ideals. In Britain, young men were turning
away from family values to create new forms of cultural expression, or subcultural style.
Among these subcultural groups were the Teddy Boys, a group of young middle class men
whose style of dress was inspired by Edwardian dress suits. Usually in dark shades, the suit
coat consisted of a velvet-trim collar and pocket flaps, "drainpipe" trousers, a brocade
waistcoat, and a loose-collared shirt with a Western tie. The preferred hairstyle was long,
greased back with a quiff in the front and combed back into a "ducks arse" at the back.
They wore Oxford shoes, brogues, or suede loafers known as "brothel creepers," and
listened to American rock 'n' roll, by the likes of Bill Haley and the Comets.[24]

The 1960s was a period of great social and political change, with the emergence of
movements like the Women's Liberation Movement, Civil Rights, and Gay and Lesbian
Liberation, and was marked by protest and upheaval that changed the cultural landscape.
It was a decade nostalgically referred to as the age of counterculture because of the
experimentation and relaxing of taboos concerning drugs, music, sexuality, fashion, and
the body. The cultural movement "Black is Beautiful" began in the United States and
challenged ideas about race and beauty that were embedded in colonial discourses of
slavery and perceived European superiority. It called for Black Americans to stop trying to
emulate Caucasian physical traits, such as straightening curly hair and whitening the skin
by bleaching, in an effort to erase their African-American identity by internalizing racism.
The movement would later spread across the world redefining dominant ideas of beauty.

Another important change in bodily awareness came in 1969 with the Stonewall riots
in New York, that was an important marker for gay men and lesbians that saw them
aggressively speak out for an independent and recognized identity. The subsequent
celebration of gayness and lesbianism, albeit fraught and far from smooth in its struggle
up to this day, caused a new consciousness of body and dress for all. It led to the term
"queer," not in use in the 1970s, that is applied to people with practices, ideas, and
identities that do not comply with "heteronormative" convention. Body ideals and style
for lesbians was essentially androgynous. Feminists rejected the butch and femme roles
that were prevalent from the 1920s through to the 1960s because they believed that they
mimicked the repressive gender roles ascribed to women in a patriarchal society. Instead,
feminists promoted an androgynous style of comfortable dress characterized by loose-
fitting flannel shirts, loose jackets, and baggy pants. Hair was cut short and they wore
Birkenstock sandals, tennis shoes, or Frye boots.

The physical desexualisation of the body in mainstream fashion was a response to the
overblown femininity of the 1950s that perpetuated the ideal woman as sexual object. As
such, the new body ideal in mainstream fashion shifted to a thin, waif-like, and pubescent
figure. It was the Swinging Sixties and Aretha Franklin was singing "You make Me Feel
like a Natural Woman" (1967) in the same year that designers Mary Quant and André
Courrèges launched their mini-skirts (Figure 3.7).

The mini-skirt changed the ideal body shape for women producing a straight silhouette
without waist or hips. Instead, the body became a set of geometric shapes that shifted

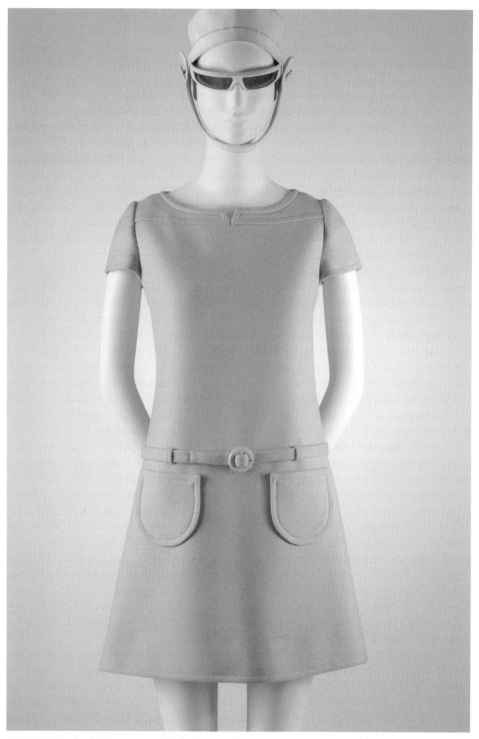

FIGURE 3.7: André Courrèges. Mini-dress. Light gray wool, c. 1968. Gift of Bernie Zamkoff. Photo: The Museum at FIT, New York.

attention away from the body to the legs. British model Twiggy, with her thin flat-chested boyish look became the fashionable ideal of the 1960s (Figure 3.8).

Within this climate of relative permissiveness and new assertiveness, non-gay men became conscious of looking gay or "camp," while male gays were keen to slough off the

FIGURE 3.8: Trimfit pantyhose. Blue nylon pantyhose in cardboard packaging. 1967–8. Gift of Dorothy Twinning Globus. Photo: The Museum at FIT, New York.

stereotype of effeminacy. From the 1970s onward, gay men began fashioning clothing styles that allowed them to "blend in" to mainstream culture. "The idea was to look more masculine," writes Joseph Hancock, "somewhat straight become accepted by the social order, and thus appear more attractive to each other."[25] It was the birth of the hypermasculine "clone" with a standardized dress style consisting of flannel shirt, baseball hat, jeans, army fatigues, and hiking boots. This culture of manliness anticipated the full-scale body culture of bodybuilding when anabolic steroids became more freely available in the 1980s. "Unlike the straights, gay men," Hancock observes:

> . . . overcompensated and recontextualized these traditional masculine appearances with rituals that included: weight lifting and body building routines to pump-up their muscles; engaging in extensive grooming regimes that kept their hair, skin, nails, and teeth nicely polished; and wearing their new ensembles fitted to every curve and crevice of their muscular bodies.[26]

Masculinizing gay male identity cannot be seen in isolation as an impatience to the effeminized stereotype but as a touchstone for opening up the possibility for different queer identities; to claim masculinity for gay as well as heterosexual males and to re-embody the desire for "maleness." An outstanding model, and symptom, of the shift of ideal body types among gay men was the illustrations of muscular gay men by the illustrator Touko Laaksonen, known as Tom of Finland. Touko dressed in leather, "becoming" Tom, and dreaming up a whole menagerie of pumped, "ripped" guys, "a gay utopia" in the words of Guy Snaith, that was "full of horny lumberjacks, sailors, policemen and construction workers, all bursting out of their uniforms or their jeans and T-shirts. Tomland is a fantasy world in which masculinity is held up as the highest ideal."[27] Laaksonen invented a universe in which jutting chins and full, pursed lips gazed longingly at biceps and pectorals that bulged with exaggerated rotundity, or to use the correct gay expression: "big pecs, tight abs and bubble butt."[28] The effect of Tom of Finland on the male gay community was immense, liberating many from inhibitions, and allowing them to assert that "maleness," such as it is, is an idea to be shared between gay and heterosexual men.

In the 1970s, celebrity culture heavily influenced ideas about the body. Popular media constantly reported on designers, rock stars and their muses, including Yves St Laurent, Catherine Deneuve, and Mick Jagger and Nicaraguan socialite, Bianca Jagger. Bianca's entry into the nightclub Studio 54 on a white horse made the disco the most famous club in the world. Celebrities including Liza Minelli, Gloria Vanderbilt, Grace Jones, Diana Ross, Margaux Hemingway, Cher, John Travolta, and Brooke Shields flocked through the club's doors wearing Halston, Calvin Klein, and Bill Blass. These celebrities represented ideal beauty, glamor, excess, and aspirations of luxury. People turned to celebrities and glamor as fashion influences, and they began to pay attention to the fashion labels that these celebrities wore. Most significantly, celebrities molded and influenced fashionable ideals and became icons of a generation. With the 1977 release of the now cult film *Saturday Night Fever* starring John Travolta with music by the Bee Gees, disco became a major phenomenon in Europe and America with clubs emulating Studio 54 opening internationally. Discotheques and nightclubs brought a whiff of excitement to young people where the working week would end and everyone would indulge in the escape from the everyday. Cocaine became the drug of choice and the enthusiasm for dressing up and exhibitionism, combined with gay and lesbian subculture, generated an atmosphere of hedonism. Studio 54 even launched a dedicated gay Sunday night, and Jerry Rubin Business Networking Salon night on Wednesdays, from 5 till midnight—the only time the disco opened at 5pm.[29] The confident, strident moves of disco-dancing are complemented by the exaggerated, splayed lines of the fashions inspired by the 1960s. Disco wear for women included sequined tops and halter-neck shirts, blazers, mini-skirts, tight spandex shorts, loose bell-bottom pants or form-fitting spandex pants, maxi-skirts and dresses with long thigh-high slits, jersey shoes ranged from knee-high boots to kitten heels. Men wore jackets with wide lapels, wide-legged or flared trousers and high-rise waistcoats. Neckties became wider and bolder, and shirt collars became long and pointed. In 1972, Diane von Fürstenberg designed the wrap around jersey dress, which became popular as daywear and disco attire (Figure 3.9).

The figure hugging fabrics used for fashion at the time enhanced the ideal body shape for male and female bodies that returned to the ideal of slim (and preferable tall) figure of the 1960s. Motown Records played an important role in the cultural landscape with artists such as Diana Ross and the Supremes, The Jackson Five, Donna Summer, Gladys Knight and the Pips, Sister Sledge, and Marvin Gaye influencing fashion and style.

FIGURE 3.9: Diane von Fürstenberg. Wrap dress. Multicolour printed acrylic knit. 1973. Gift of Diane von Fürstenberg. Photo: The Museum at FIT, New York.

THE POSTMODERN MALLEABLE BODY

We have already drawn a demarcation at about 1970, which was the visible emergence of queer as a political and physical statement of difference against the codes of heterosexuality and the traditional nuclear family, and thus the entry of diverse and perverse conceptions of the body. We might draw a new line in the history of the body at 1981 and the date of the first diagnosis of the AIDS in the Western world. This date marks the beginning of a definitive set of changes to the era of the cyborg and the technologized body. The body is henceforward a site of infinite modification and transformation that oscillates between paranoia and mania. The body is one that, thanks to the information revolution and media hype, is acutely conscious of agents that threaten the body, such as unwelcome chemicals in the air or chemical additives in food. The body is also terrified of ageing, for men and women alike. This fear of ageing overlaps with the body that is obsessed with "body maintenance"—the connotations of body and machine ought not to go unnoticed—and bodily improvement. Gym culture is born.

The fitness movement that emerged from California in the late 1970s gave rise to bodybuilding among men and women, gay and straight, and led to an increased consumption of supplements and products aimed at creating physical strength and muscular bodies. According to Marc Stern, it was these "same people who watched the same movies and television shows, who saw the same advertising and who consumed the same products and cultural images of beauty, sexuality, masculinity, femininity power and identity."[30] These representations of bodies—worked, pumped, drugged, and shaped by "pumping iron" and lifting weights—were articulated in visions of ideal bodies seen in fashion advertising and film. There is a discernible difference between the body builders from the 1980s onward, and in the female body. In both cases, the lack of fat and the presence of muscles is more pronounced. The body turns to any means available to push to the extremes of "perfection," a notion that exceeds the limits of a body. Anabolic steroids were available before this era, and instances of cosmetic enhancement surgery such as breast augmentation and silicone cheek-bones are evident since the mid-twentieth century. But it was only in the 1980s that these means of radical body mediation became widespread. Photographic technology had advanced to a degree that it could confer on its subject an imposing verisimilitude. The capitalist boom before the 1987 economic crash, together with photographic sophistication, led to the rise of the supermodel. Catwalk "supermodels" such as Cindy Crawford, Elvira Herzigova, Helena Christensen, Christie Brinkley, Naomi Campbell, Linda Evangelista, and others reached a marketability and celebrity hitherto unknown. The development of Photoshop technology meant that images of these fashion figureheads that appeared in fashion editorials would have enviable longevity; it would also mean that any model could be corrected with a flick of a computer mouse. The bodily ideal was never more present—and more remote.[31]

Olivia Newton John's music video *Physical*, in which she wore a trend-setting short hairstyle with a headband and spandex leggings, became a world number one hit in 1981. In the video she is the lone female (trainer?) in a stylized gym full of overweight men who, in a magical transformation involving exercise, evolve into becoming trim and muscular. The corollary is far too blatant to miss: fitness is sexy and good sex requires fitness.

Gyms, fitness centers and "wellness" centers are now commercial institutions in the developed world with a definable culture. There are specialized departments for "classes" such as Pilates, spin, and zumba, and many more, which attract the interest of different age groups and body types, which are often tied to social interests, and are also social gatherings in themselves. All of those mentioned are regimes groomed and refashioned from other activities and disciplines, namely yoga, cycling, and salsa dancing respectively. But they now have their discrete syntax and following, and are taken very seriously. Gym culture gave rise to a new form of dress style—work out or aerobics' fashion—and popular items included leotards in bright neon colors that covered the torso and sometimes the arms, worn with leggings or tights, as well as gadgets and accessories. Men often wore drawstring sweatpants with oversized crew neck sweatshirts that were also popular as women's fashions. Leg warmers bunched around the ankles, popular "high top" workout shoes such as Reebok and sweatbands completed the gym outfit. Fitness is now big business, as is fitness clothing, with large multinational brands like New Balance, Adidas, and Nike controlling a large portion of the market.

From the perspective of body and dress, a key turning point in this era was Madonna's *Blonde Ambition* tour that was launched in 1990. The costume designs by Jean Paul Gaultier had an indelible effect on both performer and designer, since both continued to make use of fetishistic, pseudo-BDSM (bondage, discipline, sadism, and masochism) fashions (figure 3.10).

Madonna, and Gaultier also presaged Lady Gaga who would pronounce herself to be a cyborg, thereby renouncing any claim or interest in naturalness. The modern world, with its dream of its polar opposite, placed nature clearly well and truly behind us. Instead, where the body is concerned, there are only degrees of technological intervention.

The 1980s and 1990s came and went, and along with it came the buffed body conscious metrosexual embodied by British football celebrity David Beckham and Australian swimmer Ian Thorpe. Heroin chic, influenced by the popularity of "designer drugs" like ecstasy was a look that became popular in the 1990s and was characterized by emancipated and androgynous bodies with pale complexions, dark circles under their eyes, unkempt hair, and prominent collar bones. The waif-like body of British supermodel Kate Moss and the androgynous slender look of model Jenny Shimizu became synonymous with Calvin Klein's underwear and *CK One* perfume commercials. Fashion editorials were no longer depicting clean and glamorous bodies that were unattainable, instead they were raw and rugged and mostly black and white to depict the brutality and harshness of reality. Heroin chic was the de-glamorization of fashion and the glorification of neglect and despair at the end of the twentieth century.

THE POST-MILLENNIAL PLASTIC BODY

The twenty-first century has witnessed the emergence of a new stylized type of body that is best described as the "porn" body and exists in exponential iterations thanks to the Internet, which has revolutionized pornography into a billion-dollar industry. Fashion has not been immune to the workings of the porn industry, often using pornographic codes to sell garments and accessories in a fiercely competitive market. "Fashion and pornography are connected in many ways,"[32] Pamela Church Gibson and Vicki Karaminas argue in a special issue of the journal *Fashion Theory* dedicated to the meeting of fashion and porn. "Both expose the body, fragmenting it by cropping and foregrounding the culturally eroticized parts of it, and both use stereotypically gendered, eroticized tropes."[33] In fashion media, pornographic bodies appear as *ideal* bodies placed in *ideal* and desirable

FIGURE 3.10: Jean Paul Gaultier. Dress. Orange shirred velvet, 1984. Photo: The Museum at FIT, New York.

lifestyles. This mutually exclusive relationship between fashion, the body, and pornography which is being played out in popular culture and the mass media has been described by Annette Lynch as porn chic and by Ariel Levy as raunch culture or raunch eroticism.[34] The definition of porn chic includes, "fashion and related trend based behaviors linked to the porn industry that have now become mainstreamed into the dress of women and girls."[35] The amalgamation of pornographic stylistic and visual codes by the fashion industry has resulted in what Pamela Church Gibson calls pornostyle, a new unacknowledged system of design and fashion promotion that has emerged in the last decade. As Gibson explains,

> This new fashion system has its own leaders in young female celebrities, its own magazines to chronicle their activities and showcase their style, its own internet presence, and its own retailing patterns. These young women often resemble in their self presentation the "glamour models" or pin-up girls of popular men's magazines, whose "look" is a muted version of the styling associated by many with that of hardcore pornography.[36]

The pornification of contemporary Western culture has given rise to ideal body types that are enhanced and superadded with technologies of beauty; faces pumped with Botox and Restalyne, and lawless foreheads free of wrinkles and expressions. Cosmetic surgery is, as Meredith Jones puts it, "makeover cultures quintessential expression."[37] The beautiful bodies of men and women of the twenty-first century are the products of a considerable amount of "work." Work here is understood as the euphemistic shorthand for plastic and cosmetic enhancement surgery. But this work is effort without material productivity. Note also that the work done on woman's long nails creates the condition that renders her deficient at manual labor. In both cases the notion of work is alien to the conventional meaning of work in the sense of labor and production.[38]

CONCLUSION. GIRLS WILL BE BOYS WILL BE GILRS WILL BE BOYS

In Paris Fashion Week *Haute Couture* Spring 2011, a tall, slender blond model strides down the catwalk wearing a white Jean Paul Gaultier wedding dress. Later in the evening the same model appears in Marc Jacobs men's collection dressed in a black suit. Andre (Andreja) Pejic was the first male model to parade for a womenswear collection, Isis King followed, and then came Casey Legler, the first woman to be signed to the men's board at Ford Models in New York. "I am a Woman who Models Men's Clothes. This is not about Gender," was the title of an article that Legler wrote for *The Guardian* newspaper in 2013. "The contemporary cultural landscape supports a larger interpretation than the one we currently have" of female-masculinity and masculine-femininity, wrote Legler, "to believe otherwise is to be deceived by a myopic view which is influenced by capitalist gain and profit."[39] Fashion has embraced a new masculine and feminine body ideal, one that does not equate beauty with biology and gender, rather the new condition of the body is one of shifting possibilities. To alter and modify one's appearance is no longer criminal or bizarre, although the results might entail either. Fashion and popular culture is so rife with examples and exhortations to bodily variation that it is sometimes invisible. We are presented with celebrities who, with plastic surgery, chemical peeling, Botox, and hair dye appear to have drunk from the fountain of youth. The perfected body in which perfectability and youth is an endlessly flowing sequence with no end, is embroiled in the flows of capital. The body becomes more and more machine: and the procedures are referred to as "maintenance." One maintains one's body as one does one's car. The ideal fashionable body of the twentieth and twenty-first century has always preferred (in fact insisted) on a young and slim physique, ignored plump and older bodies. As Julia Twigg fittingly writes, "fashion and age sit uncomfortable together. Fashion inhabits a world of youthful beauty, of fantasy, of imagination, allure. Its discourses are frenetic and frothy; its images glamorous and—above all—youthful."[40]

CHAPTER FOUR

Belief

SUSAN J. PALMER AND PAUL GAREAU

Every religion has its own sacred form of dress. Whether the tradition is Christian, Muslim, Judaic, Buddhist, Hindu, each has its own style of religious clothing—a style that is unique, yet shares certain common features. Most religions promote cleanliness and respect for the human body, and clothing is a means of safeguarding members' modesty and chastity. For the laity, clothing proclaims membership in a specific faith. For the clergy, whether they are bishops, rabbis, imams, or monks, their distinctive garb is a sign of their special ministry. Liturgical vestments are, typically, based on the fashions of antiquity and express a link with the past. The color and design of religious dress may denote rank in the priestly hierarchy, or may reflect the liturgical season.[1]

Conservative, sectarian "fundamentalist" religious communities in particular, such as the Amish, the Hutterites, the Hassidic Jews, and certain branches of Sunni Islam tend to preserve the fashion conventions of previous centuries, which advertise their religiously-based gender roles and family patterns. The hijab, for example, has been interpreted by journalists and feminists in the West as a symptom of Muslim men's entrenched prejudices and sexist attitudes towards women, and a sign of their confinement to the domestic sphere. Muslim women, however, have defended the hijab as a protest against the degradation of women in Western fashion, which defines them as sex objects.[2] The niqab debate in Europe has generated many statements about patriarchal control and the subjugation of Muslim women. For French politicians, one argument for the banning of the niqab in the public sphere was that it implies a rejection of the rights and responsibilities of French citizenship.[3]

Thus, religious dress can be a "flash point" between "fundamentalists" and their neighbors. Spiritual symbols, overtly displayed, in dress, jewelry, hairstyles, tattoos proclaim the individual's most intimate inner world and spiritual identity. But the secular observer might interpret these symbols as a defiant declaration of elite "otherness." What true believers wear advertises their affiliation with a mother church or community, but for the outsider, these beliefs might appear strange, irrational, and even subversive or threatening. Since traditional clothing can be a source of friction with the larger society, as it appears archaic, even anachronistic as it is worn in the venerable world religions. Thus, it is not surprising that an even higher level of popular concern—or hostility—is evoked when the "cults" appear on the street in "costumes" that broadcast their unfamiliar, heterodox beliefs and unconventional lifestyles.

In this chapter, we will describe and interpret sacred dress (and undress) in several unconventional minority religions, known to sociologists as "new religious movements" or "NRMs" (although journalists the general public tend to label them more pejoratively, as "cults"). Most of the NRMs referred to in this chapter emerged in the late twentieth century, after the Second World War. Fashion plays an important and dynamic role in these new religious communities, because NRMs are "deliberate heresies."[4] NRMs might be seen as utopian societies in the process of forging new myths, new rituals, and new doctrines. As micro-societies, they are in flux, undergoing rapid development, and they are oppositional by their very nature. NRMs tend to pose a challenge (overt or implied) to mainstream churches, governments, and the scientific or educational institutions of their host society. As the British sociologist, Eileen Barker, notes: "Throughout history, new religions have been treated with fear and suspicion—they are, after all, challenging the status quo with their new beliefs and practices."[5]

If examined within the historical context of twentieth century America, these new religious fashions are significant as laboratories of social experimentation. Warren Lewis writes: "New religions in the history of the American people have served at least one particular function; they have allowed the nation to explore, work out and relieve deep cultural needs . . . to solve within the laboratories of these new religions some more general cultural problem."[6] America in the twentieth century was a period of rapid change and diversification. The liberalization of immigration policies led to an influx of new, exotic populations from Asia and the Middle East. The hippie counterculture and other radical social movements like the Black Panthers and the women's feminist movement and Gay Pride expressed in their dress codes new, idealized, almost utopian visions of race, gender, and sexuality. Compared to the dress codes of the nineteenth century or before the Second World War, the second half of the twentieth century was a period of amazing flexibility, diversity, and creativity in fashion. America's new, eclectic, and syncretic spiritual movements appropriated and combined fashion codes and concepts from these larger social movements. Thus, the extraordinary forms of new religious dress and undress described below might be analyzed as extreme forms of, almost parodies of, the multicultural and multifaceted experiments in fashion found in twentieth-century "mainstream" secular society.

NEW RELIGIOUS MOVEMENTS IN THE TWENTIETH CENTURY

North America has provided a haven to persecuted religious minorities from Europe since the *Mayflower* landed at Plymouth Rock in 1620.[7] Since then, the continent has proven to be a fertile environment for spiritual innovations and communal "cities on a hill." If we survey the "alternative altars" in twentieth century North America, many of the most "successful" (in terms of size and longevity) attracted attention simply because of their dress codes.[8]

At the turn of the twentieth century, the Theosophical movement, based on the teachings of Madame Blavatsky, as well as Rudolf Steiner's Anthroposophy, gained a certain visibility due to the Greek tunics worn in their pageants and Eurythmics dance demonstrations. The disciples of Katherine Tingley's (1847–1929) theosophical community in California, for example, wore Greek togas and wreaths as part of the Theatrical Work of the Universal Brotherhood and Theosophical Society (1898–1929), costumes which signaled their "pagan" distance from Christianity.[9] The African-American "Black Nationalist" spiritual movements that emerged in the US

FIGURE 4.1: Noble Drew Ali's Moorish Science Temple Conclave, Chicago, 1928. Photo: Wikimedia Commons.

in the early twentieth century were—and still are—conspicuous due to their distinctive un-American dress. Noble Drew Ali's Moorish Temple in Philadelphia combined Egyptian and Muslim fashions (the fez, hijab, dishdasha, and shalwar) with esoteric symbols from Freemasonry (Figure 4.1). The Nation of Islam is conspicuously conservative, for its brothers still wear 1950s-style suits and red bow ties. The Rastafarians are highly visible in their dreadlocks and tams which display the colors of the Rasta flag: red for the blood of black people, yellow for the stolen gold, and green for the lost lands of Africa.[10]

If analyzed within the African-American struggle for equal rights and dignity, the quite different dress codes found in Black Nationalist groups all address the issue of the role of place of the "Black Man" in US society. Father Divine's Peace Mission, which refused to recognize racial differences, the Nation of Islam, whose aim is to separate the races into all-white/all-black states within the US, and Martin Luther King's Protestant congregation, who marched to demand their right to exercise their vote, all wear conservative symbols of urban respectability and responsible citizenship—suits and ties. The exotic, foreign garb of the Moorish Temple, which embraces Egyptian culture, and of the Rastafarians, who dream of Africa, are visible symbols of their conscious rejection of White American identity and culture (Figure 4.2).

FIGURE 4.2: African Rastafarian, c. 1990. Photo: ruffraido/Getty Images.

SYMBOLS OF AUTHORITY: CORONATION AND REGENCY IN FOUR APOCALYPTIC NRMs

Thomas Carlyle, the nineteenth-century Scottish philosopher and satirical essayist, writes of the symbolic value of clothing. He invites his readers to visualize an assembly of British dukes, colonels, and generals in their pompous military uniforms, and to imagine that, suddenly, their clothes should vanish! "Live there a man," Carlyle asks rhetorically, "who can figure a naked Duke . . . addressing a naked House of Lords? Imagination . . . recoils on itself."[11] Carlyle's playful passage points to how all clothing is imbued with symbols. Some symbols speak of authority. As anthropologist David Kertzer claims, "We can recognize, through symbols, who are the powerful and who are the weak. Through the manipulation of symbols, the powerful reinforce their authority. Yet the weak, too, can try to put on new clothes and strip the clothes from the mighty."[12]

Many examples of how the weak "try to put on new clothes and strip the clothes from the mighty" are found in marginal new religions. Charismatic prophet/founders of NRMs are indeed "weak" in the sense that the larger society does not lend them institutional support nor grant them social legitimacy. Many of them are relatively uneducated and come from ghettos or the margins of society. But through the deliberate manipulation of symbols, they may gain strength, attract a following, and bolster their precarious charismatic claims. One way they accomplish this is by appearing in public in the appropriate symbolic apparel. The American political scientist, Harold L. Nieburg, observed that "creating a symbol, or . . . identifying oneself with a popular symbol, can be a potent way of gaining power, for the hallmark of power is the construction of reality."[13] One often finds the symbols of royalty in new religions; the trappings of kings and queens, and rituals of coronation. The messianic leaders described below all expressed their divine status and leadership aspirations through the wearing of royal garments and rituals of coronation.

MANDAROM

In June 1990, the cover of *Paris Match* featured a photograph of the messianic leader of Mandarom in the act of crowning himself the "Cosmoplanetary Messiah" in a new, magical ritual whose purpose was to unite the world's faiths and usher in the Golden Age. Gilbert Bourdin (1923–98), was initially a yoga teacher who came to France from Martinique, and with his disciples founded the Association of the Knights of the Golden Lotus in 1967. In 1969, they purchased land in the French Alps where they built the Holy City of Mandarom Shambalasalem, a new, original religion indigenous to France that combines *advaita* Hinduism with Western esotericism.[14]

Bourdin prepared his disciples, the "Aumistes," for his messianic role in stages; first unveiling himself as Shri Swami Hansananda Sarasvati, then as the Lord Hamsah Manarah, next as the Hierokarantine, and finally as the Cosmoplanetary Messiah. His mission, Aumistes believe, was to come to Earth at the end of time to unite all the world's religions, to reveal the Unity of the Face of God, and to usher in the Golden Age.[15] He guided his *chelas* (disciples) through seven steps of Revelation. Each revelation focused on one of the world's religions, and was marked by the enactment of Buddhist, Hindu, Muslim, Jewish or Christian rituals. In 1990 they all culminated in the supreme "Revelation of Unity."

In May 1990, the Aumistes held a press conference to announce the glad tidings of the advent of the Cosmoplanetary Messiah to the world. The gates of Mandarom were opened, and the public was invited to attend a series of climactic coronations during the Feast of Wesak (the Buddhist full moon celebration). Lord Hamsah Manarah sat enthroned as the Aumistes performed five hours of circumambulations, prostrations, genuflections, chanting, drums, bells, and cymbals. One by one, the guru placed a series of elaborate crowns on his own head. Each represented one of the major faiths: Hindu, Buddhist, Jewish, Christian, and Muslim. At the climax of the ceremony, accompanied by drums and clashing cymbals, the guru placed the magnificent crown of the Cosmoplanetary Messiah upon his own head, symbolically enacting the Unity of All Religions and the Advent of the Golden Age (Figures 4.3, 4.4).

For journalists, the coronation yielded a veritable arsenal of colorful, exotic photographs. These were used in a less-than-reverent manner by UNADFI (France's major "anticult" organization) and by the French media to illustrate the weird and dangerous aspects of irrational *sectes* in France. The eight-meter high statue of the Cosmoplanetary Messiah, which dominated Mandarom and the surrounding landscape, became a focus of conflict. In June 2001, the prefect of *les Alpes de Haute Provence* asked for authorization to invade Mandarom and proceed with the demolition of the statue. On September 5, 2001 the

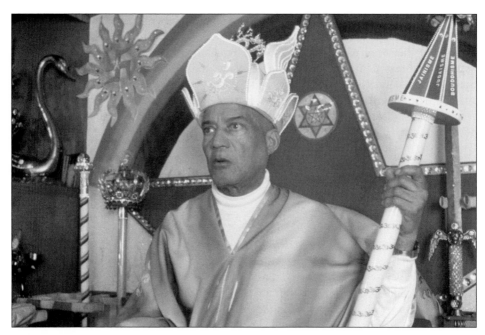

FIGURE 4.3: Crowning of his holiness the Messiah Hamsah Manarah in Castellane, France, on March 1, 1991. Photo: Alain Benainous/Gamma-Rapho via Getty Images.

FIGURE 4.4: The King Messiah in the Mandarom Shambhasalem Monastery, Castellane, France on March 1, 1991. Photo: Alain Benainous/Gamma-Rapho via Getty Images.

prefect led a surprise raid, invading the monastery with 200 soldiers from the French army accompanied by journalists. For forty-eight hours, France watched the preparations for the detonation unfold on television. The following morning at 5:20, the statue exploded and toppled down the side of the mountain. The face of the Cosmoplanetary Messiah, that bore an obvious resemblance to Hamsah Manarah, fell to the ground intact, so the army pulverized it with a shovel.[16] Mandarom's fashions, art and architecture were outstanding in terms of its eclecticism and syncretism. This event provides a vivid example of an "allergic reaction" to alien cultures, and of how spiritual clothing might be perceived as threatening to the secular public when its very intent was to bring about unity and peace.

THE NATION OF YAHWEH

The Nation of Yahweh (NOY) is one of America's Black Hebrew groups, and was founded in 1979 in Miami, Florida by Hulon Mitchell Jr., known to his "worshippers" as Yahweh ben Yahweh (YBY) meaning "God, Son of God" in Hebrew. He established a commune called the Temple of Love in Miami where he would appear on stage wearing white robes and a white turban. He was surrounded by bodyguards called the Circle of Ten, men evidently chosen for their height and strength, who wielded African spears. All NOY members dress in white robes and turbans, emulating their messianic leader, and embrace a strong ethic of hard work, vegetarianism, and conservative family values. White clothing is of course a perennial and universal symbol of cleanliness and purity, and in the NOY their white flowing robes and white turbans ("crowns") also express their collective identity as a "Royal Priesthood" (Figure 4.5).

The majority of the first converts came from the socially disadvantaged ranks of Miami's black ghettos. YBY, in his recorded speeches, talks to and refers to homeless beggars, pimps, prostitutes, and drug addicts; the petty criminals or gangsters in his congregation (see the documentary film, *Judas, The Parable of the Leaven*). But these people experienced a dramatic improvement in their living conditions and "mentality." By surrendering to YBY as the Black Messiah in the Last Days, symbolically and psychologically, they embraced their own divinity, as "Hebrew Israelites." The NOY's "From Poverty to Riches" program combined cooperative sharing, voluntary labor, and strict adherence to "Hebrew" rules governing morality, cleanliness, and diet. By this means, members (many of whom were erstwhile "wretches") achieved economic success, social respectability, and enjoyed the security of a strong, dynamic community that supported the nuclear family.[17]

By 1990, it appeared that YBY had achieved his dream of building a material "Kingdom of Heaven" on earth, based on each brother's and sister's realization of their own divinity as Hebrew Israelites, part of the body of the Living God, which literally promised them physical immortality in this life. NOY literature refers frequently to YBY's divinity and draws on metaphors of royalty:

> These subsequent events shall be the most . . . readily visible . . . to the so-called Black people of America . . . [Yahweh Ben Yahweh] is also the Savior and Redeemer of the whole world. He shall be crowned "King" of kings and "Lord" of all lords.[18]

In 2007, Yahweh Ben Yahweh died shortly after getting out of prison. He had been convicted of conspiracy in murder, racketing, and extortion. Suddenly, his worshippers were forced to confront the problem of "cognitive dissonance," since YBY was believed to be God-in flesh, hence immortal.[19] Within a year, a new leader emerged opportunistically, who called himself, Yahweh ben Yahweh ben Yahweh (Son of the Son of God), and claimed that YBY's soul had

FIGURE 4.5: Portrait of Yahweh leader Yahweh ben Yahweh, December 1986. Photo:
Bettmann/contributor.

transmigrated into his consciousness. In important part of YBYBY's "charismatic display" was to appear in royal garments and gold medallions.[20] His robes were positively flashy compared to those of his father's white garment. He created an asymmetrical closed coat of shiny satin with high standing collar. One side was white, the rest navy with a rippled textures satin in the sleeves and yoke. It was trimmed with a wide panel of silver braid.

An ex-member of the NOY named Khalil Amani attacks the upstart's credentials in his article, "YBYBY the Interloper," posted on his website. In pithy, satirical ghetto prose, he deplores YBY's negligence in appointing no successor and makes the point that clothes do not make the man (or, in this case, the God):

> I don't care how fancy your robes are! You're still just a wannabe bald-headed, emaciated-looking black man who appears to be two-weeks off the crack pipe! Yahweh ben Yahweh was a beautiful man! (Pause) His skin was like fine brass! His fingernails were immaculately groomed. His eyes were like a "flame of fire" (blue/green/gray)! His hair on his head was long and like pure wool!

Khalil Amani questions the usurper's charismatic claims (of soul transmigration) by launching into an *ad hominem* attack:

> But let YBYBY tell it—Yahweh ben Yahweh jumped into his body! He is the reincarnation of YBY! Such bullshit that borders on blasphemy! And, of all the bodies YBY could've jumped in—why did he downgrade his looks by entering the body of a frail, fragile, skinny, boney, girlie-man with hydrocephaly (a jug head)? Dude is straight skint (that means ugly) compared to Yahweh ben Yahweh.

Thus it appears that the pretender's "fancy robes" were not enough to qualify him to become YBY's successor as the NOY's God-in-Flesh—at least for Khalil Amani.

UNARIUS ACADEMY OF SCIENCE

The theatrical costumes of Unarius, the UFO religion outside San Diego, CA appear to be inspired by American TV and pop culture of the 1950s and 1960s. The queenly apparel of the group's charismatic late leader, Uriel (Ruth Norman), might have been taken from sci-fi movies, *Star Trek* or *Planet of the Apes*. But for Unarians, their fashions refer to the visions of past lives and other planets received by Uriel.

Ruth E. Norman (1900–93) became the leader and psychic channel known as "Uriel" of the Unarius Academy of Science after her husband, Ernest Norman, passed away in 1971. She began to receive messages from extra-terrestrials, as well as Nikola Tesla, Mary Magdalene, and Leonardo da Vinci. In 1974, Norman predicted that a space fleet of benevolent aliens, the Space Brothers, would land on Earth that year, and purchased a property to serve as their landing site. After the extraterrestrials failed to appear, undaunted, Norman embarked on a publicity campaign, claiming to have united the Earth with an interplanetary confederation, and postponed the landing date to 2001.[21]

The Unarians have filmed many dramatic re-enactments of their past lives, which involves the designing, sewing, and wearing of historic costumes in the style of 1950s Hollywood films. Unarius video programs were frequently aired on public access TV channels across the USA and many were hosted by Uriel wearing sparkly blue eye shadow and face glitter (Figure 4.6).

In 1973, Norman revealed to her followers an important event occurring on a higher spiritual plane—her spiritual marriage to Archangel Michiel. This wedding had culminated

FIGURE 4.6: Uriel, cosmic visionary and co-founder of the Unarius Educational Foundation, in the Flame Room, 1980s. Photo: Unarius Educational Foundation.

in her coronation as Queen of Archangels, Uriel. She and her close assistant, Charles Spiegel (who would became her successor) experienced the event over a twenty-one-day time period and re-enacted the ceremony for the Unariuns, with Spiegel standing in for the Archangel Michael.[22] This wedding ceremony marked an escalation in Norman's charismatic claims and status. Her students subsequently referred to Ruth Norman as "Uriel", an acronym of "universal, radiant, infinite, eternal light," and the Unarians still hold an annual celebration of this cosmic wedding.[23]

Throughout her charismatic career, Uriel was often photographed by media in her queenly gowns, fancy wigs, and royal scepters. She said her dress style imitated the fashion of extraterrestrials, whose attire was brighter and more radiant than any clothing on Earth. At the Unarius headquarters in San Diego, Uriel would sit on a golden throne decorated with peacock feathers. Scholars Kirkpatrick and Tumminia speculate that Uriel's charismatic clothing was primarily responsible for gaining publicity for the group and spreading the Space Brothers' invitation to join the Intergalactic Federation.[24] Uriel's creative inspiration seemed to be derived from her psychic memories of past live events, but her charismatic performances might be compared to the performance art of popular musicians, Liberace, Cher, or Elton John.

THE ARMY OF MARY

The Army of Mary is a highly conservative Catholic organization that evolved out of a Marian devotional group in Lac Etchemin, Quebec (a village 100km south of Quebec

City). In 1971, Marie-Paule Giguère (1921–2015), a Quebecoise housewife and mother of five, founded the Army of Mary under the auspices of the Catholic Church. Despite her group's fundamentalist orientation and subordination to the authority of the Holy See, the Army of Mary was excommunicated in 2007 for their heterodox beliefs and practices. Since then, the Army of Mary has successfully negotiated their transition into a new religion, bolstered by the members' belief in the authenticity Giguère's charismatic claim to be the Virgin Mary incarnate.

Through her mystical experiences and the communication of her ongoing divine revelations, Giguère has shaped and transformed the "Catholic" worldview of her followers and reshaped their understanding of prophecy, theology, and the apocalypse. But Giguère perceives God's revelations through a "gendered lens" that underscores women's perspective and agency—and this applies to the sacred apparel of the Army of Mary, most notably in Giguère's writings on the *Five Dresses Asked of Heaven*.

In 1958, Giguère writes, she received the mystical revelation that she was indeed the Virgin Mary incarnate. As Christ was the incarnation of God, so she is to her acolytes the physical embodiment of Mary on earth.[25] This concept became the foundation for the Army of Mary's religious worldview, and the driving force behind their future actions.

In 2000, the Army of Mary inaugurated an impressive building at Lac Etchemin called *Spiri Maria* that currently serves as headquarters for the Church of John. This Church is understood to be the transmutation of the Church of Rome into the apocalyptical Church of John the Evangelist—a new symbolic Vatican, in tandem to the Holy See. Within this new space, the Army of Mary has elected a new Pope, ordained its own priests, performed canonizations, and promulgated a new Marian dogma. Moreover, the Church of John has issued new Trinitarian doctrine they call the *Quinternity*,[26] adding two new persons to the traditional Holy Trinity—the Immaculate Conception (the Virgin Mary) and Marie-Paule Giguère. This transmuted, parallel Church and its new doctrines is understood by Army of Mary acolytes as a necessary condition before humanity can be saved in the impending apocalypse, according to their understanding of Christian salvation history.

Despite the Army of Mary's evident piety and conservative Catholic stance, in 2007 the Vatican excommunicated several of their members who "knowingly and deliberately embrace the "heretical" teachings of the Army of Mary."[27] The Vatican excommunicated Father Jean-Pierre Mastropietro—the current pope of the Church of John under the name Padré Jean-Pierre, and other members of the movement for performing ordinations of priests and deacons, and "enter[ing] into schism by participating in the ordinations despite Church warnings."[28]

The Five Dresses Asked of Heaven

The *Five Dresses Asked of Heaven*, written by Giguère, is summarized in one important edition of the Army of Mary's newsletter.[29] These dresses are significant because they underscore key moments in Giguère's charismatic career, acting as signposts in the development of the Church of John and of her role in Christian salvation history. They define her sacred gendered identity, and the Five Dresses have had an impact on the identity development of the Army of Mary as an institution.

Early in her career, there was a prefiguration of the divine dress theme on Giguère's own wedding day, July 1, 1944.[30] After slipping into her wedding dress, she prayed to God to bless her marriage with the gift of children. Suddenly, she beheld herself flying above the earth wearing a flowing white gown, floating from country to country on a mission of caring for the world—a mission that she would only come to comprehend at a later time. In hindsight, this vision was interpreted as the first step down the road that would eventually lead to her divinity. But centrally, the wedding dress represented her connection to conservative Catholic vision of women's engagement within a gendered domesticity in what Robert Orsi spoke of as "the Catholic Family Romance"[31] that underscores a moral framework from which mothers are asserted as religious pillars of the family and society. Symbolically, it prefigured her role of Mother on a cosmological scale.

The First Dress

In 1972, Giguère claims, she heard the voice of God instructing her to find a white dress to wear at the Mass inaugurating the Army of Mary as a pious organization.[32] But God's instructions were rather vague, and after searching the clothing shops of Quebec City without any luck, Giguère's daughter finally spotted the fateful dress. Fashioned from a silky white fabric, it had a modest cut with high collar and long sleeves, but was fitted with a fashionable white belt and accented with a sharp light blue taffeta kerchief. It is a conventional, feminine dress that affirms modesty. Later, while attending Mass, Giguère heard God's voice saying she should wear white in imitation of the priests. Giguère would wear this dress when she set out on her pilgrimages; to Lourdes in 1974, and to the Holy Land in 1975.

This First Dress narrative places Giguère in a parallel role with the priests who are the legitimate religious experts in the Catholic Church. Also, it introduces the theme of Holy Motherhood.[33] This assures her social network of friends and family that they will not be excluded from Christian salvation. This emphasis on motherhood and family is found throughout Giguère's lengthy, twenty-volume hagiography.

The Second Dress

In 1969, Giguère received a vision in which God told her to find a more elaborate white gown with a train and veil to wear on three separate occasions. The first would be at the sanctuary at Lac Etchemin (1976); the second at her mother's house at Lac Etchemin at the time of a papal visit to Quebec (1992); and the third in Rome (2000).

Giguère chose a wedding dress with a long veil of light, transparent material that produced an aura enveloping her body. On the back of the dress was pinned a white bow that drew in her waist. This dress featured fancy details and brocade work. Giguère writes of her first time wearing and of how it represents her connection to the Virgin Mary.[34] In humble tones, she declares she is unworthy of this honor. She wore the dress again for the visit of a high-ranking clergyman and supporter of the Army of Mary, Monseigneur van Lierde from Holland. Giguère regarded him as a stand-in for the Pope, since he was the Vicar General for the Vatican at the time. This occasion was understood as a major step toward legitimizing the work of the Army of Mary. The third occasion she wore the Second Dress was during her visit to Rome in 1992, but the Vatican officials refused to participate with her in a church ceremony that would operationalize God's "third request." This was a significant blow for Giguère, and it undermined the legitimacy of the Army of Mary. Her leaders viewed the Vatican's refusal as a "betrayal" of the Church that would have dire consequences to the salvation of mankind. In 2000, however, the Vatican was bypassed and God's will was obeyed when Giguère and one of her high-ranking priests performed the ceremony inaugurating the Spiri Maria building as the Church of John.

The Third Dress

In 1974, God spoke to Giguère again, asking her to find another white dress, this time giving her a clear vision of its appearance. She beheld a full-length dress like a priest's cassock, with long sleeves, a high Nehru collar, and metallic appliqué adorning the entire front length of the dress. Giguère searched the shops in Quebec City, but to no avail. The following summer of 1975, while on a pilgrimage to Jerusalem, a woman stranger who was part of their group of pilgrims unwittingly pointed out a dress in a gift shop. To Giguère's surprise, this was the Third Dress, destined for future important events. This dress was similar to the first dress asked by God, but more elaborate, and it emulated the traditional vestments of the Catholic male clergy, thereby marking Giguère's growing stature in her alternative Catholic worldview through ecclesiastical parallel.

The Fourth Dress

On March 25, 1977, Giguère tried on a dress that the women in the Army of Mary choir were already wearing. It was a simple polyester white dress with high button-up collar, long sleeves, and blue satin sash—in the style of the Marian apparition of Lourdes. In contrast to her previous divine dresses, this was particularly plain. Upon donning this modest Marian apparel, Giguère had a vision of her three long-term women friends (co-founders of the Army of Mary) all wearing this dress to commemorate the Immaculate Conception. At that moment, Giguère and her three friends were receiving a benediction from a priest, and she had a revelation that they were standing on hallowed ground. Giguère noted, however, that they were in Lac Etchemin and not in Rome. For her, this moment was a clear signal of the importance of Lac Etchemin in God's plan as the New Rome.

Although Giguère never required that the women or men of the Army of Mary should imitate her divine dress style, at this point the Fourth Dress (with a white sash) became the standard ritual dress for both female and male members, on the occasion of their initiation into the Army of Mary, referring to the Immaculate Conception and their unity as a moral community. It is a practical costume and economical to reproduce on a mass scale.

The Fifth Dress

This dress was worn in 2007 as a penultimate expression of Giguère's divine status—at the inauguration of the Church of John and at the Army of Mary's subsequent excommunication. This dress was modeled on the iconic Marian apparition, the Lady of All Peoples, a powerful Marian apparition in a post-Second World War Holland that called for a new Marian Dogma that would elevate the Virgin's salvific role in the Catholic Church by way of intersession and popular devotion.[35] Army of Mary acolytes venerate the Lady of All Peoples and view Giguère as the incarnation of this particular apparition. The dress is a modest cassock of white polyester with a beige-colored belt and thin veil at the back of the head and a waist-length white cloak. The cloak became the ritual garb for both male and female members of the Army of Mary. These cloaks, however, are a deep blue with golden fringe.

Army of Mary members are spiritual warriors at the end of time. Their ritual garb is white cassocks and deep blue Marian-colored cloaks with gold fringe to help them brave the challenges of the apocalypse. But the Fifth Dress is the most significant divine dress of all. It imitates the traditional style of previous Marian apparitions, particularly those at Lourdes and Fatima. The color blue connects these apparitions to the current Army of Mary uniform. But for Guiguère as the Lady of All Peoples, the gold fringes refer to her penultimate divinity as a golden light from the Godhead received through the Holy Spirit.

The Fifth Dress serves a teleological and Christological function that elevates Guiguère from her mere earthly role to her role in Christian eschatology. It denotes Guiguère's divinity and salvific role at the head of an army girded for a cosmic battle. Recalling the vision, Guiguère received on her wedding day, the Fifth Dress is depicted in images of Guiguère walking above the earth, like the Lady of All Peoples. Guiguère becomes a goddess, dressed in white fringed in gold.

Toward the end of her hagiographic narrative on divine fashion, Guiguère reflects on her role in Christian salvation history and its challenges. She notes that, like Christ, her suffering, humiliations, and frustrations have a special salvific power that extends to all suffering humanity. Thus, the Five Dresses are a significant part of God's divine plan.

The apocalyptical worldview of the Army of Mary, with its powerful images of the feminine divine, is interesting from a feminist perspective. It is important to note, however, that Guiguère is not a proponent of gender equality. As a mother of five children, a steadfast wife and a grandmother, she remains a staunch conservative, advocating a gendered and heteronormative complementarity.[36] But since she is believed to be the Virgin Mary incarnate, for her followers the androcentric Catholic faith is infused with the feminine divine and a gendered complementarity cosmology.

The Five Dresses Asked of Heaven are powerful symbols They mark the evolution of the Army of Mary's work and make God's will in the world palpable. In Max Weber's typology of dominance, the Five Dresses function as a form of "charismatic display"[37] serving to reinforce Guiguère's claims and to legitimize the Church of John as the new Rome. By wearing them to important occasions, Guiguère fully embraced her role as savior of the universe and justified her "seemingly" unorthodox actions concerning the Church of John. It appears extraordinary that a matter of such *gravitas* as salvation history could be signaled, transformed, and safeguarded by a woman wearing a symbolic dress. These actions prove that religious and symbolic meanings have myriad means of transmission. The Army of Mary has provided us with a spectacle of divine authentication through evolving and carefully crafted divine fashion.

SACRED UNDRESS: THE POLITICS AND SYMBOLS OF NUDITY IN THREE RADICAL NRMs

Sacred clothing does not always denote authority; it can also denote humility. Protestant ministers, for example, may attend church in sports clothes so as to "blend in" with their flock. Ministers from the Christian Motorcycle League who infiltrate biker clubs, intent on saving the souls of their fellow sinners, will assume the leather garments and tattoos of these outlaws, their unwitting "flock." Religious vestments are necessarily clean. Holiness is associated with purity, but cleanliness might be discarded for certain sacred occasions. Devout Christians mark their foreheads with ashes during Lent, Franciscan monks vowed to poverty wear rags, and Rastafarians let their hair form dreadlocks.

While religious clothing and ritual vestments, in most religious traditions, are usually modest, reflecting their conservative sexual *mores*, the principle of modesty has been discarded certain radical religious groups. In India, for example, Hindu renunciates, the *sadhus* who reject clothing, walk around "sky-clad."[38] The Lakota Sioux and other Native

American tribes practice a sweat lodge ceremony, which requires nudity in sex-segregated lodges. In contemporary Wicca, there are skyclad gatherings.[39] Two examples of ritual nudity in the twentieth century can be found in the Doukhobors of British Columbia and the International Raëlian Movement. Both of these contemporary NRMs exhibits anarchistic, antinomian qualities. If clothing is a source of friction between a minority religion and its host society, the naked body constitutes an even greater flash point.

THE DOUKHOBORS

The Doukhobors ("Spirit Wrestlers") originated in Russia and the Ukraine in the eighteenth century and might be described as radical Christian anarchists who refused to pledge allegiance to a secular government. Until the late 1960s, they were strictly communitarian, refusing to sign contracts or to serve in the military.

In the Doukhobor worldview, God resides in every living thing. As radical anarchists, they rejected the outer trappings of the Orthodox Church: the clergy, the sacraments of baptism, marriage, the mass, and religious icons. Because of their radical pacifism, the early Doukhobors came into conflict with the Russian czars, Alexander I and Nicholas I. In 1899, persecuted for their refusal to serve in the Russian army, around 7,500 Doukhobors emigrated from Russia to Canada and settled in Manitoba and Saskatchewan, and eventually British Columbia.

On arrival in Canada, the Doukhobors' conflict with the state continued, due to their refusal to pledge allegiance to the Crown, and to register marriages, births, and deaths. Also they refused to register the ownership of land under the names of private individuals. Between 1908 and 1912, the Doukhobors bought land in British Columbia where they cultivated farms and planted fruit trees.

The very first Doukhobor nudist demonstration occurred in 1903 when a schism formed called the Svobodniki, who later became the "Sons of Freedom", or "Freedomites." This radical branch of the Doukhobors became infamous for public protests, for burning money and possessions, and parading in public nude. Their rationale for nudity was that human skin, as God's creation, was more perfect than clothing, which was the imperfect work of human hands. Also, public nudity became a form of protest against the materialist tendencies of society.

The Sons of Freedom rejected their Russian leader, Peter Verigin's claim to be the Christ, and protested against his leadership, since Verigin had persuaded his followers to sign contracts with the British Columbian government, so by April 1903, over 2,000 quarter sections of Doukhobor land were legally registered.[40] Fifty-odd Doukhobors went underground to form a resistance movement. In May 1903, they marched naked from village to village. The historian Zubek and Solberg write:

> They were back in [Eden], the pre-figleaf era, before sin and evil entered the world. They marched, free as the birds in the air. Not a shred of clothing was in evidence, except the rubbers protecting their feet from the pebbles and gravel.[41]

In Doukhobor teachings, nudity symbolizes a state of Edenic innocence and holiness. In Doukhobor utopian thought, their communal society was based on the original Garden of Eden where Adam and Eve rested in pleasure, with no need to work, prepare cooked food, exploit animals, or make and wear clothing. Only after the Fall of Man did Adam and Eve wear the fig leaf, which the Doukhobors saw as a symbol of man's corruption by Evil. Thus, by marching in the nude these "zealots" were "finding a way to symbolize freedom." [42] The demonstrators in 1903 were met by twenty guards, sent out by Verigin, who ordered them to "Go home and behave!" and whipped them with willow switches, eventually taking the women and children into their care. Two naked men marched through the cold night and were rounded up the Royal Canadian Mounted Police (RCMP) assisted by a hundred local citizens. The naked zealots were herded into Immigration Hall where lanterns were hung overnight to attract mosquitos which persuaded the prisoners to get dressed. These twenty-eight Doukhobors were sentenced to three months in prison. Until they were charged, these farmers had been unaware of any existing laws that banned such exhibitionism and were astonished to find that nudism was a criminal and civil offence in Canada. Their own accounts of their prison experience in Regina, Saskatchewan, report of brutal beatings and torture at the hands of the prison guards.

Ten of the released prisoners formed the core leadership of the Sons of Freedom. Their experience had convinced them that Peter Verigin was no longer the Christ and that the Doukhobors had abandoned their faith by compromising with secular society and buying "satanic" farm equipment like metal binders and rollers made in factories.[43] Their suffering in prison made them martyrs for a cause, and they were Christ-like figures. They had also discovered that nudity could be a powerful tool, for "whenever such a parade was repeated it would result in wide publicity and in confinement and 'martyrdom'"[44] (Figure 4.7).

In the early 1950s, reacting to the Canadian government's seizure of their lands and the pressure to place their children in public schools, the Sons of Freedom continued to stage nudist marches and launch arson attacks on public buildings, police cars, and

FIGURE 4.7: Doukhobor nude protest, January 1, 1930. Photo: Archive Photos/Getty Images.

motorcycles. In the 1960s, their leader was a farmwife nicknamed "Big Fanny." The photograph of her wearing nothing but knee-high nylons, heeled shoes, and a hair net, escorted on each side of her ample bulk by embarrassed RCMP officers, appeared in many newspapers.[45]

In 1953, a rumor spread among the Doukhobors that the RCMP were setting off bombs and initiating burnings in an effort to frame and destroy their community. This resulted in a new wave of protest that was expressed in bombings, arson attacks on public buildings and more nudist marches. Between 1953 and 1957, the RCMP raided the Doukhobor communities of Kretova and other villages, seizing approximately 200 children who were loaded on buses and forcibly placed in a boarding school in the north of British Columbia for six years. The government's rationale for these raids was to protect the children's rights, as Canadian citizens, to receive an education and to literacy. The Doukhobors spoke Russian inside their British Columbian community, and had always made it their policy since the 1700s in Russia, to reject the written Bible in favor of the "Living Book" (the community) and the prompting of the Holy Spirit within each person. Thus, their history and beliefs had never been written down, but were enshrined within an oral history tradition, notably in their hymns and polyphonic choral works.[46]

The Doukhobor notion of the naked body, as archaic and innocent, contrasts with contemporary sexualized or fashionable ideas of human nudity that are found in the two examples that follow.

THE INTERNATIONAL RAËLIAN MOVEMENT

The International Raëlian Movement is a "UFO religion" founded in France by Claude Vorilhon (1946–) after his alleged close encounter with an extraterrestrial.[47] The "Eloha" dubbed him "Raël" and taught him that human beings were originally "implanted" on earth by a team of "Elohim" scientists, who set up a laboratory on a barren planet and proceeded to create life from DNA matter.[48] Thus, the first "Adams and Eves" were created from the Elohim's own genetic material. The two aims of the Raëlian Movement are to spread the message (concerning humanity's true origins) and to build the Embassy to welcome the Elohim, who are expected to land sometime before the year 2035.[49]

The dress and undress in this group is clearly codified and gendered; Raël himself wears a white padded jacket, similar to an astronaut's space suit. Early in his career he wore his hair long, as antennae, to facilitate telepathic communication with the Elohim, but today, he wears his thinning hair in a samurai topknot. Raëlians, as members of "the world's first atheistic religion," dress like anybody else but are identified by the medallion worn around the neck. This medallion is a swastika inside the Star of David, a symbol of eternity and infinity, first noted by Raël on the hull of the space ship during his Close Encounter of the Third Kind, when he met extraterrestrials face to face.

Raëlians practice a form of ritual nudity during their annual two-week seminars, held at camps in rural settings in various countries. The campers discard their clothing, in emulation of the Elohim, who Raël describes as a nudist society in his second book, written after he was taken aboard a spaceship to visit their planet in 1976. The nudist campers, however, do wear name tags on strings and white open sided togas on hot days.

The meaning of nudity in Raëlian culture is threefold. It refers to the Elohim who created us in "their image," and who live in a nudist society on their planet. It implies a rejection of Christian sexual ethics, viewed as oppressive and unrealistic. Finally, the naked body is a testimonial to the power of science, its potential for human cloning, and the joys of unlimited sexual expression.[50]

Through the "wonders of science," Raël has argued, humanity has reached its maturity. Today, men and women may freely choose their sexual orientation, and even their gender. In his 2001 book, *Yes to Human Cloning: Immortality Thanks to Science*, Raël argues that biological reproduction has become obsolete, since the Elohim created us to feel sexual desire as a panacea for men's violent impulses and as a way to bring about world peace. Through sexual pleasure, Raël claims, new pathways between the neurons in the brain are forged that enhance the individual's intelligence, and increase his/her eligibility for "regeneration" (i.e. cloning) by the Elohim, thereby evading death. Thus, for Raëlians, sex brings hope of eternal life and individual salvation; a kind of physical, quasi-immortality (Figure 4.8).

Another example of Raëlian symbolic dress is the jewelry adorning the necks and bosoms of a select cadre of beautiful Raëlian women at the Sunday meetings. They wear the feathered necklaces reserved for members of the Order of Raël's Angels that was founded on December 13, 1997, when Raël announced he had received a revelation from Elohim, who instructed him to create a new order comparable to "nuns in the Catholic Church." Raël then proceeded to found an all-female religious order at the heart of his movement called, the Order of Raël's Angels.[51] Raël claimed his mission was to prepare a select group of Raëlian women to serve the Elohim when they descend in their space ships on the Embassy's landing pad. Raël's Angels would then serve as liaison officers between the alien visitors and the world's politicians and mass media. Only women are eligible to become Raël's Angels. As Raël explains, the male Elohim are extremely gentle, delicate, and sensitive: "the most feminine woman on earth is only 10% as feminine as the Elohim."[52]

White Angels wear white feathers on their necklaces, live in the world, and may choose their own (human) lovers. Pink Angels, who wear pink feathers, must "reserve their sexuality" for the Elohim and for the thirty-nine prophets, including Raël. The number and color of feathers on the Angels' necklace is significant, for they denote rank and level of commitment. Gold Ribbon Angels are chosen among the most beautiful Raëlians, they have an important role in the Apocalypse and meanwhile function as Raël's bodyguards.

A new form of public semi-nudity has been practiced by Raëlians since 2007, when Raël founded the GoTopless organization that holds public parades in which women march topless. Raël's Angels lead the vanguard of these demonstrations. The first GoTopless Day was held in 2008 at Venice Beach, California. By August 2011, the Raëlians had held rallies in twelve US states, and GoTopless rallies were also held in Canada, Paris, Japan, and India.[53]

In Canada, the first GoTopless Day rally was staged on August 28, 2011 in Toronto, Ontario. Nearly twenty women rode topless on a pickup truck between Queen Street East and Kew Beach to the Beatles' song, "Revolution" blared over a loudspeaker. The Toronto chapter's Raëlian spokeswoman was quoted saying, "This is not a beauty contest. It is about freedom."[54] Members of the GoTopless Canadian chapter were annoyed that Toronto's parks' department rejected a request to "exercise our freedom," said Sylvie Chabot, one of the event's planners. One of their stated aims is to promote gender equality in Third World countries. Raëlian protesters displayed signs that read, "Equal topless rights for all or none." Men marching in the demonstration wore bras and bikinis to protest against Canadians' double standards regarding the baring of the chest in public. Raël was quoted saying, "As long as men are allowed to be topless in public, women should have the same constitutional right. Or else, men should have to wear something to hide their chests"[55] (Figure 4.9).

FIGURE 4.8: Raël, the leader of Raëlian sect ready to perform human cloning experiment at a press conference in Tokyo, Japan, April 4, 2002. Photo: Kurita KAKU/Gamma-Rapho via Getty Images.

FIGURE 4.9: GoTopless, a group associated with Raëlians help a protest against not getting a permit to be topless on Ashbridges Beach, Toronto, 2011. Photo: Rick Madonik/*Toronto Star* via Getty Images.

The rationale for this ritual semi-nudity may be found in Raël's philosophy of "eschatological feminism."[56] In Raël's view, women are superior to men because we are living in the "Age of Apocalypse." Women resemble more closely the Elohim, our enlightened and godlike Creators. Therefore, Raël proposes, "because women, who give birth and cherish their children, know . . . life in all its fragility . . . if women were in power, there will be no more war."[57] Thus, the serious purpose behind the (apparently frivolous) GoTopless demonstrations is to stop war and save the world from nuclear destruction.

THE SIGNIFICANCE OF "SKYCLAD"

The two minority religions described above are quite distinct from each other. The Doukhobors are Russian Orthodox anarchists and the Raëlians are a "flying saucer cult" that originated in France. Each group has its own rationale for nakedness. But if one examines their common practice of ritual nudity within the framework of anthropologist Victor Turner's theories on the ritual process, a deeper interpretation of their ritual behavior might be rendered.[58]

Turner addresses the meaning of nudity in the context of the liminal phase of the ritual process, based on his study of African Ndembu tribe. First, he notes that the attributes of liminality do not fit the classification systems that normally locate states and positions of persons in cultural space. He writes, "their ambiguous and indeterminate attributes are expressed by a rich variety of symbols. . . . Their liminality is frequently likened to death, to being in the womb, to invisibility, to darkness, to bisexuality, to being in the wilderness."[59] Turner then offers a fascinating explanation of nudity as a liminal state:

> Liminal entities such as neophytes in initiation or puberty rites, may be represented as possessing nothing. They may be distinguished as being monsters, wear only a strip of clothing, or even go naked, to demonstrate that . . . they have no property, insignia, or secular clothing indicating rank or position.[60]

Thus, nudity that occurs within the symbolic milieu found in the liminal phase of a rite of passage creates a sense of *communitas*; that emotionally intense, intimate, egalitarian, roleless, non-hierarchical, irrational, androgynous community, the transitional and temporary brother/sisterhood that is experienced within the rite of passage. The nudist marches of the Doukhobors and the Raëlians' GoTopless marches might be understood as creating a sense of *communitas*, uniting Raël's Angels in a new sisterhood.

As Turner explains, the symbols of liminality refer to both the grave and the womb.[61] Thus, it is appropriate to find ritual nudity in rites of passage that speak of rebirth or of dying to the world. Johnson makes a similar point about the meaning of "skyclad" in contemporary Wicca: "To be naked indicates freedom from conventional mundane thought. [. . .] you are free to place your mind into a sphere of magickal thought where anything is possible."[62] Certainly the Doukhobors' emphasis on public nudity is consistent with their rejection of artifice and the trappings of civilization.

Preparation for the millennium has often involved a ritualized overthrow of traditional norms. Allisson notes, "Primitive millenarian movements have engaged in breaking of hallowed taboos and in a desecration of their most valued religious symbols, thus disassociating themselves from their traditional culture."[63] Certainly, ritual nudity can imply a critique of the Catholic Church. Raël, in founding a sexy order of "nuns" is challenging the Catholic Church almost appear to be deliberately designed so as to challenge and offend the Catholic clergy.

CONCLUSION

Religious dress and undress are both replete with the symbols of power that refer to an invisible world, the world of the afterlife or spirit, or to a mythic past before the Fall. New spiritual leaders grasp traditional myths and symbols, then combine and craft them to create new visions of the New Man or New Woman, of utopia or of an apocalyptic future.

Myths and symbols of the Bible come to life and take on new meanings. For the Doukhobours and the Raëlians, marching in the nude is a way of identifying with their mythic ancestors; Adam and Eve for the Doukhobors, and the Elohim for the Raëlians. For Uriel of Unarius, as well as for Raël's Angels, the heavenly symbols of feathers, haloes, and wands speak of divine union between the female soul and her (alien) god. Marie-Paule Giguère's five dresses co-opt the spiritual authority of the Pope; they refer to the

Book of Revelation, and to previous apocalyptic Marian apparitions. These symbols are worn to bolster Giguère's claim to be the Virgin Mary incarnate, come to usher in a new Church and a new age.

These new forms of dress and undress might be interpreted as reflecting some of the tensions resulting from social changes in the twentieth century—changes in our perceptions of race, gender, class, and authority. The new religious fashions at times predict future trends, as for example the loose, un-corseted Grecian-style robes of the Theosophists, and the 1950s respectable prosperous suits of African-Americans in the Divine Light Mission. Or the absence of clothing might imply a critique of secular society, as in the case of the Doukhobors and Raëlians, or of the Catholic Church. As the historian Frank E. Manuel said, commenting on the utopian impulse, "The utopia may well be a sensitive indicator of where the sharpest anguish of an age lies."[64]

CHAPTER FIVE

Gender and Sexuality

ANNAMARI VÄNSKÄ

In 1923, the American painter Romaine Brooks wrote to her lover Natalie Barney about her social life in London:

> Never have I had such a string of would-be admirers, and all of my black curly hair, and white collars. They like the dandy in me and are in no way interested in my inner-self or value."[1]

And in 1990, the American philosopher Judith Butler established the idea of gender as performative in her now classical book *Gender Trouble*:

> As much as drag creates a unified picture of "woman" [. . .], it also reveals the distinctness of those aspects of gendered experience which are falsely naturalized as a unity through the regulatory fiction of heterosexual coherence. In imitating gender, drag implicitly reveals the imitative structure of gender itself—as well as its contingency.[2]

Both excerpts remind us that social status, gender, and sexuality are discursive and historically constructed. They also remind us that clothing plays a central role in their construction and in theorization of gender. An understanding of dress practices and fashioning oneself illuminate ways in which social changes are experienced by individuals and how they are used in theorizing gender and sexuality—in this case by an independent modern woman and a lesbian artist and a philosopher who established and popularized the idea of gender as performative.

In the first decades of the twentieth century, dress practices highlighted women's changing social identity and at the end of the millennium, they were used to highlight the constructedness of gender. The period after the devastating First World War has been described as a time when women's societal visibility and assertive sexuality came to the forefront of scientific and public debate in Europe and America. It was also the time when fashion became a "woman's thing," and dress a political tool in advocating women's rights. At the beginning of the twenty-first century, sexual minorities, fashionable men and children are gaining more visibility—as are even fashionable pets, especially little lap dogs, which we have begun to dress fashionably.[3] During the past one hundred years, fashion has become a central factor that defines and expresses the real and imagined status of humans in relation to gender. But fashion also expresses and defines what it is to become, or rather, *to look like*, human, as lap dog fashions testify.

THE 1920s: WOMEN IN TROUSERS

After the demise of feudal class societies, clothing increasingly became a marker of gender. Up until 1920s, in Western societies, being a woman was largely associated with wearing skirts and dresses, while being a man was associated with wearing trousers. When a child was born, it was clothed in a dress regardless of gender, but when the child grew up, its clothing practice changed according to gender. When a boy became an adult at the age of thirteen, he discarded his dress and started wearing trousers.[4] Becoming a woman, on the other hand, did not include this kind of rite of passage. Women never seized wearing a dress, and therefore remained more like infants throughout their lives.[5] Wearing a skirt was thus also an important marker of women's social inferiority. This is one of the reasons why societal changes in women's lives after the First World War changed women's social status and employment patterns, and led women to adopt masculine tailoring and comfortable clothes. The independent young modern woman, the *flapper* or *garçonne* in French, was able to move about, ride a bicycle, and even play golf. Her style became the emblem of modernity, embodying novelty, change, youth, glamor, and sexual subjectivity.[6] The flapper's societal freedom changed her figure into an androgynous, flat, and geometrical boyish form.[7] She abandoned the Edwardian model of fashion, the frilly petticoats, S-shaped corsets, and large hats, and started wearing loosely fitting tunics— and trousers. For the first time in history, adult women's fashion drew from girl's dress: the dropped waistline and short skirts.[8] While young girls had worn flapper styles since 1914, the adult flappers appeared only in mid-1920s.[9]

Perhaps the best-known designer re-interpreting the modern woman's boyish look was Gabrielle "Coco" Chanel. She changed the dominant paradigm of femininity by rejecting the hour-glass silhouette, by creating the Chanel-look and by introducing trousers to middle and upper class women.[10] Another often-mentioned designer is Jean Patou. Before the war, he had already designed tailor-made jackets for women, and after the war, he started designing sportswear for women. In his designs, he borrowed from men's wear and emphasized women's natural waistline.[11] Social change was also apparent in the modern woman's short hairstyles: the "bob," the *coupe carrée*, the *coupe à la Jeanne d'Arc*, and the *coupe à la garçonne*[12] (Figure 5.1).

After returning home from the battlefield, men's wardrobes were intact, but their spirits were shattered from the horrors of war. The unchanged wardrobe represented the old world order and the precarious political atmosphere fed a pleasure-seeking life of jazz, partying, and cocktail drinking. Soon a range of casually-dressed androgynous *new men*— businessmen, sports idols, film stars, gigolos, middle class youth, and artists—took the floor of fashionable clubs in Europe and America. These cosmopolitan men aspired to get rid of men's strict dress code and took inspiration from sports clothing, work uniforms, and avant-garde art.[13] The post-war male's casualty and effeminacy was directly linked to war. Men wished to distance themselves from wartime masculinity, and from values associated with it.

In fact, men's wardrobe had never been so limited as it had become by the twentieth century. Before the so-called "great masculine renunciation" in the eighteenth century, men were the fashionable peacocks. But now the variety of clothing available to men had been reduced significantly. While men had been wearing skirts and sarongs in the previous centuries, now these garments were regarded feminine, exotic, and deviant, and therefore unsuitable for an average man.[14] The new man's interest in comfort and casual style aimed to free men from hard warrior-like masculinity, and materialized in soft materials: linen, silk, and fine wool flannel. Men also got rid of stiff collars in favor of the softer ones,

FIGURE 5.1: Actress Ina Claire wearing a herringbone tweed skirt and jumper by Chanel, *Vogue*, 1924. Photo: Edward Steichen/Condé Nast via Getty Images.

exchanged their formal suit jackets for informal ones, and started wearing sweaters—a garment that in the pre-war era was mostly worn by sailors, workers, and athletes. Men also "dared to remain in flannels . . . all day long," in other words challenged the strict middle class dress codes of a proper dress for each time of the day.[15] The changes evoked modern sensations of leisurely outdoor life and free bodily movement and eroticized the male as the soft cloth accentuated the body underneath the clothes (Figure 5.2).

FIGURE 5.2: Man's two-piece wool leisure suit with knickerbockers, c. 1920, as worn by the Prince of Wales (left) and the Duke of York (right). Photo: Sean Sexton/Getty Images.

While men's look softened, women's look hardened. Women's trousers became a political garment, signifying women's liberation and intellectual independence.[16] But trousers also signified class and sexuality. Most middle and upper class women wore skirts and dresses because they did not have to work, while working-class women wore trousers because they had to work. But trousers also signified sexuality: while long skirts and dresses hid women's legs and made them look "respectable," trousers made the legs visible and the look therefore "improper" and "immoral."[17] The sexual meanings of trousers transformed the garment into a key in defining and explaining deviant sexuality: lesbianism. These meanings were largely produced by sexology, a new science about sexuality. It popularized the idea that a person's sexual identity was not only an inner quality but could be discerned from appearance.[18] Women's masculine behavior and masculine appearance were read as signs of homosexuality. The sexually and economically independent woman, who took over the streets and the work place, was thus characterized as a lesbian. The same applied to men who took on the more feminine look with softer materials: their appearance was read as proof of homosexuality. Sexologists, who drew heavily on the meanings of garments, thus constructed the stereotypes of masculine lesbian and the effeminate homosexual. In the years to come, cross-dressing—women wearing masculine, men feminine garments and materials—played a significant role in self-identification of lesbians and gay men.[19] Inter-war years thus established the notions of modern women and men as well as homosexual and lesbian identities, and how they could be discerned from clothing.

1930s: MANNISHNESS RULES!

On October 29, 1929, the Wall Street stock market crashed and triggered an economic depression in the United States and Europe. Only two years later, 2.5 million people in Britain, five million people in Germany and over eight million people in the United States were unemployed. It was a sudden end of the post-war reality. In contrast to the "gay twenties," the political and social atmosphere tightened. With the rise of fascism, Nazism, and communism, a call for moral, aesthetic, and social order swept Europe. Traditional gender roles of masculinity and femininity were back in fashion again, and simplicity, sensibility, and realism became the defining words. Interest in traditional warrior-masculinity was apparent in the uniformed body. When Hitler came to power in 1933, military uniforms became the symbol of totalitarian authority in constructing the racially pure male. Even some avant-garde movements, especially the Italian futurism and the Russian constructivism, underlined the centrality of uniform clothing in creating the new nation and the new citizen.[20] Men's fashions became harder: padding and the defined shape of a double-breasted suit accentuated a broad chest while long broad lapels accentuated the shoulders, and the high waist and wide trousers, the column-like shape of the figure. The outfit signaled a stronger masculinity and "served as the base for an athletic silhouette that placed a neoclassical stamp on masculine elegance."[21]

Contrary to this, women's designs accentuated femininity—like Christopher Breward has noted, economic depression and political uncertainty lessened optimism that the modern woman's dress had symbolized in the 1920s.[22] Women's hemlines dropped and clothing hugged the body, revealing the feminine form. Still, female masculinity[23] was not altogether absent: the female figure became a mixture of femininity and masculinity. The avant-garde fashion designer Elsa Schiaparelli, for example, saw the body as a playground where rules about gender could be broken. Fashion periodicals also published reports about women's suits and other clothing made in "masculine fabrics" of wool flannel, and plaids. Women's dress was structured and styled according to traditional men's wear and broad, padded shoulders, notched lapels, and deeply cuffed trousers were in fashion. Women's upper body was defined by shoulder pads originally popularized by Elsa Schiaparelli in 1930, while the lower body was defined by narrow waist-line and leg-hugging materials.[24]

FIGURE 5.3: Young woman on a bicycle, wearing a three-piece Aquascutum trouser suit, October 1939. Photo: *Daily Herald* Archive/SSPL/Getty Images.

Female masculinity became a trend and it was called "mannish." It contrasted feminine fashions that favored the slim and soft silhouette and body-hugging materials. The mannish look continued to underline women's changed social standing: a growing number of women worked outside of the home, and necessitated a masculine professional dress (Figure 5.3).

The new and popular cinema and film stars became important fashion setters and their appearance was sold to the public by popular press. Film stars were styled by leading designers: Gilbert Adrian, Howard Greer, Edith Head, Elsa Schiaparelli, and Travis Banton.[25] They constructed a new type of femininity on screen: the powerful and career-oriented woman whose toughness was accentuated through glamorized costuming. They also highlighted appearance as a discourse of illusion and artifice; how dress simultaneously represses the body and highlights it. Joan Crawford wore a dress with dramatic and large ruffled sleeves designer by Adrian in the film *Letty Lynton* (1932), accentuating the film star's feminine figure with masculine shoulders. Marlene Dietrich, the heroine of the mannish look, on the other hand, was represented wearing low-heeled shoes, mannish hats, and ties—and reported to purchase boys' suits for her daughter, Maria.[26] Department stores had specialized areas under the title "cinema fashions," and sold garments and accessories worn by the favorite film stars making the adoption of Hollywood styles easy for the audience.[27] Thousands of women also curled their daughters' hair into innocent and cute ringlets after Shirley Temple, the most famous child star of 1930s,[28] while thousands of men followed the masculine elegance of Gary Cooper, Fred Astaire, and Cary Grant who made English stylishness known by wearing Savile Row suits.

Despite the mannish trend in women's clothing, cross-dressing was still seen as a sign of non-normative sexuality. Elsa Schiaparelli who was interested in excess of gendered appearance, nevertheless warned women against going "too extreme" with their masculine appearance. Coco Chanel, on the other hand, underlined that her suits were "boyish," not masculine. She wanted suits to "harmonize femininity," not to produce an air of masculinity.[29] This may have some bearing to the fact that the mannish suit was established as the sign of the modern lesbian identity in the 1930s, epitomized in the British novelist Radclyffe Hall's *The Well of Loneliness* (1928). Its protagonist Stephen Gordon is described as a woman with a masculine appearance and personality in contrast to her female body. Gordon's image not only made cross-dressing a sign of lesbianism but also standardized it.[30]

POST-WAR: SPECTACULAR FEMININITY AND INVISIBLE GAY MEN

During the Second World War, appearance and fashion lost their relevance in defining individuals' gendered and sexualized identity, and styles remained practically unaffected throughout the war. But once the Second World War was over, Paris made an effort to re-establish its position as the fashion capital with Christian Dior's "New Look" in 1947[31] (Figure 5.4). It represented an opposite to wartime fashions and a deliberate attempt to break free from the masculine appearance with its square-padded shoulders.[32] The style was exaggerated, Victorian-inspired, and ultra-feminine. It consisted of crinoline skirts which emphasized the full bust, the corset that underlined the hour-glass waistline and high-heeled shoes that accentuated the length of the legs. It has been interpreted as a figure of the modern, post-war fertility goddess[33] in accordance with the "baby-boom generation." This may well be the case—Dior is known to have emphasized the rehabilitation of femininity after the uniforms that constructed "women like boxers."[34] In its nostalgic reach to a supposedly more stable time, the "New Look" represented traditional femininity. It was not the look for the emancipated woman. But it can also be interpreted as reaction against the war and disvaluing of femininity. Furthermore, the look was so exaggerated that it was almost a caricature of femininity and in this sense represented a more contemporary tendency of articulating femininity as thoroughly constructed. The

FIGURE 5.4: French fashion designer Christian Dior arranging one of his evening dresses. Paris, mid 1950s. Photo: Mondadori Portfolio via Getty Images.

"New Look" represented what the philosopher Simone de Beauvoir wrote in her classical book *Second Sex* in 1949: "One is not born, but rather becomes, woman."[35] The ultra-feminine new look made the post-war woman.

Simultaneously, the look raises other questions regarding the relationship between a designer's sexuality and his/her designs, taken up in a recent fashion exhibition, *A Queer*

History of Fashion: From the Closet to the Catwalk (2013). The exhibition listed many gay designers, among them Christian Dior.[36] Analyzing the "New Look" from this perspective, it can be asked, how much did the fact that homosexuality was still a crime, and the sexological and psychoanalytical discourses about homosexuality as inversion, affect Dior's designs? During the 1940s, it was still commonplace to think that a gay man was a woman trapped in a man's body and vice versa. Was the hyperbolized "New Look" an expression of Dior's "inner femininity" when he stated that dress was "an expression of personality?"[37] Or, did he emphasize femininity as constructed and performed because he knew about female impersonators, a popular form of entertainment in homosexual subcultures and in the war front?[38] Be that as it may, but in its overstated femininity, the "New Look" represented femininity as female impersonation or, in contemporary terms, femininity as drag.

Analysis of Christian Dior's styles as expressions of the designer's closeted homosexual identity has its problems. Nevertheless, a reading of the look as an effect of closeted sexuality has a point: in the 1940s, being openly homosexual meant the threat of public exposure, blackmail, and imprisonment not to mention violence and trials. Being gay meant remaining invisible. Invisibility was even advocated by the first gay rights organizations such as Mattachine Society (1950) for gay men and Daughters of Bilitis (1955) for lesbians. Both advised their members to adhere to normative gender roles and dress codes. Lesbians were advised to wear skirts and blouses, and to discard signs of masculinity and the established style of the mannish lesbian.[39] Gay men were urged to abandon femininity, to stick to restrained colors, and to dress according to conventions of male fashion: dark suits, simple shirts, tie, and sports jackets. The fear of exposure was reflected in lists of "don'ts" for gay men: "Don't masquerade . . . in women's clothes . . . don't be too meticulous in the matter of your own clothes, or affect any extremes in color or cut; don't wear conspicuous rings, watches, cuff-links, or other jewelry; don't allow your voice or intonation to display feminine inflection—cultivate a masculine tone and method of expression."[40]

The list of don'ts clearly indicates the central role of clothing in creating gendered and sexualized identity. One may wonder, however, how gays and lesbians recognized each other in this hostile atmosphere. Perhaps through excessive designs like in Dior's case, but mostly by speaking about sexuality by not naming it directly: through small details of their clothing, style, and behavior.[41] In fact, the detail became a symbol of a special kind of clothing technique and a crucial marker of sexual difference. Gay men, for example, used accessories, red ties, suede shoes, and non-masculine associated colors in "speaking" to other gay men through their clothing.[42] It is noteworthy that the modern notion of homosexuality coincides with the rise of ideas about the modern society as a society of appearances[43] and clothing as a language-like institution from which individual styles are differentiated as parole.[44] Of course, not all accepted invisibility. Working-class lesbians in the lesbian bar scene in England and in the United States invented a new norm for the lesbian: the butch–femme couple. While the butch wore masculine attire, the femme dressed in traditional feminine outfit. The butch–femme thus resisted dominant norms of gender and transformed gender into role-playing.[45] This preceded the 1960s maxim of showing one's sexuality openly, advocated by the Gay and Lesbian Liberation Movement.

1950s: REBELS AND PLAYBOYS

But women, gays, and lesbians were not the only groups to use clothing as a sign of their gendered or sexualized identity. Post-war Western culture also saw the birth of the youth culture and the new consuming man: the bachelor. This also created new categories of clothing: casual wear and youth wear.[46]

The idea of leisure had been linked to clothing of the upper classes already at the turn of the century[47] but in the post-war culture it had trickled down to middle classes. Again, a *new man* emerged: the hedonistic and consumer-oriented bachelor whom the founder of the *Playboy* magazine, Hugh Hefner, popularized in 1953. The bachelor was a man, who was always (allegedly) heterosexual, lived in a penthouse, and spent most of his time "mixing up cocktails and an hors d'oeuvre or two, putting a little mood music on the phonograph and inviting in a female acquaintance for a quiet discussion on Picasso, Nietzsche, jazz, sex . . ."[48] His lifestyle included a fascination for a conservative yet casual dress, a red velvet smoking jacket, loafers, and a pipe, and who had a taste for the latest technological devices (radio, tape recorder, record player, and a television set), gin and tonic, and pretty girls[49] (Figure 5.5). The idea of the bachelor was constructed through his

FIGURE 5.5: A man wearing a smoking jacket from Christian Dior's collection at the Dior Men's Boutique in Paris, 1955. Photo: John Sadovy/BIPs/Getty Images.

activities, wardrobe, appearance and luxurious life-style—much in the same way as ideal femininity was defined in women's high fashion magazines.[50]

Alongside the bachelor, post-war culture also produced youth culture, symbolized in the concept of the teenager. The teenager designated an age stage and white middle class youth already in the 1940s, but in the 1950s it referred to youth's novel visibility in public culture and to a stylistic identity. The fashion- and consumer-oriented teenager was constructed and popularized by such films stars as James Dean and Marlon Brando who represented the "rebellious youth," a new market niche through their filmic characters.[51] The film *A Streetcar Named Desire* (1951) fashioned Brando as the rebellious and sexually alluring "working-class stud" through his costume: his leather jacket, jeans, and the stained, greasy, and sweaty-looking and body-hugging white T-shirt with rolled-up sleeves.[52] James Dean's character, Jim Stark in the film *Rebel Without A Cause* (1955), popularized the red bomber-jacket. Both characters made the white T-shirt, still an undergarment in the 1930s, and jeans—a garment mainly worn by children in the 1930s[53]—into a fashionable and defiant outfit. The characters also constructed "rocker-look" and the "Teddy-look," the earliest youth subcultures or "style tribes."[54] Brando and Dean, but also Montgomery Clift and Paul Newman, were ambassadors of teenage fashion.[55] Paradoxically, while these styles were defined as "rebellious," they centered on a normative understanding of masculinity and femininity. The young boys wore masculine attire while the girls sported a girlish feminine look: panniers that accentuated waistline, padded bra, ponytails, and ballerina shoes.

1960s: SEXUAL REVOLUTION AND SINGLE GIRLS

Even if youth culture, with its different style tribes, was established in the 1950s, it was only fully developed in the 1960s and included also girls and young women. The decade brought about many novelties: the first orally consumed contraceptive, the Pill, liberation movements, and new technologies in clothing manufacturing which made mass production of new materials and cheap clothing possible. The decade also saw the "second wave" of feminism: the Women's Liberation Movement aimed at ending women's social discrimination in work and at home, and pursued women's right to make decisions about their own bodies.[56] Young women became less dependent on men and a new type of young woman emerged: the single girl. Helen Gurley-Brown describes her in *Sex and the Single Girl* (1962) as financially independent and sexually experimental. This new girl was encouraged to take on a job as a sales clerk, shop assistant, or a model, giving her economic independence. At the end of the decade, the Gay and Lesbian Liberation Movement pursued equal rights for non-heterosexuals, encouraging people to show their sexual identity openly.[57] A new politics of visibility ensued via street theater, drag shows, demonstrations, and finally the first Gay Pride parade in 1972 with people wearing T-shirts with slogans such as "Gay is Good" printed on them.[58]

Liberation movements affected change in the gendered appearance of women and men. Sexuality was detached from marriage and family life and defined exceedingly as a personal matter. This materialized in unisex and minimalist styles at the first part of the decade, and in more natural, ethnic, and simple clothing at the second part of the decade. The ideology of "free love" epitomized in the hippie look: casual, colorful, loose, and ethnic clothes, and naturally-grown body hair—long hair for women and men, unshaven beards, legs, and armpits. A new belief in the future and the human's capacity of conquering distant planets materialized in man-made synthetic materials and futuristic looks by such designers as Courrèges and Pierre Cardin. Their designs included "space age clothing" made of plastic: transparent coats, dresses, and shoes—clothes "with nothing or next to nothing under them,"[59] underlining the new approach to gender, body, and sexuality.

In youth cultures, the English mod culture embraced a more androgynous and unisex look. It represented a more equal relationship between girls and boys, and made the mod style more conceptual and political.[60] Mod boys rejected the "crude conception of masculinity" of the previous decade and embraced a more feminine, and visually understated style. It consisted of slick suits, parkas, polo shirts, turtlenecks, clean jeans, and Clark's boots.[61] The style also represented a reaction against the upper class somber elegance of the "establishment of men's fashion," Savile Row. It represented a new attitude towards male dress accentuating hedonism instead of asceticism, stirring a label of "Peacock Revolution" in the British press.[62] The dandyesque yet androgynous and unisex looks were visible in appearance of the pop stars. *The Beatles* and *The Who* were the incarnation of mod style while the *Rolling Stones* embraced a more decadent dandy-look.

The mod girls' style is illustrated in the designs of Mary Quant, a designer not much older than those she designed for. Quant is credited for creating the miniskirt, the "Chelsea girl," and the "London Look"[63] (Figure 5.6). Her designs represented a new breath of fresh air and mixed femininity with young girls' social, economical and sexual independence. The "Queen of the Mods" was a lesbian singer: Dusty Springfield. She masqueraded black American soul singers through her outfits and the high beehive hairstyle, heavy mascara,

FIGURE 5.6: Models wearing clothes by Mary Quant at the Carlton Hotel, August 15, 1967. Photo: Keystone-France/Gamma-Keystone via Getty Images.

and false eyelashes and peroxide-blonde hair, killing any naturalistic ideas about femininity.[64] Furthermore, Springfield's performances were impersonated by drag queens. But Springfield did not only lend her look to drag queens, she also impersonated them. She thus popularized her own style and the styles impersonated by drag queens, making gay male sub culture's camp performances known for a mainstream audience.[65]

Even though the above-mentioned example may indicate otherwise, the "swinging sixties" was an era of sexual license that mainly liberated heterosexual men and women. The romantic view of liberating sexuality was made possible with social changes, and its materializations through technological advancements and the rise of popular and youth culture. The 1960s was an era of fantasizing a better future and it gained tangible results through fashion. The next decade began with optimistic views about the future but ended in a bleak pessimism, materialized in punk aesthetics.

1970s: ANTI-FASHION AND ARTIFICIAL GENDER

In the 1970s, the "street" became an important symbol of revolutionary ideas. It was a stage for political activism for oppressed groups and a place that democratized fashion by becoming a source of inspiration and a market place. The street became the symbol of "anti-fashion" put forth by musical and sexual subcultures that opposed the prevailing (adult) social and gender order. Even though "fashion was not in fashion," as Valerie Steele has put it, the decade is remembered for certain garments and materials: hot pants, vinyl maxi-coats, Lycra pantsuits, Lurex tops, polyester suits, bell-bottoms, wide lapels, wide ties, and unisex platform shoes.[66] Men's shirts were open to the waist which accentuated the eroticism of the male torso, while women's dresses were slit up to the crotch highlighting the erotic power of women's legs. The decade was not without style; it was a decade interested in excesses, distortions, and non-natural fibers. This intensified the idea that codes of taste, propriety, and gender were class-bound and culturally constructed, not natural facts.

Artificiality of gender is visible in the image and style of androgynous glam-rockers such as David Bowie and Marc Bolan. Their look challenged normative ideals about beauty, gender, and sexuality. Bowie's influences came largely from the gay and drag queen culture which made a journalist describe him as a "swishy queen, a gorgeously effeminate boy" and "as camp as a row of tents, with his limp hand and trolling vocabulary."[67] Bowie's "genderfuck" style had a huge influence on youth in general and gay men in particular.[68] Another influential group was the New York Dolls, a proto-punk band who dressed, in their own words, as "Puerto Rican sluts," and promoted "polymorphous pan-sexuality." Their appearances owed much to such drag queens as Jackie Curtis, one of the most famous stars of Andy Warhol's Factory (Figure 5.7). Warhol himself is known to have impersonated the stereotype of the "dumb blonde," and he rarely appeared in public without his signature peroxide-blonde wig.

The ideas of trashing established norms of gender were taken to extreme in the mid-1970s punk, in its DIY music and sartorial aesthetics (Figure 5.8). Punk's anti-establishment values and critique of capitalism and beauty norms laid down by the "dominant classes" were embodied in Mohawk haircuts in shock-colors, overtly visible make-up, and piercings, safety pins, and lavatory chains as jewelry.[69] Punk produced clothes from found materials, torn fabrics, and waste: plastic bags, rubber, tin, and old tires.[70] This was intended to assault the hegemonic ideology of fashion and expose the unnaturalness of beauty, decency, and the standards of acceptable femininity and masculinity. Punk aesthetics helped

FIGURE 5.7: Transvestite superstar Jackie Curtis photographed in 1970, the year Curtis began filming *Women in Revolt*. Photo: Jack Mitchell/Getty Images.

construct gendered and sexualized identities for the disadvantaged, highlighting fashion as an important arena of sexual politics. The subcultural fascination in gender-bending clothing practices signaled a willingness and interest in blurring the boundaries between "normal" and "perverse" sexuality—themes that were fully developed in the fashions of the next decade.

FIGURE 5.8: Sid Vicious, Vivienne Westwood, and punks in audience at a Sex Pistols gig,
November 15, 1976. Photo: Ian Dickson/Redferns.

1980s: IRONY OF FASHION

In *Fashion Zeitgeist,* Barbara Vinken describes 1980s fashion as "postfashion." The concept refers to the ways in which fashion took up ideas set forth in the previous decade and became self-aware and self-reflective about its own histories and practices. Fashion changed direction: instead of trickling down from the upper classes to the lower ones, it moved upwards, from the street to the catwalk. Fashion became more conceptual and abstracted, and in terms of gender and sexuality, it decidedly aimed to deconstruct prevailing ideals. "Nothing could be more out of date than to clothe oneself as 'woman,' as 'man' or as 'lady'," Vinken sniffs.[71] Blurring gender categories visualized, again, in the fashion-oriented *new man.* This time around, his figure was circulated in men's fashion media and his look drew from the "stylistic homosexual identity," offering heterosexual men new ways of shopping and looking at other men and at themselves.[72] A *new woman* was also re-invented: she was (again) assertive and economically independent. This time around her powerfulness materialized in the "power dress": the boxy-shaped masculine pinstripe suit expressing strength, aggressiveness, and upward mobility.

Gender bending was also visible in popular culture and sexual subcultures. Pop stars such as Annie Lennox, Robert Smith from the Cure, Pete Burns from Dead or Alive, Boy George from Culture Club, and Michael Jackson mixed masculinity and femininity through pierced ears, noses and lips, nail polish, and visible make-up regardless of gender. They were the style ambassadors for the youth as their image was disseminated globally through music and style press and the newly established music television, the MTV. The new media landscape also made sexual minorities more visible and legitimate, and made their distinctive sartorial styles known outside the subculture. One such figure was the ultra-masculine Tom of Finland-type clone. He dressed in bomber jackets, Levi's jeans, and Doc Marten boots. The figure was a counter-attack on the stigmatized effeminate gay man but it was also the effect of the heterosexist and homophobic culture that had pathologized gay men after the AIDS crisis.[73] The macho look accentuated the muscular and healthy body in contrast to the prevailing stereotype of the homosexual man's ill and diseased effeminate body.

The lesbian-feminist style, on the other hand, celebrated androgyny or gender blending that aimed to reveal the "real woman" beneath cultural constructions of femininity. It critiqued fashion as a time-consuming practice and women's oppression. Like the clone, gender blending also rejected femininity. It was defined as structurally secondary and personally vulnerable to violence and exploitation. Androgyny was a strategy to minimize the stigma of femaleness and to accentuate that lesbians did not dress for men. Stylistically, androgyny was a combination of flat shoes, baggy trousers, unshaven legs, and faces bare of make-up. Another distinct style was the S/M lesbian who dressed in leather, rubber, and uniform styles. The butch or the "top" wore vests, waistcoats without shirts, or no clothes on the upper body, revealing the body from the waist up. The "bottom" or the femme wore skirts, dresses, lingerie, and high heels, revealing her body from the waist down.[74]

In the spirit of a wider ethos of postmodernism, defined by such philosophers as Jean Baudrillard, Jacques Derrida and Jean-François Lyotard, fashion underlined that it is an effective tool in constructing and deconstructing gendered appearance. This is exemplified in the work of Jean Paul Gaultier and Vivienne Westwood. They are both designers known for their attempts to question taste, propriety, and categorical boundaries of gender. Gaultier mainstreamed stereotypes of gay culture: the sailor, the clone, the cross-dresser and the gay S/M leather fetishist. He also transformed the figure of the drag queen into a campy and excessive representation of femininity. Gaultier's designs are openly camp; they

FIGURE 5.9: Jean Paul Gaultier. Man skirt, Paris, c. 1987. Photo: The Museum at FIT.

embrace the unnatural, the artificial, and the exaggerated. He became one of the first popular household names through the costumes he designed for Peter Greenaway's film *The Cook, the Thief, His Wife & Her Lover* (1989). His signature garments, underwear-as-outerwear, the cone-bra, popularized by Madonna in *Blond Ambition* tour (1990), and the male-skirt converted the seriousness of gender into frivolous role-play (Figure 5.9). Unlike Christian Dior, Gaultier openly employed gay culture's bombastic mannerisms of gender performance and produced clothing full of double entendre. His designs also transformed the pejorative definitions of sexuality—gay, whore, slut—into symbols of powerfulness. He erased negative connotations historically attached to gays and sexually active women and transformed them into acceptable styles and popular fetish looks. The Italian designer Giorgio Armani claimed, in his turn, that there are no gender-specific garments, colors or styles and moved constantly between women and men in constructing their new social identities in the rumpled, baggy, shapeless and still yuppie chic linen suit.

The 1980s also saw the rise of women designers. Vivienne Westwood, who had already brought the punk style into the world of fashion, dressed her models in bodysuits with fig leaf -designs placed on genitals. The design simultaneously referred to and drew from the biblical narrative of the "The Fall," describing the transition of the first man and woman from a state of innocence to the state of sexuality, and how they covered their sexual organs, the genitals with these "first clothes." Westwood suggested that all clothing is sexually charged and that it centers on a paradox of hiding and revealing. While dress hides the forbidden and the secret body, it also draws attention to it. The Japanese designer Rei Kawakubo explored the gendered nature of color and cut, designing collections with "genderless" colors of black and white, and creating dresses that accentuated body parts that are not typically seen as sexual. She also experimented with class in her Poor Chic clothing, transforming class into masquerade.[75] And Jil Sander, one of the few openly lesbian designers, created minimalistic and androgynous looks for the modern fashion-conscious (lesbian) woman.

The 1980s witnessed a conceptual move in fashion. It highlighted dress as disguise and costume, and in doing so, the artificiality of gender and sexuality. But it was the next decade that normalized the idea that it is not only the extreme examples but the ordinary aspects of dress that construct gender and sexuality.

1990s: QUEERING FASHION

The 1990s was a decade when fashion visualized in an accelerating speed and was increasingly represented in image-form. Even though visuality has defined fashion since the birth of the modern fashion system and the modern fashion media at the turn of the 20th century[76] it was now intertwined in the lives of people through advertising, music videos and lifestyle magazines with glamorous advertising. In the twenty-first century this development has only increased with the invention of "new media," the Internet, social media with its different image-based applications, and blogs.[77] Images produced new visibility for fashion and became important means of influencing how fashion was perceived, marketed, and disseminated. Images of clothes became more important than clothes, and fashion became a field where editors, photographers, graphic designers, stylists, and art directors could use their creative freedom and intuition in producing fantastical narrative-like scenarios that created an alluring atmosphere around the designs and imagined consumers. While films such as Sally Potter's *Orlando* (1992) and Neil Jordan's *The Crying Game* (1992) mainstreamed non-heterosexuality, new music genres such as grunge, hip-hop, and techno blurred gender categories and

FIGURE 5.10: A New York billboard displaying Kate Moss for Calvin Klein, shot by photographer Steven Meisel. Photo: Niall McInerney, Bloomsbury Fashion Photography Archive.

introduced more conceptual and gender-neutral club clothing. Through such avant-garde fashion and lifestyle magazines as *i-D*, *Dazed & Confused*, and *The Face*, fashion advertising became an art form of its own right.

In these publications, fashion advertising became decidedly *queer*. This meant that fashion advertising not only used snapshot aesthetics in their attempt to create an air of "realism" and "authenticity" around the brand. It also meant using unconventionally gendered models and marketing strategies addressing a newly found niche market: the homosexual consumer.[78] In its academic form, as *queer theory*, queer makes critical questions about naturalness of gender and sexual identity. While queer has historically been used as a colloquial and abusive word about homosexuality, in the 1990s academics started using it as a concept that challenges ideas about the naturalness of gender and heterosexuality.[79] Queer is against identity, it is its deconstruction. In terms of visuality, queer attempts to make clear-cut categories of gender and desire—whether gay or straight, female or male, feminine or masculine—impossible. This is visualized in fashion advertising which underlines the multiplicity and mobility of identification and desiring possibilities through the unisex and androgynous styling of the fashion models. In terms of clothing, queer accentuates cross-gender identification. Perhaps the most cited queer theorists Judith Butler[80] and Judith Halberstam[81] have both used the figures of the drag queen and the drag king in theorizing the cultural constructedness of gender.

Furthermore, the role of constructing gendered and sexualised identities largely shifted from garments to models and visual images. In fact, when clothes became more ordinary and casual—t-shirts and jeans for everybody—advertising became more interested in sexual subcultures. Benetton and Calvin Klein were the forerunners of queering fashion. They introduced advertising that had little to with promotion of clothes, but everything to do with playing with the accepted norms of gender and sexuality. Benetton represented unconventional families consisting of Caucasian and African mothers holding a Chinese child, while Calvin Klein advertised jeans, underwear and perfumes with androgynous and ordinary-looking models including Kate Moss, Stella Tennant, Eve Salvail and Jenny Schimitzu (Figure 5.10). *Haute couture* fashion houses from Versace and Gucci to Dolce & Gabbana soon followed this trend and used sexually daring advertising in selling affordable accessories: underwear, bags and sunglasses.[82] Diesel and Sisley offered basic everyday clothes but glamorized them with provocative images created by the brands' marketing departments and famous fashion photographers Oliviero Toscani, Helmut Newton, Corinne Day, Jürgen Teller and Steven Meisel. Many of the advertising campaigns created by these photographers became the target of heated public debate, and some of the campaigns were abandoned because of their non-normative and sexually explicit content.[83]

In the 1990s, high fashion advertising decidedly drew from the past. One much-used visual theme was the 1920s androgyny and the tradition of cross-dressing. It even produced a trend called *lesbian chic*.[84] It was a nostalgic style that drew from visual representations of aristocratic female dandies: from Romaine Brooks' paintings and filmic representations of cross-dressed Marlene Dietrich and Greta Garbo. In 1998, the British footballer David Beckham wore the famous sarong and gave the concept *metrosexual*[85] a manly face. Paradoxically, fashion, which had been seen as the most immoral part of culture, had become the forefront of progressive queer politics. It had recognized and made visible the new consumer, the affluent, fashion-conscious homosexual and his/her new field of economics, the pink dollar.[86] A growing number of companies advertised for this new consumer, making it increasingly hard to separate homosexuality from heterosexuality.

However, even though queer became visible in fashion, the prerequisite lies in social change, advocated by the LGBT movement and especially the American-based AIDS-activism groups such as Queer Nation and Act Up who fought for ending violence and prejudice against homosexuals. The groups used t-shirts with slogans such as "We're Here! We're Queer! Get used to it!" in normalizing non-heterosexuality. To be gendered was now theorized as a function of dress.[87] At the beginning of the new millennium, visualization of fashion has only increased and gender construction extended from women, men and children to our pets.

2000s: FROM *SEX AND THE CITY* TO FASHIONABLE LAP DOGS

Contemporary fashion is thoroughly intertwined with visuality. A new genre has been created: the fashion film.[88] It is an attempt to intertwine brand image with moving image, and to go from costume drama into a film that mediates fashion and narrates a desirable lifestyle. One of the most influential fashion films was actually a television series: *Sex and the City*. It first aired on TV in 1998 and went from a cult hit into a globally watched award-winning success over six seasons. The series featured four single women discussing sex and relationships, and made fashion into a tool for constructing the new millennial woman. The series also made fashion into a character of its own, mainstreamed exclusive designer labels—especially the shoe designers Manolo Blahnik and Christian Louboutin—and granted the series' costume designer, Patricia Field, a position as fashion guru.[89] It connected characters with reality: clothes worn by the characters were auctioned in reality. While the series offered viewers a virtual shopping spree, it also provided some viewers with actual designer clothes.

Sex and the City conjured up an image of the contemporary glamorous and fashion-conscious single girl. It made dressing-up into a fun and empowering game, and transformed the main-character, Carrie Bradshaw, into "a stiletto-heeled role model for women in our time, click-clacking her way through the politics of fashion."[90] *Sex and the City* not only managed to popularize big *haute couture* brand names, it transformed high heels and ultra-feminine dress into a "third-wave feminist" tool for constructing femininity. The four characters underline the idea that there is no single femininity or a model to be a woman.

The fashion industry has continued its search for new consumer niches. The new fashion consumers that used to occupy a marginal spot in fashion are children and pets. As families have become smaller in size, both emotional and economical investment in children and pets has increased. Children are important players in and for the global and local fashion markets, and childhood has become an essential point in the social formation of fashion-oriented global consumers. Little girls especially are represented as "mini-fashionistas" who know how to dress and which brands to consume. This has increased the supply and demand of children's designer clothes. High-fashion brands such as Dior, Versace, Calvin Klein, Burberry, Armani, Alberta Ferretti, and Gucci all have children's wear collections (Figure 5.11). Childhood is shaped by fashion, but fashion has also become an important means to construct gendered childhood: girlhood and boyhood. Separate clothing for girls and boys was introduced in the 1930s, after which gender division has only increased. Gendering starts early: babies, whose gender cannot always be

FIGURE 5.11: The new millennium has seen the rise of children's high fashion. All the major brands have their children's lines, New York, 2010. Photo: Annamari Vänskä.

FIGURE 5.12: Clothing does not only make gender, it makes the human. In 2010s, fashion's search for ever-new markets is going to our pets. Fashionable clothing for lap-dogs sold in a specialized boutique, Tokyo, 2014. Photo: Annamari Vänskä.

recognized at first glance, are dressed in colors and materials associated with gender of children—pink and frilly dresses for girls, blue jeans for boys.[91] Children's gendered clothes exemplify how gender is inscribed in clothing: in the design, cut, color, pattern, and material. Clothing makes gender, not the other way round.

But clothing does not only make gender, it also makes the human. This is specifically visible in the world of pets. Little lap dogs are increasingly dressed in fashionable outfits, they have their own pet fashion weeks, and pay regular visits to pet salons.[92] Fashion humanizes dogs: their clothing follows same patterns, colors, and designs as clothes designed for humans. There are more conservative and grown-up looks such as pullovers with Burberry tartan, or oilskins by Barbour. Dog wear is also gendered: there are pink dresses, underwear with bows and laces for girly dogs, and leather jackets and hoodies for more streetwise dogs. Furthermore, dog clothes accentuate signs of race (!) and class familiar from the human world of fashion. It is revealing how straightforwardly the visual signs of gender have trickled from one species to another. This is proof of how profitable gender is for the fashion industry. It has transformed gender into a set of signs that can easily be attached to new things, and even species. In the post-industrial commodity domain, fashion has reached, what I would call, its posthuman phase. It is not only a tool that constructs gender; it is a tool for constructing the human. Dress neither needs a body to signify gender nor humanity.

Some designers are clearly taking up on posthumanism. The late Alexander McQueen's collection "Plato's Atlantis" (2010) and the Dutch avant-garde designer Bas Kosters' 2015 collection entitled "Permanent State of Confusion" blur the categorical boundaries of gender, human, and the animal. While McQueen's designs such as the Armadillo Boot drew from the world of animals and non-humans, Kosters' models were dressed in childishly patterned gender- and human-bending outfits. Both designers seem to state that the tendency to sell ready-made gender is mind numbing. The new millennium should be less about gender than the previous one, and more about humanity.

CHAPTER SIX

Status

JANE TYNAN

POWER AND STATUS

Roland Barthes observed that clothing links the body to society.[1] In this chapter, I explore various ways in which fashion and dress mark the body as a site of social power. Fashion is a cultural phenomenon; it generates meaning in the social area. However, the contingency of fashion prevents an easy interpretation of its status markers. While it may be an industry, it is unpredictable, illustrated throughout the history of fashion by the subversive styles that have emerged from above and below.

As Fred Davis observes, "to merely be 'in fashion' is to be one-up on those who are not as yet."[2] To be fashionable is to be modern—to have the competitive edge—an attitude inspired by a dynamic and youthful consumer culture. So in this context what exactly do we mean by status? Despite shifts in social structures during the past century, class continues to be a useful term to describe social difference in terms of education, wealth, and occupational status. If dress stabilizes identity to connect us with our social group then our social class could be determining what we wear.[3] However, class is not static; it describes collective identities that are themselves constantly changing.

In the late twentieth century, studies of class suggest a term that is deeply resonant yet also regularly dismissed as unfashionable.[4] Looking at the dynamics of social class help to explore clothing as a marker of status and site of social power. What do dress habits reveal about shifting perceptions of social class? Popular dress emerged from community tradition, but once the relationship between the urban and the rural changed in the West, consumer fashion became the dominant system to determine what people wore. The emergence of a consumer culture occurred alongside access to better wages and consumer credit for a range of social groups.

Fashionable status

Fashion was, and is, an urban phenomenon, as Patrizia Calefato observes, "fashionable dress is cosmopolitan."[5] The social importance of clothing, how it is worn and how meaningful it might be, is determined by the distribution of power and resources in any given society. Fashion has long been an urban phenomenon, whereas costume survived in many rural areas against the backdrop of traditional culture. Costume was a social practice to mark rituals and to bind communities together. In contrast, cities concentrate labor power, and consumerism we associate with a dynamic fashion society. Models of industrial organization determine how people access clothing and the aesthetic choices they make to fashion their bodies. Where consumer fashion prevails, aspirational images proliferate.

If fashion is about one-upmanship, then it can play on insecurities about social status. Fashion changes with ever-shifting collective identities, with each new look a seductive image shapes the desires and dreams of consumers. When people shop, they seek more than the acquisition of inanimate things, they are purchasing new identities. Consumer fashion has enlarged the social role of clothing, creating a whole aesthetic system through which people can stabilize their identities and ostensibly, connect with their social group. Most of all, though, fashion is about projecting social aspirations.

Fashion embodies status through a fluid, shifting, and unstable structure echoing the dynamics of capitalism itself. According to the sociologist, Georg Simmel, fashion derives from tension between "the tendency towards social equalization with the desire for individual differentiation and change."[6] He describes an unwritten system of emulation whereby new fashions descend through the status hierarchy.[7] This balancing act bears a resemblance to the dynamics of capitalism itself and the elasticity of liberal democracy. Once certain fashions lose their capacity to communicate status distinctions, they are redundant, making room for new fashions, and so on. Hence the fast pace of change in fashion. Simmel's principle that fashion "is the product of class distinction" is most significant.[8] His theory looks to the stratification of society to understand how the resulting tensions and divisions create a fashion system.

Inside the fashion industry, mysterious rituals are enacted to express its power to designate fashionable status. *London Fashion Week* was examined for a sociological study on how boundaries are used to stratify participants in this important event in the fashion calendar. *London Fashion Week*, like other events of its kind, reproduces key divisions and hierarchies, designed to sustain the whole fashion system. Entwistle and Rocamora found participants stratified according to their social capital, mirroring the boundaries set

FIGURE 6.1: The Royal Family watch the annual Trooping the Colour ceremony at Horse Guards Parade, London, June 13, 2015. Photo: Samir Hussein/WireImage.

FIGURE 6.2: A fashion show at Centrum Warenhaus department store at Alexanderplatz in East Berlin, April 1974. State socialism encouraged East Germans to think of themselves as workers first and consumers second. Photo: Mehner/ullstein bild via Getty Images.

in the wider field of fashion.[9] Status marking, ritualized within the fashion industry, reflects the investment participants make in the surfaces of glamour and seduction. These surfaces are socially meaningful; they represent and reproduce the very inequalities the fashion system is built on (Figure 6.2).

The fashion system trades in images of social power, addressing a seemingly exclusive club of youthful, thin, educated, healthy, rich people. Entwistle considers how fashion markets work to balance cultural and economic calculations, when fashion buyers, models, and brokers mediate between producers and consumers.[10] A system that exploits the potential aesthetic power of the styled and pimped body claims to let an eager public in on its powerful fashion's secrets. Status is critical to the fashion system and there are few concessions to notions of equality or fairness. Fashion appears to embody the harsh world of commerce. A few cities in the world, such as Paris, London, New York, Tokyo, and Milan, hold disproportionately high status in terms of the influence they have over what people wear in other countries and regions. Historically, fashionable dressing has been linked with cultural power; it signals social status, ritualizes status marking, and the industry creates glamorous looks to interest "cultured" cosmopolitan consumers. Fashion is an expression of capitalism, incorporating its structural inequalities by encouraging people to strive, behavior so critical to creating illusions of success in an unequal society.

Consumerism directed to self-improvement encourages people to maximize their social power by maintaining the youth and beauty of their bodies.[11] A key study on fashion and social class by Diana Crane traces shifts in the relationship between fashion and gender from the class fashion of the nineteenth century to the globalized consumer fashion of the early twenty-first century.[12] It looks at discourses that surround clothing, and to the communicative role of fashion, in particular to consider "how tensions between social groups manifest in social space."[13] Clothes signify social status but do so in complex ways, particularly in contemporary society, where codes are less rigid and carry multiple messages. This is further complicated by the drive for self-improvement amongst fashion consumers; creating the illusion of youth and beauty maximizes social power. Thus, the high status body is presented as something that can be made.

The key historical fact about clothing—its capacity to indicate status and to express social power—lies in its availability. Sumptuary laws regulated what kind of fabrics and ornaments people from different social classes could wear, a reflection of the power of clothing to express social class in the Middle Ages.[14] With the industrialization of Western societies, the social meanings of particular clothes altered, built on what Lipovetsky saw as a more democratic and fluid system for "social regulation and social pressure."[15] It was the appearance of the sewing machine and the introduction of the science of measurement in the nineteenth century that altered the relationship people had to their clothes; innovations that paved the way to mass fashion. Indeed, this regulation of clothing supply is intimately bound up with a system of social stratification.

Economists who give status-seeking a socio-biological basis describe fashion as the desire within human societies to develop effective signals of status.[16] For them, the status-seeking incentive is paramount to understanding consumer behavior in relation to fashion. Crane argues that, while certain types of social information were less easy to read from a person's clothing, such as occupation and regional origin, fashion has become a primary carrier of meanings about class and gender.[17] Thus, fashion offers visual information about a person's class and gender, signals that are meaningful to social participation in modernity.

Dress is a significant marker of gender. Our clothing choices change as gender intertwines with age, occupational, and other social roles throughout our lives.[18] Thus, fashion is a complex social practice, reflecting (self) consciousness of our age, class position, gender role(s), and sexuality. Fashion is also a device to avoid social embarrassment; we develop certain types of useful knowledge about the forms of appearance that befit our social role. For instance, the social practice of fashioning the self nurtures an awareness of age-appropriate clothing. Fashion is about surfaces, not depth. However, the role of fashion in performing the self throughout a lifetime represents one of the ways in which a person can gauge expectations and monitor their position within the social group. Fashion communicates class, gender, and sexuality but is also the arena for challenges to fixed identity positions.

Women

Feminist concerns about the link between the discomforts of fashion and the lowly status of women gave rise to rational dress reform in the nineteenth century. In 1914 at a series of talks at Cooper Union in the United States, fashion became associated with a patriarchal agenda, when a group of women sought "the right to ignore fashion," which they believed was weakening the status of their gender.[19] Since then fashion has been a preoccupation for many in the women's movement who sought to improve the status of women in society (Figure 6.3).

Women have been particularly vulnerable to the pressures of a fashion society, a problem that led many second-wave feminists to view fashion as a tool of women's oppression. Betty Friedan felt that fashion created false desires to make women passive and Andrea Dworkin raged against the male objectification of women's bodies in fashion, which she characterized

FIGURE 6.3: American feminist, journalist, and political activist, Gloria Steinem (left) with art collector Ethel Scull and feminist writer Betty Friedan (lower right) at a Women's Liberation meeting at the home of Ethel and Robert Scull, Easthampton, Long Island, New York, August 8, 1970. Photo: Tim Boxer/Archive Photos/Getty Images.

as an oppressive system "created by men for women."[20] Along with many second-wave feminists, they believed that fashion kept women in their place, policing their sexuality and drawing attention away from their intellectual capabilities. They blamed fashion for maintaining women's lowly status. On the other hand, a body of theory emerged in the late twentieth century to challenge the feminist rejection of fashion. Elizabeth Wilson and Caroline Evans have systematically argued that fashion has a distinctive role in women's culture, giving women pleasure and opportunities for self-expression.[21]

Others argue that fashion drew women into the cultural arena, as producers and consumers, to experience modernity first hand.[22] If fashion was part of the popular culture of modernity, then it held the promise of a democratic age for women. The relationship between fashion and status for women is clearly fraught. Women are under considerable pressure to take responsibility for maintaining standards of femininity, often measured by their engagement with fashion practices.[23] However, fashion is not always a mask; it can also be viewed as an embodied social practice. Studying fashion as a meaningful body practice offers insights into the micro-practices that make up women's everyday lives.[24] Fashioning the self can be conforming to social pressure, but can equally be a challenge to established social rules.

Men

Men's clothing has not attracted the same level of criticism, but various changes in the history of men's wear reflect changes in the transformation of gender politics and social hierarchies in modernity. The debate on fashion and status has pre-occupied fashion historians for some time, particularly the move to more modest and uniform appearance for men in the nineteenth century.[25] A separation of private and public spheres saw gender marked by distinctive fashionable identities; men wore the uniform of the sober suit, while women bore a more decorative appearance.

In 1930, Flügel coined the term "Great Masculine Renunciation" to describe these changing ideals in masculine appearance: "As commercial and industrial ideals conquered class after class . . . the plain and uniform costume associated with such ideals has, more and more, ousted the gorgeous and varied garments associated with the older order."[26] Sartorial excess, he wrote, was renounced by men in the nineteenth century, due to the growing dominance of bourgeois values, expressed by the middle classes through a disapproval of brightly colored and decorated costume.[27] This became the dominant theory to explain distinctive fashionable appearances for men and women in the modern period.

This emergent masculinity was represented by uniformity in men's dress. In practice, it saw the rise of the sober suit for men, and the widespread use of the color black as a symbol of masculine power and confidence.[28] However, Christopher Breward has argued against Flügel's limited interpretation of men's clothing habits in the modern period in his study of the clothing habits of young men in London from 1860 to 1914. He says that they were not excluded from consumer culture, but their sartorial choices were constrained.[29] For David Kuchta, uniformity in men's dress was the result of earlier political upheavals that led the middle classes to seek in men's clothes the "ideology of inconspicuous consumption."[30] As social class became more significant to the formation of a person's identity, clothing became a visible form of social stratification. However, this was expressed very differently for women than men (Figure 6.4).

FIGURE 6.4: The pinstripe suit is emblematic of upper class power. Photo: Shutterstock/Zhu Difeng.

Clothing reflected social mobility in many ways, not least the growth of ready to wear, which affected availability, cost, and consumer choice for both men and women. The means of its production and distribution amplified already visible social class shifts. By the mid-twentieth century, innovations in promotion and retailing responded to the growing desire for fashionable dress in the mid-twentieth century. A greatly increased mass production sector made fashion a significant part of modern culture. The rise and fall of couture is one of the dominant stories of fashion in the twentieth century.[31] What Breward calls the "myth of sartorial individualism" maintained the symbolic dominance of couture, from the mid-century onwards, but paradoxically also drove the market for mass-produced, ready-made clothing.[32] The houses continued with ready-to-wear lines, licensing contracts and fragrances. Fashion consumption became a symbolic social practice to articulate social identities, which led to the growth of a commercial system of production, an expansion of retailing and the subsidiary industries of fashion promotion, styling, marketing, and media.

Children

Children's dress is less prominent in discussions of fashion historically, but no less an indicator of social identity. Clare Rose examines the contexts for the consumption of children's clothing in late nineteenth and early twentieth century Britain, to consider what fashionable dress meant for wearers and their families. She speculates on why boys and their clothing are marginalized in academic debate about dress and identity: "marginal to masculinity because of their youth, to consumption because of their low economic status, to fashion because of their masculinity."[33] In addition, the problem of parents acting on behalf of the child meant that consumption took place at a remove, making it more difficult to assess the social significance of clothing consumption for children (Figure 6.5).

Children's clothing is often excluded from serious analysis of fashion consumption, yet it involves all of the social and economic considerations made for women and men. Rose's study of boys' dress reveal efforts to code clothes for age and gender, a system of clothing practices for children that sought to embody family relationships, to reflect attitudes to masculinity, and to mark educational status.[34] If clothing links the body to society, then fashion systematizes that relationship, creating desirable images of bodies improved and transformed. For women, men, and children very different systems of meaning govern the consumption of their clothing.

Children's clothing consumption has large market value and now studies suggest that adults no longer determine their symbolic use of clothing.[35] A "myth of sartorial individualism" has driven the market for mass-produced, ready-made clothing and sustains a fashion system ever more reliant on the logic of branding. Men, women, and children are drawn in through their desire to express their social roles. Consumer fashion creates a whole aesthetic system for people to stabilize and communicate their identities in a society with increased social mobility.

CLOTHING AS SYSTEM OF REGULATION

Regulation clothing ascribes status within a closed social grouping. Fashion is about improving social status, but the rules are unclear, and the grounds more perilous. Does the spectacle of fashion draw consumers in with the promise of enhanced status and cultural power? Not long ago, every day dress was codified—hats for men are a case in point. Up until the 1960s, hats signified men's social status; their headgear dictated by

FIGURE 6.5: Fashion clearly identifies age and gender, 1940s. Photo: H. Armstrong Roberts/
ClassicStock/Getty Images.

occupation and social position. In the public sphere, hats were ideal markers of class and status, but also when a man "tipped" his hat he was deferring to his social superiors.[36] Cloth caps endured for working class men until after the Second World War, and to this day retain connotations of working class authenticity.

The bowler hat began as an occupational hat for gamekeepers and hunters in the mid-nineteenth century, was then adopted by the upper classes for sports, to eventually move to the city to be transformed into a symbol of bourgeois masculinity in the twentieth century.[37] Neckwear had a similar role to embody occupational position, with those in the higher social positions wearing high, stiff collars and those "who had to bend their necks, like clerks and shop assistants, had lower ones while the labourer abandoned the collar completely when at work and wore a muffler or neckerchief with his coloured shirt" all of which served to communicate the social position and occupational status of the wearer. [38]

To distinguish between manual and skilled workers, the collar also became significant, whereby those who were uniformed became known as blue-collar workers. Their social superiors in the professions, who perhaps wore suits and shirts, were referred to as white-

FIGURE 6.6: A white-collar worker stands with a blue-collar worker at an office, c. 1940. Photo: FPG/Hulton Archive/Getty Images.

collar workers. These terms have become shorthand for describing social distinctions in the English-speaking world in terms of the work that people do. Fashion is the flip side of uniform, but regulation plays an important part in the meanings that clothes can communicate in any context. Regulated clothing projects a particular kind of power that is only potent if situated and maintained through agreed social rituals and mores. On the other hand, fashion thrives in a mobile society, with access to cheap, mass-produced clothing and a dynamic popular culture (Figure 6.6).

Uniforms

Uniform and fashion are equally concerned with self-presentation but modern uniform enforces rigid social identities.[39] Fashionable dress is not proscribed in the same way, is subject to changing ideas of style, and is by definition an unstable system. However, it is clear that uniform and fashion both re-design the body; fashion advocates "play" and creativity, whereas uniform promotes conformity. For instance, the standardizing of British sailors' uniform in the early nineteenth century brought them under more official control, reflecting the move from a privatized to a publicly owned body.[40] The new design of the sailors' clothes made them more publicly accountable (Figure 6.7).

FIGURE 6.7: School uniforms worn by students at the Liceo Diurno Avenida Independencia (Chile) March 2008. Photo: Wikimedia Creative Commons.

Uniform embodies the interests of the institutions that set it to work. The image of the uniformed body is critical to the kind of power it exerts. When prison clothing was implemented in Europe and America in the nineteenth century, it was a form of "conspicuous punishment."[41] Thus, prison uniform reflects the dynamics of power within the institution, rather than the individual status of prisoners. Ash suggests that the return to conspicuous clothing, such as the orange jumpsuit, might signify the re-institution of harsh punishment regimes for prisoners. Here, the orange jumpsuits conspicuously announce the power the state has over those it incarcerates.

If uniform physically directs and coerces activity for the wearer, it also signals authority. Regulation dress came into its own when consumer capitalism reached new heights, which was when institutions demanded that prisoners and workers start to wear uniforms.[42] At the same time, the British military was standardizing and modernizing the khaki uniform dress. Uniform is an embodied social practice that reinforces or undermines wider social hierarchies; it fits with the needs of the nation state and its forms of standardization, bureaucracy, and centralized systems of organization. Uniforms later became part of the construction of citizenship in various regimes, where regulation clothing was valued for its transformative power.

There is another sense in which uniform was embraced in the modern period, through fascist and quasi-fascist projects that sought to build a culture of the body. These projects deployed clothing to signify and embody ideals of masculinity, patriotism and action. Wendy Parkins brings together a collection of essays on the inter-connected concerns

FIGURE 6.8: A foreign detainee is walked by two US Army MPs at Guantanamo Bay, Cuba, in March 2002. Photo: Peter Muhly /AFP/Getty Images.

of dress, gender, and citizenship dealing with, amongst other things, the black shirt of Italian fascism and the uniforms worn by the *Falange Española*.[43] Here, clothing is central to discussions of citizenship through the material formation of collective disciplines. If uniform is thought to stabilize identities and embody specific forms of citizenship, this is because clothing publicly intervenes in the private lives of soldiers or workers (Figure 6.9).

FIGURE 6.9: Past and present members of the Irish Guard on parade in Whitehall, London, March 15, 1965. Photo: Terry Fincher/Express/Getty Images.

Sartorial proscription is part of a complex network of normalizing standards and discursive practices, but is not as constraining as it appears, inserting various uniforms into a vocabulary of conformity and subversion. The resulting modernized uniforms that dominated in the twentieth century were not designed to reflect a rigid class position of the wearer, but to negotiate the complex mechanisms of social mobility. Uniforms were not so much about service, but marked social status as people laid claim to particular roles, professions, and sporting activities. Traditional working clothes in Britain were modernized, to reflect a more democratic society, such as the Metropolitan Police uniform, which started as an elegant gentlemanly costume, to be replaced by a military-style outfit.[44] An upsurge in democratic ideas at the start of the twentieth century was reflected in the move from picturesque occupational costume to practical and protective clothing for work.[45] In Britain, railway and road transport workers started to wear smart uniforms.

Working clothes

By the 1920s, the number of uniformed workers had greatly increased, to enhance the prestige of the employer and to provide them with protective clothing. Regulation clothing proliferated when a range of institutions sought control over populations. Uniform had the power to encode social inequalities. But that power could also be subverted. When codified clothing sets bodies apart, they are also invested with a kind of magic, as Keenan argues, in his study of sacred dress.[46] He demonstrates how sacred dress as sign-symbol has been eroticized by a postmodern fashion culture keen to mine any sign-system for shock value. Hierarchies set down by a church institution and represented by specific time-honoured forms of dress, are regularly subverted by the refashioning of sacred dress on the catwalk.

Closed systems of meaning constructed to mark status and confer authority upon certain participants, has made regulation dress an ideal sign system to raid for fashionable looks. Fred Davis was fascinated by the identity change that blue jeans underwent, from a garment "associated exclusively with hard work to one invested with many of the symbolic attributes of leisure."[47] So, too, a range of garments designed for work or sport gained fashionable status, such as the trench coat, first designed for upper class leisure, adapted to be worn by British army officers in wartime, to then become a twentieth century design classic.[48] The symbolic transformation of various garments from work to leisure reflect how fashion works to appropriate styles rooted in social systems and meaningful to institutional settings.

As social life constantly changes, status markers transform, mirroring the fluid condition of social identity itself. Regulation clothing can ascribe status within a specific social grouping, but codes only hold their meaning within this context. What is clear is that uniform clothing systems are prey to fashionable appropriation. It is precisely the situated meanings of regulation clothing, their power to signify hierarchy and status within a closed social system that attracts fashion designers and stylists. By exploiting the novelty of uniforms and sacred dress, the fashion media display a fascination with the stability of traditional institutions, their capacity to create arresting images of social power.

FASHION, CLOTHING, AND SOCIAL CLASS

Consumer culture is part of the experience of modernity. The term "consumer culture" suggests consumption practices have come to actually represent cultural values.[49] Consumer practices and perceived needs are constructed through specific social, economic, and political structures that cannot be defined universally. Thus culture shapes practices of consumption and defines needs according to how we imagine we should live. Luxury goods have specific cultural meanings, what Douglas and Isherwood describe as "marking services" rather than "physical services."[50] It is other consumers who endow goods with value and meaning. People make judgments about one another's class position through their perception of, for example, how well-dressed a person might be. Thus, clothing, can unite and divide, can be used as an instrument of inclusion and exclusion. Luxury goods have social rather than intrinsic properties that enable identification with a peer group and signify social status.

Clothing, in particular, socializes the body making it meaningful in the social world. Returning to the history of consumerism clarifies how the logic of fashion—and style— came to permeate so much of everyday life. Methods of production were once organized around fixed ideas about status groups. Fordism, so called after Henry Ford, who produced the first Model T car in Detroit in 1908, describes assembly-line methods that produced cheap, uniform commodities in high volume and paid good wages. This represented a stage in the development of consumer culture, replaced by more flexible methods of production, and later became known as post-Fordism. What Crane describes as class fashion probably approximates the Fordist approach; a single style widely disseminated.[51] In 1926, *Vogue* called Coco Chanel's famous little black dress a "Fashion Ford" for its simplicity, clean lines, and rejection of decoration. Chanel's dress was a challenge to the bourgeoisie and a bold statement on the newfound democracy of taste.

Fashion operated in the first half of the twentieth century according to this cycle, whereby designers set styles for each season. This has been replaced by a much less predictable market, characterized by "bottom-up models," such as youth subcultures, catering to market niches rather than to the masses. A style of capitalism emerged that used technology and people management techniques, focused on targeting consumers. From the 1980s, post-Fordism meant outsourcing production to newly industrializing economies.[52] Technological innovations introduced flexible specialization methods of production such as "Just in Time Production" (JIT) and fast fashion, thereby replacing economies of "scale" with economies of "scope." Fashion, like many other parts of popular culture, displayed a postmodern pluralism that coincided with the rise of neoliberal economic models.

It became clear that consumer lifestyles were undermining more fixed traditional ideas about status groups. Post-Fordist consumption was apparently more responsive to the needs and interests of the consumer.[53] Knowledge of the consumer, and what they wanted, became valuable to producers, and technology was directed to harvesting data and creating systems to respond quickly to their desires. Academic debates on consumerism center on whether post-Fordism can be viewed as a reflection of human desires or represent the emergence of a social force to perpetuate capitalism.

It has been argued that the focus on "constant change" in the fashion mechanism allows for temporary solutions. Lipovetsky saw fashion as a system to disrupt the established principle of inequality in dress laid down by sumptuary laws, in favor of the permanent revolution of modern democracy.[54] In a modern society, status is not fixed, but actively sought, giving fashion a key role in the endless construction and reformulation of the self. This has been attributed to the link between fashion and sexual desire, where people seek to create alternative ways of being in their bodies, to explore the deviant pleasures of rebellion, evil, and danger through masquerade.[55] Others are more convinced by theories around status seeking, ideology and belonging.[56]

Conspicuous Consumption

Miles argues that "people are not merely consuming products or fashions, but they are also reproducing consumerism as a legitimate way of life."[57] Various theorists link consumption with cultural change. Conspicuous consumption, a concept developed by Thorstein Veblen in 1899, made a clear distinction between the use value of goods and their prestige value, arguing that the desire to enhance social status drives people to purchase things that they do not need, to simply display their wealth. Veblen offers a critique of economic inequality, explaining the concern a leisure class might have with the appearance of consumption.[58] He locates aesthetic principles in the economic choices they make. A closer look at the goods and services favored by them reveals that by indulging in luxury goods they offer conspicuous evidence of their leisure. The leisure of women and children and even servants acts as further proof of the rich man's power over others, whether he can indulge his dependents in impractical activities. Such is his wealth that his family is conspicuous by their economic inactivity and by their consumption.

Consumption is only useful to display social status if it is highly conspicuous. This is no less true today with the explicit branding that allows consumers to display their social status. Logos are a signaling process to fuel the desire for a whole network of consumers to "keep up." Theories of conspicuous consumption have become very influential, whether analyzing the shopping habits of middle class women or gauging the role of luxury brands in the emerging industrial economies. Social envy is pivotal to signaling social status, particularly in the light of the visibility of fashion, and its links with ideas of taste and culture.

Bourdieu examines systems of classification in French life to explore this wider category of taste. When people make aesthetic choices they are distinguishing themselves from other social classes. His study demonstrates that choices of clothing, furniture, leisure activities, and food reveal taste as a system of social and political power, a means by which social classes are organized and their class interests reproduced. "Taste classifies, and it classifies the classifier" is a formulation that describes how social subjects distinguish themselves by the commodities they consume, but more significantly, by those for whom they have distaste.[59]

The science of taste is made powerful by its capacity to create classes. This leads to stylized forms of eating or dressing. For the middle classes, a heightened sense of anxiety about outward appearances makes them susceptible to concerns about fashionable clothing. The choices people make, to say, be "on-trend" or even their efforts to avoid "being too fashionable," constitute an elaborate system of classification. The styles of dressing people embrace, but also what they repudiate, reveal much about the social group they belong to, and what they aspire to become. The level of interest they have and the time they devote to self-presentation can also be telling:

> The interest the different classes have in self-presentation, the attention they devote to it, their awareness of the profits it gives and the investment of time, effort, sacrifice and care which they actually put into it are proportionate to the chances of material or symbolic profit they can reasonably expect from it.[60]

Status symbols do not have a fixed value, and lose their value when eventually adopted by the masses. But as Veblen suggests, in consumer culture, wealth is aestheticized and luxury goods promise to ascribe high social status to the owner. If taste creates social classes, then the consumption of goods becomes a very delicate matter indeed. It heightens the anxiety the middle classes have about outward appearances, their furniture, their clothing and, of course, the food they eat. Daniel Miller observed, "On the surface is found the clothing which may represent us and may reveal a truth about ourselves, but it may also lie."[61] This drives people to invest in the duplicity of appearances, to look to clothes to enhance their social status, which accounts for the special role fashion plays in expressing social aspiration.

Politicizing Consumption

With so much fear about failing to live up to expected social standards, no wonder status anxiety drives the consumption of luxury goods. Fashion consumption, in particular, involves a complex range of feelings. The role of emotions in the practice of fashion consumption for women has been described as a competitive psychosocial mechanism.[62] Drawing on the work of Bourdieu, Rafferty offers a complex portrait of women's self-fashioning practices acting as a "tool of distinction, identification and segregation for social collectivities."[63] Woodward's ethnographic study of women's clothing choices is much more optimistic. She demonstrates how women negotiate being fashionable, revealing a balance of external and internal forces influencing their decisions.[64] She concludes that the act of getting dressed is reflexive, which involves accessing ideas of the authentic self, as well as the choices offered by "fashion."

It would be a mistake to see consumer culture and self-fashioning exclusively through the lens of western society. Consumer practices in other regions are shaped by perceived needs, constructed through specific social, economic, and political structures. However people imagine they should be living, it is their specific social aspirations that shape their practices of consumption. Critical to this is the role of goods within a given culture or micro-culture, whether they mark social standing or sustain physical existence. If they are of the former variety, then they have a strong role in symbolic systems. Behind the Iron Curtain, as in the case of the German Democratic Republic (GDR), state socialism encouraged East Germans to think of themselves as workers first and consumers second. Concerns about quality, price, and value were constructed as equally important to matters of taste and aesthetics in the consumption of goods.[65] Fashion was not divorced from a society organized around socialism, which created its own form of consumer culture, generated its own dreams and desires (Figure 6.10).

As an alternative socialist consumer culture emerged in many countries, the desire for luxury goods was managed through the model of consumer-citizen, which was how women's roles were constructed in the GDR. Fashion may be capitalist, but consumption is not, and can even take on the character of institutions and states with a high degree of control and regulation. And yet, consumption can be fraught, particularly when goods are conspicuously luxurious. Breda Luthar, in her analysis of desire and consumption under state socialism, draws on personal memories of former shoppers from 1950s and 1960s Yugoslavia, to discover their motivations and experiences of border crossing.[66] They crossed the border to purchase consumer goods associated with the West. Here consumption becomes politicized through the means by which luxury goods were acquired "against dominant definitions of socialist subjectivity and collectivity and the corresponding definition of human needs."[67] Thus, border crossing was a transgressive act, a risk worth taking, to acquire desirable commodities that represented the social aspirations of people living under state socialism.

Status is not just about how people position themselves within a given social collectivity, but also how nations and regions compete with one another. Historically, fashion has been the ideal status symbol for nations to project their economic power. If a fashion industry is evidence of the status of a nation, then the rush to purchase luxury goods is a sign of a strengthening economy. This is most conspicuous in the emerging industrial economies of the world, where luxury goods act as status symbols and there is a strong desire for brands from the big European fashion houses. China has become one of the fastest growing markets for luxury labels and by 2004 it was the third largest luxury goods consumer in the world.[68] Consumer culture symbolized the way of life in the West over at least the past century, which was then exported, to generate new forms of status anxiety in other cultures and regions.

Consumption has become a way of life, a means by which we communicate everything from wealth, occupational status, to education and social class. Luxury goods, in particular, are forms of conspicuous consumption that hold prestige value and enhance social status. This is why a leisure class is so concerned with the appearance of consumption, to offer conspicuous evidence of their leisure by indulging in luxury goods. Wu argues that the appetite for luxury goods in China is bound up with a desire to reject the aesthetics of communism, in favor of a more "global" style, while enthusiastically adopting a Western kind of stratified society. She finds a social class system emerging in China, predicated on social envy, and promoting fashionability as a visible marker of taste and culture.

FIGURE 6.10: Shop display window, East Berlin, Germany, c. 1960. Photo: Dominique
Berretty/Gamma-Rapho via Getty Image.

BREAKING THE RULES

The body practices of fashion and dress connect us with our social group. In this discussion of fashion and status, I explored power and asked how it is distributed and regulated in relation to fashion, clothing and style. Throughout the discussion, I identified dominant patterns in social behavior, but styles of resistance are also significant, perhaps even more so, revealing lifestyles constructed in opposition to consumer culture. Historically, artists challenged the constraining standards of the fashion system on women and men. From the Arts and Crafts Movement in Britain to second-wave feminists, groups sought clothing reform in their attempts to create a utopian way of life. Various movements experimented with systems of dress; amongst them rational and aesthetic dress, British men's dress reform, Futurism and Russian Avant-Gardists.[69] Anti-fashion represented a rejection of capitalism, its illusions and the conspicuous waste it generates.

Later, a more systematic theorizing of anti-fashion took place, largely through subcultural theory, an approach that emerged in the 1970s from the Centre for Contemporary Cultural Studies (CCCS) at the University of Birmingham in Britain. *Resistance Through Rituals* was one of the first studies to theorize British subcultures as a form of working-class resistance to a dominant capitalist culture.[70] Subsequently, Dick Hebdige interpreted subcultural style as an interruption of the normal order through the various styles adopted by young people to challenge the status quo. What he highlighted was the power of style to expose and contradict "the myth of consensus."[71] The CCCS characterized the stylistic practices of youth groups in the 1970s as a response to social change in Britain. While fashion presents a limited and largely manufactured consensus on the correct styles of body presentation, Hebdige and others saw "spectacular subcultures" subverting dominant ideas on how to look. In particular, punk was a focus for much analysis, articulating the frustrations of working-class youth in 1970s Britain, using rebellious attitudes, style and music (Figure 6.11).[72]

Subcultural style was an alternative symbolic system of dress, which offered a fractured alternative to the fashion system, and a style that could be described as deviant. There have since been many challenges to the CCCS "youth cultures" approach to understanding the behavior of young people. Evans finds it more useful to think of subcultural identities as "fluid and mobile, rather than fixed." Moving through subcultures allows young people to resist recuperation, to be in a constant state of voyage through a complex array of identities and stylistic possibilities.[73] This view is echoed in Woodward's study, a mass observation of the style choices of young people in Nottingham in Britain, where she detects a shift towards "subtly differentiated style groupings, which incorporate mainstream high street fashions."[74] For her, young people do not represent street style in the mythical sense, nor are they immersed in fashion, but assemble their clothes from a variety of sources. Thus, their identities are not so much fractured as layered, reflecting the complexities of fashion practices.

More recent work explores youth transitions under "consumer capitalism," such as Greg Martin's study of underclass responses to social division, exclusion, and inequality, through stylized solutions such as designer clothes. These expressions of social aspiration he identifies in a so called "chav" style, not necessarily a subculture, but a British phenomenon reflecting how social deprivation is negotiated against a backdrop of rampant consumerism.[75] The parodying and subversion, of say, the Burberry check is, for Martin, a subcultural attempt to resolve real social relations symbolically.[76] He emphasizes continuity rather than novelty in youth transitions under consumer capitalism, where he

FIGURE 6.11: A group of punks in London, late 1970s. Photo: Virginia Turbett/Redferns.

views a tribal dress code as overcompensation for the sense of uncertainty and crisis. He echoes Hebdige in the 1970s, particularly when he argues that "chav style" is an attempt to symbolically resolve the contradictions of poverty in a consumer society. These styles of resistance demonstrate that lifestyle is not just an invention of consumer culture, but a way of life, often constructed in opposition to dominant narratives.

CONCLUSION

Fashion is cultural and generates meaning in the social area. According to Bourdieu, avant-garde couturiers "speak of fashion in the language of politics."[77] It is no wonder. There are so many ways in which fashion marks people out: education, gender, race, sexuality, nationality, social position, occupation, and ideology. Status marking is ritualized within the fashion industry; reflecting and reproducing on a symbolic level the dividing practices so critical to the workings of commercial capitalism. Perhaps uniform practices interest fashion designers because social hierarchies are so cleverly designed into the clothes. However, fashion is an aesthetic system where people can express either their conformity or opposition to this established order. Once in the public sphere, both uniform clothing and fashion garments become part of a vocabulary of conformity and subversion.

This discussion explores fashion as a status marker, a tool of social aspiration, an object of conspicuous consumption, an instrument of rebellion, and a source of status anxiety. Clothing is regulated in various ways, from the normalizing standards of institutional cultures, to the means of production and distribution that determine what people wear in their everyday lives. In a society of increased social mobility, fashion consumption is a tricky business. Class belonging, gender, and age-appropriate behavior are not as rigid as they once were. Fashion might articulate social aspiration, but cultural consumption also brings with it uncertainty and anxiety. And what about those who cannot participate in consumer culture, or do so at a remove? When young people parody and subvert status markers they remind us that clothes are both personal and political. Clothing links the body to society in ways that are ever more ambiguous, fragile, complex, and elusive.

CHAPTER SEVEN

Ethnicity

SIMONA SEGRE REINACH

I want to be honest about the world we live in, and sometimes my political persuasions come through my work. Fashion can be really racist, looking at the clothes of other cultures as costumes . . .[1]

DRAPING AND SEWING

The first great semantic opposition in human dress was that between flat, uncut, unsewn, two-dimensional fabric, typical of Asia, with its many definitions and workmanship—ao-dai, hanbok, kimono, lungi, sari, and many others, which all stand in the various languages for "a piece of cloth"—and three-dimensional fabric, i.e. cut and sewn, characteristic of the European sartorial silhouette. The Issey Miyake collection *APOC* (launched in 1971) is a good example. It is described as clothing made from "a Piece of Cloth," a concept that explores not only the relationship between the body and clothing, but also the space that is born between them. Roberto Rossellini had noted this distinction between the sartorial traditions of the Asian world and those of the West. The Italian director even described the Indian leader, Pandit Jawaharlal Nehru, in terms of his non-Western, untailored attire saying: "Like all Indians, Nehru is a 'draped' man. He seeks to open his spirit to all knowledge and to achieve a poetic synthesis of the world. We Europeans are 'sewn men'; we have become specialists; we excel in the field of our activity, but are unable to understand what lies outside our specialization. We are prisoners of our habits; I say 'we', but I am striving to become a 'draped man.'"[2]

Roberto Rossellini, who often filmed in India and married an Indian woman, saw Indian sartorial habits as an expression of a possible different approach to creativity. He considered draping as a continual creative act, as opposed to the fixity of a Western garment. For Winston Churchill, the Indian leader Gandhi, landing in England in the rain before the curious eyes of the public gathered on the quay to get a close look at the man who was leading India toward independence, dressed only in a lungi draped around his loins, was instead only a "half naked fakir."[3] Indirectly, Rossellini and Churchill are re-proposing a typical theme of the debate on dress between the nineteenth and twentieth centuries: fashion versus costume, i.e. civilized dress versus that of the savages. The great voyages of discovery leading to European colonial domination between the sixteenth and nineteenth centuries had also confronted the colonizers with the physical aspect of other populations, dressed up and clothed in a highly diversified way, from the nakedness of the "American Savage" to the dress of India, China, and Japan (Figure 7.1).

The British colonizers in India, for example, occasionally adopted the Indian way of dress, but only partially, and with many precautions, to avoid the feared possibility of

FIGURE 7.1: A model presents a hanbok, traditional Korean dress, during a fashion show in Hanoi, September 8, 2013. Photo: Luong Thai Linh/AFP/Getty Images.

"going native." The fear, was that if they did, they would lose their identity and position of privilege which, evidently, is assured by a way of dress that is considered symbolically important and appropriate. In a word, superior. On the other hand, the British prevented the Indian rulers, their subjects, from wearing Western dress on their journeys to the UK. Deference toward the British Empire had to be maintained, and it started with dress.

Western fashion was considered the opposite to costume. The term was applied to all forms of dress that the Europeans encountered in the countries they dominated. The still frequent reciprocal attraction between European dress and non-European, non-Western or ethnic dress, in the course of time did not affect the Euro-centric background of a theory of dress that was then taking shape. Within the classifying principle opposing fashion and costume, change and fixedness, there were of course ambivalences and contradictions. Non-Western materials, styles, and articles of dress have, however, constituted, at least from the eighteenth century, an on-going source of inspiration for European fashion.[4]

This Western fashion theory was consolidated by the mid-nineteenth century with the invention of Parisian *haute couture* at the peak of the domination of European culture and economy. It still resonates today in an age of globalized exchange and new emerging sartorial identities, it conditions the overall view.[5] It is not easy to outline the ethnic contribution to modern and contemporary fashion, because the very meaning of "ethnic" escapes a single definition. As Karen Tranberg Hansen writes on the subject of fashion in Africa, it is a question of "global encounters and local reinventions."[6] We may, however, seek to highlight the process through which the initial Euro-centrism transformed into poly-centrism, and those elements that are profiled within this process, defining the components at stake within the system of contemporary fashion.[7]

EURO-CENTRISM AND FASHION

In the early twentieth century, the French millionaire Albert Khan, banker and philanthropist, promoted the first major photographic research on "world costumes." The result, today on show at the Musée Albert Khan in Paris, in a documentary and in a book collecting all the images,[8] is a sort of enormous catalog of dress. Khan's collection of images, which he never succeeded in completing, is in many ways similar to another celebrated catalog completed in the sixteenth century by an Italian painter, Cesare Vecellio. Their difference lies in the fact that Khan's collection contains the written foundations of a middle class hierarchical order deduced from dress that we might still find today: the West and the Rest. In a way, Khan's project was to make it possible to attribute to everyone a place, and one place only according to the ordered ideal started and promoted by the Industrial Revolutions and French society and culture. Between the sixteenth and the twentieth centuries, a process took place that led Europe, and later Europe and the United States, to have the financial and cultural lead over the rest of the world, in particular over Asia. The Western world somehow forgot that Asia had been the leader in the textile trade in the previous centuries.[9] The invention of *haute couture* in Paris can be considered in several dimensions, and not only from the point of view of style. It was a manufacturing and cultural industry that turned into a system, consolidating a long history of production of luxury goods, and exchange between the court and city. The relation between the fashion system and urban life became increasingly direct.[10] The *couturiers*—from Charles Frederick Worth and Paul Poiret right down to Coco Chanel, Christian Dior, and Yves Saint Laurent—strengthened the lead of Paris as the capital of good taste. Paris rivaled London, the other great European capital and center of male elegance. Women's *haute couture* in Paris, and male elegance that was defined by the craft of tailoring in London, celebrated the leadership of these cities and the European urban lifestyle that was instrumental in depreciating other models, other cultures, and other dress systems. European and later Western fashion was not only the expression of modernity, but also the only accepted representation of it. There may have been other sources of inspiration, but their authority was denied in agreement with the colonial project (Figure 7.2).

Colonial expansion, which in the nineteenth century reached a new impetus (second and third colonial periods), was based on an ideology of an evolutionist and positivist mould, within which the system of middle class taste was presented as a strongly ambivalent construct, a confirmation of the superiority of Western culture. Fashion, however, had an ambivalent status. It was frivolous and feminine, and hence inferior, compared with male rationality, which with the, so-called "Great Masculine Renunciation," abandoned all frivolity.[11] It is important to observe how fashion and dress came to represent stereotyped ideal types that are loaded with ideology, rather than real oppositions between ways of dressing. This is so despite the fact that there were differences between the European fashion of Paris and London in the early twentieth century and the way of dress of Asia, China and Japan, in South America, and in rural and peasant Europe. As cultural and ideological constructs, fashion and costume re-appear in the present day globalized fashion:

> The conception of time is central in this division between Western and non-Western dress practices, epitomized by the all too prevalent discussion of non-Western dress in terms of an "ethnographic present" as opposed to the "perpetual future" associated with Western fashion's constant rush to the next season.[12]

Fashion is therefore both the expression and the manifestation of a superior social system, and in particular of the lifestyle of the major cities[13] and a sign of Western cultural superiority, in that the rest of the world dress in ethnic costume. The construction of the East as a great imaginary and undifferentiated "elsewhere," later theorized by Edward Said, took shape as a further strengthening of Western identity, the place and time of modernity. At the same time, this vision of fashion, which considers it a mainly feminine attribute, places it in the ambiguous position of inferiority, the same, as Said shows, places the feminized, passive East opposite a masculine, active West.[14]

The Euro-centric and Franco-centric theory of the origins of fashion have been revised, scaled down, and criticized by anthropologists, costume historians, and fashion theorists. On the one hand, dress is defined as the set of modifications and body supplements to the body, thus widening the notion of fashion in the anthropological sense.[15] On the other hand, specific studies based on historical and iconographic sources have demonstrated that there was fashion, i.e. more or less swift change in styles, even in past periods, before the fourteenth and fifteenth centuries, the period in which the origin of fashion is usually collocated, and also in places outside Europe.[16] The total fixity of costume not only does not exist; like every human phenomenon, costume also changes, but the very concept of costume is identified as an ideological construction. As the anthropologist, Karen Tranberg Hansen writes:

> "Ethnic" dress is dynamic and changing: it even has fads. People everywhere want the "latest" by whatever changing definitions of local preferences. Widespread desire "to move with fashion" and to be "in style" now.[17]

It is the lack of knowledge of different dress phenomena that leads Western scholars to wrongly attribute an almost complete staticity to clothes which they were or are not able to de-codify or of which they have indirect knowledge.

FIGURE 7.2: A model walks the runway during the Stella Jean show as a part of Milan Fashion Week Womenswear Spring/Summer 2014. Photo: Antonio de Moraes Barros Filho/WireImage.

As Sarah Grace Heller affirms, the origin of fashion is found wherever it is sought and its various attributions, in place and time, only indicate the uselessness of wishing to attribute it to a single historic period and a single place.[18] The concepts of authentic and local are also strongly problematic. We may just think of the case of African wax, which becomes authentic African, while it is a print technique created in Indonesia, re-invented by the Dutch, and introduced by the latter in Africa and hence authenticated there (Figure 7.3).[19]

The Globalization of Fashion: The West and the Rest

Many recent studies have analyzed the effects of globalization on people's dress, tastes, and habits, seeking to pinpoint those models, constant factors, and features that disseminate fashion in order to trace a sort of globalized map of fashion's paths.[20] Fashion simply cannot be reduced to a form of cultural imperialism and to a mere commercial expansion of brands from the West to the rest of the world. According to some authors, the very expression "expansion of fashion" from Europe to other parts of the world is not correct, in that it is already an ethnocentric expression.[21] It would be a further proof of the persistence of the preconception that fashion was born in Europe, the cradle of civilization. The first axiom to question is, therefore, not that concerning the European and Western origin of fashion, but that that associates fashion with Western modernity, while it links the dress of the Rest to the pre-modern tradition. The first opposition to be overcome is that between "fashion" and "dress," which we may replace with exchange, hybridization, and inspiration.

The concept of "cultural authentication," i.e. the process in which the members of a cultural group incorporate extraneous cultural elements and make them their own, is put forward by fashion anthropologists to realize the complexity with which extraneous elements of dress to one's own dress tradition are included and absorbed into local habits.[22] Even the global spread of jeans and T-shirts, as Margaret Maynard has demonstrated, for example, is not as uniform and pervasive as it might seem, but is always subject to local interpretation.[23] Karen Tranberg Hansen has underlined that the introduction of acquired or donated second-hand Western clothes in Africa, a phenomenon she studied in Zambia, has in many ways overturned the local textile market.[24] However, considering only this side of the coin, i.e. the negative impact on the local equilibrium, would be misleading. Tranberg Hansen has in fact demonstrated that second-hand clothes have been set in a wider discourse that defines the person's role and his/her position in a world defined as globalized. Every individual or collective choice to adopt an item of the Western wardrobe in locations and cultures, use other sartorial grammars, and it is always linked to the local reference context.

China is an emblematic case in hand. Since 1978, with Den Xiao Ping's "Open Door Policy," the country has been transformed from being a producer of fashions designed elsewhere, to a country of consumers.[25] The new global luxury in Asia is not only a translation of the European one, i.e. of Western brands expanding their network in Asia, but a complex new cultural construct enriched by the Asian interpretation, which is rapidly influencing the image and identity of European fashion. The collocation of Western brands in Chinese shopping malls is subject to local negotiations, which bring about a continual re-semantization of their value and their image.

On the other hand, the "non-Western" responses cannot be isolated from a market context defined by the West, nor can they be traced back to a single model, as they are

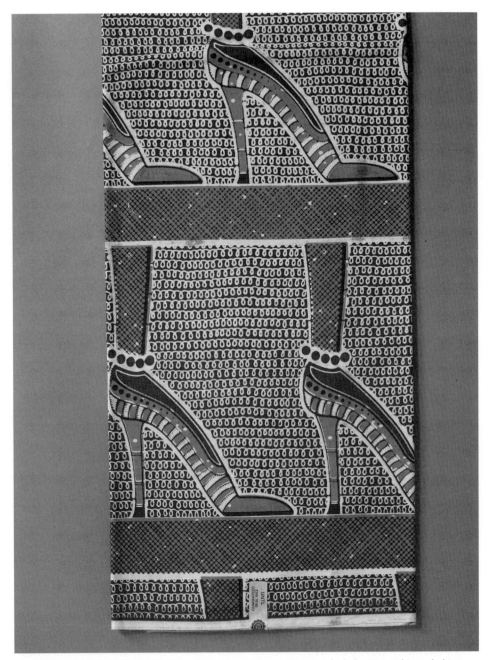

FIGURE 7.3: *High Heels* Dutch Wax style printed cotton factory cloth for East African fashion market, 2005. CHA Textiles (Hong Kong) founded United Nigerian Textiles Ltd. (UNTL) in 1964 in Nigeria and has factories in Ghana. This acquisition was made possible by the generous support of the ROM Reproductions Acquisitions Fund. Photo: Royal Ontario Museum © ROM.

part of an extremely variegated, constantly evolving picture. What the West calls ethnic fashion is in reality the result of complex vicissitudes, never extraneous to the fashion system. On the subject of Africa, Victoria L. Rovine writes:

> Africa is home to some of the world's most dramatic dress practices, including textiles, jewelry, coiffures, and apparently infinite combinations of all of these elements. These include embroidered boubous and intricately woven strip cloth in West Africa, richly beaded blankets in southern Africa, and vibrantly patterned kangas in the east— some of the most famous of African adornments. In popular imagination, both in Africa and elsewhere, such garments often represent African culture. All are in fact the result of global interactions and historical change; in short, they are part of fashion systems.[26]

Stating that fashion has always been, in the past and in places outside Europe, and that costume is not radically "other" with respect to fashion, does not solve the question of the relationship between the West and the Rest. Nor is it possible to distinguish between local fashion and Western fashion, because of the very ambivalence and complexity characterizing the process of the circulation of clothes, brands and creativity in the twenty-first century. The contradictions in the simple binary model contrasting modernity and backwardness, already evident in the past, are exploding in our time, highlighting a model of greater complexity.

> By situating Western "interpretations" as superior to Eastern "originals", cultural intermediaries helped to re-establish the authority of the Western subject and the value of their creativity. In doing so, they reaffirmed the West as the true source of fashion-inspiration from elsewhere notwithstanding being authorized to set for the rest of the world.[27]

European fashion and ethnic costume are constitutive opposites of a modernity that is not consistent with present-day reality. Even in the past it was an ideological construct more than an actual reality. Anthropologist Zhao, for example, unequivocally questions whether fashion is an expression of modernity, and whether the modernity to which fashion is linked is that of a Western stamp:

> [This book] aims to demonstrate that the rise of the Chinese fashion industry not only involves economic development, but also social and political dynamics, that fashion is not just a means to a rags-to-riches style modernization, but also a medium through which a Chinese notion of modernity is articulated and contested, and that the globalization of the fashion industry is always met by various forms of localization practices and simultaneously shaped by the global political economy . . . According to this Chinese notion of modernity, China becomes modern not because of the adoption of Western styles of clothing (hence becoming more Westernized) but because clothing styles now are considered better than the ones in the past.[28]

It is therefore more correct to see fashion and dress as an overall process, and not as single entities with established boundaries. Starting more or less from the 1990s, the relation between European fashion and other sources of inspiration began to be strained, due to the increasingly evident contribution of non-European creativity and the shaping of an increasingly vast receiving market (Figure 7.4).

FIGURE 7.4: A model presents a creation by Pakistani designer Sarah Gandapur during Bridal Couture Fashion Week in Karachi, June 2015. Photo: Asif Hassan/AFP/Getty Images.

DECONSTRUCTING GLOBAL FASHION

Theorists from various cultural and geographical backgrounds are thus committed to modifying the consolidated Eurocentric view on which fashion is based, and to revising, broadening, narrowing, and redefining the concept of fashion in the West and in a global perspective. The view of the relationship between colonial West and colonized East, in particular, has been worked through, made relative, and enriched by the awareness of a whole series of ambivalences, which colonialism, post-colonialism, and globalization bring about. The relation between modernity and tradition, which was once simple and clear cut—modernity is the Western one which sooner or later the Rest are also bound to catch up with—has shattered into many possible modernities, often placing dress at the center of many stylistic and cultural contradictions, to say nothing of those of generation and identity. A study of women's dress in India shows that Indian women's choice of a dress from various possible options—sari, salwar kameez (the Punjabi tunic) and Western dress—is not presented in opposite terms between modernity and tradition.[29] Although the influence of Western styles of consumption is evident, particularly in the large Indian cities, new hybrid or purely Indian styles are equally evident, especially in dress. The globalization of fashion proceeds according to an uneven pattern, which we may describe as "leopard spotted." Its flow responds to a logic that is the outcome of the very history of fashion, a history made up of differences and inequalities in the relation between Europe and the rest of the world. Historical, political, economic, and power relations have marked specific directions. In our times, marked by continual global interactions, it is therefore useful to know the directions in which ideas and trade have moved to overcome old stereotypes, and also to renounce claims to "pure" sartorial identities, those of product, consumption, and communication, which perhaps never existed and certainly do not exist today. As the Indian economist, Amartya Sen writes: Historically the direction of the shifts of ideas from one part of the world to another varies according to the times, and it is important to know these changes in direction because the global movement of ideas is sometimes seen as the ideological imperialism of the West, as a one-directional shift which merely mirrors an asymmetry of power, and which we must resist.[30]

We may distinguish at least two points of view according to which "ethnic" fashion relates with Western fashion. The first is the East–West perspective; the second, the North–South slant. East–West and North–South may partly overlap, as it is always a question of power relations between the West and the rest of the world, between European fashion, originating in Paris, and the other fashions; but for the reasons we will be looking at, it is preferable to consider them separately. Orientalism continues a tradition that goes back to the ancient world and a celebration of the Silk Road, and continues to contemporary exoticisms, while the North–South relation is more directly determined by colonial and post-colonial events. To paraphrase Chakrabarty, we may say that provincializing Western-European fashion is necessary to construct a global fashion theory of our times, in the awareness that it is itself an imaginary figure, which remains deeply intertwined in its constituent schematic and stereotyped forms.[31]

The East–West Perspective or Orientalism

Orientalism is an essential part of fashion's complex and protean composite on an astonishing number of levels: from cotton, the textile we take for granted, to silk, the eternal luxury textile; from floral motifs to paisley; from dressing gowns to tie-dye.[32]

The Early Twentieth Century In the first decades of the twentieth century, there was a mania for Orientalism or anything coming from a rich, exotic, remote East—from ancient Persia and Arabia, to the Russian ballet brought to Paris by Diaghilev, and the colors of the *fauve* artists. The goods from these far-off colonial countries also spread, thanks to stores, such as Liberty in London. The Parisian millinery trade created turbans trimmed with ostrich or peacock feathers or those of other exotic birds. The kimono was used as "at home" wear, in the original version, or as inspiration for dressing gowns, often with paisley patterns which was by then an established decorative motif, or for caftans or other garments it inspired, like the sumptuous creations of the Maison Callot Soeurs. Turkish, Moroccan, Japanese effects, and the related "kimonomania" picked up some of the old ideas on the wardrobe of the Rest, blending them with the new demands of fashion, such as the peplos-like clothes mourned by Oscar Wilde, and re-invented by Mariano Fortuny and Paul Poiret for Parisian *haute couture*. Fortuny's celebrated pleated tunic (later to be re-elaborated by Issey Miyake in the *Pleats Please* collection) was in fact called the Delphos tunic. We may say that early twentieth century Orientalism was filtered through Classicism and undifferentiated in inspiration, as were Morocco and Turkey in the magic and undefined nineteenth century paintings by Delacroix. Martin and Koda wrote that it is difficult to pinpoint a specific period or a definite Oriental item of clothing in the proposals made by couturiers described as Orientalist.[33] The two inspirations—neo-classicism and Orientalism—often blend in their creations. Elsewhere and the past are part of the same imaginary of pre-modern otherness from which to draw elements.

The Nineteen Sixties The vision of the Orient constructed by the hippie counter-culture in the 1960s is the opposite of that in the early twentieth century. The protest counterculture typical of the period produced the first Western attempt to look closely at and from within the cultures of exoticism, seeking to transform them, in many ways in a naïve fashion, into an original, freer body culture, with new lifestyles set free from middle class constrictions. It was an East idealized as a place immune from the consumer society under attack. Ethnic and Oriental dress was not complicated, rich, luxurious—as it had been for Poiret and Fortuny—but informal and soft. There were multiple Oriental inspirations: saris, djellaba, shirts with a Nehru collar, Mao jackets, and much more. The journeys of the hippies contributed to strengthening the idea of an uncontaminated, poor, simple, and thus to a certain extent, happier world, or one at least closer to nature. They introduced the idea of a new relationship between the West and elsewhere, between capitalism and other cultures whose code was not transvestism, theater, fiction, opulence, but in many ways a utopian, naïve search for a lost authenticity and simplicity: an East "within reach," but equally exoticized, and therefore as unreal as that of the early twentieth century. The implicit ideology contrasting Western civilization and the primitivism of elsewhere did not seem to be grasped by the Western counterculture (Figure 7.5).

The Nineteen Eighties With the so-called "Japanese revolution"[34] with Yohji Yamamoto, Issey Miyake, and Rei Kawakubo's fashion shows, the Western fashion world discovered new silhouettes. The collections were not the usual Oriental tribute of flowers and butterflies, but showed a new, disturbing aesthetic, made up of asymmetries, irregularities, imperfections, dark colors, large shapes, and bias cuts. Japanese fashion constituted a watershed in the history of global fashion, for at least two fundamental reasons. The first was the statement, for the first time, of a fashion, which was both avant-garde and

FIGURE 7.5: A pair of young women in a crowd of hippies dance at an outdoor event, late 1960s or early 1970s. Photo: David Fenton/Getty Images.

Oriental. The second was the break with the idea that the fashion designer must be Western. The result was a shift in perception that was reflected in the Western media at the time—the famous Paris fashion show of the three Japanese designers in 1981 was described as the Japanese revolution—the revision of the concept of ethnic inspiration. The result was the unique position of Japan, in many ways still Orientalist, as a Western outpost for the success of its fashion in the East. Dorinne Kondo, however, underlines that this revolution was partial. Paris remained the fashion center in the 1980s, and that to achieve international success, Yohji Yamamoto, Issey Miyake, and Rei Kawakubo had to pass through Paris and show all three together, as Japanese, although they were already well known in Japan as individuals with distinct and different aesthetics.[35] "I realized that I was Japanese only when I arrived in Paris, because they called me the Japanese," Yamamoto stated in the Wim Wenders film devoted to him.[36]

The North–South Perspective

> States as Singapore, Vietnam, China, and Indonesia touted versions of Asian modernity in which economic prosperity could coexist with, or even be achieved through, commitment to traditional values.[37]

Western dress spread to various parts of the world, not only along the customary paths of fashion but also through the missionaries, dealers, colonial administrators, their wives, and the military. Apart from evangelization, one of the first objectives of the missionaries in the colonies was that of clothing the savages. The Spanish elite in Peru had the habit of moving about accompanied by slaves dressed in elegant clothes to confer greater prestige on their masters. However, as Tamara J. Walker shows this habit was also used by the slaves themselves to acquire status in an economy based on honor.[38] In this sartorial perspective, a rich, privileged North contrasted with a South, which was very often directly or indirectly dependent on and exploited by the North in various ways. The countries that freed themselves from European and Western domination reflect the ambivalences in interpretations of dress and the ideological role of choices. Simplifying greatly, we may state that, as far as Asia and Africa in particular are concerned, the first phase of the de-colonization process by European, mainly Dutch, English, and German rule, was from 1945 to 1954, the year of the Geneva Conference. At this time, Western dress was invested with considerable symbolic value and was even preferred in some cases, even by local governments who identified the West with modernity. The early years of the so-called post-colonial period, which concerned Asia above all, were marked by a trend to adopt the Western uniform. In the following years, i.e. the 1960s, 1970s and 1980s when most of the decolonization process had been concluded, an opposite attitude took shape in the policy of dress. Many political leaders from various parts of the ex-colonial world thus challenged, through new rules of dress, the fact that modernity and progress should be exclusively Western, and their having to follow Western models for development. Going back to the local way of dress to so-called ethnic, popular, autochthonous, and authentic traditions, although they were very often culturally constructed and in any case always hybrid—became part of a necessary search for stating their own identity and political and cultural autonomy, as well as the expression of alternative modernities. Fashion became a marker of identity and political questions, sharply undermining the opposition between modernity and tradition, male and female, and accentuating the theme and the ambivalences of the relation between personal identity and collective identity. On the subject of Islamic dress, Emma Tarlo and Annelies Moors write:

> During the twentieth century in many Muslim majority countries, elements of a Western lifestyle, including the adoption of European styles of dress, became widespread especially amongst the middle and upper classes. Contesting this trend, the 1970s and 1980s saw the ascendency of an Islamic revival movement which encouraged a growing number of women to adopt Islamic covered styles of dress. Some authors have referred to this as "the new veiling" (Mc Leod 1991) in order to underline that it entailed a new style of covered dress that was worn by young, well-educated women who consciously chose to adopt it.[39]

As Reina Lewis explains, today the veil is again being worn with various meanings: it may be a free choice made by a generation of young women rejecting the secular modernization in many post-colonial states in the Islamic world; it may symbolize belonging to communities for the women in the diaspora; it may be a strategy against highly aggressive male behaviors or also be imposed by Islamic integralist movements (Figure 7.6).[40] Analyzing the themes of the North–South sartorial vector, therefore, means reconsidering, in a way less mediated by Orientalist charm, the various phenomena of empowerment linked to the relation between fashion and so-called costume. In post-colonial India, Saloni Mathur describes this process in this way:

> No longer simply showcases of imperial possession, nor appropriation of the latter by agents of nationalism, the spectacle of culture in the post-colonial present is increasingly mediated by the ideological conditions of the production of 'heritage', the tension and competition between the local and the global, and the mediations of South Asian diaspora in a transnational landscape of cultural production.[41]

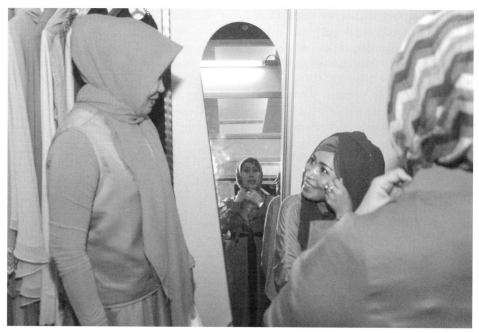

FIGURE 7.6: An Indonesian Muslim woman fits a headscarf or hijab at Indonesia Moslem Fashion Expo, 2013. Photo: Yermia Riezky Santiag /Pacific Press/Corbis via Getty Images.

At the end of the twentieth century, the major post-colonial transformations intersect in various ways with the new production and financial set-up of fashion, with the delocation of production fragmenting the various fashion processes and with the globalization of markets that puts brands, images, and persons into circulation. Thus, understanding fashion as a global phenomenon is further supported by shifts in the organization of garment production across the globe as well as by the vast economic significance of garment production in world trade.[42]

From being the concern of the European middle class elite, fashion is becoming a cultural universal characterizing our times in various ways. Non-Western future designers increasingly attend fashion schools in the West. The web, and above all fashion blogs, contribute to spreading aesthetics and mixing the languages of global tribes.[43] Throughout Asia, national promotion strategies for local fashion and brands have been launched in the last decade in reaction to the West which thinks of Asia as only a low-cost place for production. Since 2001, Vietnam has launched a "Speed Up Strategy for 2010" in which the government plans financial aid and incentives for manufacturing companies that design their own brands. The governments of India and China have done the same with similar initiatives linked to the promotion of creativity and innovation. "Creative China" is one of the projects in which the Chinese government is investing in a more significant way to transform China into a country of innovation instead of lost-cost manufacture.[44] Brazil, a country with a strongly expanding economy, aims to construct a new national fashion going beyond the "football, bikini, and samba" stereotype. We may say that the majority of the countries are interested in the creative expression of fashion. A change in the role of culture is taking place in the new global economy.[45] Fashion is part of a country's culture, as Alexandra Palmer writes:

On one hand, fashion is becoming more multinational, in terms of both design and manufacture, making trade and international borders increasingly irrelevant. On the other hand, the role of design identity has become an increasingly important marketing tool in creating a unique fashion product, particularly when there is little distinction between designs.[46]

The process is, however, complex and not devoid of ethicizing traps.[47] On the one hand, to demonstrate their ability to produce fashion, nations have to demonstrate that they are modern. However, to establish their original contribution, they have to emphasize national markers and their ethicizing traditions. On the other hand, it is the very definition of modernity, which by progressively including national and distinctive contributions, continuously contributes to also redefining the meaning of "modern fashion." As Thuy Linh Nguyen Tu notes on the subject of the young generation of Asian American designers: These material connections were manifested in the symbolic realm not through the use of exotic images and styles, but through a particular approach to design.[48]

In Africa, fashion is presented as a tool for emancipation for those producing, designing, and creating it, and in a more general way as an opposition to the stereotype of poverty and corruption generally ascribed to this continent. In the process of emancipation and affirmation of identity, the ideologies of the Sixties blur, assimilated in the national and market policies. National fashion, i.e. the recognizability of a country's aesthetic style, therefore regains vigor in an age of globalization. In the early years after the Second World War, the textile industry promoted the birth of national fashions. In the 1980s and 1990s, it was a convergence of private and public interests, now also on the agenda of many governmental bodies, the star system, distribution, fashion design, fashion schools, media, new media, distribution, tourism, tertiary industry, cultural industries, and manufacturing industries which convey the identity of national aesthetic production. Presence on the global stage always seems to imply the recognition of an authoritative aesthetic, as well as economic presence, as is demonstrated by the exponential spread of fashion weeks.[49]

For a country or a city, expressing an immediately recognizable aesthetics has become an important corollary to communicate political and economic strength. Much more than in the past, fashion has not only the task to reflect and represent social or individual needs, but has equipped itself with the chance to construct *ex novo* territories in which the imaginary is creatively set free. This is because, as Diana Crane explains, unlike most of the types of production and commercial activities, fashion expresses a very elaborate culture, composed of symbols, ideologies, and lifestyles to draw on.[50] Nationality, or rather the various forms of identity construction[51] which fashion is able to enact, are often supported by governments themselves, for example in the case of Canada[52] and the Scandinavian countries which have realized its importance. In the present-day "catwalk economy," a concept expressed by Lofgren and Willim, each nation has a vested interest in being recognized as a place of creativity and aesthetics.[53] We might call this a dressed power, as a consequence of the catwalk economy. Fashion itself is no longer an issue regarding ways in which people dress up and ways in which brands are distributed, but the chance for countries to take part in the global exchange, the interconnections marking our period. Fashion is not just making clothes, but also an attribute that nations no longer seem to be able to do without it.

If fashion is rediscovering terms such as ethnicity and identity, it is not to re-affirm the old myths of pre-modernity, but to use them as dynamic processes constructed through the practices of cultural contacts. We may generalize what Hildi Hendrickson has written concerning Africa: "Africa and the West are mutually engaged in a semiotic web whose implications are not completely controlled by any of us."[54] The encounter between historic European brands and non-Western designers gives place to hybrid narrative weavings, as is the case of the Anglo-Kenyan Ozwald Boateng for Givenchy, and the Indian Manish Arora for Paco Rabanne.

The spectacularization of national fashion also involves countries such as France, Great Britain, the USA, Italy, and Japan, with an established sartorial identity, and not only those who, until now, for historical and cultural reasons have not enjoyed the conditions to express it fully. Even in France, with a concentration on luxury also thanks to the more recent acquisitions, the concept of "economic patriotism," coined by the member of Parliament Bernard Carayon in 2006, shapes the actions of groups such as Kering (former PPR) and LVHM. The biographies of tailors and dressmakers, artisans and shoemakers, and the rediscovery of textile archives are part of a trend in the new cultural history. Concepts such as heritage, craftsmanship, and artisan creativity are at the center of the communications strategies of many brands, from Louis Vuitton to Salvatore Ferragamo. Fashion is used by governments to promote tourism, to weave celebratory, and competitive relationships in a sort of contemporary potlatch in which the objects traded are garments, designers, and images in the media. As Hendrickson writes, the negotiation of national and international identity is expressed in dress and in the treatment of the body, and today significance is sought within the oscillation between local and global (Figure 7.7).[55]

CONCLUSION

Fashion is an abstraction for a mass of different sartorial events which cannot possibly be observed as a totality.[56]

As we learn from Arjun Appadurai, the circulation of objects and people, the real or virtual journeys that individuals undertake in the contemporary world, arouse a sort of active imagination, but, unlike regressive and consolation fantasies, is in its turn able to generate desires and bring about changes.[57] Like any other product, dress is an economic and political fact, but, more than other products, it is linked to the theme of pleasure and the various expressions of identity. As Dwyer and Jackson write, there remains an underlying, innate tension to fashion itself that lies between a "materialist" analysis of fashion production, which cannot escape highlighting the conflict between the demands of the Western world and the exploitation of labor in other economies, and the "culturalist" exploration of the pleasures of fashion consumption, rapidly expanding in many parts of the world.[58]

Fashion reproduces two opposing and partly complementary visions that characterize the various theories on globalization: that of a historical, economic perspective, of a neo-Marxist type, and theories, which instead place emphasis on diversity: i.e. on the cultural component and on multiplicity, as in Giddens interpretation.[59]

How can we then de-codify the polyphony of discourse on global fashion? How can we understand the various contributions and interlocutors? Making fashion speak instead of speaking of fashion may be the change of perspective demanded.[60] It is not so much the garments themselves, or their iconic representation, but what is said of fashion which leads us to its truth. Today we may clearly see how the entire culture of fashion, and

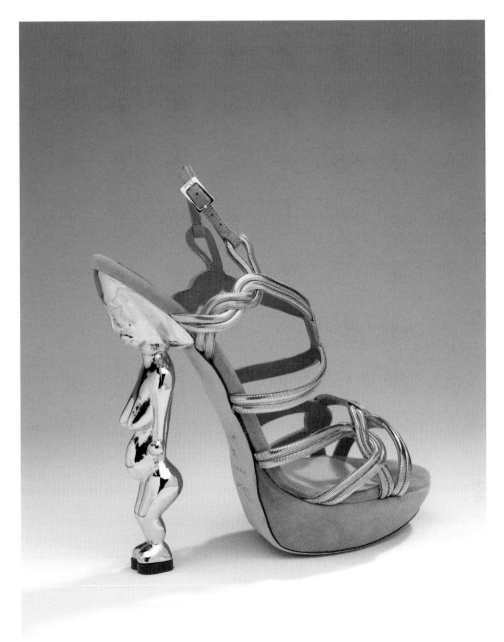

FIGURE 7.7: *Deese* "goddess" sandal by John Galliano for Christian Dior Spring/Summer 2009, prêt-à-porter collection. Gift of Christian Dior Couture. Photo: Royal Ontario Museum © ROM.

not only its words, supplies us with information: advertising, editorials, blogs, company strategies, the convictions and visions of fashion designers, garment morphology, organization of collections, representations in stores, and in the increasingly numerous exhibitions devoted to fashion. Whereas in the past it was thought that fashion was in a way the almost automatic reflection of the social—fashion as the "mirror of history"— today a less passive interpretation is preferable. The imaginary of fashion also makes it possible to penetrate deeply beneath the surface of society, and to reveal the schemata, archetypes, and consequently, the major anthropological structures defining a period and giving it meaning. In the monographic volume *Fashion Theory* she edited, devoted to African fashion, Victoria Rovine entitles her editorial, "Viewing Africa Through Fashion."[61] Fashion has, in fact, become a discourse able to create a dialogue between the various components of a global culture, revealing what are at the same time emerging truths, stereotypes, and commonplaces, still present at the level of narrative, production, and consumption. More than anticipating the present, fashion in its globalized version therefore represents the present itself. Making fashion speak in its own language at the crossroads between materiality and immateriality of the fashion object. In all its various manifestations, this leads us back to the system of differences within which we live: individual and collective aspirations, ideals of femininity and masculinity, body practices, the relationship with age, time, and places, i.e. all the main fields with which fashion has always been expressed and whose status quo it has continued to change (Figure 7.8).[62]

The blurring of the old antinomies—local/global, traditional/modernity, Western/ Oriental, folklore/luxury—is visible in many aspects of the present-day context of global fashion. A trend may be seen in many cases where garments, which were once traditional (costume), are brought up to date again in different contexts. "Local" fashion is therefore a hybrid, often brought back under the ambiguous label of authenticity, made up of many possible fashions inscribed in various forms in the global and which implies a dialectic relation between European ontology and epistemology and the impulse to create or recreate independent local identities. In this sense, authentic does not signify the return to something that has never been, as history teaches, or the impossible creation of something which is not "contaminated," but a different vision related to the pluralist position of the various subjects which today flank each other on the stage of global fashion. A world which exists outside the "Orientalist" glance, and which no longer seeks, as Nirmal Puwar writes, to be translated for the public, but simply states its existence.[63] Rey Chow shows in "Il sogno di Butterfly," the visual reveals something very profound concerning identity construction, in which she takes a new look at the myth of Puccini's *Madame Butterfly* through the interpretation of the director Cronenberg (1993).[64] Like Nirmal Puwar, Rey Chow also rejects the attitude that idealizes cultural otherness, wishing in reality to flatten its specificity, conflicts, and multiplicity (Figure 7.9).

Parading the features of a global wardrobe is thus definitely an abstraction. Many styles and variations have apparent homogeneity that the large-scale Western fashion brands spread. The immediate result is a minor westward loss of balance, the relativization of the customary perspective, the exit from the tradition of a fashion that identifies with the culture of ready-to-wear of European designers or of the great American brands. The wardrobe dictionary is broader and the garments speak with each other, enriched with their roots. As the American anthropologist Marshall Sahlins has noted, dress relates to multiple cultural categories and to the various relations between them, almost forming a sort of map of cultural universes.[65] Different dress cultures are confronting each other and their differences are what questions the concept of "ethnic dress" and re-inscribes

FIGURE 7.8: Model wearing a Krel Wear hijab during Miami Fashion Week Funkshion Fusion 2005, Florida. Photo: John Parra/WireImage.

FIGURE 7.9: An Indian woman combines her sari with a sweater in February 2015. Photo: Money Sharma/AFP/Getty Images.

new dress solutions in the international circuits. The result is a sort of cosmopolitan ethnography of dress that includes processes of de-territorialization and de-localization to which cultures, and the individuals that make them up, are increasingly frequently exposed. The only possible *authenticity* is therefore that of the present, that is, of the many different ways in which fashion is made today.

CHAPTER EIGHT

Visual Representations

RACHAEL BARRON-DUNCAN

I have before me a series of fashion-plates dating from the Revolution and finishing more or less with the Consulate. These costumes, which seem laughable to so many thoughtless people—people who are grave without true gravity—have a double natured charm, one both artistic and historical. They are often very beautiful and drawn with wit; but what to me is every bit as important, and what I am happy to find in all, or almost all of them, is the moral and aesthetic feeling of their time. The idea of beauty which man creates for himself imprints itself on his whole attire, crumples or stiffens his dress, rounds off or quests his gesture, and in the long run even ends by subtly penetrating the very features of his face. Man ends by looking like his ideal self.[1]

— Charles Baudelaire, 1863

When Charles Baudelaire sat down with his set of engraved fashion plates, he was at a remove of sixty to seventy-five years from their making. He discovers in the old illustrations a "double natured charm"—they speak to the aesthetic and historic sensibility of the bygone era. His musings, which take him on an extended consideration of beauty, clothing, and modernity, critically begin with the artistic rendering of garments, not with garments themselves. He does not see the mores of the Revolution in an actual collar, but one mediated by art. More than one hundred years later, critic Anne Hollander went as far as to assert that artistic representations provide the only "true view" of clothes. Human bodies lack the ability to biologically morph and adapt as fashions change. Artists, she writes, help us recast the clothed bodies around us through the lens of a perfected interpretation of fashion; "the authoritative fiction creates the received truth."[2]

When we take a page from Baudelaire and look back from our current vantage point at the visual representations of the past century to see the aesthetic and historical past, there is one prominent difference. While Baudelaire looked at engraved fashion plates, we look at photographs, as photography has become the preferred medium to document fashion. A number of factors contribute to this bias. First and foremost is photography's general rise to the level of ubiquity in the twentieth and twenty-first centuries, whereby the medium's facile and inborn reproducibility has been wedded to the vehicles of mechanical reproduction and mass media via newspapers, magazines, television, and the internet. Additionally, because fashion prides itself on being new, up-to-date, and always current, fashion found a special affinity for the most modern of the art mediums. With its ever-advancing technological processes (glass plates, tintype, Kodachrome, Polaroid, digital), photography cast the traditional media of painting, sculpture, and printmaking in an aging light.

To chart a complete history of the past century's fashion imagery in one chapter would be impossible, even for Baudelaire. So instead, this chapter considers the history of fashion photography over the last one hundred years as it sorts into distinct aesthetic and historical impulses. At the conclusion of the First World War, the newly formed genre of fashion photography was preoccupied with its own status and relationship to art. Then moving to the middle of the twentieth century, fashion photographs let go of the inward focus on their own artfulness to acknowledge the active, athletic modern woman. Finally, radical social changes in the last quarter of the twentieth century challenged the traditional boundaries of femininity and masculinity, and fashion photographs became public forums for these cultural anxieties. By considering the "double natured charm" of a small set of images, this chapter underscores how fashion photographs mirror their contemporary cultural paradigms and aesthetic concerns.

ARTFUL PICTURES

Initially, photographs in fashion magazines had an elucidating role. Publishers included photographs as a way to communicate visual information to their readers. Publisher Condé Nast turned increasingly to photography instead of illustration after the First World War, "in support of *Vogue's* mission in life—to serve those one hundred and more thousands of women who were so literally interested in fashion that they wanted to see the mode thoroughly and faithfully reported—rather than rendered as a form of decorative art."[3] For him, photography had an inherent "truth" quality that a hand-drawn rendering lacked. While magazines may have introduced photography with the aim of factual reportage, in practice, the fashion photograph functioned in a more nuanced manner. *Vogue's* art director, and later editorial director, Alexander Liberman reflected, "a fashion photograph is not a photograph of a dress; it is a photograph of a woman."[4] Liberman's line is pithy, but pointed: we are drawn to fashion photography not because of its ability to accurately relay the texture of bouclé or depict precisely how a garment fastens, but rather because the world created in the photograph captivates us. Coexisting with its "factual" nature, photography has a second quality, which is the ability to evoke an enigmatic world around the woman in the dress—a hallucinatory vision that encourages not just consumption, but also erotic engagement and/or identification. To look at a fashion photograph is both to forecast what clothes one might wear, and also to imagine a mirror self, a fantasy projection of how we might be seen by others.

In the 1920s and 1930s, the aesthetics of the fashion photograph engaged with the larger trends of the art world. However, fashion photography entered the 1920s, still holding onto pre-war aesthetics. A *belle époque* gentility pervaded the images, suffusing the pages of *Vogue* and *Vanity Fair* in a gentle radiance, thanks to the work of Baron Adolph de Meyer. De Meyer's aesthetic—soft, gauzy views of women surrounded by fabric or bouquets of flowers—was an innovation in the realm of fashion photography, but one that borrowed from long-standing trends in art. The Pictorialist movement arose in the mid-nineteenth century as a countermeasure to the prevailing understanding of the photograph as mere document, best suited for capturing likenesses in portraiture and chronicling the world exactly as it is seen. The photograph, in the mind of the Pictorialist, functioned no differently than any other medium in its ability to be shaped by the maker. To underscore the composed nature of the photograph, artists frequently chose to soften the focus, print in colors, or physically manipulate the print in the darkroom. When de Meyer brought the Pictorialist aesthetic to *Vogue* in 1914, it brought the fashion pages in line with more recent innovations in photography, and infused the magazine with images that felt artful.

De Meyer's photographs at times failed to capture the details of trim and patterning on a dress, but instead generated the evocation of a light-hearted, soft, carefree mood (Figure 8.1). One of his oft-employed techniques was soft focus, which he achieved

FIGURE 8.1: Baron Adolph De Meyer. Elsie Ferguson in a Callot gown. *Vogue* [New York], February 1, 1921, p. 40. Photo: Adolph de Meyer/Condé Nast via Getty Images.

through a variety of methods. He favored a Pinkerton-Smith lens, which is calibrated for sharp focus at the center and a progressively fuzzy halo of focus at the edges. Other times, he shot through a sheer fabric, which would uniformly blur the image.[5] The resultant images de-emphasized specificity, disintegrated detail, and instead gave a broader sense of form. His photographs have their parallel in James Abbott McNeill Whistler's tonal work, in which paint does not bound and delineate form, but evokes sensation.

De Meyer's second trademark technique was his use of soft, diffuse light, frequently radiating from behind his model. Backlighting his sitter further obliterated the garment's detail, while illuminating the silhouette of the body in a halo. In this light, limbs appear lyrical, diaphanous fabrics glow, and pretty profiles take on an angelic cast. His photographs turned heiresses and models alike into lily-white spring flowers, impossibly unblemished and rarified. His lens had transformative powers akin to Gatsby's vision of Daisy Buchanan: it made everything ever virginal, ever glowing, ever white.

Condé Nast wanted *Vogue* and *Vanity Fair* to be elite amongst all other society and fashion magazines. He capitalized on the technical innovations in photographic publishing to fill the pages of his magazines with high quality imagery. In 1923, Nast hired Edward Steichen, who had already made his name as a prestigious painter and a photographer, to be his chief photographer for *Vogue* and *Vanity Fair*. When the tides of history shifted towards war, Steichen became an aerial photographer for the United States Army. Upon his return to New York, Nast offered him the prized role, replacing de Meyer. During the negotiations, Nast proposed that Steichen's name might be only printed next to society portraits, offering the artist a chance to keep his fashion photographs anonymous. Steichen retorted, "If I made a photograph, I would stand by it with my name; otherwise I wouldn't make it."[6] This was a big departure from Steichen's previous alignment with Alfred Stieglitz, who was vehemently against using photography as an agent of commerce.

Steichen quickly pushed fashion photography's aesthetic into a new era. De Meyer's penchant for the dewy embellishment and gauzy soft focus gave way to Steichen's bolder and more streamlined clarity that showed the garments' details. This was a conscious effort to relay greater information to the viewer. He felt "that a woman, when she looked at a picture of a gown, should be able to form a very good idea of how that gown was put together and what it looked like."[7] Steichen's objective aesthetic mirrored a new sentiment in fine art photography, which moved away from the manipulated romanticism of Pictorialism in favor of unaltered shots with sharp focus, clear lighting, and a full range of tones. "Straight photography" embraced the medium of photography "as is," privileging the autonomous and objective nature of the camera lens as an agent of cool, modern, technical urbanity. The resulting photographs not only took on a sharper resolution, but favored a more direct subject matter. While de Meyer's women gazed wistfully out of the frame, or contemplated a bouquet, Steichen's women confidently looked into the lens and directly at the viewer. In many of Steichen's photographs, the image blurs the distinction between portrait and fashion photograph. Nast once remarked to Steichen, "Every woman de Meyer photographs looks like a model. You make every model look like a woman."[8]

In the pages of *Vogue*, Steichen employed a modernist aesthetic in harmony with the new taste for Art Deco. The 1925 Paris *Exposition International des Arts Décoratifs et Industriels Modernes* catalyzed a new aesthetic, transforming the world of art and design. Named for the trend already brewing before the exposition and clearly on display during its run, Art Deco combined the geometric abstraction of extant art movements like Cubism, Futurism, and Purism, with the clean lines of the Machine Aesthetic. Art Deco as a style influenced the rectilinear forms appearing everywhere from teacups, to graphic fonts, to the boxy cut of a flapper dress. Steichen took the angular lines of the dresses and incorporated these into the staging and composition of his photographs. In one photograph, his favorite model, Marion Morehouse, stands in an iridescent Chéruit evening wrap in front of a piano that Steichen designed for the photo shoot (Figure 8.2). The piano's decoration glistens linearly in syncopation with the sheen bouncing off of the

FIGURE 8.2: Edward Steichen. Marion Morehouse wearing a dress by Chéruit and jewelry by Black, Starr, and Frost. *Vogue* [New York], May 1, 1928, p. 64. Photo: Edward Steichen/Condé Nast via Getty Images.

wrap's metallic plaid detailing. The strong light that rakes across the background draws diagonals that overlap just above the model's head and disappear behind screens. Steichen knew just how to use light as a tool for abstraction. "We use light to dramatize, to build up," he said. "We use it to transform. We use it to express an idea."[9] In Steichen's photograph, the light solidifies into form and rises to equal Morehouse as the center of attention. She is both in shadow and highlighted, both glamorously lit and a mere compositional element in the overall image.

As the 1920s progressed, another style appeared in the pages of *Vogue* alongside Steichen's modernism. George Hoyningen-Huene's photographs, while benefiting from the clear, clean lines of Steichen, brought an architectural quality to the notion of glamor. Huene carefully calibrated negative space, so that his photographs feel not only composed, but sculpted (Figure 8.3). Huene was a master of theatrical illusion. Born into nobility in St. Petersburg, the revolution displaced him at a young age and he landed in Paris. Huene studied painting and drawing, and first applied his training to his sister Betty's dressmaking business, eponymously named Yteb. Not long after, he was hired by *Vogue* to illustrate for the magazine and recruit models. Huene helped out around the *Vogue* studios, absorbing various parts of the magazine's daily business, and chanced into the role of photographer in 1926 by stepping in when the scheduled photographer didn't show.

A few years later, another assistant in *Vogue*'s studios, Horst Bohrmann, also transitioned to the role of photographer and began working professionally under the name Horst. He had originally come to Paris from Germany to study under the architect Le Corbusier. When Horst gave up architecture, he found himself assisting Huene in the studio by arranging lights, dressing sets, and modeling. It was *Vogue*'s art director, M.F. Agha, who encouraged him to pick up the camera.[10] Together, Horst and Huene were the photographers of the 1930s, filling the pages of *Vogue* with a theatrical elegance that relied heavily on props and artifice.

Both Huene and Horst embraced a neo-classical aesthetic that matched the lengthened hems and bias-cut gowns of the 1930s offered by designers such as Augustabernard, Vionnet, and Alix (who gained popularity later under the name Madame Grès). Huene photographed Grecian-inspired gowns interposed with marble-faces, evoking a fashion that speaks through the ages, a timeless, unchanging sense of elegance and beauty. Horst and Huene traveled together to Greece and frequently spent hours studying the marble sculptures in the museums of Paris and London. Horst would later recall: "I tried to learn from the marvelous old Greek statues, from the shapes and proportions—even the poses—of the bodies in Greek art . . . I stood in front of the Acropolis and cried like a baby."[11] In the 1936 photograph of Edwina d'Erlanger, he juxtaposed the long, fluted form of her white Alix dress with a plaster ionic capital, thus creating the overall impression of a classical column. Shot from a low angle, the image lengthens d'Erlanger and transforms her into the architectural pillar—cool, soaring, and monumental (Figure 8.4). Horst would say that he photographed women like goddesses: "almost unattainable, slightly statuesque, and in Olympian peace."[12]

For both Huene and Horst, the studio was a substitute for the world at large. Horst was one of the first photographers to use a blank white backdrop. Inside the empty shell of the studio, props and backdrops created the illusions. He favored strong raking light, but unlike Steichen, who used shadow to create form (the strong orthogonal lines above Marion Morehouse), Horst's strong spotlight instead shaped and added drama to the figure. In their carefully staged studio images, Horst and Huene created a new icy, stilled glamor in the pages of fashion magazines.

FIGURE 8.3: George Hoyningen-Huene. The publication of this image in *Vogue* was reversed. Models wearing dresses by Germaine Lecomte and Callot Soeurs. *Vogue* [New York], May 15, 1932, p. 48. Photo: George Hoyningen-Huene/Condé Nast via Getty Images.

FIGURE 8.4: Horst. Mrs. Leo (Edwina) d'Erlanger wearing a dress by Alix. *Vogue* [New York], February 15, 1936, p. 43. Photo: Horst P. Horst/Condé Nast via Getty Images.

MOTION PICTURES

When former *Vogue* editor Carmel Snow switched over to *Harper's Bazaar* in 1933, the Hearst publication began to pose a serious threat to *Vogue*'s dominance as the preeminent fashion magazine. Snow gathered a leadership team that shaped the magazine for years to come, by hiring art director Alexey Brodovitch and editor Diana Vreeland. *Harper's*

Bazaar had already picked up de Meyer when he fell out of favor at *Vogue*, and Snow continued the tradition by hiring other former *Vogue* photographers, like Man Ray and Erwin Blumenfeld. When Huene broke with *Vogue* in 1935 after a bitter dispute, she hired him as well. Snow encouraged experimentation, and the magazine championed a looser, freer kind of photography that frequently liberated the model from the studio. Photographers like Toni Frissell, Louise Dahl-Wolf, Martin Munkacsi, and Herman Landshoff took images that felt connected to how women experienced fashion in the world, infusing the images with what was understood to be an American aesthetic. While Horst was staging upper class goddesses in artificial dream worlds, these *Harper's Bazaar* photographers were showing fashion as integral to a modern lifestyle, and offering up a less controlled idea of glamor for a liberated, sporty beauty. Hungarian photographer Martin Munkacsi not only took models out of the studio (which Steichen and Huene had done, but only from time to time), but he placed them in the world of action: running, leaping, reaching with a tennis racket, swinging a golf club. The images were blurred and rushed, not crisp and posed. His images were particularly well suited to sportswear, with their notion of active femininity. Against the tradition of airless studio shots, which now looked highly constructed, Munkacsi's work felt vital and fresh.

In the late 1920s, Munkacsi was working as a photojournalist for the Ullstein Press in Berlin, which published the largest illustrated weekly in the world, the *Berliner Illustrirte Zeitung*. Photographing picture stories of anything and everything that sparked public interest, from politics to high society to everyday life, Munkacsi's time with the Ullstein Press equipped him with unique skills which he would later bring to fashion photography: realism and relevance.[13] In her autobiography, Snow recounts how on a November day, with December's resort issue ready to go to print, she looked again at the photographs for bathing suit features taken indoors with painted backdrops. In a last minute change of plans, Snow had Munkacsi re-photograph the fashions and took the photographer and a model out to Long Island on a cold, grey day. There were some difficulties communicating as the Hungarian didn't speak English, and the gestures were not easily understood at first. Snow recalled: "It seemed that what Munkacsi wanted was for the model to *run toward him*. Such a 'pose' had never been attempted before for fashion (even 'sailing' features were posed in a studio on a fake boat), but Lucile [the model] was certainly game, and so was I. The resulting picture, of a typical American girl *in action*, with her cape billowing out behind her, made photographic history" (Figure 8.5).[14]

Richard Avedon began working for *Harper's Bazaar* at the conclusion of the Second World War and quickly developed a carefree sense of fashion. Characterizing Avedon's woman, Winthrop Sargeant wrote, "The model became pretty, rather than austerely aloof. She laughed, danced, skated, gamboled among herds of elephants, sang in the rain, ran breathlessly down the Champs-Elysées, smiled and sipped cognac at café tables, and otherwise gave evidence of being human."[15] Avedon's early post-war images were very much about the fashionable woman as she engaged in the vitality of the city. Setting and situation were critical. His models were wasp-waisted beauties flirting with a gaggle of male suitors on the streets of Paris or smoking archly at a café, hand on hip and shoulders curved to accentuate the extremes of the New Look silhouette. In the 1950s, the women in his photographs donned ball gowns and went to lavish restaurants, swank casinos, and risqué nightclubs on the arm of a tuxedoed paramour.

Avedon had a retainer of regular models who became recognizable and marked a photograph as an "Avedon": Dovima with her dramatically balletic arms; her sister Dorian Leigh whose image became synonymous with Revlon's Fire and Ice advertisement; Suzy

FIGURE 8.5: Martin Munkacsi. Lucile Brokaw. *Harper's Bazaar*, December 1933, pp. 46–7.
Photo: © Estate of Martin Munkacsi, courtesy of Howard Greenberg Gallery, New York.

Parker the spunky redhead who launched bikini mania and whose natural ease behind the
camera was parlayed into an acting career. Later it would be Veroushka and Jean
Shrimpton. Avedon made his models into stars through the devotion of his photographic
concentration. Stanley Donen's 1957 film *Funny Face* fictionalized this model/
photographer dynamic, with Audrey Hepburn playing the bookish girl who blooms under
the lens of Avedon's screen alter-ego, Dick Avery. At times, Avedon's relationship with his

models assumed the status of an all-supreme maestro; correcting Parker when she complained that she looked dreadful, he asserted: "It doesn't matter how you look—it is *I* who make you beautiful."[16]

Though many of Avedon's early images took full advantage of extant settings, he favored a studio setting for portraits. His portraits stood in contrast to those taken by Arnold Newman, who would capture the celebrity sitter in their "natural" environment, surrounded by the props of their genius. For years, Avedon placed eminent figures in front of a neutral gray backdrop, refining it down over time to an empty, pure white void. "The white background isolates the subject from itself and permits you to explore the geography of the face," Avedon remarked.[17] The severity of his backgrounds can either be interpreted as a denial of naturalism ("look at the construction of this photograph which clearly could only be taken in the carefully constructed setting of a studio") or else a pinnacle of naturalism ("look at how there is nothing in this photograph to distract me from seeing the person as they truly are"). While initially used more for portraiture, Avedon integrated the emptied out studio backdrops into his fashion images. For Avedon, as well as his contemporary colleague Irving Penn, the line between portraiture and fashion photograph frequently blurred. "A fashion picture is a portrait," Penn said, "just as a portrait is a fashion picture."[18]

In his white background fashion photographs, Avedon continued to play with the idea of a liberated and embodied subject. Where in the past, the model responded to the world, skipping over rain puddles or leaning against the felt roulette table, now the model moved in a void. Avedon continued the active prototype that Munkacsi had begun before the war, but it took a few decades for his models to rediscover the pure athletic abandon that the Hungarian photographer had captured so easily. Regarding Avedon's photographs of the 1960s and later, Susan Sontag commented that his neutral, ideal spaces worked because the beauty created in the photographs did not require the validation or explanation by a given setting.[19] The model's movement was no longer situational and naturalized but somehow internal to her, a dance that had no physical limits.

In his 1970 photograph of Jean Shrimpton in a dress by Pierre Cardin, she animates the diaphanous print dress more as spirit than body, her form having melted into pure movement (Figure 8.6). Avedon's image is perhaps the most disembodied fashion photograph to date, as we are only aware of the model as one foot, two hands . . . and otherwise, she is just a suggestion of density amidst the sheer fabric. A ruffle flares at the top while the dress surges forward, and the many delicate layers billow and stream in the wake. Body, dress, and air have conjoined into one united lunge, and the resultant photograph harkens back to Futurist sculptures where the figure was "flung open" to merge with the energy and speed of the world around it.

DIRTY PICTURES

In the 1970s and 1980s, as women participated increasingly in the workforce and claimed control of their bodies and their rights, Helmut Newton photographed strong, bold, vital women. His women do not glamorously lounge in idealized idyll, nor do they dwell in a pantheon of goddesses on pedestals. They dominate. They desire. They devour. They know the power of their bodies and their minds. His are in-charge women who have benefitted from the sexual revolution by being able to own their sexuality.

Newton's fashion photographs value nudity and fashion equally, if not nudity over fashion. They make blatant the sexual desires primly kept under wraps in the fashion

FIGURE 8.6: Jean Shrimpton in dress by Pierre Cardin, Paris, January 1970. Photograph by Richard Avedon. © The Richard Avedon Foundation.

photographs of others. This earned him the moniker of "King of Kink" and his photographs were dubbed "porno-chic."[20] While his images indulge in a fantasy of voyeurism, they also subvert the easy scopic possession that voyeurism normally entails (Figure 8.7). His women exude a fierceness that ices out any possibility of sexual possession.

Berlin-born Newton fled Germany in 1938 at the age of eighteen, but his work of the 1970s frequently harkens back to an interwar "noir" sensibility: women stride through dark cobble-stone streets exposing pubic hair; the lady of the house embraces her chauffeur in the privacy of the service entrance; a seemingly endless number of women sprawl in some state of undress in lavish hotel rooms. Newton's images return to a 1920s play on androgyny, frequently pairing women in erotically charged encounters. When he shot Yves Saint Laurent's gender-bending *le smoking* on a female model with slicked down short hair, he underscored the ambiguity inherent in adopting men's wear for women.

Newton's photography frequently feels filmic, as if each photograph were a glimpse of a moment in time, inviting speculation about how the figures got here, and what they will do next. Theirs is a world that suggests narrative unfolding temporally in both directions. Newton's evocation of an on-going saga parallels rising trends in fashion editorials. Beginning in the 1960s, magazines developed style essays, which transmitted a narrative across successive pages. More than showing a collection of the season's latest fashions, the style essay connects disparate designers and times of day to an over-arching dramatic storyline.[21] Newton's 1975 "Story of Ohhh . . ." photo essay might be considered an early forerunner of those that can still be seen in fashion magazines. In it, Newton created a narrative of the sexual tension and jealousy between two women and one man as they lounge poolside at a villa. In one image, model Lisa Taylor sits back on a couch in with her legs spread apart, skirt hitched above the knees. The photograph subverts traditional gender norms, as Taylor sprawls with a masculine casualness that doesn't worry about being ladylike while she coolly appraises the shirtless, faceless man.

Newton's photography flourished at *French Vogue* where European permissiveness allowed for overt sexuality and nudity. In America, his photography faced a puritanical reaction. The "Story of Ohhh . . . didn't go over well in the Bible Belt—and brought a spate of angry letters and cancelled subscriptions."[22] In 1975, art critic Hilton Kramer singled out Newton in the *New York Times,* stating that his "interest in fashion is indistinguishable from an interest in murder, pornography and terror."[23] Here Kramer conflates Newton's sexually charged images with those by French photographer Guy Bourdin, whose campaign for Charles Jourdan shoes included a photograph of a stark crime-scene, the shoes discarded helter-skelter near a chalk outline on a blood-stained sidewalk. Like Newton, Bourdin was a storyteller in his photography, though the stories were darker, and his women were not impervious Amazons but vulnerable (if fictive) victims. Francine Crescent, editor of *French Vogue,* felt that Bourdin had his finger on the pulse of a changing cultural ethos. "He knew before everyone else that sex and violence were going to be very important factors in our society. But I think that he was interested in and wanted to describe, life itself."[24] Together, Bourdin and Newton ushered in a new frankness to fashion photography that reflected the shifting social norms of the 1970s.

FIGURE 8.7: Helmut Newton. Verushka, Nice, 1975. Photo: *From Private Property, Suite II,* 1989. © Helmut Newton Estate.

PUBLIC PICTURES

While fashion photography resided firmly within the pages of the magazine for most of the twentieth century, in the 1980s photographs began to leap out from the confines of serial publications and into everyday spaces: i.e. billboards, sides of buildings, subway posters, and bus stops. This broader public address corresponded with a shift in how clothing was marketed. As ready-to-wear lines from fashion designers are beyond the financial reach of the average fashionable consumer, designers began exploring diffusion lines, and sports and leisure wear dominated the market. Labels, which had always rested discreetly on the inside of garments were replicated and were now displayed prominently on the exterior, in the form of logos and brand names. In this environment of pervasive visual marketing on the clothes themselves, fashion photography entered into the public visual field as never before. In a busy field of visual clutter, fashion photographs had to be as aesthetically arresting as possible, to compete with soft drinks and cigarettes. The photographers who arose in this climate found a way to use the strategies of those who came before them to maximum effect.

Calvin Klein, a designer synonymous with American classic minimalism, used Richard Avedon to direct and shoot his 1980 advertising campaign that featured fifteen-year-old Brooke Shields telling the world that nothing came between her and her Calvins. The photographs ran in magazines and the commercial appeared on television. Avedon's pure white backdrop complemented the brand's minimalist aesthetic, and became something of a trademark of Calvin Klein campaigns for decades. A case in point was a 1982 campaign launched by the brand for its men's underwear. Bruce Weber's erotic photograph of a pole-vaulter focused on the tanned, muscular torso, contrasted against the crisp whiteness of the briefs (Figure 8.8). Shot from below against a whitewashed

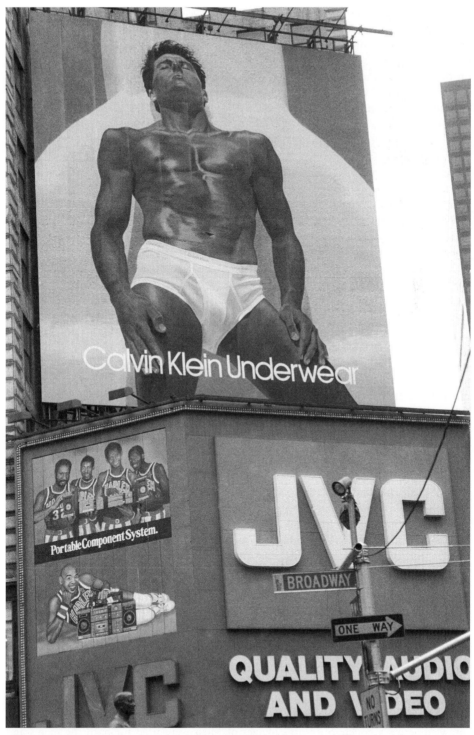

FIGURE 8.8: Bruce Weber. Tom Hintinhous for Calvin Klein, on a billboard in Times Square, New York City, October 1982. Photo: Bettmann/Getty Images.

wall, the heroic male body loomed over cities, and even earned a privileged spot in Times Square, where he became "a colossus looming over a crossroads."[25] The passive, inactive body of the pole-vaulter expresses physical power and maintains its masculine identity even in a languid state, due to the emphasis on muscle tone.[26] The overt sexuality, focused on the erotics of the male body, marked a new social moment. If Newton had shown us not the desired woman, but the desiring woman, Weber focused us on the desired man, thus interjecting the male body into the role traditionally reserved for women's bodies.

Weber's photographs reimagined the male body within the realm of the fashion photograph. Historically, women's fashion shots have marginalized if not eliminated the presence of men, and men's fashion magazines employed stiff, "freeze-dried male models and their female props." By contrast, Bruce Weber's photographs "suggest a way of being a man that is fluid, playful, artful, and at once straight-acting and gay-friendly."[27] This latter attribute was a large stumbling block for many, as the homo-erotics of Weber's images was a shake up to the heteronormative masculinity traditionally embraced by magazines. Weber recalled the prevailing attitude at *GQ* in the late 1970s: "They were really frightened of seeing men's skin, pushing up the sleeves was an amazing adventure."[28] Weber's multi-storied and unavoidable images of male torsos loosened the social restrictions surrounding images of men. "I also want men to be a little bit more open about looking at another man in a photograph and respecting him as he would a film actor on screen, or a sculpture in a museum," he said.[29]

Weber's imagery was part of a shift towards the "new man," the term for a consumer-group-cum-cultural-construct developing in the mid-1980s that as a category "was somewhat ambiguous and loosely-defined, and was gradually used to sum up several different masculine typologies, from style leaders in fashion to the more emotionally-centered, caring, sharing partner or father figure."[30] This idea of a new generation of men interested in their appearance corresponded to a proliferation of products from clothes to grooming to magazines catering to this new man. This began a golden age magazines aimed at the fashionably inclined male: *FHM* (1985), *Arena* (1986), *Men's Health* (1987), *Men's Journal* (1992).

The 1980s became the "designer decade"[31] of visible brand names (Calvin Klein's moniker quickly moved onto the waist bands of his underwear), supermodels with household recognition by first name (Cindy, Naomi, Linda, et. al.), and a suite of power photographers (including Weber, Herb Ritts, Steven Meisel, and Patrick Demarchelier). Fashion and celebrity were inextricably linked. In the following decade, the focus on celebrity didn't fade, but rather merged with a new interest in the everyday and ordinary, resulting in pictures that looked behind the glassy surface of fame. Photography emphasized a kind of naturalism, dramatizing the close relationship between the model and the photographer.

This was especially true in Mario Sorrenti's photographs of a young Kate Moss for the Calvin Klein Obsession campaign of 1992. A couple at the time, Sorrenti (twenty-one) and Moss (eighteen), were sent to an island alone to shoot the campaign. The resultant photographs transmit a fragile intimacy. Sorrenti's black and white photographs pull in close to Moss's naked body, capturing the graceful-awkward slump of her shoulders, the bird-like arrangement of her limbs, the seemingly pre-pubescent curve of her rear as she sprawled across a couch. Sorrenti's images of Moss were used for both the men's and women's versions of the scent, suggesting a kind of androgyny of desire evoked by the perfume, and reflected in Moss's teen body.

The campaign went against 1980s glamazon advertising not only in the physique of the model, but in the seeming deconstruction of beauty. Sorrenti's photographs stressed not the trappings of fashionability, but the intangible: the self beneath the clothes. In her writing, Sontag pointed out that fashionability goes beyond whether or not one is well-dressed.

> Many images that show nothing to emulate, nothing to buy, are still part of fashion. The gestures that create or inspire fashions are defined by the camera. It is the photograph that confers celebrity, that makes something fashionable, that perpetuates and comments on the evolving idea—that is, the fantasy—of fashion.[32]

The photographs for Obsession thrust Moss into the advertising pages of magazines, but also plastered her body on the sides of buses and subway walls. Quickly, fashion photography became the subject of public debate, as articles appeared in newspapers and mainstream media, critiquing Moss's "waifish" form, leveling accusations of pedophilia, and questioning the model's eating habits.[33] The increased public nature of fashion photography entered Moss's body into an international discourse on media body types and the new aesthetic of "heroin chic." *Esquire* magazine published a spoof ad in January 1994 repurposing the Kate Moss image for a Feed the Waifs advertisement, with text telling readers that "for 39 cents a day, less than the cost of a cup of coffee" they could help keep supermodels alive. Thousands called the printed telephone number, 1-800-SOS-WAIF (a number that connected callers to the Federal Wage and Labor Law Institute in Houston).[34] Some viewers of the Obsession advertisement took their critique directly to the image itself, scrawling "FEED ME" with spray paint and permanent marker on every poster they encountered (Figure 8.9). As fashion photography integrated into the urban

FIGURE 8.9: Mario Sorrenti. Kate Moss for Calvin Klein on a bus panel, defaced, 1994. Photo: Paul Harris/Getty Images.

wallpaper, the images engaged an even wider audience, and increasingly viewers were speaking back to the photographs.

MOTION PICTURES 2.0

What viewers saw in magazines and on billboards had always been a constructed product, an image chosen from a bevy of similar but not-as-good shots, cropped, reprinted for greater contrast, etc. There had also been dark room dodging and burning, and editorial splicing and airbrushing. But the transition to digital photography, with its ease of alteration, encouraged new, nearly limitless possibilities of manipulation and artifice.

Now in the twenty-first century, fashion photography has taken on a new incarnation that shatters the traditional understanding of photography. Historically, photography allowed for a singular, stilled image; in the digital age, fashion "photography" is no longer limited to a fixed moment, but can now include movement and sound. Fashion films allow for a garment to be seen in motion, on a body, over time, from multiple directions. Munkacsi freed the model from her rigidity, and now the digital technologies have finally enabled a platform to match the model's mobility. In 2000, Nick Knight founded Showstudio as an online site for fashion film. Knight earned a reputation in the 1990s for his anti-establishment, grunge sensibility that questioned and deconstructed notions of beauty. Knight's alternative photographs initially fit best in the newer European magazines, like *i-D*, *Purple*, and *Dazed & Confused*, which catered to a growing appetite for idiosyncratic manifestations of fashionability. However, as we spend less and less of our time with printed matter in favor of a world of screens, fashion imagery has been moving

FIGURE 8.10: Audience members use smartphones and cameras to photograph the Hervé Leger by Max Azria fashion show during Mercedes-Benz Fashion Week Spring 2015, New York. September 6, 2014. Photo: Michael Nagle/Bloomberg via Getty Images.

from magazines and billboards to the internet. Knight has embraced the immediate, interactive, and independent nature of working online:

> It felt like the medium I'd been waiting for all the time I'd been doing photography. I've always worked predominantly in fashion, and fashion is created to move. Showing that movement isn't possible in print. Other mediums like film and TV were too bureaucratic—it needed to be something that's accessible, fast, moving: the internet's very good at that.[35]

The internet is also very good at democratizing fashion imagery, wresting control from the hands of the professionals and passing it over to the layperson equipped with social media. Fashion shows have become so synonymous with social media image sharing that designers now plan for audience members and backstage personnel to flood Instagram during Fashion Week (Figure 10).[36] In our new digital world, the insta-image of an outfit can circle the globe in seconds. The information distribution of fashion imagery has been sped up and decentralized. The fashion consumer will probably already know this season's designer offerings before the advertisements and magazines are printed or the films posted to the internet. In this way, the photographer and filmmaker are liberated from communicating the fact of fashion, and can now focus entirely on crafting its fiction.

CHAPTER NINE

Literary Representations

IRENE GAMMEL AND KAREN MULHALLEN

People thought twice before they were rude to anybody wearing a good fur coat; it was protective colouring, as it were.

— Jean Rhys, *After Leaving Mr Mackenzie* (1930)[1]

I flung my jacket over my shoulder, Frank Sinatra style. I was full of references.

— Patti Smith, *Just Kids* (2010)[2]

What happens when an object, whether real or imaginary, is converted into language? . . . isn't written Fashion a literature?

— Roland Barthes (1967; emphasis in original)[3]

Twentieth-century literature reveals fashion to be central in the construction of identity. More than a reflection of social change, fashion is an agent in it, involved both in normalizing characters in social identities and roles, and in affording them opportunities for rebellion. The first fifty years of the twentieth century are rich in literary depictions of women's, and sometimes men's, clothing. In fiction, women's clothing in the first half of the century initially signals their class, often their age, and eventually their occupation, as the role of women and the presence of women in the workplace change. It also signals the changing sexual identities, the breakdown of heterosexual relationships after the First World War, and the advent of more fluid gender roles.

After the Second World War, particularly in the 1960s, literature registers a marked shift in Western fashion culture. The hippie movement, the rise of feminism, San Francisco's Haight-Ashbury, and London's Chelsea, all see the distance between male and female fashion diminishing, a trend that continues with the punk movement of the 1970s. Postmodern writings, which extend into the twenty-first century, perform a deliberate and self-conscious parody play, recycling popular culture and historical tropes alike, as in Patti Smith's epigraph above. The reverence for couture (and the use of dressmakers who might imitate couture) also begins to erode as fashion is democratized, male and female clothing blends, and branding takes priority. So what exactly is the function of fashion in twentieth-century literature? How does fashion fuel character, narrative and genre? How is fashion embedded in the texture of literary forms of the twentieth-century from modernism to postmodernism? We begin with a brief consideration of the intersecting theories of fashion and literature.

KEY CONCEPTS: FASHION, LITERATURE, AND MODERNITY

Over the past decade and a half, the study of fashion in literature has become an emerging subfield of the discipline of literary studies. The twentieth century produced leading fashion theorists such as John Flügel, Georg Simmel, Walter Benjamin, and Roland Barthes, all of whom make distinctions between clothes (functional garments) and fashion (decorative garments). Flügel focuses on the shifting erogenous zones and the accentuation of various body parts through fashion, drawing on Sigmund Freud's idea that any part of the body can be eroticized,[4] and Simmel articulates the dynamics of social imitation and distinction through clothing, while Benjamin reads fashion (*die Mode*) as the epitome of modernity, in that fashion, like modernity, is ephemeral and tethered to the new. In *The Fashion System* (1967), Barthes builds on these earlier theories of fashion's signifying function by distinguishing between "image-clothing" and "written clothing":

> The first is the one presented to me as photographed or drawn—it is image-clothing. The second is the same garment, but described, transformed into language; this dress, photographed on the right, becomes on the left: *a leather belt, with a rose stuck in it, worn above the waist, on a soft shetland dress*; this is the written garment.[5] (Emphasis in original.)

Written clothing, according to Barthes, is both dependent on and resistant to language. "'Real' clothing is burdened with practical considerations (protection, modesty, adornment)," he writes. In contrast, "only written clothing has no practical or aesthetic function: it is entirely constituted with a view to signification."[6]

Departing from traditional (and male-dominated) fashion theory, Elizabeth Wilson notes that "in modern western societies no clothes are outside fashion; fashion sets the terms of *all* sartorial behaviours."[7] In this process, "fashion does not negate emotion, it simply displaces it in the realm of aesthetics."[8] As a representation of embodied cultural practice, clothing in literature, or written clothes, has one distinctive advantage. As Randi S. Koppen observes, the sensations—the touch, smell, and even sounds—of clothing that are absent in the photograph can be evoked through literature. In this way, then, clothes represent "the threshold where the modern subject/object relation plays itself out in a series of encounters and ruptures."[9] Ultimately, as Koppen sums up, "clothes are the place where character becomes image, the place where one's inscriptions in culture and the system of exchange become visible."[10]

As for the method of analyzing fashion in literature, our chapter builds on Peter McNeil, Vicki Karaminas, and Cathy Cole's edited volume *Fashion in Fiction: Text and Clothing in Literature, Film and Television* (2009), which is less interested in "extract[ing] the fashion trace in literature and literary sources" than it is concerned "with the imaginative capacity of fashion to perform several . . . functions simultaneously."[11] These editors engage with how fashion's mythologies are constructed and disseminated through fictional texts. Their approach also foregrounds "fashion metaphors as central to literary tropes, the realm of poetics, and the shaping of societies through mechanisms such as race and gender difference."[12]

Thus, our chapter highlights the various functions of fashion in shaping the literature of the long twentieth century from the turn of the century through the modernist into postmodernist literature, revealing fiction and non-fiction to be an important anchor for twentieth-century sartorial styles. While we include British and transatlantic examples—both highbrow and popular—our primary focus is on American literature. By setting thematic emphases along chronological lines, the themes we explore include fashion, consumerism, and economics; glamor and the gaze; fashion as a normalizing and resisting agent; fashion and anti-fashion; cross-dressing; fashion as performance of identity; and fashion at the intersections of class, race, gender, sexuality, and age. This chapter argues that, far from being a passive presence and reflection, fashion is an active and dynamic force shaping the literatures and characters of the twentieth-century; in turn, literature engages fashion in ways that help render certain styles iconic. Fashion and literature intertwined configure the modernist and postmodernist sartorial fiction of the twentieth century.

FASHION, CONSUMPTION, AND CLASS: THE SOCIAL REALISTS

"A woman should some day write the complete philosophy of clothes. No matter how young, it is one of the things she wholly comprehends,"[13] Theodore Dreiser (1871–1945) writes in his controversial novel *Sister Carrie* (1900). As eighteen-year-old Caroline (Carrie) Meeber leaves rural Wisconsin and enters Chicago, and later New York, she reads her world through sartorial signifiers, decoding social position and power through garments and accessories. Even though a passive character with no money and no connections, she assumes remarkable agency in and through the realm of fashion. The clothes in *Sister Carrie* literally speak to her: "'My dear,' said the lace collar she secured from Partridge's, 'I fit you beautifully; don't give me up.'"[14] Fashion quickly becomes a necessary part of Carrie's identity and social rise: "She could possibly have conquered the fear of hunger and gone back [to a life of factory work]; [. . .] but spoil her appearance?—be old-clothed and poor-appearing?—never!"[15] Seductive and persuasive, garments and accessories speak of desirable social roles; they help assert status and power, but they also proclaim the lack thereof. If clothes afford pleasures and possibilities, the social realism of Dreiser's sartorial fiction also documents the opposite effect: clothes have the power to instill shame and an acute sense of failure in the wearer. Dreiser's sartorial fiction achieves a timely and timeless articulation of social criticism by balancing Carrie Meeber's spectacular rise as an actress with George Hurstwood's tragic fall. Carrie's one-time husband sheds his expensive suits and accessories in a downward spiral; by the novel's end, Hurstwood's "one-time coat of buff had been changed by soot and rain" to proclaim him a Bowery bum.[16] It becomes a tool in his last act, as he stuffs the coat in the cracks of the door before turning on gas and stretching out on a dingy bed.

Although the world of fashion glamor and the haute bourgeoisie are the domains of Edith Wharton's New York, she too is attuned to social realism and satire. Thus, Wharton takes readers from drawing rooms to city streets, from private ballrooms to the opera box, depicting these spaces as privileged sites for sartorial display and glamour. In *The Age of Innocence* (1920), the scandal-plagued Countess Ellen Olenska enters the novel as an object of spectacle. She is by birth American but married to a European aristocrat. At the opera, which she attends immediately upon her mysterious return to New York, scrutiny and judgment of her clothing align with speculation about the state of her marriage. Dressed in "what was then called a 'Josephine look',"[17] Ellen's dress evokes the empire-waisted designs of Paul Poiret (Figure 9.1).

Her style appears deliberately to assert her foreignness and artistic independence, even as it carries vague suggestions of impropriety to the watching representatives of New York society. "'I wonder if she wears a round hat or a bonnet in the afternoon,' Janey speculated.

FIGURE 9.1: Design for a Poiret-style empire waist evening gown by Paris couturier Jeanne Paquin, 1911. Watercolor drawing. Victoria and Albert Museum. Photo: © Victoria and Albert Museum, London.

'At the Opera I know she had on dark blue velvet, perfectly plain and flat—like a night-gown.'"[18] As Wharton's fiction reveals, the glamor of such public and class-conscious entertainment had an underside. In her book *Displaying Women: Spectacles of Leisure in Edith Wharton's New York*, Maureen E. Montgomery considers the spaces of upper class display of fashion such as debutante balls, engagements, and other society events. She notes that women's public performances of their sartorial choices opened them up to intense sexual innuendo, rumors, and misrepresentation during an era when women were beginning to assert their sexual rights.

FASHION AND SUBVERSION: THE RACIALIZED DRESS

If Wharton and Dreiser are focused on fashion as the site through which women and men are integrated into finely-calibrated social hierarchies, their fictions also discern fashion's potential as a site of social subversion and creativity, a theme explored more fully by several American writers. Sara Smolinsky, the Polish girl heroine of Anzia Yezierska's (1880–1970) *Bread Givers* (1925) is depicted as undergoing a similar Cinderella-like transformation as Dreiser's Carrie. As an immigrant, and a Jewish outsider, Sara enters the American middle class with the purchase of a suit made of "plain Serge only! Yes. But more style in its plainness than the richest velvet."[19] As Meredith Goldsmith writes, "Yezierska's fiction mines the possibilities and limitations of Jewish female self-affirmation within that culture."[20] Such self-affirmation from a marginal position is also evident in the work of African-American novelist Jessie Redmon Fauset (1882–1961), a writer of the Harlem Renaissance, and author of *The Chinaberry Tree: Novel of American Life* (1931) and *Comedy: American Style* (1933). Lori Harrison-Kahan argues that all main (non-white) characters adjust their identities by becoming designers. Moving beyond the focus of fashion as a method of deterministic social integration, Harrison-Kahan suggests that becoming a fashion designer creates a more significant opportunity for rebelling against social norms as they relate to gender, class and race. She explains: "fashion becomes a vehicle for racial pride and a means of exposing the co-construction of race and gender."[21] The figure of the fashion designer in early twentieth-century ethnic American literature, then, is key as a figure of empowerment. Rather than functioning to impose conformity to racial and gender norms, fashion is employed by Fauset's female characters "as a form of resistance against the ways that identity was dictated by the dominant culture."[22] The breakdown of the dichotomies of black and white, female and male, immigrant and American is enabled through fashion.

The potential to use fashion for imaginative acts of social resistance is also seen within a transatlantic setting of the Jamaican-American author Claude McKay's novel *Banjo: A Story Without a Plot* (1929). The protagonist, African-American Lincoln Agrippa Daily, aka Banjo, is a drifter in 1920s Versailles, and the novel chronicles his adventures with a band of unemployed sailors and vagabonds. Addressing Banjo's "sartorial self-fashioning," Graeme Abernethy explores how, throughout the novel, "clothes are shown to rival other principal expressions (especially speech and music) of the contingencies inhering in interwar identity."[23] Abernethy argues that Banjo's castaways represent a transnational proletarian blackness, which in turn provides a different perspective to the "Harlem-centered notion of 'subversive dandyism.'"[24] Flamboyant in a blue jean shirt "with knotted scarf bearing an 'elaborate pattern of black, yellow and red at both ends',"[25] Banjo proclaims his proletarian roots with a counter punch of the dandy's color. McKay's *Banjo* describes skin color as a kind of racialized dress that ranges from "gold-brown" to "chocolate-black."[26] The diasporic aspects of fashion, facilitated by the novel as a fashioner of taste also draw attention to the differences of European and American fashion as representing differing conceptual perspectives. In the novel, Banjo's vagabondage becomes a geopolitical and personal journey, as he takes pleasure in "perpetually transform[ing] his sartorial self . . . by adopting (and adapting) the fashion idioms of his temporary home":[27] as he arrives in Marseille, "Banjo bought a new suit of clothes, fancy shoes, and a vivid cache-cool. He had good American clothes, but he wanted to strut in Provençal style."[28] McKay's novel presents vagabondage as a metaphor for the process of writing identity, a self-fashioning of black masculinity, and a seeking of freedom, all of which make Banjo's collaged clothing a double of the doubly marginalized leftist author (Figure 9.2).

FIGURE 9.2: Claude McKay in Paris c. 1930, dapper and formal in a suit and dress coat, a testament to his sartorial versatility. Photo: Universal History Archive/Getty Images.

FASHION AND SEX: THE MODERNISTS

McKay and Fauset's examples illustrate the transition from literary realism to modernism with its increased focus on queering and cross-dressing identities and literary styles, both of which become self-consciously experimental for literary modernism on both sides of the Atlantic. Although D.H. Lawrence was one of the most renowned of the English modernists, his work was considered highly controversial, even pornographic. The body and its clothing are crucial tropes in Lawrence's work. In the opening chapter of *Women in Love* (1920), Gudrun Brangwen stands out from the ashy, dark Midlands colliery town to which she has recently returned from her bohemian life in London. Her unusual style of dress attracts attention:

> She wore a dress of dark-blue silky stuff, with ruches of blue and green linen lace in the neck and sleeve and she had emerald-green stockings. . . . The provincial people, intimidated by Gudrun's perfect sang-froid and exclusive bareness of manner, said of her: "She is a smart woman."[29]

Throughout the novel, Gudrun's clothing marks her modernity and her estrangement from their community. Her artistic and intellectual nature is expressed in her elaborate and individual choices of dress, which is met with resentment and aggression by the townsfolk: as Gudrun walks through the town, someone behind her says, "What price the stockings!"[30] emphasizing the class-difference that underlies her modern appearance.

Lawrence's interest in the relationship between women's clothing and their changing social position is further demonstrated in his war writing. In his war novella *The Fox* (1922) in particular, Lawrence depicts women whose assumption of male roles involves the wearing of male clothing. In *The Fox,* Henry Grenfel, a soldier, returns to his grandfather's farm during the war and finds it being run by women. In England during both world wars a Women's Land-Army was assembled as a back-up for the war effort. These women, known as land girls, wore male clothing and worked on farms, filling in for men who had gone to the battlefields (Figure 9.3).

The land girls running Henry's grandfather's farm are Nellie March and Jill Banford. The women call one another by their last names, and while Banford dresses in conventionally feminine attire, March dresses in a masculine fashion, in the tightly-buttoned workman's tunic of a land girl's uniform, and she does the heavy work. The plot of the novel focuses on Henry's sexual pursuit of March, and his perception of her as a sexual object evolves in relation to her clothing. After seeing her in a dress and delicate women's shoes and stockings for the first time, he is struck by her femininity: seeing her always in "hard-cloth breeches, wide on the hips, buttoned on the knee, strong as armour, and in the brown puttees and thick boots it has never occurred to him that she has a woman's legs and feet. Now it came upon him. She had a woman's soft, skirted legs, and she was accessible."[31] Clothing is central to Lawrence's sexual philosophy and thus to his modernism: the tenuousness of heterosexual relationships and fluidity of gender were popular tropes in modernist literature shaping modernist sartorial fiction.

A case in point is F. Scott Fitzgerald, a male style icon of the jazz age (Figure 9.4), and author of *The Great Gatsby* (1925), which widely popularized glamorous flapper styles and bent boundaries of class. The book's titular hero, Jay Gatsby, uses his clothing to present a specific version of masculinity, which he uses to reconnect with the affluent Daisy Buchanan, with whom he had a brief wartime love affair. Originally from a poor

FIGURE 9.3: Recruitment poster for female land-workers during the First World War, showing the functional, masculine uniforms worn by the "land girls." Photo: Buyenlarge/Getty Images.

family, Gatsby has recreated himself as a wealthy member of the leisure class. In one of the most dramatic sartorial scenes, Gatsby and Daisy gather at his two wardrobe cabinets, where his shirts are:

> piled like bricks in stacks a dozen high . . . shirts of sheer linen and thick silk and fine flannel . . . shirts with stripes and scrolls and plaids in coral and apple-green and lavender and faint orange, and monograms of Indian blue.[32]

On one level, Gatsby's shirts signal his immense wealth, and therefore, his attractiveness. However, they also reveal the incompleteness of his self-transformation. Since shirts had moved from their status as formal under-layer to mass-produced and multi-colored daywear, as Shaun Cole describes in *The Story of Men's Underwear*, "the shirt ceased to be a symbol of social rank."[33] The excess showcased by Gatsby has a sobering effect for status-conscious Daisy: the collection of colorful shirts reveals something akin to Cole's "working class dandy" who tried to impress with flashy colors.[34] Thus fashion exposes Gatsby, the self-made man, as a social outsider in Daisy's world of old money. As the examples of Fitzgerald and Lawrence reveal, the breakdown of heterosexual relationships was a modernist trope that went hand in glove with gender crossings and anxieties regarding the woman who assumed masculine roles: driving cars, earning a salary, wearing male clothing, and even displaying dubious ethics like their male counterparts.

Such cross-dressing gestures assume even more radical dimensions in the more experimental and avant-garde sartorial fictions of the era. Today an examplar for feminists,

FIGURE 9.4: F. Scott Fitzgerald, an icon of jazz-age style, 1925. Photo: Hulton Archive/Getty Images.

American writer Djuna Barnes (1892–1982), who had sexual relationships with men and women and captured sexual bohemianism on both sides of the Atlantic, repeatedly employs cross-dressing in her interrogation of modern sexuality and sexual politics. Her chapbook *Book of Repulsive Women* (1915) explores Manhattan's lesbian culture, while *Ladies Almanack* (1928), a *roman à clef*, satirizes the Paris lesbian circle of Natalie Barney, whose habituées signaled their alternate identities by celebrating Sappho and dressing in white Greek robes. Discarding the traditional undergarment, they lived their homoerotic fantasies, dancing in sandals or barefoot in Barney's garden at rue Jacob. Many of the novel's arcane words (such as "underkirtel," "gusset," "snood") reference clothing that is "pointedly out of fashion" as Tyrus Miller has observed.[35] These arcane words, Miller suggests, act like the top hat donned by painter Romaine Brooks (Barney's lover), in that the verbal and sartorial codes combine to encode the secret language of "the love that dare not speak its name" in public (Figure 9.5). Thus to be a "lady of fashion" is to be a flamboyant, untamed, and even suspicious figure.

FIGURE 9.5: Romaine Brooks's self-portrait, showing her signature top hat, 1923. Photo: Smithsonian American Art Museum, gift of the artist.

In Barnes's novel, *Nightwood* (1936), the trope of cross-dressing is even more prominent. *Nightwood* defies all the conventions of the realistic novel, following the interlocking stories of Nora Flood, an American drifting through cosmopolitan Europe, Robin Vote, her mercurial lover, and Dr. Matthew O'Connor, an impoverished transvestite whose medical bona fides are suspect. The doctor appears wearing make-up and a woman's flannel nightgown.[36] Other characters also participate in this crossing of genders and epochs, even in dreams. Love of the androgyne or the cross-dresser, we are told, is a search for one idealized gender in another: "the girl lost" is but "the Prince found," the pretty lad is a girl.[37] In Robin's case, gender-crossing expands further: she is "a wild thing caught in a woman's skin," "the third sex,"[38] performing a kind of species-crossing and creating a new gender identity in a radical sartorial fiction. *Nightwood* functions as a device for destabilizing gender and unsettling binary logic, affirming an inherent mutability of gender. As Warburton writes:

> Both [Barnes and Virginia Woolf, in *Orlando*,] construct subjects . . . who are never finally male, female, nor androgynous, without capitulating to sexlessness. Instead, the writers construct subjects whose genders, desires, and meanings are perpetually deferred and destabilized.[39]

Gender is represented through Barnes's use of polarity: night and day, animal and human, child and adult. Thus, Barnes challenges "the assumptions of mimetic language and the gendered presumptions of the realist representational mode."[40]

THE LITTLE BLACK DRESS: FROM CHANEL TO HOLLY GOLIGHTLY

In 1926, Ernest Hemingway's *The Sun Also Rises* introduced Lady Brett Ashley, a war nurse who drinks, smokes, and takes lovers. Lady Brett is the love interest of Hemingway's sexually-incapacitated narrator, Jake Barnes, who is also one of the war-wounded. The terms with which Jake describes her initially highlight her attractiveness, her modernity, and her androgyny: "Brett was damned good-looking. She wore a slipover jersey sweater and a tweed skirt, and her hair was brushed back like a boy's."[41] Later she makes a striking appearance at a party in "a black, sleeveless evening dress," which is charged with a disturbing sexuality: the men, and most notably her former lover Robert Cohn, "could not stop looking at her."[42] Where black clothing was previously linked to mourning, Hemingway's novel associates it with women's sexual agency. By coincidence, Gabrielle "Coco" Chanel's crêpe de chine "little black dress" made its first appearance in *Vogue* on October 1, 1926. Not nearly as sexually-charged as Brett's garment, Chanel's modest, long-sleeved design made its debut as "a sort of uniform for all women of taste."[43] The modernist designer provided freedom of movement for women through practical, simple, yet well-tailored designs that afforded women sartorial mobility for their working lives. Brett's jersey sweater is further evidence of the innovation in fashion that Chanel represented: wool jersey, fabric formerly used for male underwear, was a frequent feature in her designs. Brett Ashley's clothing thus signals her modernity, which is at the heart of her sexual appeal, just as Hemingway signals his modernity by shaping twentieth-century sartorial fiction through cross-dressing.

The little black dress would come to typify the fashion revolution of the twentieth century. It was dubbed a "Ford" because it was reproducible in so many fabrics, and so many prices, and rapidly came to denote a powerful modern type of independent femininity (Figure 9.6).

FIGURE 9.6: Dancer and choreographer Desiree Lubovska wearing a dress of georgette crepe decorated with bands of cock feathers in front, designed by Jean Patou, 1923.

In Jean Rhys's novels of the 1930s, women repeatedly imagine the power of the black dress to transform their lives. Rhys, born in the colony of Dominica but transplanted to England as a teenager, was acutely concerned with women's powerlessness in a man's world, and the ability of women's clothing to confer upon them agency and respect. Julia Martin, the heroine of *After Leaving Mr. Mackenzie* (1930), recognizes the protective power of clothing. In the first epigraph with which we began this chapter, she laments the sale of her fur coat, which acted as "protective colouring" from the rudeness of others and so would help her in her painful return to her family after being abandoned by her lover.[44] Later, in a moment of disappointment, she imagines herself "in a new black dress and a little black hat with a veil that just shadowed her eyes," which she equates with "happiness."[45] As she walks through Paris, she returns to the imaginary black dress, using the image "like a charm"[46]: it signals the respectable and happy existence she so desires. Sasha Jansen, the heroine of Rhys's 1939 *Good Morning, Midnight*, similarly endows a black dress with transformative powers: she hopes to buy "a black dress with wide sleeves embroidered in vivid colors—red, green, blue, purple. It is my dress. If I had been wearing it I should never have stammered or been stupid."[47] The fashionable black dress is thus invested with a transformative power, affording the wearer the privileges of poised, successful modern femininity.

By the 1950s, New Orleans-born Truman Capote had become the torchbearer for intertwining the literary and the sartorial in a profoundly sartorial fiction. His 1958 novella, *Breakfast at Tiffany's* tells the story of Holly Golightly, who has lived on in popular mythology through the film adaptation starring Audrey Hepburn (1961) (Figure 9.7).

FIGURE 9.7: Audrey Hepburn as Holly Golightly, in a promotional photograph for *Breakfast at Tiffany's*, 1960. Photo: ullstein bild via Getty Images.

In Capote's novella, improvisational identity is tied to clothing. Holly uses clothing to recreate herself from an insecure country girl to a sought-after society woman. Where in Hemingway's *The Sun Also Rises*, Lady Brett Ashley's little black dress is charged with post-war sexual tension, for Holly the little black dress is the costume of elegance, refinement and versatility. However, Holly's performance remains imperfect. Gabrielle Finnane, in her discussion of the waif figure, compares *Breakfast at Tiffany's* to its predecessor, *Goodbye to Berlin* (1939) by English writer Christopher Isherwood. The archetype of the waif, Finnane argues, is dependent on sartorial description. Sally Bowles, Isherwood's protagonist, is the model for the later Golightly and for both waifs the scarf is used as a visual trope indicating the bohemian sensibility as "an object that is tied yet flying free."[48] Black clothing indicates the women's "loose morals," as Finnane observes: "The view of the beat girl's life as morally ambiguous is suggested by Holly Golightly's dark glasses with their connotations of concealment."[49] While Holly's image may be iconic, in its original iteration it is also ambiguous. Holly is a Manhattanite but is still rooted in her hillbilly past. She goes riding in Central Park wearing jeans, then still considered as work clothes, tennis shoes, and a windbreaker, appearing in clothing that is a clear breach of social convention. She is wearing this outfit when she is arrested for her alleged role in a drug-smuggling racket. In the newspaper, the photograph shows her wedged between two muscular detectives, one male, one female: "In this squalid context even her clothes (she was still wearing her riding costume, windbreaker and jeans) suggested a gang-moll hooligan: an impression dark glasses, disarrayed coiffure and a Picayune cigarette dangling from sullen lips did not diminish."[50] That it is the image of Holly in the black dress that has endured, eliding the ambiguity of Holly herself, is a testament to its aspirational status. The image of modern womanhood pioneered by Chanel remains powerful to this day, connoting a femininity that is not diminished but sustained by confidence and independence.

GLAMOR, FASHION, AND PROSPERITY: AGENT 007

By the mid-century, sartorial fiction had embraced branding as a theme exemplified and popularized globally by British Secret Service agent James Bond. Set during "a new era of fashion and prosperity,"[51] Ian Fleming's best-selling James Bond stories have sold more than 100 million copies. The first Bond book, *Casino Royale* (1953) sets the template for the future novels and short story collections, in which action plots involving beautiful women and innovative technology are combined with the meticulous evocations of luxury consumer culture (Figure 9.8). Everything in Bond's world is bespoke, specially chosen and constructed, and expensive, with brands listed by name. Bond's cigarettes are "a Balkan and Turkish mixture made for him by Morlands of Grosvenor Street";[52] his French aide smokes "Caporals." Bond's car is a 1933 4½ litre convertible Bentley,[53] and his cigarette lighter is a Ronson. It is not only Bond's clothing and possessions that are meticulously catalogued: the clothing of Vesper Lynd, Bond's colleague who later proves to be a double-agent, is also described in detail. On their first meeting, she wears a "medium-length dress of grey 'soie sauvage' with a square-cut bodice . . . The skirt was closely pleated . . . She wore a three-inch, hand-stitched black belt. A hand-stitched black 'sabretache' rested on the chair beside her together with a wide cartwheel hat of gold straw, its crown encircled by a thin black velvet ribbon which tied at the back in a short bow. Her shoes were square-toed of plain black leather."[54] Later, she wears a (borrowed) black velvet Christian Dior dress.[55]

FIGURE 9.8: Sean Connery as James Bond in *Goldfinger*, 1964. Photo: Michael Ochs Archives/ Getty Images.

Dior had shown his first collection in Paris only in 1947, establishing Paris as a center of post-Second World War fashion. The choice of Dior shows just how attentive Fleming was to the luxury items of the moment.

Fashion branding returns four decades later in Bret Easton Ellis's third, and best-known novel, *American Psycho* (1991), whose central figure is a serial killer, a Manhattan businessman called Patrick Bateman. Every page presents myriad brands to the reader who becomes enveloped in a haze of consumerism. In a typical example, Patrick describes his preparations for a date: "I go into the bedroom and take off what I was wearing today: a herringbone wool suit with pleated trousers by Giorgio Correggiari, a cotton oxford shirt by Ralph Lauren, a knit tie from Paul Stuart and suede shoes from Cole-Haan. I slip on a pair of sixty-dollar boxer shorts I bought at Barney's and do some stretching exercise."[56]

The details Ellis provides are excessive and satirical, and although the character is overtly heterosexual, his clothing descriptions are slightly homoerotic and pornographic, as well as autoerotic and solipsistic. His brand awareness includes the clothing of those around him; in this case, that of his date: "a silk gazar blouse with rhinestone cufflinks by Louis Dell'Olio and a pair of embroidered velvet pants from Saks, crystal earrings by Wendy Gell for Anne Klein and gold sling-back pumps."[57] By interrupting these lists of brands with explicit descriptions of Patrick's sexual activity and the gruesome violence of his killings, Easton Ellis emphasizes a connection between consumerism, sexuality, and violence, each one which is latent but less self-conscious in the Bond novels.

POSTMODERNIST SELF-FASHIONING

Just like fashion which channels earlier styles, so postmodern literature is characterized by flashbacks and recycling of earlier literatures, styles, and genres through parody. With the postmodern frame of 1920s Harlem, Toni Morrison's *Jazz* (1992) evokes American jazz consumerism through references to beauty salons and fashion. At the novel's sartorial center is a green dress, passed down through generations, a garment imbued with love and racism, with memory and history. In her study of Morrison's use of clothing, Natalie Stillman-Webb concludes that Morrison's depictions "can be seen as an emphasis on both the perils and possibilities associated with consumer culture and its relationship with racial desire and identification."[58] The green dress in the novel can be seen as "a signifier for the cultural constraints and opportunities characters face in construction of subjectivity" and Morrison "demonstrates how this culture at the same time contributes to new opportunities for self-fashioning."[59]

Like Morrison, Margaret Atwood dramatizes the mediation of clothes between private and social selves, whereby clothing is the threshold between the two spheres. As an extension of the body, clothing becomes invested with memories and emotions. A long black coat too big for her frame clothes the narrator, a young woman, in "Hair Jewellery," a story in *Dancing Girls and Other Stories* (1977). "That's my technique, I resurrect myself through clothes," the narrator observes, continuing: "In fact, it's impossible for me to remember what I did, what happened to me, unless I can remember what I was wearing, and every time I discard a sweater or a dress I am discarding a part of my life."[60] Building "a patchwork self"[61] through clothes pieced together from Filene's bargain basement store, the narrator approaches her clothing in a way that mirrors the workings of the writing of postmodern fiction, which is also made of patchworks, collaged together through memory and fragments of identity. Examining Atwood's fictional self-fashioning, Cynthia Kuhn suggests that Atwood's "characters are often compelled by the dictates of style yet troubled by the coding abilities of dress. In many cases, they seek to challenge limitations by performing resistance sartorially."[62] Kuhn focuses on how trends contribute to the dystopic picture offered in the sci-fi novel *Oryx and Crake* (2003) and Atwood's vision more specifically. The notion of self-fashioning is represented as temptation and frustration in the novel, and, Kuhn concludes, *Oryx and Crake* is a "cautionary tale," in which "bodies remain unstable signifiers while fashionable desires and anxieties are foregrounded."[63]

In contrast to Atwood's dystopian universe, Alice Munro, recipient of the 2013 Nobel Prize for Literature (Canada's first) sets her sartorial fiction in small-town Ontario. She explores women's self-identification through clothing in an early work, *Who Do You Think You Are?* (1978). These stories, all but two originally published separately in various magazines, together constitute an experimental novel, a *bildungsroman* of the protagonist Rose covering time from before the Second World War until the early sixties. Rose's clothes in part mimic her class: she comes from the poor part of town where East and West Hanratty are divided not only by a bridge, but also by what people eat for breakfast and where their toilet is located. Rose's stepmother Flo has a friend, Mavis, who looks like the American movie star Frances Farmer.

Mavis consciously emphasizes that resemblance through her clothing: she "bought herself a big hat that dipped over one eye and a dress made entirely of lace."[64] Mavis, in her clothing, mimics the appearance of the film star she resembles and goes to a resort on Georgian Bay in the hopes folks will think she is Francis Farmer herself: "She had a little cigarette holder that was black and mother-of-pearl. She could have been arrested, Flo said. For the *nerve*" (emphasis in original).[65] Flo's shock at Mavis's mimicking of Farmer is perhaps due to Farmer's notoriety: the actress was famously arrested in Santa Monica in the winter of 1943, having failed to pay the final installment of the penalty after drunk driving. The event was captured in a photograph that showed her disheveled and defiant, cigarette in hand (Figure 9.9). Glamorous, Farmer was also rebellious, refusing aspects of the Hollywood glamor industry and her career forever shadowed by her brief commitment to a mental asylum. The mimicking of celebrity clothing thus provides the opportunity for both glamor and rebellion: in adopting the style of a sexualized and rebellious film star, Mavis subversively re-makes herself in defiance of her poor and conventional background.

In postmodern engagement of, and playing with, the past, a final tour de force takes us back more than forty years through the history of twentieth-century fashion. Singer-songwriter Patricia Lee (Patti) Smith's memoir, *Just Kids* (2010) recapitulates many of the earlier themes of clothing in twentieth-century literature: the importance of black clothing, the development of beat and hippie culture in clothing, the elevation of used clothing into vintage, the merging of male and female styles, and the influence of films on the way women dress. In Smith's case, another rich vein is not only the importance of film stars and their dress, but also the impact of literature, of literary figures, such as William Blake, Arthur Rimbaud, and Jean Genet, and of musicians and of visual artists on one's personal styles. *Just Kids* provides a textured history of an important period in Western culture, when the center of art shifted from Paris to New York City. Its primary focus is a little more than a decade of New York culture, 1967–79, but Smith's narrative takes us up to the death of Robert Mapplethorpe in 1989. When Patti Smith arrives in New York in 1967, she is wearing dungarees, a black turtleneck, and an old second-hand gray raincoat.[66] The memoir becomes a nostalgic sartorial narrative, the self fueled by the clothing styles of the era, which the mature writer itemizes. Within a tension of irony and nostalgia, she dons and sheds selves that present a fashion tour of the beatnik generation. Looking for

FIGURE 9.9: Dishevelled and rumpled, the notorious silver-screen movie star Frances Farmer smokes a cigarette, 1943. Photo: Bettmann/contributor.

work, she describes herself as cultivating a "good beatnik ballet look."[67] When John Coltrane dies, Smith remembers the event by the clothing of the day: the boys in the village wear striped bell-bottoms and military jackets, the girls are wrapped in tie-dye.[68] Smith and her sexual partner, Robert Mapplethorpe, search out used clothing in the Bowery, "tattered silk dresses, frayed cashmere overcoats, and used motorcycle jackets."[69]

The pair don identities self-consciously by using the fragments of literature, film, and pop culture. Descriptions of the wearing of used clothing, or vintage, once seemed to be confined to prostitutes, who rented attractive clothes in order to sell their bodies. For Smith, in contrast, questions of sexual identity are in the foreground of this sartorial narrative. Mapplethorpe is in the process of discovering both his homosexuality and his vocation as an avant-garde photographer who would soon shock America with edgy homoerotic portraits. Detailing the transformation of their relationship and of her identity as a budding artist, Patti Smith's memoir becomes a literary experiment in postmodern autobiographical sartorial narrative, which she sums up best in the epigraph to our chapter. "I was full of references," she states of the photo shoot staged for Mapplethorpe's camera. In the apartment of Mapplethorpe's new lover, Sam Wagstaff, Smith poses cross-dressed in black pegged pants and white shirt (Figure 9.10).[70]

FIGURE 9.10: Robert Mapplethorpe photograph of Patti Smith, 1975. Photo: Michael Ochs Archive/Getty Images.

The resulting photograph has "magic": "When I look at it now, I never see me. I see us," she observes.[71] Her possessive feelings toward the photograph point to the dissolution of boundaries of authorship, with Mapplethorpe shooting the picture, Wagstaff fussing with the lights, and Smith staging herself. Her sartorial narrative is the result of the dissolution of boundaries, with the self written in the threshold space where literature and dress intertwine.

CONCLUSION

As we have argued in this chapter, fashion and literature have co-produced the sartorial fiction and non-fiction of the long twentieth century. The modernist era explored gender-bending fashion and fueled the eroticism and sexuality of bared arms and legs that affirmed women as sexual agents in modernist literature. The literature of the postmodern era plays exuberantly with the earlier sartorial and genre styles, self-consciously alluding to literary and fashion styles through parody and metafictional commentary. As we have argued, literature both reflected and, in the case of Holly Golightly, coproduced iconic styles. The black dress made its appearance in literature simultaneously with Chanel's invention while literature charged the invention with sexuality. Many literary luminaries such as Dreiser, Woolf, and Barnes started their careers in writing or editing for fashion magazines. Profoundly steeped in the world of fashion and fashion consumption, these authors also struggled against their background in fashion writing. They tried to overcome their roots to become literary writers, so that the relationship between literature and fashion is both reinforcing but also fueled by critical tension. Many twentieth-century literati used fashion and glamor to stage themselves as celebrity authors in public while also ensuring their legacies through careful presentation of themselves in journals and autobiographies. Fitzgerald's glamor made him the representative author of the flapper era, while Hemingway's head bandage and open shirt made him the lost generation author. Modernist and avant-gardist writers and poets staged themselves in expensive portrait photographs taken by Man Ray and Berenice Abbott, who also photographed fashion designers such as Coco Chanel and Elsa Schiaparelli. In these portraits, hats, ties, scarves, and veils are the tools of identity construction, used simultaneously to reveal and disguise the self, just as doubleness would preoccupy literature during the twentieth century.

Finally, in the postmodern era, the backward look dominates, the past impinging on the present in both literature and fashion. In the later twentieth century, vintage carried with it a number of charges, a cocking of the snoot at the contemporary, at luxury, at commodity culture, but it also presented a way of taking on the past in all its guises. Fashion and literature entwined are fueled by history, with the freedom—and constraints—that this evocation of the past engenders.

NOTES

Introduction

1. Marie Riegels Melchior, "Introduction: Understanding Fashion and Dress Museology," in *Fashion and Museums: Theory and Practice*, Marie Riegels Melchior and Birgitta Svensson (eds), (London: Bloomsbury, 2014), 3–5.
2. George H. Darwin, "Development in Dress," *Macmillan Magazine* (1872): 410–16.
3. Edmund Bergler, *Fashion and the Unconscious* (Madison: International Universities Press (1953) 1987), vii, xii.
4. Ibid., vii, xxiii, 14.
5. Sarah Fee, "Anthropology and Materiality," in Sandy Black et al. (eds), *Handbook of Fashion Studies* (London: Bloomsbury, 2013), 302.
6. James Laver, *Clothes* (London: Burke, 1952).
7. Polly Feele, "Fashions and the Seven-year Schedule," *The Globe and Mail*, February 13, 1915: 10.
8. Alexandra Palmer, "Chanel: American as Apple Pie," in *The Chanel Legend* (Draiflessen Collection, Mettingen, Germany, 2013), 170–81; "Du fil au vêtement. La production de textiles pour la haute couture" in *La mode en France, 1947–1957*, Alexandra Bosc (ed.+) (Musée Galliera, Musée de la mode de la ville de Paris, 2014): 98–113.
9. Barbara Vinken, *Fashion Zeitgeist: trends and cycles in the fashion system*, trans, Mark Hewson (Oxford & New York: Berg, 2005), 63.
10. Alexandra Palmer, *Couture & Commerce: the transatlantic fashion trade in the 1950s* (University of British Columbia Press and Royal Ontario Museum, 2001).
11. Vanessa Friedman, "Saint Laurent is Creating a Line Even More Exclusive Than Couture," *New York Times*, July 29, 2015, http://www.nytimes.com/2015/07/29/fashion/saint-laurent-is-creating-a-line-even-more-exclusive-than-couture.html [accessed August 3, 2015].
12. Lawrence Langer, *The Importance of Wearing Clothes* (New York: Hastings House, 1959), 303.
13. Alexandra Jacobs, "Smooth Moves: how Sara Blakely rehabilitated the girdle," *The New Yorker*, March 28, 2011, http://www.newyorker.com/magazine/2011/03/28/smooth-moves [accessed August 2, 2015].
14. Vinken, *Fashion Zeitgeist*, 119–28.
15. Laver, *Clothes*, ix–x.
16. Dick Hebdige, *Subculture: the meaning of style* (London: Routledge, 1979); Lauren D. Whitley, *Hippie Chic* (Boston: MFA Publications, 2013).
17. Rebecca Arnold, *Fashion, Desire and Anxiety: image and morality in the 20th century* (New Brunswick: Rutgers University Press, 2001), 68.
18. Bergler, *Fashion and the Unconscious*, 99–116.
19. George Simmel, "Fashion," *International Quarterly*, 10, no. 1 (1904): 130–55.
20. http://www.wmagazine.com/fashion/2010/05/nan_kempner/ [accessed July 25, 2015].
21. http://www.metmuseum.org/about-the-museum/press-room/exhibitions/2003/bravehearts-men-in-skirts [accessed July 26, 2015].
22. Alan Feuer, "Do Real Men Wear Skirts? Try Disputing a 340-Pounder," *New York Times*, February 8, 2004, http://www.nytimes.com/2004/02/08/nyregion/08skirts.html [accessed July 26, 2015].

23. Angela McRobbie, *In the Culture Society: art, fashion and popular music* (London, New York: Routledge, 1991); *Zoot Suits and Second-hand Dresses: an anthology of fashion and music* (Boston: Unwin Hyman, 1988); M.E. Davis, *Classic Chic: music, fashion, and modernism* (Berkeley: University of California Press, 2006).

24. Simmel, "Fashion."

25. Armand Limnander, "Miguel Adrover, Fall 2001 Ready-to-Wear," February 11, 2001, http://www.style.com/fashion-shows/fall-2001-ready-to-wear/miguel-adrover [accessed July 30, 2015].

26. http://www.style.com/fashion-shows/spring-2001-ready-to-wear/miguel-adrover [accessed July 30, 2015].

27. Cathy Horyn, "Fashion: some things new, most borrowed," *New York Times*, September 11, 2001, http://www.nytimes.com/2001/09/11/nyregion/review-fashion-some-things-new-most-borrowed.html [accessed July 30, 2015].

28. Colleen Nika, "Whatever Happened to Miguel Adrover?" February 1, 2011, http://fashionetc.com/fashion/influencers/439-whatever-happened-to-miguel-adrover [accessed July 30, 2015].

29. Julia Twigg, *Fashion and Age: Dress, the Body and Later Life* (London: Bloomsbury, 2013), 2, 18.

30. Langer, *The Importance of Wearing Clothes*, 301, 307.

1 Textiles

1. Mary Schoeser, *World Textiles: A Concise History* (London: Thames & Hudson, 2003), 183.

2. Alexandra Palmer, "Du fil au vêtement. La production de textiles pour la haute couture," in Alexandra Bosc (ed.), *Les années 50. La mode en France, 1947–1957* (Paris: Paris Musées, 2014), 98–112.

3. Jacqueline Field, "Dyes, Chemistry and Clothing: The Influence of World War I on Fabrics, Fashions and Silk," *Dress* 28, no. 1 (2001): 77–91; Regina Lee Blaszczyk, *The Color Revolution* (Cambridge, MA: MIT Press, 2012).

4. See Dorothy Siegert Lyle, *Focus on Fabrics* (Silver Spring: National Institute of Drycleaning, 1964 (revised edition)), http://www.cs.arizona.edu/patterns/weaving/books.html#L [accessed July 19, 2010]; Helen Anstey and Terry Weston, *The Anstey Weston Guide to Textile Terms* (London: Weston Publishing Ltd., [1997] 2005); R.W. Moncrieff, *The Man-Made Fibres* (New York and Toronto: John Wiley & Sons, 1975 (6th edition)).

5. Kaori O'Connor, "The Other Half: The Material Culture of New Fibres," in Susanne Küchler and Daniel Miller (eds), *Clothing as Material Culture* (Oxford: Berg, 2005); Kaori O'Connor, *Lycra: How a Fiber Shaped America* (New York and London: Routledge, 2011), 58–61; Susannah Handley, *Nylon: The Story of a Fashion Revolution* (Baltimore: Johns Hopkins University Press, 1999), 22–8.

6. Field, "Dyes, Chemistry and Clothing": 86–7.

7. Susan Hay (ed.), *From Paris to Providence: Fashion, Art, and the Tirocchi Dressmakers' Shop, 1915–1947* (Providence: Museum of Art, Rhode Island School of Design, 2000).

8. Madelyn Shaw, "H.R. Mallinson & Company, Inc., of New York, New Jersey and Pennsylvania," in Jacqueline Field, Marjorie Senechal, and Madelyn Shaw, *American Silk 1830–1930* (Lubbock: Texas Tech University Press, 2007).

9. Ibid., 209

10. Field, "Dyes, Chemistry and Clothing": 81, 83.

11. Whitney Blausen, "Rodier," in *Contemporary Fashion* (Farmington Hills: St. James Press, 1994), 575; Hay, *From Paris to Providence*, 185–7.

12. Mary Lynn Stewart, *Dressing Modern Frenchwomen: Marketing Haute Couture, 1919–1939* (Baltimore: Johns Hopkins University Press, 2008), 78.

13. Hay, *From Paris to Providence*, 185–6.

14. Edwina Ehrman, "Glamourous Modernity: 1914–30," in Christopher Breward, Edwina Ehrman, and Caroline Evans, *The London Look: Fashion from Street to Catwalk* (New Haven: Yale University Press/Museum of London, 2004), 106–7.

15. Amy de la Haye and Shelley Tobin, *Chanel: The Couturiere at Work* (London: Victoria & Albert Museum, [1994] 2003), 16.

16. Ibid., 24–6

17. Amy de la Haye, "Patou, Jean," in Valerie Steele (ed.), *Encyclopedia of Clothing and Fashion* (Detroit: Thompson Gale, 2005); Meredith Etherington-Smith, *Patou* (New York: St. Martin's/Marek, 1983), 56–68; Emmanuelle Polle, Francis Hammond and Alexandra Keens, *Jean Patou: A Fashionable Life* (Paris: Flammarion, 2013), 90–101, 198–214.

18. Dilys E. Blum, *Shocking! The Art and Fashion of Elsa Schiaparelli* (Philadelphia: Philadelphia Museum of Art, 2003), 13–20.

19. Quoted in Guillaume Garnier (ed.), *Paris-Couture-Années Trente* (Paris: Musée de la Mode et du Costume, Palais Galliera, 1987), 18.

20. Betty Kirke, *Madeleine Vionnet* (San Francisco: Chronicle Books, 1998), 69; see also ibid., 38.

21. Patricia Cunningham, "Swimwear in the Thirties: The B.V.D. Company in a Decade of Innovation," *Dress* 12, no. 1 (1986): 20–2; Susan Ward, "Swimwear," in Valerie Steele (ed.), *Encyclopedia of Clothing and Fashion* (Detroit: Thompson Gale, 2005), 253.

22. Blum, *Shocking!* 60–5; Handley, *Nylon*, 27.

23. American Fabrics, *Encyclopedia of Textiles* (Englewood Cliffs: Prentice-Hall, 1960), 453–6.

24. Handley, *Nylon*, 31–48; O'Connor, *Lycra*, 62.

25. Colin McDowell, *Forties Fashion and the New Look* (London: Bloomsbury, 1997); see also Fabienne Falluel and Marie-Laure Gutton, *Elégance et Système D: Paris 1940–1944* (Paris: Paris Musées, 2009), Dominique Veillon, *Fashion Under the Occupation* (London: Berg, 2002), and Irene Guenther, *Nazi "Chic"?: Fashioning Women in the Third Reich* (London: Berg, 2004).

26. McDowell, *Forties Fashion*, 156–68, and Alexandra Palmer, *Couture & Commerce: The Transatlantic Fashion Trade in the 1950s* (Toronto: Royal Ontario Museum, 2001), 16–40.

27. Metropolitan Museum of Art. *American Textiles, '48* (exhibition brochure) (New York: Thomas J. Watson Library, Metropolitan Museum of Art, 1948).

28. See "American Fabrics Presents a Key to the Man-Made Fibers," *American Fabrics* 26 (Spring 1953): 70–4; "Guide to some well known finishes and finishing terms," *American Fabrics* 28 (Spring 1954): 80–3; Lyle, *Focus on Fabrics*.

29. Handley, *Nylon*; Regina Lee Blaszczyk, "Styling Synthetics: DuPont's Marketing of Fabrics and Fashions in Postwar America," *The Business History Review* 80, no. 3 (2006): 485–528; Regina Lee Blaszczyk, "Designing Synthetics, Promoting Brands: Dorothy Liebes, DuPont Fibres and Post-war American Interiors," *Journal of Design History* 21, no. 1 (2008): 75–99; O'Connor, "The Other Half"; O'Connor, *Lycra*.

30. Frank D. Barlow, Jr., *Cotton, Rayon, Synthetic Fibers—Competition in Western Europe* (Washington: US Department of Agriculture, 1957).

31. Palmer, "du Fil au vêtement," 103–4; Blaszczyk, "Styling Synthetics," 506–14; Handley, *Nylon*, 77–97.

32. Blaszczyk, "Styling Synthetics," 490–1.

33. Ibid.; Lyle, *Focus on Fabrics*.

34. American Fabrics 1960, 453–6; Perkins H. Bailey, "Report on Men's Wear," *New York Times* (May 1, 1955), SMA7; Isadore Barmash, "Men's Shirts Get Permanent Press," *New York Times* (February 21, 1965): 43.

35. Richard Martin, *American Ingenuity: Sportswear 1930s–1970s* (New York: Metropolitan Museum of Art, 1998); Kohle Yohannan and Nancy Nolf, *Claire McCardell: Redefining Modernism* (New York: Abrams, 1998).

36. Jessica Daves, *Ready-Made Miracle: The Story of American Fashion for the Millions* (New York: G.P. Putnam's & Sons, 1967), 113–20.

37. Ibid., 132–6.

38. Valerie Steele and Gillian Carrara, "Italian Fashion," in Valerie Steele (ed.), *Encyclopedia of Clothing and Fashion* (Detroit: Thompson Gale, 2005), 254–5; Nicola White, *Reconstructing Italian Fashion: America and the Development of the Italian Fashion Industry* (Oxford and New York: Berg, 2000), 113–22.

39. Luigi Settembrini (ed.), *Emilio Pucci* (Florence: Skira, 1996), 34–40.

40. Bailey, "Report on Men's Wear."

41. Pendleton Woolen Mills, Pendleton Company History, http://www.pendleton-usa.com/custserv/custserv.jsp?pageName=CompanyHistory&parentName=Heritage [accessed June 15, 2014]; William R. Scott, "California Casual: Lifestyle Marketing and Men's Leisurewear, 1930–1960," in Regina Lee Blaszczyk (ed.), *Producing Fashion: Commerce, Culture, and Consumers* (Philadelphia: University of Pennsylvania Press, 2008); Daves, *Ready-Made Miracle*, 120–2.

42. Susan Ward, "Chemise Dress," in Valerie Steele (ed.), *Encyclopedia of Clothing and Fashion* (Detroit: Thompson Gale, 2005).

43. Lesley Ellis Miller, *Cristóbal Balenciaga* (London: B.T. Batsford, Ltd., 1993), 48; Cristóbal Balenciaga Museoa, *Cristóbal Balenciaga* (New York: Thames & Hudson, 2011), 382.

44. Valérie Guillaume, *Courrèges* (London: Thames & Hudson, 1998), 9.

45. Lyle, *Focus on Fabrics*, 219; Daves, *Ready-Made Miracle*, 131–2.

46. Jacqueline Field, "Bernat Klein's Couture Tweeds: Color and Fabric Innovation, 1960–1980," *Dress*, 36, no. 1 (2006): 41–55; Handley, *Nylon*, 113–4; Lyle, *Focus on Fabrics*, 301–4.

47. Handley, *Nylon*, 88–90.

48. Ibid., 106–8; Mary Quant, *Quant by Quant* (London: Cassell & Co., 1966), 135.

49. Alexandra Palmer, "Paper Clothes: Not Just a Fad," in Patricia A. Cunningham and Susan Voso Lab (eds), *Dress and Popular Culture* (Bowling Green: Bowling Green State University Popular Press, 1991), 85–104.

50. Peggy Moffitt, *The Rudi Gernreich Book* (Köln: Taschen, 1999), 90.

51. Richard Martin, "Missoni," in *Contemporary Fashion* (Farmington Hills: St. James Press, 1994).

52. Bernadine Morris, "Jogging Suits Are Off and Running in a Race for Style," *New York Times* (March 11, 1979): AD1; Kaori O'Connor, "The Body and the Brand: How Lycra Shaped America," in Regina Lee Blaszczyk (ed.), *Producing Fashion: Commerce, Culture, and Consumers* (Philadelphia: University of Pennsylvania Press, 2008).

53. Marianne Aav (ed.), *Marimekko: Fabrics, Fashion, Architecture* (New Haven and London: Yale University Press, 2003), 241.

54. Roy Reed, "Happy Days for Cotton," *New York Times* (July 9, 1972): F1.

55. Clare Sauro, "Jeans," in Valerie Steele (ed.), *Encyclopedia of Clothing and Fashion* (Detroit: Thompson Gale, 2005), 274.

56. Myra Walker, "Cardin, Pierre," in Valerie Steele (ed.), *Encyclopedia of Clothing and Fashion* (Detroit: Thompson Gale, 2005), 224.

57. Lauren D. Whitley, *Hippie Chic* (Boston: MFA Publications, 2013); Christopher Breward, David Gilbert and Jenny Lister (eds), *Swinging Sixties* (London: Victoria & Albert Museum, 2006).

58. Blaszczyk, "Styling Synthetics," 520–2.

59. Leonard Sloane, "Suiting Up for Leisure," *New York Times* (October 27, 1974): 178.

60. Blaszczyk, "Styling Synthetics"; O'Connor, "The Other Half"; O'Connor, *Lycra*.

61. Moffitt, *The Rudi Gernreich Book*, 20.

62. Herbert Koschetz, "Du Pont Unfurls a New Silklike Fiber," *New York Times* (June 28, 1968): 57; Handley, *Nylon*, 94–6.

63. George Wagner, "Ultrasuede," *Perspecta*, 33 (2002): 90–103; Toray Industries, "The Science of Ultrasuede®," http://www.ultrasuede.com/about/science.html [accessed June 4, 2014].

64. Handley, *Nylon*, 117–20.

65. Ibid.; Jane Schneider, "In and Out of Polyester: Desire, Disdain and Global Fibre Competitions," *Anthropology Today* Vol. 10, No. 4 (August 1994): 2–10.

66. Isadore Barmash, "Manufacturers Warned on Rising Textile Waste," *New York Times* (March 27, 1971): 35.

67. Woolmark Company, "The Woolmark brand celebrates 50 years," (March 26, 2014), http://www.woolmark.com/history [accessed June 5, 2014].

68. Cotton Incorporated. "Cotton Incorporated's History," http://www.cottoninc.com/corporate/About-Cotton-Incorporated/Cotton-Incorporated-company-history/ [accessed June 5, 2014].

69. Seth S. King, "The Restoration of King Cotton," *The New York Times* (March 2, 1980): F1.

70. Steele and Carrara, "Italian Fashion."

71. Handley, *Nylon*.

72. Lisa Birnbach and Jonathan Roberts, Carol McD. Wallace, Mason Wiley, *The Official Preppy Handbook* (New York: Workman Publishing, 1980).

73. *Jane Fonda's Workout Book* 1981; http://www.cbsnews.com/news/jane-fondas-feel-the-burn-workout-video-turns-32/ [accessed February 1, 2015]; O'Connor, "The Body and the Brand," 222–4.

74. Lauren D. Whitley, "Azzedine Alaïa," in P. Parmal, et al., *Fashion Show: Paris Style* (Boston: MFA Publications, 2006), 109.

75. Handley, *Nylon*, 157–8.

76. Ibid., 129–38; Sarah E. Braddock and Marie O'Mahony, *Techno Textiles: Revolutionary Fabrics for Fashion and Design* (New York: Thames & Hudson, 1998), 10–12, 105–9.

77. Handley, *Nylon*, 129.

78. Midori Kitamura (ed.), *Pleats Please Issey Miyake* (Köln: Taschen, 2012).

79. Ibid., 565; Hervé Chandès (ed.), *Issey Miyake Making Things* (Zurich: Scalo, 1999), 4.

80. Braddock and O'Mahony, *Techno Textiles*.

81. Ibid., 12–16.

82. Ibid., 25–7.

83. Sandy Black, *The Sustainable Fashion Handbook* (London: Thames & Hudson, 2013); Kate Fletcher and Lynda Grose, *Fashion and Sustainability: Design for Change* (London: Laurence King Publishing Ltd., 2012).

84. www.Oeko-tex.com [accessed June 7, 2014].

85. http://www.polartec.com/about_us/faq [accessed June 7, 2014].

86. Braddock and O'Mahoney, *Techno Textiles*, 16–19.

2 Production and Distribution

1. Thorstein Veblen, *The Theory of the Leisure Class. An Economic Study of Institutions* (New York: Penguin, 1899 [1994]). Georg Simmel, *Philosophie der Mode* (Berlin: Pan-Verlag, 2005). Gilles Lipovetsky, *L'empire de l'éphémère. La mode et son destin dans les sociétés modernes* (Paris: Gallimard, 1987).

2. Véronique Pouillard, "Fashion for All? The Transatlantic Fashion Business and the development of a popular press culture during the interwar period," *Journalism Studies*, 14 (5) (2013): 716–29.

3. Christopher Breward, David Gilbert (eds), *Fashion's World Cities* (Oxford: Berg, 2006).

4. Kai Raustiala, Christopher Sprigman, "The Piracy Paradox: Innovation and Intellectual Property in Fashion Design," *Virginia Law Review* 92 (1996): 1687–777.

5. Nancy J. Green, *Ready-to-Wear and Ready-to-Work: A Century of Industry and Immigrants in Paris and in New York* (Durham: Duke University Press, 1997).

6. Helen E. Meiklejohn, "Dresses. The Impact of Fashion on a Business," in Walton Hamilton, *Price and Price Policies* (New York: McGraw-Hill, 1938), 308.

7. Green, *Ready-to-Wear and Ready-to-Work*, 41–3.
8. Morris D.C. Crawford, *The Ways of Fashion* (New York: Putnam, 1941), 151.
9. Claudia B. Kidwell, Margaret Christman, *Suiting Everyone. The Democratization of Clothing in America* (Washington: Smithsonian Institution, 1994).
10. Lisa Tiersten, *Marianne in the Market. Envisioning Consumer Society in Fin-de-Siècle France* (Berkeley: University of California Press, 2001).
11. Didier Grumbach, *Histoires de la mode* (Paris: Editions du Regard—Institut Français de la Mode, 1993 [2008]), 434.
12. Pierre Vernus, *Art, Luxe, Industrie. Bianchini-Férier. Un siècle de soieries lyonnaises 1888–1992* (Grenoble: Presses Universitaires de Grenoble, 2006).
13. Crawford, *The Ways of Fashion*, 194.
14. Claude A. Rouzaud, *Un problème d'intérêt national: Les industries du luxe* (Thèse pour le doctorat d'Etat, Strasbourg: Librairie du Recueil Sirey, 1946), 115.
15. Dean Merceron, *Lanvin* (New York: Rizzoli, 2007), 20.
16. Crawford, *The Ways of Fashion*, 218.
17. Rouzaud, *Un problème d'intérêt national*, 115.
18. Véronique Pouillard, "Design Piracy in the Fashion Industries of Paris and New York in the Interwar Years," *Business History Review*, 85(2), (2011): 323.
19. Georges Le Fèvre, *Au secours de la couture (industrie française)* (Paris: Editions Baudinière, 1929), 61–2.
20. Nancy J. Troy, *Couture Culture: A Study in Modern Art and Fashion* (Cambridge: MIT Press, 2002), 22–5.
21. Florence Brachet-Champsaur, "Madeleine Vionnet and the Galeries Lafayette: The unlikely marriage of a Parisian couture house and a French department store, 1922–40," *Business History*, 54 (1), (2012), 48–66; Nancy J. Troy, *Couture Culture*, 42–7.
22. Pamela Golbin, *Vionnet, Puriste de la Mode* (Paris: Les Arts Décoratifs, 2009).
23. Marguerite Coppens, *Mode en Belgique au XIXe siècle* (Brussels: Musées Royaux d'Art et d'Histoire, 1996).
24. Véronique Pouillard, "The Rise of Fashion Forecasting and Fashion PR, 1920–1940. The History of Tobé and Bernays," in Hartmut Berghoff, Thomas Kuehne, *Globalizing Beauty: Consumerism and Body Aesthetics in the 20th Century* (New York: Palgrave, 2013), 151–69.
25. William R. Leach, *Land of Desire: Merchants, Power, and the Rise of a New American Culture* (New York: Vintage, 1994), 311–13; Thierry Maillet, *Histoire de la médiation entre textile et mode en France: des échantillonneurs aux bureaux de style (1825–1975)*, PhD thesis (Paris: EHESS, 2013).
26. Betty Kirke, *Madeleine Vionnet* (San Francisco: Chronicle Books, 1991 [2005]).
27. Mary Lynn Stewart, *Dressing Modern Frenchwomen: Marketing Haute Couture, 1919–1939* (Baltimore: Johns Hopkins University Press, 2008), 111–33.
28. Véronique Pouillard "Design Piracy": 319–44; Scott C. Hemphill, Jeannie Suk, "The Fashion Originators' Guild of America. Self-help at the edge of IP and antitrust," in Rochelle C. Dreyfuss, Jane C. Ginsburg, *Intellectual Property at the Edge: The Contested Contours of IP* (Cambridge, Cambridge University Press, 2014), 159–79.
29. Andrew C. Mertha, *The Politics of Piracy: Intellectual Property in Contemporary China* (Ithaca: Cornell University Press, 2005), 118–63.
30. Annallee Saxenian, *Regional Advantage: Culture and Competition in Silicon Valley and Route 128* (Cambridge MA: Harvard University Press, 1994 [1996]), 1–9.
31. Caroline Rennolds Milbank, *New York Fashion: The Evolution of American Style*, (New York: Harry N. Abrams, 1989); Jessica Daves, *Ready-Made Miracle: The American story of fashion for the millions* (New York: Putnam, 1967), 112–18.
32. Beryl Williams, *Fashion is Our Business* (New York-Philadelphia: Lippincott, 1945), 138.
33. Ibid., 155–70.

34. Crawford, *The Ways of Fashion*, 234–5.
35. Meiklejohn, "Dresses," 312–3; Green, *Ready-to-Wear and Ready-to-Work*.
36. Crawford, *The Ways of Fashion*, 14.
37. Meiklejohn, "Dresses," 314–15.
38. Crawford, *The Ways of Fashion*, 171; Meiklejohn, "Dresses," 343.
39. Saskia Sassen, *The Global City: New York, London, Tokyo* (Princeton: Princeton University Press, 1991), 4.
40. Crawford, *The Ways of Fashion*, 171.
41. Green, *Ready-to-Wear and Ready-to-Work*, 60.
42. Leon Stein, *The Triangle Fire* (Ithaca: Cornell University Press, 1962); David von Drehle, *Triangle: The Fire that Changed America* (New York: Grove Press, 2003); Hasia R. Diner, *Roads Taken. The Great Jewish Migrations to the New World and the Peddlers Who Forged the Way* (New Haven: Yale University Press, 2015), 15–16.
43. Adam Davidson, "Economic recovery, Made in Bangladesh?" *New York Times*, May 14, 2013: MM16.
44. Naomi Klein, *No Logo. Taking Aim at the Brand Bullies* (Toronto-New York: Knopf, 1999); Marie-Emmanuelle Chessel, *Consommateurs engagés à la Belle Epoque. La Ligue sociale d'acheteurs* (Paris: Presses de Sciences Po, 2012), 179–201.
45. European Parliament briefing, Workers' conditions in the textile and clothing sector: just an Asian affair? Issues at stake after the Rana Plaza tragedy, August 2014, http://www.europarl. europa.eu/EPRS/140841REV1-Workers-conditions-in-the-textile-and-clothing-sector-just-an-Asian-affair-FINAL.pdf
46. On the Rana Plaza tragedy, see for example the webpage set up by *The Guardian*: http://www.theguardian.com/world/rana-plaza
47. Robert Ross, *Clothing: A Global History* (Cambridge: Polity Press, 2008).
48. Alexandra Palmer, *Couture & Commerce: The Transatlantic Fashion Trade in the 1950s* (Vancouver: University of British Columbia Press and Royal Ontario Museum, 2001); Mary Lynn Stewart, "Copying and Copyrighting Haute Couture: Democratizing Fashion, 1900–1930," *French Historical Studies*, 28(1), (2005): 103–30.
49. Green, *Ready-to-Wear and Ready-to-Work*, 29.
50. Meiklejohn, "Dresses," 310.
51. Roland Barthes, *Système de la mode* (Paris: Seuil, 1967).
52. Yuniya Kawamura, *Fashion-ology: An Introduction to Fashion Studies* (London: Bloomsbury, 2005).
53. Grumbach, *Histoires de la mode*, 30–1.
54. http://www.modeaparis.com/1/news/article/membres-invites-janvier-2015?archive=1 [accessed March 4, 2015].
55. *Lilly Daché, Glamour at the Drop of a Hat* (New York: The Museum at FIT, 2007).
56. Daves, *Ready-Made Miracle*, 112–18.
57. New York Public Library, Fashion Group International Archives, 73, Meeting, New York, January 26, 1928: 11–12; Caroline Rennolds Milbank, *Couture: The Great Designers* (New York: Stuart, Tabori, and Chang, 1989).
58. Valerie Wingfield, *The Fashion Group International, Records c. 1930–1997* (New York: New York Public Library, 1997), 4–5.
59. Ibid., 9.
60. Dominique Veillon, *La mode sous l'occupation. Débrouillardise et coquetterie dans la France en guerre (1939–1945)*, (Paris: Payot, 1990); Irene Guenther, *Nazi Chic?: Fashioning Women in the Third Reich* (New York: Berg, 2004); Eugenia Paulicelli, *Fashion under Fascism: Beyond the Black Shirt* (New York: Berg, 2004).
61. Veillon, *La mode sous l'occupation*, p. 229.
62. Guenther, *Nazi Chic*; Paulicelli, *Fashion under Fascism*.
63. Crawford, *The Ways of Fashion*, 30.

64. Solange Montagné-Villette, *Le Sentier, un espace ambigu* (Paris: Masson, 1990).
65. Lourdes Font, "Dior before Dior," *West 86th: A Journal of Decorative Arts, Design History, and Material Culture*, 18, 1 (2011): 26–49.
66. Alexandra Palmer, *Dior* (London: Victoria & Albert Museum Publishing, 2009), 32.
67. Claire Wilcox (ed.), *The Golden Age of Couture: Paris and London 1947–57* (London: Victoria & Albert Museum, 2009), 122–7.
68. Palmer, *Dior*, 76–98.
69. Wilcox, *The Golden Age of Couture*, 102–6.
70. Florence Brachet-Champsaur, "Un grand magasin à la pointe de la mode: les Galeries Lafayette," in Michèle Ruffat, Dominique Veillon, *La mode des sixties, l'entrée dans la modernité* (Paris: Autrement, 2007), 174–9.
71. Sophie Chapdelaine de Montvalon, *Le beau pour tous* (Paris: L'Iconoclaste, 2010); Maillet, *Histoire de la médiation entre textile et mode en France*.
72. Shoshana-Rose Marzel, "De quelques Success Stories dans la creation vestimentaire parisienne des années 60," *Archives juives*, 2, 39 (2006): 72–84.
73. Wilcox, *The Golden Age of Couture*, 122–3.
74. Tomoko Okawa, "Licensing Practices at Maison Dior," in Regina L. Blaczszyk (ed.). *Producing Fashion. Commerce, Culture, and Consumers* (Philadelphia: University of Pennsylvania Press, 2007), 88–102.
75. Elisabetta Merlo, Francesca Polese, "Turning Fashion into Business: the emergence of Milan as an international hub," *Business History Review*, 80 (3) (2006): 415–47.
76. Lou Taylor, "L'English Style: les origines de la mode en Grande-Bretagne de 1950 aux années 1970," Ruffat, Veillon, *La mode des sixties*, 27–30.
77. Green, *Ready-to-Wear and Ready-to-Work*, 37–39.
78. Mary Quant, *Quant by Quant. The Autobiography of Mary Quant* (London: Victoria & Albert Publications, [1965] 2012), 67.
79. Marnie Fogg, *Boutique: A 60s Cultural Phenomenon* (London: Mitchell Beazley, 2003), 21–2.
80. Barry Eichengreen, *The European Economy Since 1945. Coordinated Capitalism and Beyond* (Princeton: Princeton University Press, 2007), 129–30.
81. Djurdja Bartlett, *Fashion East: The Spectre that Haunted Socialism* (Cambridge MA: MIT Press, 2010); Larisa Zakharova, *S'habiller à la soviétique. La mode et le dégel en URSS* (Paris: CNRS, 2011).
82. Olga Klymenko, "Fashion Week(s) in Kyiv—The Attempt to create Fashion Industry in Post-Soviet Ukraine," paper presented at Fashioning the City Conference, Royal College of Art, London, 2012.
83. Sabine Chrétien-Ichikawa, *La réémergence de la mode en Chine et le rôle du Japon*. PhD thesis (Paris: EHESS, 2012).
84. Yuniya Kawamura, *The Japanese Revolution in Paris Fashion* (Oxford: Berg, 2004).
85. Barbara Vinken, *Fashion Zeitgeist: Trends and Cycles in the Fashion System* (New York: Berg, 2005), 139–51.
86. Olivier Saillard (ed.), *Fashion Mix. Mode d'ici. Créateurs d'ailleurs* (Paris: Flammarion, 2014).
87. Roy Y.J. Chua, Robert G. Eccles, *Managing Creativity at Shanghai Tang*, Harvard Business School Case 410-018 (2009); Chrétien-Ichikawa, *La réémergence de la mode en Chine et le rôle du Japon*.
88. Simona Segre Reinach, "China and Italy: Fast Fashion versus Prêt- à -Porter. Towards a New Culture of Fashion," *Fashion Theory: The Journal of Dress, Body and Culture* 9 (1) (2005), 43–56.
89. Klein, *No Logo*.
90. Liesbeth Sluiter, *Clean Clothes: A Global Movement to End Sweatshops* (London: Pluto Press, 2009); Lucy Siegel, *To Die For: Is Fashion Wearing out the World?* (London: Harper Collins, 2011).

91. Djurdja Bartlett, Shaun Cole, Agnès Rocamora (eds), *Fashion Media: Past and Present* (London: Bloomsbury, 2013).

3 The Body

1. Adam Geczy and Vicki Karaminas, *Queer Style* (London: Bloomsbury, 2013).
2. Paul Poiret, *En habillant l'époque* (Paris: Grasset, 1930), 64.
3. Adam Geczy, *Fashion and Orientalism* (London: Bloomsbury, 2012).
4. Valerie Steele, *Fashion and Eroticism* (Oxford and New York: Oxford University Press, 1985), 232–3.
5. Geczy, *Fashion and Orientalism*, ch. 4 and passim.
6. Cit. Amy Homan Edelman, *The Little Black Dress* (New York: Simon and Schuster 1997), 15. See also Caroline Evans, *The Mechanical Smile: Modernism and the First Fashion Shows in France and America, 1900–1929* (New Haven and London: Yale University Press, 2013); Emanuelle Polle, Francis Hammond, and Alexandra Keens, *Patou: A Fashionable Life* (Paris: Fammarion, 2013); and Meredith Etherington-Smith, *Patou* (London: St Martin's Press, 1983).
7. Barbara Burman, "Better and Brighter Clothes, The Men's Dress Reform Party, 1929–1940," *Journal of Design History*, vol. 8, no. 4 (1995): 275–90.
8. Patricia Campbell Warner, "The Americanisation of Fashion: Sportwear, the Movies and the 1930s," in Linda Welters and Patricia Cunningham (eds), *Twentieth Century American Fashion* (London: Bloomsbury, 2005), 79.
9. Ibid., 79–98.
10. Ibid., 79–80.
11. See Emily Mayhew, *Wounded: A New History of the Western Front in World War I* (Oxford: Oxford University Press, 2013).
12. Mario Lupano and Alessandra Vacari, *Fashion at the Time of Fascism* (Rome: Damiani, 2009), 156.
13. Elizabeth Bosch, cited in Irene Guenther, *Nazi Chic? Fashioning Women in the Third Reich*, (Oxford: Berg, 2004), 100.
14. Khasana advertisement, cited in ibid., 104.
15. Richard Gray, *About Face: German Physiognomic Thought from Lavatar to Auschwitz* (Detroit: Wayne State University, 2004).
16. Allison Nella Ferrara, "Fashion's Forgotten Fascists." VICE, April 8, 2015, http://www.vice.com/read/fashions-forgotten-fascists [accessed November 18, 2014]; http://www.vice.com/read/fashions-forgotten-fascists [accessed March 20, 2015].
17. Eugenia Paulicelli, *Fashion Under Fascism: Beyond the Black Shirt* (London: Berg, 2004), 14.
18. Katie Milestone and Anneke Meyer, *Gender and Popular Culture* (London: Polity Press, 2011).
19. Marianne Thesander, *The Feminine Ideal* (London: Reaktion, 1997), 135.
20. Joseph Hancock II and Vicki Karaminas, "The Joy of Pecs. Representations of Masculinity in Fashion Advertising," *Clothing Cultures* (Bristol: Intellect, 2014).
21. Hugh Hefner, cited by Steven Cohan (1996) "So Functional for its Purposes: Rock Hudson's Bachelor Apartment in *Pillow Talk*," in Joel Sanders (ed.), *Stud. Architectures of Masculinity* (New York: Princeton University Press, 1996), 30.
22. Ibid., 29.
23. Jessica Sewell, "Performing Masculinity Through Objects in Postwar America. The Playboy's Pipe," in Anna Moran and Sorcha O'Brian (eds), *Love Objects. Emotion, Design and Material Culture* (London: Bloomsbury 2014), 64.
24. Ray Ferris and Julian Lord, *Teddy Boys: A Concise History* (London: Milo, 2012).
25. Joseph H. Hancock II, "Chelsea on 5th Avenue: Hypermasculinity and Gay Clone Culture in the Retail Brand Practices of Abercrombie and Fitch," *Fashion Practice* 1, vol. 1 (May, 2009): 75.

26. Ibid., 78.
27. Guy Snaith, "Tom's Men: The Masculinization of Homosexuality and the Homosexualization of Masculinity at the end of the Twentieth Century," *Paragraph* 26 (2203): 77.
28. Ibid., 78.
29. Interview with Paul Mathiesen, lighting designer, July 26, 2015.
30. Marc Stern, *The Fitness Movement and Fitness Centre Industry 1960–2000*, Business History Conference 2008, 5–6, http://www.thebhc.org/publications/BEHonline/2008/stern.pdf [accessed February 20, 2014].
31. See also Kiku Adatto, *Picture Perfect: Life in the Age of the Photo Op* (Princeton: Princeton University Press, 2008), passim.
32. Pamela Church Gibson and Vicki Karaminas, Letter from the Editors, *Fashion Theory: The Journal of Dress, Body and Culture, Special Issue, Fashion and Porn*, 18.2 (April 2014): 118.
33. Ibid., 119
34. See Ariel Levy, *Female Chauvinist Pigs: The Rise of Raunch Culture* (London: Free Press, 2006).
35. Annette Lynch, *Porn Chic. Exploring the Contours of Raunch Eroticism* (London: Berg, 2012), 3.
36. Pamela Church Gibson, "Pornostyle: Sexualized Dress and the Fracturing of Feminism," in *Fashion Theory: The Journal of Dress, Body and Culture, Special Issue, Fashion and Porn*, 18.2 (April 2014): 189–90.
37. Meredith Jones, *Skintight: An Anatomy of Cosmetic Surgery* (London: Berg, 2008), 1.
38. See also Adam Geczy, "Straight Internet Porn and the Natrificial: Body and Dress," *Fashion Theory: The Journal of Dress, Body and Culture, Special Issue, Fashion and Porn*, 18.2 (April, 2014): 169–88.
39. Casey Legler, *"I am a Woman Who Models Male Clothes. This is not about Gender,"* The *Guardian*, Friday November 1, 2013, http://www.theguardian.com/commentisfree/2013/nov/01/woman-models-mens-clothes-casey-legler [accessed March 21, 2015].
40. Julia Twigg, *Fashion and Age* (London: Bloomsbury, 2013), 1.

4 Belief

1. Paul Gwynne, *World Religions in Practice: A Comparative Introduction* (Oxford: Blackwell Publishers, 2008), 257–8.
2. Marnia Lazreg, *Questioning the Veil: Open Letters to Muslim Women* (Princeton, N.J.: Princeton University Press, 2011), 67.
3. Dounia Bouzar, *Laïcité, mode d'emploi: Cadre légal et solutions pratiques, 42 études de cas* (Paris: Eyrolles, 2010), 175; Ahmet Kuru, *Secularism and State Policies towards Religion: The United States, France and Turkey* (New York: Cambridge University Press, 2009), 13.
4. Susan Palmer and David G. Bromley, "Deliberate Heresies: New Religious Myths and Rituals as Critiques," in David G. Bromlet (ed.), *Teaching New Religious Movements* (New York: Oxford University Press, 2007), 135–58.
5. "What is a Cult?" May 29, 2009, www.theguardian.com [accessed March 1, 2015].
6. Warren Lewis, "Coming Again: How Society Functions through its Religions," in Eileen Barker (ed.), *New Religious Movements: A Perspective for Understanding Society* (Lewiston, N.J.: Edwin Mellen, 1982), 191.
7. Michael Ashcraft, *The Dawn of the New Cycle: Point Loma Theosophists and American Culture* (Knoxville: University of Tennessee Press, 2002).
8. R.S. Ellwood, *Religious and Spiritual Groups in North America* (Englewood Cliffs: Prentice Hall, 1979).
9. Ashcraft, *The Dawn of the New Cycle*.
10. Barry Chevannes, *Rasafari: Roots and Ideoloy* (Syracuse: Syracuse University Press, 1994).
11. Thomas Carlyle, *Sartur Resartus: On Heroes, Hero Worship and the Heroic in History* (London: J.M. Dent, 1908), 45.

12. David L. Kertzer, "Ritual, Politics and Power," in Ronald Grimes (ed.), *Readings in Ritual Studies* (New Jersey: Prentice Gall, 1996), 337

13. Harold L. Nieburg, *Culture Storm: Politics and the Ritual Order* (New York: St. Martin's Press, 1973), 54.

14. See Susan J. Palmer, *The New Heretics of France: Minority Religions, la Republique, and the Government-Sponsored "War on Sects"* (New York: Oxford University Press, 2011).

15. See the Aumiste pamphlet: *Aumisme Religion Universelle de 'Unite des Visages de Dieu'* (n.d.)

16. Palmer, *The New Heretics of France.*

17. Susan J. Palmer, *The Nuwaubian Nation: Black Spirituality and State Control,* (Farnham: Ashgate Publishing, 2010).

18. www.yahwehbenyahweh.com/pdf/. . ./coming_in_the_clouds_pt4.pdf

19. Leon Festinger, Henry Riecken, and Stanely Schachter, *When Prophecy Fails: A Social and Psychological Study of a Modern Group That Predicted the Destruction of the World* (Minneapolis : University of Minnesota Press, 1956), 44.

20. Max Weber, *Theory of Social and Economic Organization* (Glencoe: Free Press, 1947), 331–2.

21. Diana Tumminia, *When Prophecy Never Fails: Myth and Reality in a Flying-Saucer Group* (New York: Oxford University Press, 2005).

22. Ibid., 178

23. Ibid., 179.

24. K. George Kirkpatrick, Diana Tumminia, "Unarius: Emergent Aspects of an American Flying Saucer Group," in James R. Lewis, *The Gods Have Landed: New Religions from Other Worlds* (New York: SUNY Press, 1995), 97.

25. Marie-Paule Giguère and Jeanne d'Arc Demers, *Vie d'Amour*, 2nd ed., 15 vols. Vol. 1, Vie d'Amour (Québec: Limoilou, 2004), 326.

26. Marc Bosquart, *De La Trinité Divine À L'Immaculée-Trinité* (Quebec: Limoilou, 1985).

27. Canadian Conference of Catholic Bishops, *Doctrinal Note of the Catholic Bishops of Canada Concerning the Army of Mary*, 1999: 4.

28. John Thavis, "Vatican Excommunicates Some Members of Canadian Sect," *Catholic News Service*, 2007: 6.

29. Sylvie Payeur Raynauld, "Cinq Robes Demandées Par Le Ciel," *Le Royaume*, May–June (2007): 12–13.

30. Giguère and Demers, *Vie d'Amour,* 73.

31. Robert A. Orsi, *Thank You, St. Jude: Women's Devotion to the Patron Saint of Hopeless Causes* (New Haven: Yale University Press, 1996).

32. Payeur Raynauld, "Cinq Robes Demandées Par Le Ciel": 12.

33. Paul L. Gareau, "Unveiling the Army of Mary: A Gendered Analysis of a Conservative Catholic Marian Devotional Organization," MA dissertation (Montreal: Concordia University, 2009).

34. Payeur Raynauld, "Cinq Robes Demandées Par Le Ciel": 12.

35. Raoul Auclair, *The Lady of All Peoples* (Quebec: Limoilou, 1982).

36. Gareau, "Unveiling the Army of Mary": 101–37.

37. Weber, *Max Weber: The Theory of Social and Economic Organization*, 152–64.

38. B.A. Robinson, "Jain Dharma" Ontario Consultants on Religious Tolerance, 2005. www.religioustolerance.org /jainism.htm [accessed October 28, 2014].

39. Rick Johnson, "Ritual Nudity or Skyclad," Amethyst's Wicca Website, www.angelfire.com/realm2/amethystbt/ skyclad2.html [accessed September 1, 2006]

40. J.P. Zubek and P.A. Solberg, *Doukhobors at War* (Toronto: The Ryerson Press, 1952).

41. Ibid., 65.

42. Ibid., 62.

43. Ibid., 68.

44. Ibid., 68.

45. Simma Holt, *Terror in the Name of God: The Story of the Sons of Freedom Doukhobors* (Toronto: McClelland & Stewart, 1964).

46. George Woodcock and Ivan Avakumovic, *The Doukhobors* (London: Faber & Faber, 1977).

47. Susan J. Palmer, *Aliens Adored: Raël's UFO Religion* (New Jersey: Rutgers University Press, 2004).

48. Raël, *Les extraterrestres m'ont emmené sur leur planète* (Branatome: l'Editions du Message. 1977), 12.

49. Raël, *Le livre qui dit la Vérité* (Clermont Ferrand: Les Editions du Message, 1974).

50. Raël, *Yes to Human Cloning* (Florida: Raëlian Foundation, 2001).

51. *Contact* no. 348, 25 April 1962, A.H.

52. "Free Your Breasts, Free your Mind," http://www.demotix.com/news/127402/free-your-breasts-free-your-mind, August 23, 2009 [accessed November 4, 2014].

53. "Babes Take Age-Old Prejudice off their Chests," *India Today*, http://indiatoday.intoday.in/story/Babes+take+age-+old+prejudice+off+their+chests/1/58333.html [November 16, 2014].

54. "Group denied permit to march topless," http://www.thestar.com/news/gta/2011/08/25/group_denied_permit_to_march_topless.html, August 25, 2011 [accessed November 16, 2014].

55. Susan J. Palmer, "Raël's Angels: The First Five Years of a Secret Order," in Henrik Bogdan and James R. Lewis (eds), *Sexuality and New Religious Movements* (New York: Palgrave Macmillan, 2014), 201.

56. Rosemary Reuther, *Sexism and God Talk: Toward a Feminist Theology* (Boston: Beacon Press, 1993).

57. Palmer, "Raëls Angels," 202.

58. Victor W. Turner, *The Ritual Process: Structure and Anti-Structure* (Chicago: University of Chicago, 1969).

59. Ibid., 95.

60. Ibid., 95.

61. Ibid., 96.

62. Rick Johnson, "Ritual Nudity or Skyclad," www.angelfire.com/realm2/amethystbt/ skyclad2.html [accessed January 1, 2006].

63. Dale C. Allison, *Jesus of Nazareth: Millenarian Prophet* (Augsburg Fortress: Fortress Press 1998), 34.

64. Frank E. Manuel, "Toward a Psychological History of Utopia," in Frank E. Manuel (ed.), *Utopias and Utopian Though* (Boston: Beacon Press, 1967), 70.

5 Gender and Sexuality

1. Joe Lucchesi, "'The Dandy in Me': Romaine Brooks's 1923 Portraits," in Susan Fillin-Yeh (ed.), *Dandies. Fashion and Finesse in Art and Culture* (New York and London: New York University Press, 2001), 13.

2. Judith Butler, *Gender Trouble. Feminism and the Subversion of Identity* (New York and London: Routledge, 1990), 187.

3. Annamari Vänskä, "New kids on the mall: Babyfied dogs as fashionable co-consumers," *Young Consumers,* vol. 15, iss. 3 (2014): 263–72.

4. Clare Rose, *Making, Selling and Wearing Boys' Clothes in Late-Victorian England* (Farnham: Ashgate, 2010), 158.

5. Annamari Vänskä, *Fashioning Childhood. Children in fashion advertising* (London and New York: Bloomsbury, forthcoming).

6. Liz Conor, *The Spectacular Modern Woman: Feminine Visibility in the 1920s* (Bloomington & Indianapolis: Indiana University Press, 2004), 209–52.

7. Elizabeth Ewing, *History of 20th Century Fashion* (London: Batsford, 2008), 62.

8. Phyllis G. Tortora and Sara B. Marcketti, *Survey of Historic Costume* (New York & London: Fairchild Books, Bloomsbury, 2015), 449.

9. Christopher Breward, *The Culture of Fashion* (Manchester: Manchester University Press, 1995), 185.

10. Rhonda Garelic, "The Layered Look: Coco Chanel and Contagious Celebrity," in Fillin-Yeh, Susan (ed.), *Dandies: Fashion and Finesse in Art and Culture* (New York: New York University Press, 2001), 41–3.

11. Brenda Polan and Reger Tredre, *The Great Fashion Designers* (Oxford, New York: Berg Publishers, 2009), 44–5.

12. Steven Zdatny, "The Boyish Look and the Liberated Woman: The Politics and Aesthetics of Women's Hairstyles," *Fashion Theory: The Journal of Dress, Body and Culture*, vol. 1, no. 4 (1997): 367–98.

13. Farid Chenoune, *A History of Men's Fashion,* trans. Deke Dusinberre (Paris, New York: Flammarion, 1995), 143.

14. Andrew Bolton, *Bravehearts: Men in Skirts* (London: Victoria & Albert Museum, 2004).

15. Chenoune, *A History of Men's Fashion*, 163.

16. Valerie Steele, *Fashion and Eroticism: Ideals of Feminine Beauty from the Victorian Era to the Jazz Age* (New York: Oxford University Press, 1985), 146. Suffragettes wore trousers since Amelia Bloomer introduced the "bloomer costume," an ensemble of the knee-length dress over full trousers.

17. Joanne Entwistle, *The Fashioned Body: Fashion, Dress and Modern Social Theory* (Cambridge: Polity Press, 2000), 168.

18. Annamari Vänskä, "See-through Closet: Female Androgyny in the 1990s Fashion Images, the Concepts of 'Modern Woman' and 'Lesbian Chic'," in *Farväl heteronormativitet. Papers presented at the conference Farewell to heteronormativity.* Vol. 1. Sverige: Lambda Nordica Förlag; 2003: 71–82; Adam Geczy and Vicki Karaminas, *Queer Style* (London: Bloomsbury, 2013), 24–32.

19. Shaun Cole, *"Don We Now Our Gay Apparel": Gay Men's Dress in the Twentieth Century* (Oxford: Berg, 2000). However, cross-dressing was not (yet) an everyday routine because of its illegality. Cross-dressing also relates to class: while upper class women could cross-dress, lower class women only wore mannish clothes in private (Geczy and Karaminas, *Queer Style*, 29).

20. Radu Stern, *Against Fashion: Clothing as Art, 1850-1930* (Massachusetts: Massachusetts Institute of Technology, 2004), 29–62.

21. Chenoune, *A History of Men's Fashion*, 175; see also Ewing, *History of 20th Century Fashion*, 123–5.

22. Breward, *The Culture of Fashion,* 187; Chenoune, *A History of Men's Fashion*, 174.

23. "Female masculinity" is a concept introduced by Judith Halberstam, *Female Masculinity* (Duke University Press: Durham and London, 1998). It defines masculinity constructed by women.

24. Polan and Tredre, *The Great Fashion Designers*, 52, suggest that since Schiaparelli enjoyed shocking the bourgeois she was "thoroughly Punk in spirit."

25. Drake Stutesman, "Costume Design, or, what is fashion in film?" in Adrienne Munich (ed.), *Fashion in Film* (Indiana: Indiana University Press, 2011).

26. Sara B. Marcketti and Emily Angstman, "The Trend for Mannish Suits in the 1930," *Dress,* vol. 39, iss. 2, 135–52 (2013): 7.

27. Ibid., 8.

28. Tortora and Marcketti, *Survey of Historic Costume,* 464.

29. Marcketti and Angstman, "The Trend for Mannish Suits in the 1930": 14.

30. This mainly applied to upper and middle class lesbians (Geczy and Karaminas, *Queer Style*, 29).

31. Alexandra Palmer, *Couture & Commerce: The Transatlantic Fashion Trade in the 1950s* (Vancouver: University of British Columbia, 2001); Ewing, *History of 20th Century Fashion,* 155–60.

32. Alexandra Palmer, "Inside Paris haute couture," in Claire Wilcox (ed.), *The Golden Age of Couture: Paris and London, 1947–1957* (London: Victoria & Albert Publications, 2007); Ewing, *History of 20th Century Fashion,* 139–54.

33. Polan and Tredre, *The Great Fashion Designers*, 83.

34. Christian Dior, *Christian Dior et moi* (Paris: Vuibert, [1956] 2011), 35.

35. Simone de Beauvoir, *The Second Sex*, trans. and ed. H.M. Parshley, (London: Jonathan Cape [1949] 1972), 273.

36. See also, Valerie Steele, "A Queer History of Fashion: From the Closet to the Catwalk," in Steele, Valerie (ed.), *A Queer History of Fashion: From the Closet to the Catwalk* (New Haven and London: Yale University Press, 2013), 37–8.

37. Rémy G. Saisselin, "From Baudelaire to Christian Dior: The Poetics of Fashion," *The Journal of Aesthetics and Art Criticism*, vol. 18, no. 1 (1959): 112.

38. Even though female impersonators had a role to increase the morale of the troops during wars, it was increasingly associated with homosexuality (S.P. Schacht and L. Underwood, "The Absolutely Fabulous but Flawlessly Customary World of Drag Queens and Female Impersonators," *Journal of Homosexuality* 46, no. 3/4 2004, 1–17: 5).

39. Cole, *"Don We Now Our Gay Apparel."*

40. Ibid.

41. See Roland Barthes, *The Language of Fashion* (Oxford: Berg 2006), 60–4.

42. Cole, *"Don We Now Our Gay Apparel."*

43. Richard Sennett, *The Fall of Public Man* (London: Faber & Faber, 1992), 152–3.

44. Roland Barthes, *The Fashion System*, trans. M. Ward, R. Howard (Berkeley: University of California Press, [1967] 1990).

45. Sue-Ellen Case, "Toward a Butch-Femme Aesthetic," in Fabio Cleto (ed.), *Camp: Queer Aesthetics and the Performing Subject. A Reader* (Edinburgh: Edinburgh University Press, [1988] 1999), 186.

46. Tortora & Marcketti, *Survey of Historic Costume*, 494.

47. See Thorstein Veblen, *The Theory of the Leisure Class* (Oxford and New York: Oxford University Press, [1899] 2009).

48. Becky Conekin, "Fashioning the Playboy: Messages of Style and Masculinity in the Pages of *Playboy* Magazine, 1953–1963," *Fashion Theory*, vol. 4, iss. 4(2000): 449.

49. Ibid., 453–4.

50. Ibid., 462.

51. Stutesman, "Costume Design."

52. Ibid., in reality, Brando's outfit was made to look stained and greasy.

53. Tortora & Marcketti, *Survey of Historic Costume*, 499.

54. Ted Polhemus, *Streetstyle: From Sidewalk to Catwalk* (London: Thames & Hudson, 1994).

55. Chenoune, *A History of Men's Fashion*, 239.

56. Women's Liberation Movement advocated women's rights but was largely against fashion (e.g. Naomi Wolf, *The Beauty Myth* (London: Vintage, 1990). This is symbolized in the myth of "bra-burning."

57. Annamari Vänskä, "From Marginality to Mainstream: On the Politics of Lesbian Visibility During the Past Decades," in M. McAuliffe and S. Tiernan (ed.), *Sapphists, Sexologists and Sexualities: Lesbian Histories*, vol. 2, (Cambridge: Cambridge Scholars Press, 2009), 227–35.

58. James Darsey, "From 'gay is good' to the scourge of AIDS: The evolution of gay liberation rhetoric, 1977–1990," *Communication Studies* 42, no. 1 (1991): 43–66.

59. Ewing, *History of 20th Century Fashion*, 200.

60. Angela McRobbie and Jenny Garber, "Girls and subcultures," in Stuart Hall and Tony Jefferson (eds), *Resistance Through Rituals* (New York: Routledge, [1993] 2006), 182; Schacht & Underwood, "The Absolutely Fabulous": 103.

61. They also differentiated themselves from the outspokenly white rocker- and teddy-culture and identified with black culture and its musical heritage of jazz and soul (Dick Hebdige, "The Meaning of Mod," in *Resistance Through Rituals*, 72).

62. Chenoune, *A History of Men's Fashion*, 254.

63. Ewing 2008: 178, 180. However, Quant has denied creating the mini skirt (Schacht & Underwood 2004: 103.)

64. Patricia Juliana Smith, "'You don't have to say you love me.' The Camp Masquerades of Dusty Springfield," in *The Queer Sixties*, ed. P. J. Smith, New York and London: Routledge, 1999), 105.

65. Ibid., 112–13.

66. Valerie Steele, "Anti-Fashion: The 1970s," *Fashion Theory* 1, no. 3 (1997): 280.

67. Jon Savage, "Oh! You Pretty Things," in *David Bowie Is* (London: Victoria & Albert Publishing, 2013), 108.

68. Cole, *"Don We Now Our Gay Apparel."*

69. Malcolm Barnard, *Fashion as Communication* (London and New York: Routledge, 1996), 44–5.

70. Dick Hebdige, *Subculture: The Meaning of Style* (London: Routledge, 1979).

71. Barbara Vinken, *Fashion Zeitgeist: Trends and Cycles in the fashion System* (Oxford: Berg, 2005), 64.

72. Frank Mort, *Cultures of Consumption: Masculinities and Social Space in Late Twentieth-Century Britain* (London: Routledge, 1996); Sean Nixon, *Hard Looks: Masculinities, Spectatorship and Contemporary Consumption* (London: University College London Press, 1996).

73. Martin P. Levine and Michael Kimmel, *Gay Macho: The Life and Death of the Homosexual Clone* (New York: New York University Press, 1998).

74. Holly Devor, *Gender Blending: Confronting the Limits of Duality* (Bloomington and Indianapolis: Indiana University Press, 2011). Rebecca Jennings, *A Lesbian History of Britain: Love and Sex Between Women Since 1500* (Oxford and Westport: Greenwood World Publishing, 2007), 187.

75. Karen Bettez Halnon, "Poor Chic: The Rational Consumption of Poverty," *Current Sociology*, Vol. 50(4) (2002): 501–16.

76. Yuniya Kawamura, *Fashion-ology. An Introduction to Fashion Studies* (Oxford: Berg, 2005).

77. Agnès Rocamora, "How New Are New Media? The Case of Fashion Blogs," in Djurdja Bartlett, Shaun Cole, and Agnès Rocamora (eds), *Fashion Media: Past and Present* (London: Bloomsbury, 2013), 155–64.

78. Katherine Sender, *Business, Not Politics. The Making of the Gay Market* (New York, Chichester, West Sussex: Columbia University Press, 2004.

79. Teresa De Lauretis, "'Queer Theory': Lesbian and gay sexualities," *Differences: a journal of feminist cultural studies*, Vol. 3(2) (1991): iii–xviii; Butler, *Gender Trouble*.

80. Butler, *Gender Trouble*.

81. Halberstam, *Female Masculinity*.

82. Annamari Vänskä, "Why Are There No Lesbian Advertisements?" *Feminist Theory*, 6(1) (2005), 67–85.

83. See for example Annamari Vänskä, "Seducing children?" *lambda nordica* 2-3/2011: 69–109.

84. Vänskä, "See-through Closet".

85. *Metrosexual* was first coined by Mark Simpson in 1994. It defines men who are interested in fashion and lifestyle stereotypically associated with homosexual men but who are claimed to be heterosexual. Mark Simpson, "Here Come the Mirror Men: Why The Future is Metrosexual," *The Independent*, 15 November 1994.

86. Sender, "Business, Not Politics," in Amy Gluckman and Betsy Reed (eds.), *Homo Economics. Capitalism, Community, and Lesbian and Gay Lives* (New York and London: Routledge, 1997).

87. Entwistle, *The Fashioned Body*.

88. Pamela Church Gibson, *Fashion and Celebrity Culture* (London and New York: Berg, 2012).

89. Stella Bruzzi and Pamela Church Gibson, "Fashion is the fifth character," in Kim Akass and Janet McCabe (eds), *Reading Sex and the City* (London: I.B. Tauris & Co., 2008), 115–29.

90. Anna König, "Sex and the City: A fashion editor's dream?" in ibid.: 140.

91. Vänskä, *Fashioning Childhood*.

92. Vänskä, "New kids on the mall:" 263–72.

6 Status

1. Roland Barthes, *The Language of Fashion* (Oxford: Berg, 2006).
2. Fred Davis, "Of Maids' Uniforms and Blue Jeans: The Drama of Status Ambivalences in Clothing and Fashion," *Qualitative Sociology* 12 (4) (1989): 349.
3. Elizabeth Wilson, *Adorned in Dreams: Fashion in Modernity* (London: Virago, 1985), 12.
4. Paul Fussell, *Class: Style and Status in the USA* (London: Arrow, 1984); David Cannadine, *Class in Britain* (New Haven: Yale University Press, 1998).
5. Patrizia Calefato, *The Clothed Body* (Oxford, Berg 2004), 1.
6. Georg Simmel, "Fashion," *International Quarterly* 10 (1) (1904): 133
7. Ibid., 130–55.
8. Ibid., 133.
9. Joanne Entwistle and Agnes Rocamora, "The Field of Fashion Materialized: A Study of London Fashion Week," *Sociology* 40 (4) (2004): 735–51.
10. Joanne Entwistle, *The Aesthetic Economy of Fashion: Markets and Value in Clothing and Modelling* (London: Bloomsbury, 2009).
11. Mike Featherstone, "The Body in Consumer Culture," in Mike Featherstone et al. (eds), *The Body: Social Process and Cultural Theory* (London: Sage, 1991).
12. Diana Crane, *Fashion and its Social Agendas: Class, Gender, and Identity in Clothing* (Chicago: University of Chicago Press, 2000).
13. Ibid., 3.
14. Alison Lurie, *The Language of Clothes* (London: Random House, 1981), 115.
15. Gilles Lipovetsky, *The Empire of Fashion: Dressing Modern Democracy*, (Princeton: Princeton University Press, 1994), 29.
16. Philip Coelho and James McClure, "Toward an Economic Theory of Fashion," *Economic Inquiry* 31 (4) (1993): 595–608.
17. Crane, *Fashion and its Social Agendas*, 4.
18. Ruth Barnes and Joanne Eicher, *Dress and Gender: Making and Meaning* (Oxford: Berg, 1992).
19. Nancy F. Cott, *The Grounding of Modern Feminism* (New Haven: Yale University Press, 1987), 12.
20. Betty Friedan, *The Feminine Mystique* (London: Penguin, 1963); Andrea Dworkin, *Pornography: Men Possessing Women* (New York: G.P. Putnam's Sons, 1981), 126.
21. Elizabeth Wilson, *Adorned in Dreams*; Caroline Evans and Minna Thornton, "Fashion, Representation, Femininity," *Feminist Review* 38 (1991): 48–66.
22. Cheryl Buckley and Hilary Fawcett, *Fashioning the Feminine: Representation and Women's Fashion from the Fin de Siècle to the Present* (London: I.B. Tauris, 2002), 11.
23. Rosemary Betterton, *Looking On: Images of Femininity in the Visual Arts and Media* (London: Pandora, 1987).
24. Joanne Entwistle, *The Fashioned Body* (Cambridge: Polity, 2000).
25. Farid Chenoune, *A History of Men's Fashion* (Paris: Flammarion, 1993); Jennifer Craik, *The Face of Fashion: Cultural Studies in Fashion* (London: Routledge, 1994); Christopher Breward, *The Hidden Consumer: Masculinities, Fashion and City Life 1860–1914* (Manchester: Manchester University Press, 1999); David Kuchta, *The Three-Piece Suit and Modern Masculinity: England, 1550–1850* (London: University of California Press, 2002).
26. John Carl Flügel, *The Psychology of Clothes* (London: Hogarth Press, 1930), 113.
27. Chenoune, *A History of Men's Fashion*.
28. John Harvey, *Men in Black* (London: Reaktion, 1997).
29. Breward, *The Hidden Consumer*.
30. Kuchta, *The Three-Piece Suit and Modern Masculinity*, 164.
31. Lipovetsky, *The Empire of Fashion*.
32. Christopher Breward, *Fashion* (Oxford: Oxford University Press, 2003), 53.
33. Clare Rose, *Making, Selling and Wearing Boys' Clothes in Late-Victorian England* (Farnham: Ashgate, 2010), 211

34. Ibid., 228.
35. Jane Pilcher, "No logo? Children's consumption of fashion," *Childhood* 18 (1) (2010): 128–41.
36. Crane, *Fashion and its Social Agendas*, 83–4.
37. Ibid., 84.
38. Christobel Williams-Mitchell, *Dressed for the Job: Story of Occupational Costume* (London: Blandford Press, 1982), 103.
39. Jennifer Craik, *Uniforms Exposed* (Oxford: Berg, 2005).
40. Jacqueline Durran, "Dandies and Servants of the Crown: Sailors' Uniforms in the Early 19th Century," *Things* (3) (1995): 6–19.
41. Juliet Ash, *Dress Behind Bars: Prison Clothing as Criminality* (London: I.B. Tauris, 2010).
42. Diana de Marly, *Working Dress: A History of Occupational Clothing* (London: Batsford Books, 1986), 123.
43. Wendy Parkins, *Fashioning the Body Politic: Dress, Gender, Citizenship* (Oxford: Berg, 2002).
44. Phyllis Cunnington and Catherine Lucas, *Occupational Costume in England*, (London: A.&C. Black, 1976), 251–60.
45. Williams-Mitchell, *Dressed for the Job*, 101.
46. William Keenan, "From Friars to Fornicators: The Eroticization of Sacred Dress," *Fashion Theory* 3 (4) (1999): 389–410.
47. Fred Davis, "Of Maids' Uniforms and Blue Jeans": 348.
48. Jane Tynan, "Military Dress and Men's Outdoor Leisurewear: Burberry's Trench Coat in First World War Britain," *Journal of Design History* 24 (2) (2011): 139–56.
49. Don Slater, *Consumer Culture and Modernity* (Cambridge: Polity, 1997), 24.
50. Mary Douglas and Baron Isherwood, *The World of Goods: Towards an Anthropology of Consumption* (London: Penguin, [1978] 1996), 75–6.
51. Crane, *Fashion and its Social Agendas*, 160.
52. Peter Braham, "Fashion: unpacking a cultural production," in Paul Du Gay (ed.) *Production of Culture/Cultures of Production* (London/Milton Keynes: Sage/Open University, 1997).
53. Celia Lury, *Consumer Culture* (New Brunswick: Rutgers University Press, 1996).
54. Lipovetsky, *The Empire of Fashion*, 29.
55. Valerie Steele, *Fetish: Fashion, Sex and Power* (Oxford: Oxford University Press, 1996).
56. Malcolm Barnard, *Fashion as Communication* (London: Routledge, 2002).
57. Steven Miles, *Consumerism: As a Way of Life* (London: Sage, 1998), 103.
58. Thorstein Veblen, *The Theory of the Leisure Class* (Oxford: Oxford University Press, [1899] 2009).
59. Pierre Bourdieu, *Distinction: A Social Critique of the Judgement of Taste* (Harvard: Harvard University Press, 1984), 6.
60. Ibid., 201.
61. Daniel Miller, *Stuff* (Cambridge: Polity, 2010), 13.
62. Karen Rafferty, "Class-based Emotions and the Allure of Fashion Consumption," *Journal of Consumer Culture* 11 (2) (2011): 239–60.
63. Ibid., 257.
64. Sophie Woodward, "The Myth of Street Style," *Fashion Theory* 13 (1) (2009): 83–10.
65. Judd Stitziel, *Fashioning Socialism: Clothing, Politics and Consumer Culture in East Germany* (Oxford: Berg, 2005).
66. Breda Luthar, "Remembering Socialism: On Desire, Consumption and Surveillance,' *Journal of Consumer Culture* 6 (2) (2006): 229–59.
67. Ibid., 255.
68. Juanjuan Wu, *Chinese Fashion: From Mao to Now* (Oxford: Berg, 2009), 163.
69. Radu Stern, *Against Fashion: Clothing as Art, 1850–1930* (Cambridge MA: MIT Press, 2000).
70. Stuart Hall and Tony Jefferson (eds), *Resistance Through Rituals: Youth Subcultures in Post-War Britain* (London: Routledge, 1976).
71. Dick Hebdige, *Subculture: The Meaning of Style* (London: Routledge, 1979), 18.

72. Caroline Evans, "Dreams That Only Money Can Buy . . . Or, The Shy Tribe in Flight from Discourse," *Fashion Theory* 1 (2) (1997): 180.
73. Ibid., 169–70.
74. Woodward, "The Myth of Street Style": 84.
75. Greg Martins, "Subculture, Style, Chavs and Consumer Capitalism: Towards a Critical Cultural Criminology of Youth," *Crime, Media, Culture* 5 (2) (2009): 123–45.
76. Ibid., 139.
77. Pierre Bourdieu, *Sociology in Question* (London: Sage, 1993), 113.

7 Ethnicity

1. Andrew Bolton, *Alexander McQueen: Savage Beauty* (New York: Metropolitan Museum of Art, 2011), 130.
2. Roberto Rossellini, *Quasi un'autobiografia* (Milano: Mondadori, 1987), 123–4.
3. www.kamat.com/mmghandi/churchill.htm
4. Simona Segre Reinach, *Orientalismi* (Roma: Meltemi, 2006).
5. Adam Geczy, *Fashion and Orientalism* (London: Bloomsbury, 2013), 7.
6. Karen Tranberg Hansen and D. Soyini Madison, *African Dress: Fashion, Agency, Performance* (London: Bloomsbury, 2013), 1.
7. Lise Skov "Dreams of Small Nation in a Polycentric Fashion World," in *Fashion Theory*, 15, (2) (2011): 137–56.
8. D. Okuefuna *The Wonderful World of Albert Khan* (London: BBC Books, 2008).
9. José Teunissen, "Global Fashion/Local Tradition. On the globalization of fashion," in J. Brand and J.Teunissen (eds), *Global Fashion Local Tradition: On the Globalization of Fashion* (Utrecht: Centraal Museum Utrecht/Terra, 2005), 8–23.
10. Elizabeth Wilson, *Adorned in Dreams* (London: I.B. Tauris, 2005); Ulrich Lehman, *Tigersprung: Fashion in Modernity* (Boston: MIT Press, 2000).
11. Carl Flügel, *The Psychology of Clothes* (London: Institute of Psychoanalysis/Hogarth Press, 1930).
12. Victoria Rovine, www.africulture.com [accessed December 13, 2013].
13. Thorstein Veblen, *The Theory of Leisure Class* (Oxford, New York: Oxford University Press, 2007).
14. Edward Said, *Orientalism: Western Representations of the Orient* (London: Routledge & Kegan Paul, 1978).
15. Joanne Eicher, et al., *The Visible Self: Global Perspectives on Dress, Culture and Society* (New York: Fairchild Publications, 2008).
16. Margaret Maynard, *Dress and Globalization* (Manchester: Manchaster University Press, 2004); Antonia Finnane, *Changing Clothes in China: Fashion, History, Nation* (New York: Columbia University Press, 2008); Karen Tranberg Hansen, *Salaula: The World of Second-Hand Clothing and Zambia* (Chicago and London: University of Chicago Press, 2000); G. Riello and P. McNeil, *The Fashion History Reader* (New York: Routledge, 2010).
17. Karen Tranberg Hansen, "The World in Dress: Anthropological Perspectives on Clothing, Fashion, and Culture," *Annual Review of Anthropology* 33, (2004): 387.
18. Sarah Grace Heller, "The Birth of Fashion," in G. Riello and P. McNeil (eds), *The Fashion History Reader: Global Perspectives* (London and New York: Routledge, 2010).
19. Leslie W. Rabine, *The Global Circulation of African Dress* (Oxford and New York: Berg, 2002).
20. Maynard, *Dress and Globalization*; Jennifer Craik, *Fashion: The Key Concepts* (Oxford, New York: Berg, 2009); G.I. Kunz and M.B. Garner, *Going Global: The Textile and Apparel Industry* (New York: Fairchild, 2006).
21. Diane Crane, *Fashion and Its Social Agendas* (Chicago: University of Chicago Press, 2000); Sandra Niessen, "Interpreting Civilization Through Dress," in *Berg Encyclopedia of World Dress and Fashion*, vol. 8, West Europe (Oxford and New York: Berg, 2010).

22. John E. Vollmer, "Cultural Authentication," in *Berg Encyclopedia of World Dress and Fashion*, vol. 6, East Asia (Oxford and New York: Berg, 2010), 69–76.

23. Maynard, *Dress and Globalization*; Rabine, *The Global Circulation of African Dress*.

24. Hansen, *Salaula*.

25. Christine Tsui, *China Fashion: Conversations with Designers* (Oxford and New York: Berg, 2010); Juanjuan Wu, *China Fashion From Mao to Now* (Oxford and New York: Berg, 2009).

26. http://www.africultures.com/php/index.php?nav=article&no=5754§hash.mbgtROaQ.dpuf

27. Thuy Linh Nguyen Tu, *The Beautiful Generation: Asian Americans and the Cultural Economy of Fashion*, (Durham NC: Duke University Press, 2011), 121.

28. Andrew Zhao, *The Chinese Fashion Industry* (London: Bloomsbury, 2013), 12–13.

29. Mukulika Banerjee, and Daniel Miller, *The Sari* (London: Bloomsbury, 2003).

30. Amartya Sen, *The Argumentative Indian* (New York: Allen Lane, 2005), 341.

31. Dipesh Chakrabarty, *Provincializing Europe: Post-Colonial Thought and Historical Difference* (Princeton: Princeton University Press, 2007).

32. Geczy, *Fashion and Orientalism*, 199.

33. Richard Martin and Harold Koda, *Visions of the East in Western Dress* (New York: Metropolitan Museum of Art, 1994).

34. Yunika Kawamura, *The Japanese Revolution in Paris Fashion* (Oxford and New York: Berg, 2004).

35. Dorinne Kondo, *About Face: Performing Race in Fashion and Theatre* (New York: Routledge, 1997).

36. *Notebook on Cities and Clothes*, dir. Wim Wenders, 1989.

37. Carla Jones, and Ann Marie Leschkowich, "Three Scenarios from Batak Clothing History: Designing Participation in the Global Fashion Trajectory," in S. Niessen et al., *Re-Orienting Fashion: The Globalization of Asian Dress* (Oxford: Berg, 2003), 2.

38. Tamara Walker, "He outfitted his family in notable decency": Slavery, Honour and Dress in Eighteenth-Century Lima, Peru," in *Slavery and Abolition: A Journal of Slave and Post-Slave Studies,* 30, (2009): 383–402.

39. Fadwa El Guindi, "Hijab," in V. Steele (ed.) *Encyclopedia of Clothing and Fashion*, New York: Scribner, 1 (2004): 414–16; Gole 1996, quoted in E. Tarlo and A. Moors (eds), "Introduction," *Fashion Theory* 11, no, 2/3 (2013), 22.

40. Reina Lewis, *Rethinking Orientalism* (New Brunswick: Rutgers University Press, 2004).

41. Saloni Mathur, *India by Design* (Berkeley: University of California Press, 2007), 167.

42. Hansen, "The World in Dress": 372.

43. Agnès Rocamora, "Personal fashion blogs: screens and mirrors in digital self-portraits," *Fashion Theory*, vol. 15, 4 (2011): 407–24.

44. Michael Keane, *Created in China: The Great Leap Forward* (New York: Routledge, 2007).

45. Tu, *The Beautiful Generation*.

46. Alexandra Palmer, *Fashion: A Canadian Perspective* (Toronto: University of Toronto Press, 2004), 4.

47. Craik, *Fashion*.

48. Tu, *The Beautiful Generation,* 25.

49. Craik, "Fashion, Tourism, and Global Culture," in S. Black, A. de la Haye et al. (eds), *The Handbook of Fashion Studies* (London: Bloomsbury, 2013); Carla Cooper, "Caribbean Fashion Week: Remodeling Beauty in 'Out of Many One' Jamaica," in *Fashion Theory*: 14, 3, (2010): 387–404; Wessie Ling "Fashionalization. Why so many cities host fashion weeks?" in J. Berry (ed.), *Fashion Capital* (Oxford: Interdisciplinary Press, 2012).

50. Crane, *Fashion and Its Social Agendas*.

51. Ibid.; Benedict Anderson, *Imagined Communities: Reflections on the Origin and Spread of Nationalism* (London: Verso, London, 1983); Eric J. Hobsbawn and Trevor O. Ranger, *The Invention of Tradition* (Cambridge: Cambridge University Press [1983], 2012); Emma Tarlo,

Visibly Muslim: Fashion, Politics, Faith (Oxford and New York: Berg, 2010); Simona Serge Reinach, *Un modo di mode* (Roma-Bari: Laterza, 2011).

52. Palmer, *Fashion*.

53. Skov, "Dreams of Small Nation in a Polycentric Fashion World,"; Orvar Lofgren and Robert Willim, *Magic Culture and the New Economy* (Oxford and New York: Berg, 2005).

54. Hildi Hendrickson, *Clothing and Difference: Embodied Identities in Colonial and Post Colonial Africa*, (Durham NC, Duke University Press, 1996), 1.

55. Ibid.

56. Toby Slade, *Japanese Fashion: A Cultural History* (Oxford and New York: Berg, 2009).

57. Arjun Appadurai, *Modernity at Large: Cultural Dimensions of Globalization* (Minneapolis: University of Minnesota Press, 1996).

58. Claire Dwyer and Peter Jackson, "Commodifying Difference: Selling Eastern Fashion," *Environment and Planning: Society and Space*, vol. 21 (2003): 269–91.

59. Anthony Giddens, *The Consequences of Modernity* (Cambridge: Polity Press, 1990).

60. Roland Barthes, *The Fashion System* (Berkeley: University of California Press, 1983); Annette B. Weiner and Jane Schneider, *Cloth and the Human Experience* (Washington: Smithsonian Institution Press, 1989).

61. Rovine, "Viewing Africa Through Fashion," *Fashion Theory* 13, 2 (2009): 133–40.

62. See *Critical Studies on Fashion and Beauty*, 4 (2013).

63. Nandi Bhatia, "Fashioning Women in Colonial India," *Fashion Theory. The Journal of Dress, Body & Culture*, 7.3/4 (2003): 327–44.

64. Rey Chow, *Il sogno di Butterfly. Costellazioni Postcoloniali*, P. Calefato (ed.) (Milan: Meltemi, 2004).

65. Marshall Sahlins, *Culture and Practical Reason* (Chicago: Chicago University Press, 1976).

8 Visual Representations

1. Charles Baudelaire, *The Painter of Modern Life and Other Essays*, trans. Jonathan Mayne (London: Phaidon, 1964), 1–2.

2. Anne Hollander, "Fashion and Image," in *Feeding the Eye* (New York: Farrar, Straus & Giroux, 1999), 142.

3. Nast quoted in Caroline Seebohm, *The Man Who Was Vogue: The Life and Times of Condé Nast* (New York: Viking Press, 1982), 178–9.

4. *On the Edge: Images from 100 Years of Vogue* (New York: Random House, 1992), vii.

5. Nancy Hall-Duncan, *The History of Fashion Photography* (New York: Alpine Book Company, Inc., 1979), 35–6.

6. Quoted in Edward Steichen, *A Life in Photography* (Garden City, NY: Doubleday & Co., 1963), n.p.

7. Ibid., n.p.

8. Quoted in Seebohm, *The Man Who Was Vogue*, 201–3.

9. Steichen as quoted in Patricia Johnston, *Real Fantasies: Edward Steichen's Advertising Photography* (Berkeley: University of California Press, 1997), 113.

10. Martin Harrison, *Shots of Style: Great Fashion Photographs Chosen by David Bailey* (London: Victoria and Albert Museum, 1985), 22.

11. Horst as quoted in Horst P. Horst, *Horst Portraits: 60 Years of Style* (New York: Harry N. Abrams, Inc., 2001), 182.

12. Hans-Michael Koetzle, *Photo Icons: The Story Behind the Pictures, 1928–1991*, vol. II (Köln: Taschen, 2002), 42.

13. William A. Ewing, "A Natural Means of Expression," in *Style in Motion: Munkacsi Photographs 20s, 30s, 40s* (New York: Clarkson N. Potter, Inc., 1979), 9–12.

14. Carmel Snow and Mary Louise Aswell, *The World of Carmel Snow* (New York: McGraw-Hill Book Company, Inc., 1962), 88. Emphasis original.

15. Winthrop Sargeant, "A Woman Entering a Taxi in the Rain," *The New Yorker*, November 8, 1958: 49.

16. Ibid., 70.

17. Quoted in Philippe Garner, "Richard Avedon: A Double-Sided Mirror," in *Avedon Fashion: 1944–2000* (Munich: Schirmer/Mosel, 2009), 21.

18. Penn, quoted in Susan Bright, *Face of Fashion* (New York: Aperture Foundation/ D.A.P. Distributed Art Publishers, 2007), 12.

19. Susan Sontag, "The Avedon Eye," *Vogue* [New York], September 1, 1978: 507.

20. Norberto Angeletti and Alberto Oliva, *In Vogue: The Illustrated History of the World's Most Famous Fashion Magazine* (New York: Rizzoli, 2012), 234.

21. See "A Major Innovation: The Style Essay," in ibid., 262–71.

22. *Vogue* editor Grace Mirabella as quoted in ibid, 232.

23. Hilton Kramer, "The Dubious Art of Fashion Photography," *New York Times*, December 28,1975: 100.

24. Francine Crescent, as quoted in Alison M. Gingeras, *Guy Bourdin* (London: Phaidon Press, 2006), n.p.

25. Vince Aletti, "Bruce Weber for Calvin Klein," *Artforum* 41, no. 7 (March 2003): 116.

26. See Teal Triggs, "Framing Masculinity: Herb Ritts, Bruce Weber and the Body Perfect," in Juliet Ash and Elizabeth Wilson (eds), *Chic Thrills: A Fashion Reader*, (Berkeley: University of California Press, 1992).

27. Aletti, "Bruce Weber for Calvin Klein": 116.

28. Michael Gross, "Bruce Weber: Camera Chameleon," *Vanity Fair*, June 1986: 116.

29. Bruce Weber, *Hotel Room with a View* (Washington, DC: Smithsonian Institution Press, 1992), 8.

30. Paul Jobling, *Fashion Spreads: Word and Image in Fashion Photography since 1980* (Oxford: Berg, 1999), 145.

31. Jane Pavitt, "Logos," in Valerie Steele (ed.), *The Berg Companion to Fashion*, (Oxford: Berg, 2010), 485.

32. Sontag, "The Avedon Eye": 508.

33. John Leo, "Selling the Woman-Child," *U.S. News and World Report* 116, no. 23 (June 13, 1994); Louise Lague, "How Thin Is Too Thin?" *People Weekly* 40 (September 20, 1993); and "A Fat Chance of Winning This Model Argument," *The Guardian*, October 10, 1995.

34. Ellen Gray, "'Waif' Spoof Reached out and Touched," *Philadelphia Daily News*, January 28, 1994.

35. Mark Hooper, "The Image Maker," *Observer Fashion Supplement*, Summer 2006.

36. Matthew Schneier, "Fashion in the Age of Instagram," *New York Times*, April 10, 2014.

9 Literary Representations

We would like to thank Alexandra Palmer for inviting us to contribute to this volume and for providing generous feedback on our drafts; Emma Doran and Alyssa Mackenzie for invaluable research assistance and feedback with this essay; and Jason Wang for his fashion studies expertise.

1. Jean Rhys, *After Leaving Mr. Mackenzie* (London: Penguin, 1971), 57.

2. Patti Smith, *Just Kids* (New York: Harper Collins, 2010), 251.

3. Roland Barthes, *The Fashion System*, trans. M. Ward and R. Howard (New York: Hill and Wang, 1967), 12.

4. J.C. Flügel, *The Psychology of Clothes* (London: Hogarth Press, 1950), 160–6.

5. Barthes, *The Fashion System*, 3.

6. Ibid., 8.

7. Elizabeth Wilson, *Adorned in Dreams: Fashion and Modernity* (Los Angeles: University of California Press, 1985), 3.

8. Ibid., 9.

9. R.S. Koppen, *Virginia Woolf: Fashion and Literary Modernity* (Edinburgh: Edinburgh University Press, 2009), 35.

10. Ibid., 35.

11. Peter McNeil, V. Karaminas and C. Cole (eds), *Fashion in Fiction: Text and Clothing in Literature, Film and Television* (New York: Berg, 2009), 2.

12. Ibid., 4.

13. Theodore Dreiser, *Sister Carrie* (New York: Modern Library, 1961), 5.

14. Ibid., 111.

15. Dreiser, *Sister Carrie*, 111–12.

16. Ibid., 551.

17. Edith Wharton, *The Age of Innocence* (Peterborough, ON: Broadview, 2002), 62.

18. Ibid., 86.

19. Anzia Yezierska, *Bread Givers*, (New York: Persea Books, 1975), 239.

20. Meredith Goldsmith, "Dressing, Passing, and Americanizing: Anzia Yezierska's Sartorial Fictions," *Studies in America Jewish Literature* 16 (1997): 35.

21. Lori Harrison-Kahan, "No Slaves to Fashion: Designing Women in the Fiction of Jessie Fauset and Anzia Yezierska," in C. Kuhn and C. Carlson (eds), *Styling Texts: Dress and Fashion in Literature* (Youngstown: Cambria University Press, 2007), 312.

22. Ibid., 313.

23. Graeme Abernethy, "'Beauty on Other Horizons': Sartorial Self-Fashioning in Claude McKay's *Banjo: A Story Without a Plot*," *Journal of American Studies* 48, no. 2 (2014): 445.

24. Ibid., 448.

25. Ibid., 449.

26. C. McKay, quoted in Abernathy, "'Beauty on Other Horizons'," 450.

27. Abernathy, "'Beauty on Other Horizons'," 450.

28. McKay, quoted in ibid., 450.

29. D.H. Lawrence, *Women in Love* (New York: Random House, 2000), 4.

30. Ibid., 9.

31. Lawrence, *The Fox/The Captain's Doll/The Ladybird*, ed. Dieter Mehl (London: Penguin, 2006), 48–9.

32. F. Scott Fitzgerald, *The Great Gatsby* (New York: Charles Scribner's Sons, 1953), 93.

33. Shaun Cole, *The Story of Men's Underwear* (New York: Parkstone Press, 2011), 58.

34. Ibid., 57.

35. Tyrus Miller, *Late Modernism: Politics, Fiction, and the Arts Between the World Wars* (Berkeley: University of California Press, 1999), 141, 142.

36. Djuna Barnes, *Nightwood* (New York: New Directions, 1961), 79.

37. Ibid., 136.

38. Ibid., 146, 148.

39. Rachel Warburton, "'Nothing could be seen whole or read from start to finish': Transvestitism and Imitation in *Orlando* and *Nightwood*," in Kuhn and Carlson, *Styling Texts,* 269–70.

40. Ibid., 271.

41. Ernest Hemingway, *The Sun Also Rises* (New York: Scribner, 1954), 31.

42. Ibid., 150.

43. "The Chanel 'Ford,'" *Vogue* (American), October 1, 1926, 69.

44. Rhys, *After Leaving Mr. Mackenzie*, 57.

45. Ibid., 68.

46. Ibid., 68.

47. Jean Rhys, *Good Morning, Midnight* (London: Andre Deutsch, 1969), 28.

48. Gabrielle Finnane, "Holly Golightly and the Fashioning of the Waif," in P. McNeil, V. Karaminas and C. Cole (eds), *Fashion in Fiction: Text and Clothing in Literature, Film and Television,* (New York: Berg, 2009), 138.

49. Ibid., 145.

50. Truman Capote, *Breakfast at Tiffany's and Other Voices, Other Rooms* (New York: Modern Library, 2013), 71.
51. Ian Fleming, *Casino Royale* (Las Vegas, NV: Thomas Mercer, 2013), 28.
52. Ibid., 22.
53. Ibid., 30.
54. Ibid., 32–3.
55. Ibid., 49.
56. Bret Easton Ellis, *American Psycho* (New York: Vintage/Random House, 1991), 72.
57. Ibid., 76–7.
58. Natalie Stillman-Webb, "'Be What You Want': Clothing and Subjectivity in Toni Morrison's *Jazz*," in Kuhn and Carlson (eds), *Styling Texts,* 335.
59. Ibid., 335.
60. Margaret Atwood, *Dancing Girls and Other Stories* (New York: Simon and Schuster, 1982), 114.
61. Ibid., 114.
62. Cynthia Kuhn, "'Clothes Would Only Confuse Them': Sartorial Culture in *Oryx and Crake*," in Kuhn and Carlson (eds), *Styling Texts*, 389.
63. Ibid., 390.
64. Alice Munro, *Who Do You Think You Are?* (Toronto: Penguin, 2006), 64.
65. Ibid., 64.
66. Smith, *Just Kids*, 25.
67. Ibid., 29.
68. Ibid., 30.
69. Ibid., 64.
70. Ibid., 251.
71. Ibid., 251.

BIBLIOGRAPHY

Aav, M. (ed.) (2003), *Marimekko: Fabrics, Fashion, Architecture*, New Haven and London: Yale University Press.

Abernethy, G. (2014), "'Beauty on Other Horizons': Sartorial Self-Fashioning in Claude McKay's *Banjo: A Story Without a Plot*," *Journal of American Studies* 48, no. 2: 445–60.

Adatto, K. (2008), *Picture Perfect: Life in the Age of the Photo Op*, Princeton: Princeton University Press.

Aletti, V. (March 2003), "Bruce Weber for Calvin Klein." *Artforum* 41, no. 7: 116.

Allison, D.C. (1998), *Jesus of Nazareth: Millenarian Prophet*, Augsburg Fortress: Fortress Press.

American Fabrics (Spring 1953), "American Fabrics Presents a Key to the Man-Made Fibers," 26: 70–4.

American Fabrics (Spring 1954), "Guide to Some Well Known Finishes and Finishing Terms": 28: 80–3.

American Fabrics (1960), *Encyclopedia of Textiles*, Englewood Cliffs, NJ: Prentice-Hall.

Anderson, B. (1983), *Imagined Communities: Reflections on the Origin and Spread of Nationalism*, London: Verso.

Angeletti, N. and A. Oliva (2012), *In Vogue: The Illustrated History of the World's Most Famous Fashion Magazine*, New York: Rizzoli.

Anstey, H. and T. Weston ([1997] 2005), *The Anstey Weston Guide to Textile Term*, London: Weston Publishing Ltd.

Appadurai, A. (1996), *Modernity at Large: Cultural Dimensions of Globalization*, Minneapolis: University of Minnesota Press.

Arnold, R. (2001), *Fashion, Desire and Anxiety: Image and Morality in the 20th Century*, New Brunswick: Rutgers University Press.

Ash, J. (2010), *Dress Behind Bars: Prison Clothing as Criminality*, London: I.B. Tauris.

Ashcraft, M. (2002), *The Dawn of the New Cycle: Point Loma Theosophists and American Culture*, Knoxville: University of Tennessee Press.

Ashcroft, B. et al. (1995), *The Post-Colonial Studies Reader*, London and New York: Routledge.

Atwood, M. ([1977] 1982), *Dancing Girls and Other Stories*, New York: Simon & Schuster.

Auclair, R. (1982), *The Lady of All Peoples*, Quebec: Limoilou.

"Babes Take Age-Old Prejudice off their Chests," *India Today*, August 25, 2009.

Bailey, P.H. (1955), "Report on Men's Wear," *New York Times*, May 1, 1955, SMA7.

Banerjee, M. and D. Miller (2003), *The Sari*, London: Bloomsbury.

Barlow, F.D., Jr. (1957), *Cotton, Rayon, Synthetic Fibers—Competition in Western Europe*, Washington: US Department of Agriculture.

Barmash, I. (1965), "Men's Shirts Get Permanent Press." *New York Times*, February 21, 1965: 43.

— (1971), "Manufacturers Warned on Rising Textile Waste," *New York Times*, March 27, 1971: 35.

Barnard, M. (1996), *Fashion as Communication*, London and New York: Routledge.

Barnes, D. ([1936] 1961), *Nightwood*, New York: New Directions.

— ([1928] 1972), *Ladies Almanack*, New York: Harper & Row.

— ([1915] 2003), *Book of Repulsive Women*, Manchester: Carcanet Press.

Barnes R. and J. Eicher (1992), *Dress and Gender: Making and Meaning*, Oxford: Berg, 1992.

Barry, C. (1994), *Rasafari: Roots and Ideoloy*, Syracuse: Syracuse University Press.

Barthes, R. (1967), *Système de la mode*, Paris: Seuil.

— ([1967] 1990), *The Fashion System*, trans. M. Ward and R. Howard, Berkeley: University of California Press.

— (2006), *The Language of Clothing*, Oxford: Berg.

Bartlett, D. (2010), *Fashion East: The Spectre that Haunted Socialism*, Cambridge, MA: MIT Press.

Bartlett, D., S. Cole, and A. Rocamora (eds) (2013), *Fashion Media. Past and Present*, London: Bloomsbury.

Baudelaire, C. (1964), *The Painter of Modern Life and Other Essays*, trans. J. Mayne, London: Phaidon.

Beauvoir, S. de. *The Second Sex* ([1949] 1972), trans. and ed. H.M. Parshley, London: Jonathan Cape.

Berg, M. (2005), *Luxury and Pleasure in Eighteenth-Century Britain*, Oxford: Oxford University Press.

Bergeron, L. (ed.) (1993), *La Révolution des aiguilles. Habiller les Français et les Américains 19e–20e siècle*, Paris: EHESS.

Berghoff, H. and T. Kuehne (eds) (2013), *Globalizing Beauty: Consumerism and Body Aesthetics in the Twentieth Century*, New York: Palgrave.

Bergler, E. ([1953] 1987), *Fashion and the Unconscious*, Madison: International Universities Press.

Bettany, S. and R. Daly (2008), "Figuring companion-species consumption: A multi-site ethnography of the post-canine Afghan hound," *Journal of Business Research*, no. 61: 408–18.

Betterton, R. (1987), *Looking On: Images of Femininity in the Visual Arts and Media*, London: Pandora.

Bezzola, T. (2008), "Lights Going All over the Place," in *Edward Steichen in High Fashion: The Condé Nast Years 1923–1937*, eds W.A. Ewing and T. Brandow, New York: W.W. Norton & Co.

Bhatia, N. (September/December 2003), "Fashioning Women in Colonial India," *Fashion Theory: The Journal of Dress, Body & Culture*, 7.3/4: 327–44.

Birnbach, L. and J. Roberts, C. McD. Wallace, and M. Wiley (1980), *The Official Preppy Handbook*, New York: Workman Publishing.

Black, S. (2013), *The Sustainable Fashion Handbook*, London: Thames & Hudson.

Bland, L. (2013), *Modern Women on Trial: Sexual Transgression in the Age of the Flapper*. Manchester: Manchester University Press.

Blaszczyk, R.L. (2006), "Styling Synthetics: DuPont's Marketing of Fabrics and Fashions in Postwar America," *The Business History Review* 80, no. 3: 485–528.

— (ed.) (2007), *Producing Fashion: Commerce, Couture, and Consumers*, Philadelphia: University of Pennsylvania Press.

— (2008), "Designing Synthetics, Promoting Brands: Dorothy Liebes, DuPont Fibres and Post-war American Interiors," *Journal of Design History* 21, no. 1: 75–99.

— (2012), *The Color Revolution*, Cambridge, MA: MIT Press.

Blausen, W. (1994), "Rodier," in *Contemporary Fashion*, Farmington Hills: St. James Press.

Blum, D.E. (2003), *Shocking! The Art and Fashion of Elsa Schiaparelli*, Philadelphia: Philadelphia Museum of Art.

Bolton, A. (2004), *Bravehearts: Men in Skirts*, London: V&A Publishing.

— (2011), *Alexander McQueen: Savage Beauty*, New York: Metropolitan Museum of Art.

Bosquart, M. (1985), *De La Trinité Divine À L'immaculée-Trinité*, Quebec City: Limoilou.

Bosc, A. (ed.) (2014), "Du fil au vêtement. La production de textiles pour la haute couture," in Alexandra Bosc et al, *Les Années 50. La mode en France, 1947–1957*, Paris: Paris Musées.

Bourdieu, P. (1984), *Distinction: A Social Critique of the Judgement of Taste*, Cambridge, MA: Harvard University Press.

— (1993), *Sociology in Question*, London: Sage.

Bourdieu, P. and Y. Delsaut (1975), "Le couturier et sa griffe: contribution à une théorie de la magie," *Actes de la recherche en sciences sociales*, 1.

Bouzar, D. (2010), *Laïcité, mode d'emploi: Cadre légal et solutions pratiques, 42 études de cas*, Paris: Eyrolles.

Brachet-Champsaur, F. (2006a), "La mode et les grands magasins," in *Les cathédrales du commerce parisien. Grands Magasins et enseignes*, Paris: Editions de l'Action Artistique de la Ville de Paris.

— (2006b), "Un grand magasin à la pointe de la mode: les Galeries Lafayette," in *La mode des sixties, l'entrée dans la modernit*, eds M. Ruffat and D. Veillon, Paris: Autrement.

— (2012), "Madeleine Vionnet and the Galeries Lafayette: The unlikely marriage of a Parisian couture house and a French department store, 1922–40," *Business History* 54, no. 1: 48–66.

Braddock, S.E. and M. O'Mahony (1998), *Techno Textiles: Revolutionary Fabrics for Fashion and Design*, New York: Thames & Hudson.

Braham, P. (1997), "Fashion: unpacking a cultural production," in *Production of Culture/Cultures of Production*, ed. P. Du Gay, London and Thousand Oaks: Sage in association with the Open University.

"Bravehearts: Men in Skirts," *The Metropolitan Museum of Art*, http://www.metmuseum.org/about-the-museum/press-room/exhibitions/2003/bravehearts-men-in-skirts [accessed July 26, 2015].

Breward, C. (1995), *The Culture of Fashion*, Manchester: Manchester University Press.

— (1999), *The Hidden Consumer: Masculinities, Fashion and City Life 1860–1914*, Manchester: Manchester University Press.

— (2003), *Fashion*, Oxford: Oxford University Press.

Breward, C. and D. Gilbert (eds) (2006), *Fashion's World Cities*, Oxford: Berg.

Breward, C., D. Gilbert, and J. Lister (2006), *Swinging Sixties: Fashion in London and Beyond 1955–1970*, London: V&A Publishing.

Bright, S. (2007), *Face of Fashion*, New York: Aperture.

Bromley, D.G. and S. Palmer (2007), "Deliberate Heresies: New Religious Myths and Rituals as Critiques," in *Teaching New Religious Movements*, ed. David G. Bromlet, New York: Oxford University Press.

Bruzzi, S. and P. C. Gibson (2008), "Fashion is the fifth character," in *Reading Sex and the City*, eds K. Akass and J. McCabe, London: I.B. Tauris.

Buckley, C. and H. Fawcett (2002), *Fashioning the Feminine: Representation and Women's Fashion from the Fin de Siècle to the Present*, London: I.B. Tauris.

Burke, P. (2008), *What is Cultural History*, London: Polity Press.

Burman, B. (1995), "Better and Brighter Clothes, The Men's Dress Reform Party, 1929–1940," *Journal of Design History* 8 (4): 275–90.

— (1999), *The Culture of Sewing: Gender, Consumption and Home Dressmaking*, Oxford: Berg.

Butler, J. (1990), *Gender Trouble: Feminism and the Subversion of Identity*, London and New York: Routledge.

Calefato, P. (2004), *The Clothed Body*, Oxford: Berg.

Canadian Conference of Catholic Bishops (1999), *Doctrinal Note of the Catholic Bishops of Canada Concerning the Army of Mary*.

Cannadine, D. (1998), *Class in Britain*, New Haven and London: Yale University Press.

Carlyle, T. (1908), *Sartur Resartus: On Heroes, Hero Worship and the Heroic in History*, London: J.M. Dent.

Capote, T. (2013), *Breakfast at Tiffany's and Other Voices, Other Rooms*, New York: Modern Library.

Case, S. ([1988] 1999), "Toward a Butch–Femme Aesthetic," in *Camp: Queer Aesthetics and the Performing Subject. A Reader*, ed. F. Cleto, Edinburgh: Edinburgh University Press.

Chakrabarty, D. (2007), *Provincializing Europe. Post-Colonial Thought and Historical Difference*, Princeton: Princeton University Press.

Chandés, H. (ed.) (1999), *Issey Miyake Making Things*, Zurich: Scalo.

"The Chanel 'Ford'," in *Vogue* (US), October 1, 1926: 69.

Chapdelaine de Montvalon, S. (2010), *Le beau pour tous*, Paris: L'Iconoclaste.

Chenoune, F. (1993), *A History of Men's Fashion*, Paris: Flammarion.

— (1995), *A History of Men's Fashion*, trans. D. Dusinberre, Paris and New York: Flammarion.

Chessel, M. (2012), *Consommateurs engagés à la Belle Epoque. La Ligue sociale d'acheteurs*, Paris: Presses de Sciences Po.

Chevannes, B. (1994), *Rasafari: Roots and Ideoloy*, Syracuse: Syracuse University Press.

Chow, R. (2004), *Il sogno di Butterfly. Costellazioni Postcoloniali*, ed. P. Calefato, Roma: Meltemi.

Chrétien-Ichikawa, S. (2012), *La réémergence de la mode en Chine et le rôle du Japon*, PhD thesis, Paris: EHESS.

Chua, R.Y.J. and R.G. Eccles (2009), *Managing Creativity at Shanghai Tang*, Boston: Harvard Business School Case 410–018.

Clarke, S. and M. O'Mahony (2006), *Techno Textiles 2: Revolutionary Fabrics for Fashion and Design*, New York: Thames & Hudson.

Coelho, P. and J. McClure (1993), "Toward an Economic Theory of Fashion," *Economic Inquiry*, 31 no. 4: 595–608

Cohan, S. (2006), "So Functional for its purposes: Rock Hudson's Bachelor Apartment in Pillow Talk," in *Stud: Architectures of Masculinity*, ed. J. Sanders, Princeton: Princeton University Press.

Cole, S. (2000), *"Don We Now Our Gay Apparel": Gay Men's Dress in the Twentieth Century*, Oxford: Berg.

— (2011), *The Story of Men's Underwear*, New York: Parkstone Press.

Conekin, B. (2000), "Fashioning the Playboy: Messages of Style and Masculinity in the Pages of *Playboy* Magazine, 1953–1963," *Fashion Theory* 4, no 4: 447–66.

Conor, L. (2004), *The Spectacular Modern Woman. Feminine Visibility in the 1920s*, Bloomington and Indianapolis: Indiana University Press.

Cooper, C. (2010), "Caribbean Fashion Week: Remodeling Beauty in 'Out of Many One' Jamaica," *Fashion Theory* 14, no. 3: 387–404.

Coppens, M. (1996), *Mode en Belgique au XIXe siècle*, Brussels: Musées Royaux d'Art et d'Histoire.

Cott, N. (1987), *The Grounding of Modern Feminism*, New Haven: Yale University Press.

"Cotton Incorporated's History," *Cotton Incorporated*, http://www.cottoninc.com/corporate/About-Cotton-Incorporated/Cotton-Incorporated-company-history/ [accessed June 5, 2014].

Craik, J. (1994), *The Face of Fashion: Cultural Studies in Fashion*, London: Routledge.

— (2005), *Uniforms Exposed: From Conformity to Transgression*, Oxford and New York: Berg.

— (2009), *Fashion: The Key Concepts*, Oxford and New York: Berg.

— (2013), "Fashion, Tourism, and Global Culture," in *The Handbook of Fashion Studies*, eds S. Black, A. de la Haye, et al. London: Bloomsbury.

Crane, D. (2000), *Fashion and its Social Agendas: Class, Gender, and Identity in Clothing*, Chicago: University of Chicago Press.

Crawford, M.D.C. (1941), *The Ways of Fashion*, New York: Putnam.

Cristóbal Balenciaga Museoa (2011), *Cristóbal Balenciaga*, New York: Thames & Hudson.

Cunningham, P. (1986), "Swimwear in the Thirties: The B.V.D. Company in a Decade of Innovation," *Dress* 12, no. 1: 11–27.

Cunnington, P. and C. Lucas (1976), *Occupational Costume in England,* London: A&C Black.

Darsey, J. (1991), "From 'gay is good' to the scourge of AIDS: The evolution of gay liberation rhetoric, 1977–1990," *Communication Studies* 42, no. 1: 43–66.

Darwin, G.H. (1872), "Development in Dress," *Macmillan Magazine* 26: 410–16.

Daves, J. (1967), *Ready-Made Miracle: The American story of fashion for the millions*, New York: Putnam.

Davidson, A. (2013), "Economic recovery, Made in Bangladesh?" *New York Times*, May 14: MM16.

Davis, F. (1989), "'Of Maids' Uniforms and Blue Jeans: The Drama of Status Ambivalences in Clothing and Fashion," *Qualitative Sociology* 12, no. 4: 337–55.

Davis, M.E. (2006), *Classic Chic: Music, Fashion, and Modernism,* Berkeley: University of California Press.

de la Haye, A. (2005), "Patou, Jean," in *Encyclopedia of Clothing and Fashion*, ed. V. Steele, Detroit: Thompson Gale.

de la Haye, A. and S. Tobin ([1994] 2003), *Chanel: The Couturiere at Work*, London: V&A Publishing.

de Lauretis, T. (1991), "'Queer Theory': Lesbian and gay sexualities," *Differences: A Journal of Feminist Cultural Studies* 3, no. 2: iii–xviii.

de Marly, D. (1986), *Working Dress: A History of Occupational Clothing*, London: Batsford Books.

de Meyer, A. (1976), *De Meyer*, ed. R. Brandau with text by P. Jullian, New York: Alfred A. Knopf.

Devor, H. (2011), *Gender Blending: Confronting the Limits of Duality*, Bloomington and Indianapolis: Indiana University Press.

Dior, C. ([1956] 2011), *Christian Dior et moi*, Paris: Vuibert.

Diner, H.R. (2015), *Roads Taken: The Great Jewish Migrations to the New World and the Peddlers Who Forged the Way*, New Haven: Yale University Press.

Douglas, M. and B. Isherwood ([1978] 1980), *The World of Goods: Towards an Anthropology of Consumption*, London: Penguin.

Dreiser, T. ([1900] 1961), *Sister Carrie*, New York: Modern Library.

Durran, J. (1995), "Dandies and servants of the Crown: Sailors' uniforms in the early 19th century," *Things* 3: 6–19.

Dworkin, A. (1981), *Pornography: Men Possessing Women*, New York: G.P. Putnam's Sons.

Dwyer, C. and P. Jackson (2003), "Commodifying Difference: Selling Eastern Fashion," *Environment and Planning: Society and Space* 21: 269–91.

Edelman, A.H. (1997), *The Little Black Dress*, New York: Simon and Schuster.

Ehrman, E. (2004), "Glamourous Modernity: 1914–30," in *The London Look: Fashion from Street to Catwalk*, eds C. Breward, E. Ehrman, and C. Evans, New Haven: Yale University Press/Museum of London.

Eichengreen, B. (2007), *The European Economy Since 1945: Coordinated Capitalism and Beyond*, Princeton: Princeton University Press.

Eicher, J.B., et al. (2008), *The Visible Self: Global Perspectives on Dress, Culture and Society*, New York: Fairchild Publications.

Ellis, B.E. (1991), *American Psycho*, New York: Vintage/Random House.

Ellwood, R.S. (1979), *Religious and Spiritual Groups in North America*, New Jersey: Prentice Hall.

Entwistle, J. (2000), *The Fashioned Body: Fashion, Dress and Modern Social Theory*, Cambridge: Polity Press.

— (2009), *The Aesthetic Economy of Fashion: Markets and Value in Clothing and Modelling*, New York: Berg.

Entwistle, J. and A. Rocamora (2006), "The Field of Fashion Materialized: A Study of London Fashion Week," *Sociology* 40, no. 4: 735–51.

Etherington-Smith, M. (1983), *Patou*, New York: St. Martin's/Marek.

European Parliament briefing, "Workers' conditions in the textile and clothing sector: just an Asian affair? Issues at stake after the Rana Plaza tragedy," European Parliament, August, 2014. http://www.europarl.europa.eu/EPRS/140841REV1-Workers-conditions-in-the-textile-and-clothing-sector-just-an-Asian-affair-FINAL.pdf [January 20, 2015].

Evans, C. (1997), "Dreams That Only Money Can Buy . . . Or, The Shy Tribe in Flight from Discourse," *Fashion Theory: The Journal of Dress, Body and Culture* 1 (2): 169–80.

— (2013), *The Mechanical Smile: Modernism and the First Fashion Shows in France and America, 1900–1929*, New Haven and London: Yale University Press.

Evans, C. and M. Thornton (Summer 1991), "Fashion, Representation, Femininity," *Feminist Review* no. 38: 48–66.

Ewing, E. (2008), *History of 20th Century Fashion*, London: Batsford.

Ewing, W.A. (1979), "A Natural Means of Expression," in *Style in Motion: Munkacsi Photographs 20s, 30s, 40s*, New York: Clarkson N. Potter, Inc.

Falluel, F. and M. Gutton (2009), *Elégance et Système D: Paris 1940–1944*, Paris: Paris Musées.

"A Fat Chance of Winning This Model Argument," *The Guardian*, October 10, 1995: 17.

Fauset, J.R. ([1931] 1995a), *The Chinaberry Tree: Novel of American Life*, New York: G.K. Hall.

— ([1933] 1995b), *Comedy: American Style*, New York: G.K. Hall.

Featherstone, M. (1991), "The Body in Consumer Culture," in *The Body: Social Process and Cultural Theory*, eds M. Featherstone et al., London: Sage.

Fee, S. (2013), "Anthropology and Materiality," in *The Handbook of Fashion Studies*, eds S. Black et al., London: Bloomsbury.

Feele, P. (1915), "Fashions and the Seven-year Schedule," *The Globe and Mail*, February 13: 10.

Ferrara, A.N. (2015), "Fashion's Forgotten Fascists." *VICE*, April 8, 2015, http://www.vice.com/read/fashions-forgotten-fascists [accessed November 18, 2014].

Ferris, R. and J. Lord (2012), *Teddy Boys: A Concise History*, London: Milo.

Festinger, L., H. Riecken, and S. Schachter (1956), *When Prophecy Fails: A Social and Psychological Study of a Modern Group That Predicted the Destruction of the World*, Minneapolis: University of Minnesota Press.

Feuer, A. (2004), "Do Real Men Wear Skirts? Try Disputing a 340-Pounder," *New York Times*, February 8, 2004, http://www.nytimes.com/2004/02/08/nyregion/08skirts.html [accessed July 26, 2015].

Field, J. (2001), "Dyes, Chemistry and Clothing: The Influence of World War I on Fabrics, Fashions and Silk," *Dress* 28, no. 1: 77–91.

— (2006), "Bernat Klein's Couture Tweeds: Color and Fabric Innovation, 1960–1980," *Dress* 36, no. 1: 41–55.

Fillin-Yeh, S. (2001), "Dandies, marginality, and Modernism: Georgia O'Keeffe, Marcel Duchamp, and Other Cross-Dressers," in *Dandies: Fashion and Finesse in Art and Culture*, ed. S. Fillin-Yeh, New York and London: New York University Press.

Finnane, A. (2008), *Changing Clothes in China: Fashion, History, Nation*, New York: Columbia University Press.

Finnane, G. (2009), "Holly Golightly and the Fashioning of the Waif," in P. McNeil, V. Karaminas and C. Cole (eds), *Fashion in Fiction: Text and Clothing in Literature, Film and Television*, New York: Berg.

Fitzgerald, F. Scott ([1925] 1953), *The Great Gatsby*, New York: Charles Scribner's Sons.

Fleming, I. ([1953], 2013), *Casino Royale*, Las Vegas, NV: Thomas Mercer.

Fletcher, K. and L. Grose (2012), *Fashion and Sustainability: Design for Change*, London: Laurence King Publishing Ltd.

Flügel, J.C. (1930), *The Psychology of Clothes*, London: Institute of Psychoanalysis and Hogarth Press.

Fogg, M. (2003), *Boutique: A 60s Cultural Phenomenon*, London: Mitchell Beazley.

Fonda, J. (1981), *Jane Fonda's Workout Book*, New York: Simon & Schuster.

Font, L. (2011), "Dior before Dior," *West 86th: A Journal of Decorative Arts, Design History, and Material Culture* 18, no. 1: 26–49.

Friedan, B. (1963), *The Feminine Mystique*, London: Penguin.

Friedman, V. (2015), "Saint Laurent Is Creating a Line Even More Exclusive Than Couture," *New York Times*, July 29, 2015, http://www.nytimes.com/2015/07/29/fashion/saint-laurent-is-creating-a-line-even-more-exclusive-than-couture.html [accessed August 3, 2015].

Fussell, P. (1984), *Class: Style and Status in the USA*, London: Arrow.

Garber, M. (1992), *Vested Interests: Cross-Dressing and Cultural Anxiety*, New York: Harper Perennial.

Gareau, P.L. (2009), "Unveiling the Army of Mary: A Gendered Analysis of a Conservative Catholic Marian Devotional Organization," MA dissertation, Montreal: Concordia University.

Garelic, R. (2001), "The Layered Look: Coco Chanel and Contagious Celebrity," in *Dandies: Fashion and Finesse in Art and Culture*, ed. S. Fillin-Yeh, New York and London: New York University Press.

Garner, P. (2009), "Richard Avedon: A Double-Sided Mirror," in *Avedon Fashion: 1944–2000*, Munich: Schirmer/Mosel.

Garnier, G., (ed.) (1987), *Paris-Couture-Années Trente*, Paris: Paris Musées.

Geczy, A. (2013), *Fashion and Orientalism*, London: Bloomsbury.

— (2014), "Straight Internet Porn and the Natrificial: Body and Dress," *Fashion Theory: The Journal of Dress, Body and Culture, Special Issue, Fashion and Porn* 18 (2): 169–88.

Geczy, A. and V. Karaminas (2013), *Queer Style*, London: Bloomsbury.

Gibson, P. C. (2012), *Fashion and Celebrity Culture*, London and New York: Berg.

— (2014), "Pornostyle: Sexualized Dress and the Fracturing of Feminism," *Fashion Theory: The Journal of Dress, Body and Culture, Special Issue, Fashion and Porn* 18, no. 2: 189–90.

Gibson, P. C. and V. Karaminas (2014), "Letter from the Editors," *Fashion Theory: The Journal of Dress, Body and Culture, Special Issue, Fashion and Porn* 18, no. 2: 118.

Giddens, A. (1990), *The Consequences of Modernity*, Cambridge: Polity Press.

Giguère, M. and J. d'Arc Demers (2004), *Vie d'Amour*, Québec City: Limoilou.

Gingeras, A.M. (2006), *Guy Bourdin*, London: Phaidon Press.

Gluckman, A. and B. Reed (eds) (1997), *Homo Economics: Capitalism, Community, and Lesbian and Gay Lives*, New York and London: Routledge.

Golbin, P. (2009), *Vionnet, Puriste de la Mode*, Paris: Les Arts Décoratifs.

Goldsmith, M. (1997), "Dressing, Passing, and Americanizing: Anzia Yezierska's Sartorial Fictions," *Studies in America Jewish Literature* 16: 34–45.

Gray, E. (1994), "'Waif' Spoof Reached out and Touched," *Philadelphia Daily News*, January 28, 1994.

Gray, R. (2004), *About Face: German Physiognomic Thought from Lavatar to Auschwitz*, Detroit: Wayne State University.

Green, N.J. (1997), *Ready-to-Wear and Ready-to-Work: A Century of Industry and Immigrants in Paris and in New York*, Durham: Duke University Press.

Gross, M. (2008), "Bruce Weber: Camera Chameleon," *Vanity Fair*, June 1986, 102–6, 116–18.

Grumbach, D. ([1993] 2008), *Histoires de la mode*, Paris: Editions du Regard/Institut Français de la Mode.

Guenther, I. (2004), *Nazi 'Chic'?: Fashioning Women in the Third Reich*, London: Berg.

Guillaume, V. (1998), *Courrèges*, London: Thames & Hudson.

Guindi, E.F. (2004), "Hijab," in V. Steele (ed.) *Encyclopedia of Clothing and Fashion*, New York: Scribner.

Gwynne, P. (2008), *World Religions in Practice: A Comparative Introduction*, Oxford: Blackwell Publishers.

Halberstam, J. (1998), *Female Masculinity*, Durham and London: Duke University Press.

Hall, S. and T. Jefferson (eds) (1976), *Resistance Through Rituals: Youth Subcultures in Post-War Britain*, London: Routledge.

Hall-Duncan, N. (1979), *The History of Fashion Photography*, New York: Alpine Book Company Inc.

Halnon, K.B. (2002), "Poor Chic: The Rational Consumption of Poverty," *Current Sociology* 50, no. 4: 501–16.

Hancock, J.H. II. (2009), "Chelsea on 5th Avenue: Hypermasculinity and Gay Clone Culture in the Retail Brand Practices of Abercrombie and Fitch," *Fashion Practice: The Journal of Design, Creative Process and the Fashion Industry* 1, no.1: 63–85.

Hancock, J.H. II and V. Karaminas (2014), "The Joy of Pecs. Representations of Masculinity in Fashion Advertising," *Clothing Cultures* 1, no. 3: 269–288.

Handley, S. (1999), *Nylon: The Story of a Fashion Revolution*, Baltimore: The Johns Hopkins University Press.

Hansen, K.T. (2000), *Salaula: The World of Second-Hand Clothing and Zambia*, Chicago and London: University of Chicago Press.

— (2004), "The World in Dress: Anthropological Perspectives on Clothing, Fashion, and Culture," *Annual Review of Anthropology* 33: 369–92.

Hansen, K.T. and D.M. Soyini (eds) (2013), *African Dress: Fashion, Agency, Performance*, London: Bloomsbury.

Harrison, M. (1985), *Shots of Style: Great Fashion Photographs Chosen by David Bailey*, London: V&A Publishing.

Harrison-Kahan, L. (2007), "No Slaves to Fashion: Designing Women in the Fiction of Jessie Fauset and Anzia Yezierska," in C. Kuhn and C. Carlson (eds), *Styling Texts: Dress and Fashion in Literature*, Youngstown: Cambria University Press.

Harvey, J. (1997), *Men in Black*, London: Reaktion.

Hay, S. (ed.) (2000), *From Paris to Providence: Fashion, Art, and the Tirocchi Dressmakers' Shop, 1915–1947*, Providence: Museum of Art, Rhode Island School of Design.

Hebdige, D. (1979), *Subculture: The Meaning of Style*, London: Routledge.

— (2006), "The Meaning of Mod," in *Resistance Through Rituals*, eds S. Hall and T. Jefferson, New York: Routledge.

Heller, S.G. (2010), "The Birth of Fashion," in *The Fashion History Reader: Global Perspectives*, eds G. Riello and P. McNeil, London and New York: Routledge.

Hemingway, E. ([1926] 1954), *The Sun Also Rises*, New York: Scribner.

Hemphill, C.S. and J. Suk (2014), "The Fashion Originators' Guild of America. Self-help at the edge of IP and antitrust," in *Intellectual Property at the Edge. The Contested Contours of IP*, eds R.C. Dreyfuss and J.C. Ginsburg, Cambridge, Cambridge University Press.

Hendrickson, H. (1996), *Clothing and Difference: Embodied Identities in Colonial and Post Colonial Africa*, Durham: Duke University Press.

Hobsbawn, E.J. and T. O. Ranger ([1983] 2012), *The Invention of Tradition*, New York: Cambridge University Press.

Hollander, A. (1999), "Fashion and Image," in *Feeding the Eye*, New York: Farrar, Straus & Giroux.

Holt, S. (1964), *Terror in the Name of God: The Story of the Sons of Freedom Doukhobors*, Toronto: McClelland and Stewart.

Hooper, M. (Summer 2006), "The Image Maker," *Observer Fashion Supplement*.

Horst, H.P. (2001), *Horst Portraits: 60 Years of Style*, New York: Harry N. Abrams, Inc.

Horyn, C. (2001), "Fashion; Some Things New, Most Borrowed," *New York Times*, September 11, 2001, http://www.nytimes.com/2001/09/11/nyregion/review-fashion-some-things-new-most-borrowed.html [accessed July 30, 2015].

Isherwood, C. (1939), *Goodbye to Berlin*, London: Hogarth Press.

Jacobs, A. (2011), "Smooth Moves, how Sara Blakely rehabilitated the girdle," *The New Yorker*, March 28, 2011, http://www.newyorker.com/magazine/2011/03/28/smooth-moves [accessed August 2, 2015].

Jennings, R. (2007), *A Lesbian History of Britain: Love and Sex Between Women Since 1500*, Oxford and Westport: Greenwood World Publishing.

Jobling, P. (1999), *Fashion Spreads: Word and Image in Fashion Photography Since 1980*, Oxford and New York: Berg.

Johnson, R. "Ritual Nudity or Skyclad," Amethyst's Wicca website, www.angelfire.com/realm2/amethystbt/ skyclad2.html [accessed January 1, 2006].

Johnston, P. (1997), *Real Fantasies: Edward Steichen's Advertising Photography*, Berkeley: University of California Press.

Jones, C. and A.M. Leschkowich (2003), "Three Scenarios from Batak Clothing History: Designing Participation in the Global Fashion Trajectory," in *Re-Orienting Fashion: The Globalization of Asian Dress*, eds S. Niessen, et al, Oxford: Berg.

Jones, G.J. and V. Pouillard (2009), *Christian Dior: A New Look for Haute Couture*, Boston: Harvard Business School, case 809–159.

Jones, M. (2008), *Skintight: An Anatomy of Cosmetic Surgery*, London: Berg.

Kawamura, Y. (2004), *The Japanese Revolution in Paris Fashion*, Oxford and New York: Berg.

— (2005), *Fashion-ology: An Introduction to Fashion Studies*, London: Bloomsbury.

Keane, M. (2007), *Created in China: The Great Leap Forward*, New York: Routledge.

Keenan, W. (1999), "From Friars to Fornicators: The Eroticization of Sacred Dress," *Fashion Theory* 3, no. 4: 389–410.

Kelly, K.F. (2011), "Performing Prison: Dress, Modernity, and the Radical Suffrage Body," *Fashion Theory*, 15, no. 3: 299–322.

Kertzer, D.L. (1996), "Ritual, Politics and Power," in *Readings in Ritual Studies*, ed. Ronald Grimes, New Jersey: Prentice Hall.

Kidwell, C.B. and M. Christman (1974), *Suiting Everyone: The Democratization of Clothing in America*, Washington: Smithsonian Institution.

King, S.S. (1980), "The Restoration of King Cotton," *The New York Times*, March 2, 1980, F1.

Kirke, B. (1998), *Madeleine Vionnet*, San Francisco: Chronicle Books.

Kirkpatrick, R.G. and D. Tumminia (1995), "Unarius: Emergent Aspects of an American Flying Saucer Group," in James R. Lewis, *The Gods Have Landed: New Religions from Other Worlds*, New York: SUNY Press.

Kitamura, M. (ed.) (2012), *Pleats Please Issey Miyake*, Klön: Taschen.

Klein, N. (1999), *No Logo: Taking Aim at the Brand Bullies*, Toronto and New York: Knopf.

Klymenko, O. (2012), "Fashion Week(s) in Kyiv—The Attempt to Create Fashion Industry in Post-Soviet Ukraine," paper presented at *Fashioning the City Conference*, Royal College of Art, London.

Koda, H. (2003), *Goddess: The Classical Mode*, New York: Metropolitan Museum of Art.

Koetzle, H.M. (2002), *Photo Icons: The Story Behind the Pictures, 1928–1991*, vol. 2, Köln: Taschen.

Kondo D. (1997), *About Face: Performing Race in Fashion and Theatre*, New York: Routledge.

König, A. (2008), "Sex and the City: A fashion editor's dream?" In *Reading Sex and the City*, eds K. Akass and J. McCabe, London: I.B. Tauris.

Koppen, R.S. (2009), *Virginia Woolf: Fashion and Literary Modernity*, Edinburgh: Edinburgh University Press.

Koschetz, H. (1968), "Du Pont Unfurls a New Silklike Fiber," *New York Times*, June 28, 1968: 57.

Kramer, H. (1975), "The Dubious Art of Fashion Photography," *New York Times*, December 28, 1975: 100.

Kuchta, D. (2002), *The Three-Piece Suit and Modern Masculinity: England, 1550–1850*, Berkeley: University of California Press.

Kunz, G.I. and M.B. Garner (2006), *Going Global: The Textile and Apparel Industry*, New York: Fairchild.

Kuru, A. (2009), *Secularism and State Policies towards Religion: The United States, France and Turkey*, New York: Cambridge University Press.

Lague, L. (1959), *The Importance of Wearing Clothes*, New York: Hastings House.

— (1993), "How Thin Is Too Thin?" *People Weekly* 40, September 20, 1993: 74–80.

Langer, L. (1959), *The Importance of Wearing Clothes*, New York: Hastings House.

Laver, J. (1952), *Clothes*, London: Burke.

Lawrence, D.H. (1990), *England, My England*, ed. B. Steele, Cambridge: Cambridge University Press.

— ([1920] 2000), *Women in Love*, introduction Joyce Carol Oates, New York: Random House.

— ([1922] 2006), *The Fox/The Captain's Doll/The Ladybird*, ed. D. Mehl, London: Penguin.

Lazreg, M. (2011), *Questioning the Veil: Open Letters to Muslim Women*, Princeton, N.J.: Princeton University Press.

Le Fèvre, G. (1929), *Au secours de la couture (industrie française)*, Paris: Editions Baudinière.

Leach, W.R. (1994), *Land of Desire: Merchants, Power, and the Rise of a New American Culture*, New York: Vintage.

Leglar, C. (2013), "I am a Woman who Models Male Clothes. This is not about Gender," *The Guardian*, Friday November 1, 2013, http://www.theguardian.com/commentisfree/2013/nov/01/woman-models-mens-clothes-casey-legler [accessed March 21, 2015].

Lehman, U. (2000), *Tigersprung: Fashion in Modernity*, Boston: MIT Press.

Leo, J. (1994), "Selling the Woman-Child," *U.S. News and World Report* 116, no. 23, June 13, 1994: 27.

Levine, M.P. and M. Kimmel (1998), *Gay Macho: The Life and Death of the Homosexual Clone*, New York: New York University Press.

Levy, A. (2006), *Female Chauvinist Pigs: The Rise of Raunch Culture*, London: Free Press.

Lewis, R. (2004), *Rethinking Orientalism*, New Brunswick: Rutgers.

Lewis, W. (1982), "Coming Again: How Society Functions through its Religions," in Eileen Barker (ed.), *New Religious Movements: A Perspective for Understanding Society*, Lewiston, N.J.: Edwin Mellen.

Lilly Daché: glamour at the drop of a hat: The Museum at FIT, March 13–April 21, 2007, New York, N.Y.: Fashion Institute of Technology.

Limnander, A. (2001), *Miguel Adrover, Fall 2001 Ready-to-Wear*, February 11, 2001, http://www.style.com/fashion-shows/fall-2001-ready-to-wear/miguel-adrover [accessed July 30, 2015].

Ling, W. (2012), "Fashionalization. Why so many cities host fashion weeks?" In *Fashion Capital*, ed. J. Berry, Oxford: Interdisciplinary Press.

Lipovetsky, G. (1987), *L'empire de l'éphémère. La mode et son destin dans les sociétés modernes*, Paris: Gallimard/Lipovetsky, G. ([1994] 2002), *The Empire of Fashion: Dressing Modern Democracy*, Princeton: Princeton University Press.

Lofgren, O. and R. Willim (2005), *Magic Culture and the New Economy*, Oxford and New York: Berg.

Lucchesi, J. (2001), "'The Dandy in Me': Romaine Brooks's 1923 Portraits," in *Dandies: Fashion and Finesse in Art and Culture*, edi. S. Fillin-Yeh, New York and London: New York University Press.

Lupano, M. and A. Vacari (2009), *Fashion at the Time of Fascism*, Rome: Damiani.

Lurie, A. (1981), *The Language of Clothes*, London: Random House.

Lury, C. (1996), *Consumer Culture*, New Brunswick: Rutgers University Press.

Luthar, B. (2006), "Remembering Socialism: On desire, consumption and surveillance," *Journal of Consumer Culture* 6, no. 2: 229–59.

Lyle, D.S. (rev. ed. 1964), *Focus on Fabrics*, Silver Spring, MD: National Institute of Drycleaning, available online: http://www.cs.arizona.edu/patterns/weaving/books.html

Lynch, A. (2012), *Porn Chic: Exploring the Contours of Raunch Eroticism*, London: Berg.

Maillet, T. (2013), *Histoire de la médiation entre textile et mode en France: des échantillonneurs aux bureaux de style (1825–1975)*, PhD thesis, Paris: EHESS.

Manual, F.E. (1967), "Toward a Psychological History of Utopia," in *Utopias and Utopian Thought*, ed. Frank E. Manuel, Boston: Beacon Press.

Marcketti, S.B. and E.T. Angstman (2013), "The Trend for Mannish Suits in the 1930s," *Dress* 39, no. 2: 135–52.

Martin, R. (1994), "Missoni," in *Contemporary Fashion*, Farmington Hills: St. James Press.

— (1998), *American Ingenuity: Sportswear 1930s–1970s*, New York: Metropolitan Museum of Art.

Martin, R. and H. Koda (1994), *Visions of the East in Western Dress*, New York: Metropolitan Museum of Art.

Martins, G. (2009), "Subculture, style, chavs and consumer capitalism: towards a critical cultural criminology of youth," *Crime, Media, Culture* 5, no. 2: 123–45.

Marzel, S. (2006), "De quelques Success Stories dans la creation vestimentaire parisienne des années 60," *Archives juives* 2, no. 39: 72–84.

Mathur, S. (2007), *India by Design*, Berkeley: University of California Press.

Mayhew, E. (2013), *Wounded: A New History of the Western Front in World War I*, Oxford: Oxford University Press.

Maynard, M. (2004), *Dress and Globalization*, Manchester: Manchester University Press.

McDowell, C. (1997), *Forties Fashion and the New Look*, London: Bloomsbury.

McKay, C. ([1929] 2008), *Banjo: A Story without a Plot*, London: Serpent's Tail.

McNeil, P., V. Karaminas, and C. Cole (eds) (2009), *Fashion in Fiction: Text and Clothing in Literature, Film and Television*, New York: Berg.

McRobbie, A. (1988), *Zoot Suits and Second-hand Dresses: an anthology of fashion and music*, Boston: Unwin Hyman.

— (1999a), "Art Fashion and Music in the Culture Society," in *In The Culture Society: Art Fashion and Popular Music*, New York and London: Routledge.

— (1999b), *In the Culture Society: Art, Fashion and Popular Music*, London and New York: Routledge.

McRobbie, A. and J. Garber ([1993] 2006), "Girls and subcultures," in *Resistance Through Rituals*, eds S. Hall and T. Jefferson, New York: Routledge.

Meiklejohn, H.E. (1938), "Dresses: The Impact of Fashion on a Business," in Walton Hamilton, *Price and Price Policies*, New York: McGraw-Hill.

Melchior, M.R. (2014), "Introduction: Understanding Fashion and Dress Museology," in *Fashion and Museums: Theory and Practice*, eds M.R. Melchior and B. Svensson, London: Bloomsbury.

Merceron, D. (2007), *Lanvin*, New York: Rizzoli.

Merlo, E. and F. Polese (2006), "Turning Fashion into Business: the emergence of Milan as an international hub," *Business History Review* 80, no. 3: 415–47.

Mertha, A.C. (2005), *The Politics of Piracy: Intellectual Property in Contemporary China*, Ithaca: Cornell University Press.

Metropolitan Museum of Art Thomas J. Watson Library (1948), *American Textiles,'48*, New York: Metropolitan Museum of Art.

Milbank, C.R. (1989a), *Couture: The Great Designers*, New York: Stuart, Tabori, & Chang.

— (1989b), *New York Fashion: The Evolution of American Style*, New York: Harry N. Abrams.

Miles, S. (1998), *Consumerism: As a Way of Life*, London: Sage.

Milestone, K. and A. Meyer (2011), *Gender and Popular Culture*, London: Polity Press.

Miller, D. (2010), *Stuff*, Cambridge: Polity, 2010.

Miller, L.E. (1993), *Cristóbal Balenciaga*, London: B.T. Batsford.

Miller, T. (1999), *Late Modernism: Politics, Fiction, and the Arts Between the World Wars*, Berkeley: University of California Press.

Moffitt, P. (1999), *The Rudi Gernreich Book*, Köln: Taschen.

Moncrieff, R.W. (1975), *The Man-Made Fibres*, New York and Toronto: John Wiley & Sons.

Monneyron, F. (2010), *La sociologie de la mode*, Paris: Puf.

Montagné-Villette, S. (199), *Le Sentier, un espace ambigu*, Paris: Masson.

Montgomery, M.E. (1998), *Spectacles of Leisure in Edith Wharton's New York*, New York: Routledge.

Morris, B. (1979), "Jogging Suits Are Off and Running in a Race for Style," *New York Times*, March 11, 1979, AD1.

Morrison, T. (1992), *Jazz*, New York: Alfred A. Knopf.

Mort, F. (1996), *Cultures of Consumption: Masculinities and Social Space in Late Twentieth-Century Britain*, London: Routledge.

Munro, A. ([1978] 2006), *Who Do You Think You Are?* Toronto: Penguin.

Nieburg, H.L. (1973), *Culture Storm: Politics and the Ritual Order*, New York: St. Martin's Press.

Niessen, S. (2010), "Interpreting Civilization Through Dress," in *Berg Encyclopaedia of World Dress and Fashion*, vol. 8, West Europe, Oxford and New York: Berg.

Nika, C. (2011), "Whatever Happened to Miguel Adrover?" January 2, 2011, http://fashionetc. com/fashion/influencers/439-whatever-happened-to-miguel-adrover [accessed July 30, 2015].

Nixon, S. (1996), *Hard Looks: Masculinities, Spectatorship and Contemporary Consumption*, London: University College London Press.

O'Connor, K. (2005), "The Other Half: The Material Culture of New Fibres," in *Clothing as Material Culture*, eds S. Küchler and D. Miller, Oxford: Berg.

— (2008), "The Body and the Brand: How Lycra Shaped America," in *Producing Fashion: Commerce, Culture, and Consumers*, ed. R.L. Blaszczyk, Philadelphia: University of Pennsylvania Press.

— (2011), *Lycra: How a Fiber Shaped America*, New York and London: Routledge.

Okawa, T. (2007), "Licensing Practices at Maison Dior," in *Producing Fashion: Commerce, Culture and Consumers*, ed. R.L. Blaszczyk, Philadelphia: University of Pennsylvania Press.

Okuefuna, D. (2008), *The Wonderful World of Albert Khan*, London: BBC Books.

On the Edge: Images from 100 Years of Vogue (1992), New York: Random House.

Orsi, R.A. (1996), *Thank You, St. Jude: Women's Devotion to the Patron Saint of Hopeless Causes*, New Haven: Yale University Press.

Palmer, A. (1991), "Paper Clothes: Not Just a Fad," in Patricia A. Cunningham and Susan Voso Lab (eds), *Dress and Popular Culture*, Bowling Green: Bowling Green State University Popular Press.

— (2001), *Couture & Commerce: The Transatlantic Fashion Trade in the 1950s*, Vancouver: UBC Press and the Royal Ontario Museum.

— (2003), *Fashion: A Canadian Perspective*, Toronto, Buffalo, and London: University of Toronto Press.

— (2007), "Inside Paris haute couture," in *The Golden Age of Couture: Paris and London, 1947–1957*, ed. C. Wilcox, London: V&A Publishing.

— (2009), *Dior*, London: V&A Publishing.

— (2013), "Chanel: American as Apple Pie," in *The Chanel Legend*, ed. M. Spitz, Mettingen: Draiflessen Collection.

— (2014), "Du fil au vêtement. La production de textiles pour la haute couture," in *Les années 50. La mode en France, 1947–1957*, ed. Alexandra Bosc, Paris: Paris Musée.

Palmer, A. and H. Clark (eds) (2004), *Old Clothes: New Looks*, New York: Berg.

Palmer, S.J. (2004), *Aliens Adored: Raël's UFO Religion*, New Jersey: Rutgers University Press.

— (2010), *The Nuwaubian Nation: Black Spirituality and State Control*, Farnham: Ashgate Publishing.

— (2011), *The New Heretics of France: Minority Religions, la Republique, and the Government-Sponsored "War on Sects,"* New York: Oxford University Press.

— (2014), "Raël's Angels: The first five years of a secret order," in *Sexuality and New Religious Movements*, eds Henrik Bogdan and James R. Lewis, New York: Palgrave Studies in New Religions and Alternative Spiritualities.

Palmer S.J. and D.G. Bromley (2007), "Deliberate Heresies: New Religious Myths and Rituals as Critiques," in David G. Bromlet (ed.), *Teaching New Religious Movements*, New York: Oxford University Press.

Parkins, W. (2002), *Fashioning the Body Politic: Dress, Gender, Citizenship*, Oxford: Berg.

Paulicelli, E. (2004), *Fashion Under Fascism: Beyond the Black Shirt*, New York: Berg.

Pavitt, J. (2010), "Logos," in *The Berg Companion to Fashion*, ed. V. Steele, Oxford: Berg.

Payeur Raynauld, S. (2007), "Cinq Robes Demandées Par Le Ciel," *Le Royaume* (May–June 2007): 12–13.

"Pendleton Company History," *Pendleton Woolen Mills*, http://www.pendleton-usa.com/custserv/custserv.jsp?pageName=CompanyHistory&parentName=Heritage [accessed June 15, 2014].

Pilcher, J. (2011), "No logo? Children's consumption of fashion," *Childhood* 18, no. 1: 128–41

Poiret, P. (1930), *En habillant l'époque*, Paris: Grasset.

— ([1931] 2009), *King of Fashion: The Autobiography of Paul Poiret*, London: V&A Publishing.

Polan, B. and R. Tredre (2009), *The Great Fashion Designers*, Oxford and New York: Berg Publishers.

Polhemus, T. (1994), *Streetstyle: From Sidewalk to Catwalk*, London: Thames & Hudson.

Polle, E., F. Hammond and A. Keens (2013), *Jean Patou: A Fashionable Life*, Paris: Flammarion.

Pouillard, V. (2007), "In the Shadow of Paris? French Haute Couture and Belgian Fashion between the Wars," in *Producing Fashion: Commerce, Culture and Consumers*, ed. R.L. Blaszczyk, Philadelphia: Pennsylvania University Press.

— (2011), "Design Piracy in the Fashion Industries of Paris and New York in the Interwar Years," *Business History Review* 85 no. 2: 319–44.

— (2013a), "Fashion for All? The Transatlantic Fashion Business and the Development of a Popular Press Culture During the Interwar Period," *Journalism Studies* 14 no. 5: 716–29.

— (2013b), "Keeping Designs and Brands Authentic: The resurgence of the post-war French fashion business under the challenge of US mass production," *European History Review* 20 no. 5: 815–35.

— (2013c), "The Rise of Fashion Forecasting and Fashion PR, 1920–1940. The History of Tobé and Bernays," in *Globalizing Beauty: Consumerism and Body Aesthetics in the 20th Century*, eds H. Berghoff and T. Kuehne, New York: Palgrave.

Puwal N. and N. Bhati (September/December 2003), "Fashioning Women in Colonial India," *Fashion Theory. The Journal of Dress, Body and Culture*, 7.3/4: 327–44.

Quant, M. ([1965] 2012), *Quant by Quant: The Autobiography of Mary Quant*, London: V&A Publishing.

Rabine, L.W. (2002), *The Global Circulation of African Dress*, Oxford and New York: Berg.

— (2010), *African Dress: Fashion, Agency, Performance*, London: Bloomsbury.

Raël (1974), *Le livre qui dit la Vérité*, Clermont Ferrand: Les Editions du Message.

— (1977), *Les extraterrestres m'ont emmene sur leur planète*, Brantome: l'Editions du Message.

— (2001), *Yes to Human Cloning*, Florida: Raëlian Foundation.

Rafferty, K. (2011), "Class-based emotions and the allure of fashion consumption," *Journal of Consumer Culture* 11, no. 2: 239–60.

Raustiala, K.S. (2006), "The Piracy Paradox: Innovation and Intellectual Property in Fashion Design," *Virginia Law Review* 92: 1687–777.

Reed, R. (1972), "Happy Days for Cotton," *New York Times*, July 9, 1972, F1.

Reinach, S.S. (2005), "China and Italy: Fast Fashion versus Prêt-à-Porter. Towards a New Culture of Fashion," *Fashion Theory. The Journal of Dress, Body and Culture* 9, no. 1: 43–56.

— (2006), *Orientalismi*, Roma: Meltemi.

— (2011a), "National Identities and International Recognition," *Fashion Theory* 15, no. 2: 267–72.

— (2011b), *Un modo di mode*, Roma-Bari: Laterza.

— (2013), "Luxury as a process," paper given at *The Regulation of Luxury Conference*, Bologna, December 12–13, 2013.

Reuther, R. (1993), *Sexism and God Talk: Toward a Feminist Theology*, Boston: Beacon Press.

Rhys, J. ([1939] 1969), *Good Morning, Midnight*, London: Andre Deutsch.

— ([1930] 1971), *After Leaving Mr. Mackenzie*, London: Penguin.

Riello, G. and P. McNeil (2010), *The Fashion History Reader*, New York: Routledge.

Roberts, M.L. (Spring 1992), "'This Civilization No Longer Has Sexes': La Garçonne and Cultural Crisis in France After World War I," *Gender and History* 4, no.1: 49–69.

Robinson, B.A. (2005), "Jain Dharma," Ontario Consultants on Religious Tolerance, www.religioustolerance.org /jainism.htm [accessed October 28, 2014].

Rocamora, A. (2011), "Personal fashion blogs: screens and mirrors in digital self-portraits," *Fashion Theory* 15, no. 4: 407–24.

— (2013), "How New Are New Media? The Case of Fashion Blogs," in *Fashion Media: Past and Present*, eds Djurdja Bartlett, Shaun Cole, and Agnès Rocamora. London: Bloomsbury.

Rose, C. (2010), *Making, Selling and Wearing Boys' Clothes in Late-Victorian England*, Farnham: Ashgate.

Ross, R. (2008), *Clothing: A Global History*, Cambridge: Polity Press.

Rossellini, R. (1987), *Quasi un'autobiografia*, Milano: Mondadori.

Rouzaud, C.A. (1946), *Un problème d'intérêt national: Les industries du luxe*, Thése pour ledoctorat d'Etat, Strasbourg: Librairie du Recueil Sirey.

Rovine, V.L. (2007), "Viewing Africa Through Fashion," *Fashion Theory* 13, no. 2: 133–40.

— www.africulture.com [accessed December 13, 2013].

Ruffat, M. and D. Veillon (2007), *La mode des sixties, l'entrée dans la modernité*, Paris: Autrement.

Sahlins, M. (1976), *Culture and Practical Reason*, Chicago: Chicago University Press.

Said, E. (1978), *Orientalism: Western Representations of the Orient*, London: Routledge & Kegan Paul.

Saillard, O. (ed.) (2014), *Fashion Mix. Mode d'ici. Créateurs d'ailleurs*, Paris: Flammarion.

Saisselin, R.G. (1959), "From Baudelaire to Christian Dior: The Poetics of Fashion," *The Journal of Aesthetics and Art Criticism* 18, no. 1: 109–115.

Sargeant, W. (1958), "A Woman Entering a Taxi in the Rain," *The New Yorker*, November 8, 1958, 49–84.

Sassen, S. (1991), *The Global City: New York, London, Tokyo*, Princeton: Princeton University Press.

Sauro, C. (2005), "Jeans," in *Encyclopedia of Clothing and Fashion*, ed. V. Steele, Detroit: Thompson Gale.

Savage, J. (2013), "Oh! You Pretty Things," in *David Bowie Is*, London: V&A Publishing.

Saxenian, A. ([1994] (1996), *Regional Advantage: Culture and Competition in Silicon Valley and Route 128*, Cambridge: Harvard University Press.

Schacht, S.P. and L. Underwood (2004), "The Absolutely Fabulous but Flawlessly Customary World of Drag Queens and Female Impersonators," *Journal of Homosexuality* 46, no. 3/4: 1–17.

Schneider, J. (August 1994), "In and Out of Polyester: Desire, Disdain and Global Fibre Competitions," *Anthropology Today* 10, no. 4: 2–10.

Schneier, M. (2014), "Fashion in the Age of Instagram," *New York Times*, April 10, 2014, E1.

Schoeser, M. (2003), *World Textiles: A Concise History*, London: Thames & Hudson.

Scott, W.R. (2008), "California Casual: Lifestyle Marketing and Men's Leisurewear, 1930–1960," in *Producing Fashion: Commerce, Culture, and Consumers*, ed. R.L. Blaszczyk, Philadelphia: University of Pennsylvania Press.

Seebohm, C. (1982), *The Man Who Was Vogue: The Life and Times of Condé Nast*, New York: Viking Press.

Sen, A. (2005), *The Argumentative India*, New York: Allen Lane Penguin.

Sender, K. (2004), *Business, Not Politics: The Making of the Gay Market*, New York: Columbia University Press.

Sennet, R. (1992), *The Fall of Public Man*, London: Faber.

Settembrini, L. (ed.) (1996), *Emilio Pucci*, Florence: Skira.

Sewell, J. (2014), "Performing Masculinity Through Objects in Postwar America. The Playboy's Pipe," in *Love Objects: Emotion, Design and Material Culture*, eds A. Moran and S. O'Brian, London: Bloomsbury.

Shaw, M. (2007), "H.R. Mallinson & Company, Inc., of New York, New Jersey and Pennsylvania," in *American Silk 1830–1930*, eds J. Field, M. Senechal, and M. Shaw, Lubbock, TX: Texas Tech University Press.

Siegel, L. (2011), *To Die For: Is Fashion Wearing Out the World?* London: Harper Collins.

Simmel, G. (1904), "Fashion," *International Quarterly* 10, no. 1: 130–55.

— (1905), *Philosophie der Mode*, Berlin: Pan-Verlag.

Simon, P. (1931), *La Haute Couture, Monographie d'une industrie de luxe*, Paris: Presses Universitaires de France.

Skov, L. (2011), "Dreams of Small Nation in a Polycentric Fashion World," *Fashion Theory* 15, no. 2: 137–56.

Slade T. (2009), *Japanese Fashion: A Cultural History*, Oxford and New York: Berg.

Slater, D. (1997), *Consumer Culture and Modernity*, Cambridge: Polity.

Sloane, L. (1974), "Suiting Up for Leisure." *New York Times*, October 27, 1974: 178.

Sluiter, L. (2009), *Clean Clothes: A Global Movement to End Sweatshops*, London: Pluto Press.

Smith, P. (2010), *Just Kids*, New York: Harper Collins.

Smith, P.J. (1999), "'You don't have to say you love me'. The Camp Masquerades of Dusty Springfield," in *The Queer Sixties*, ed. P. J. Smith, New York and London: Routledge.

Snaith, G. (2003), "Tom's Men: The Masculinization of Homosexuality and the Homosexualization of Masculinity at the end of the Twentieth Century," *Paragraph* 26: 77–88.

Snow, C. and M.L. Aswell (1962), *The World of Carmel Snow*, New York: McGraw-Hill Book Company Inc.

Sontag, S. (1978), "The Avedon Eye," *Vogue* (US), September 1, 1978: 460–1, 507–8.

Steele, V. (1985), *Fashion and Eroticism: Ideals of Feminine Beauty from the Victorian Era to the Jazz Age*, New York: Oxford University Press.

— (1988), *Paris Fashion: A Cultural History*, Oxford: Oxford University Press.

— (1996), *Fetish: Fashion, Sex and Power*, New York: Oxford University Press.

— (1997), "Anti-Fashion: The 1970s," *Fashion Theory* 1 no. 3: 279–96.

— (2013), "A Queer History of Fashion: From the Closet to the Catwalk," in *A Queer History of Fashion: From the Closet to the Catwalk* Steele, ed. V. Steele, New Haven and London: Yale University Press.

Steele, V. and G. Carrara (2005), "Italian Fashion," in *Encyclopedia of Clothing and Fashion*, ed. V. Steele, Detroit: Thompson Gale.

Steele, V. and J. Major (1999), *China Chic: East Meets West*, New Haven and London: Yale University Press.

Steichen, E. (1963), *A Life in Photography*, Garden City: Doubleday & Co.

Stein, L. (1962), *The Triangle Fire*, Ithaca: Cornell University Press.

Stern, M. (2014), *The Fitness Movement and Fitness Centre Industry 1960–2000*, Business History Conference, 2008, http://www.thebhc.org/publications/BEHonline/2008/stern.pdf [accessed February 20, 2014].

Stern, R. (2004), *Against Fashion: Clothing as Art, 1850–1930*, Cambridge, MA: MIT Press.

Stewart, M.L. (2005), "Copying and Copyrighting Haute Couture: Democratizing Fashion, 1900–1930," *French Historical Studies* 28, no. 1: 103–30.

— (2008), *Dressing Modern Frenchwomen: Marketing Haute Couture, 1919–1939*, Baltimore: Johns Hopkins University Press.

Stillman-Webb, N. (2007), "'Be What You Want': Clothing and Subjectivity in Toni Morrison's *Jazz*," in *Styling Texts: Dress and Fashion in Literature*, eds C. Kuhn and C. Carlson, Youngstown: Cambria University Press.

Stitziel, J. (2005), *Fashioning Socialism: Clothing, Politics and Consumer Culture in East Germany*, Oxford: Berg.

Stutesman, D. (2011), "Costume Design, or, what is fashion in film?" in *Fashion in Film*, ed. A. Munich, Indiana: Indiana University Press.

Tardiff, R.J. and L. Schirmer (eds) (1991), *Horst: Sixty Years of Photography*, New York: Universe.

Tarlo, E. (2010), *Visibly Muslim: Fashion, Politics, Faith*, Oxford and New York: Berg.

Tarlo, E. and A. Moors (2013), "Introduction," *Fashion Theory* 11, no, 2/3: 133–43.

Taylor, L. (2002), *The Study of Dress History*, Manchester: Manchester University Press.

— (2007), "L'English Style: les origines de la mode en Grande-Bretagne de 1950 aux années 1970," in (eds) Ruffat, Veillon, *La mode des sixties*, Paris: Autrement.

— (2013), "Fashion and Dress History: Theoretical and Methodological Approaches," in *The Handbook of Fashion Studies*, eds S. Black, A. de la Haye, et. al. London: Bloomsbury.

Teunissen, J. (2005), "Global Fashion/Local Tradition. On the globalization of fashion," in *Global Fashion Local Tradition: On the Globalization of Fashion*, eds J. Brand and J. Teunissen, Terra: Centraal Museum Utrecht.

Thavis, J. (2007), "Vatican Excommunicates Some Members of Canadian Sect," *Catholic News Service*.

"The Science of Ultrasuede®," Toray Industries, http://www.ultrasuede.com/about/science.html [accessed June 4, 2014].

Thesander, M. (1997), *The Feminine Ideal*, London: Reaktion.

Thompson, H. (2010), "Nan Kempler: Queen Spree," *W Magazine*, May 2010, http://www.wmagazine.com/fashion/2010/05/nan_kempner/ [accessed July 25, 2015].

Tiersten, L. (2001), *Marianne in the Market. Envisioning Consumer Society in Fin-de-Siècle France*, Berkeley: University of California Press.

Tortora, P.G., and S.B. Marcketti (2015), *Survey of Historic Costume*, New York and London: Fairchild Books/Bloomsbury Publishing Inc.

Triggs, T. (1992), "Framing Masculinity: Herb Ritts, Bruce Weber and the Body Perfect," in *Chic Thrills: A Fashion Reader*, eds J. Ash and E. Wilson, Berkeley: University of California Press.

Troy, N.J. (2002), *Couture Culture: A Study in Modern Art and Fashion*, Cambridge: MIT Press.

Tsui, C. (2010), *China Fashion: Conversations with Designers*, Oxford and New York: Berg.

Tu, T.L.N. (2010), *The Beautiful Generation: Asian Americans and the Cultural Economy of Fashion*, Durham: Duke University Press.

Tumminia, D. (2005), *When Prophecy Never Fails: Myth and Reality in a Flying-Saucer Group*, New York: Oxford University Press.

Turner, V.W. (1969), *The Ritual Process: Structure and Anti-Structure*, Chicago: University of Chicago.

Twigg, J. (2013), *Fashion and Age: Dress, the Body and Later Life*, London: Bloomsbury.

Tynan, J. (2011), "Military Dress and Men's Outdoor Leisurewear: Burberry's Trench Coat in First World War Britain," *Journal of Design History* 24, no. 2: 139–56.

Vänskä, A. (2003), "See-through Closet: Female Androgyny in the 1990s Fashion Images, the Concepts of 'Modern Woman' and 'Lesbian Chic'," in *Farväl heteronormativitet*. Papers presented at the conference *Farewell to Heteronormativity*. vol. 1. Sverige: Lambda Nordica Förlag.

— (2005), "Why Are There No Lesbian Advertisements?" *Feminist Theory* 6 no. 1: 67–85.

— (2009), "From Marginality to Mainstream: On the Politics of Lesbian Visibility During the Past Decades," in *Sapphists, Sexologists and Sexualities: Lesbian Histories*, vol. 2, eds M. McAuliffe and S. Tiernan, Cambridge: Cambridge Scholars Press.

— (2014), "New Kids on the Mall: Babyfied Dogs as Fashionable Co-consumers," *Young Consumers* 15, no. 3.

— (forthcoming), *Fashioning Childhood. Children in Fashion Advertising,* London and New York: Bloomsbury.

Veblen, T. ([1899] [2007] 2009), *The Theory of the Leisure Class*, Oxford and New York: Oxford University Press.

Veillon, D. (1990), *La mode sous l'occupation. Débrouillardise et coquetterie dans la France en guerre (1939–1945)*, Paris: Payot.

— (2002), *Fashion Under the Occupation*, London: Berg.

Vernus, P. (2006), *Art, Luxe, Industrie. Bianchini-Férier. Un siècle de soieries lyonnaises 1888–1992*, Grenoble: Presses Universitaires de Grenoble.

Vincent-Ricard, F. (1983), *Raison et Passion. Langages de société. La mode, 1940–1990*, Paris: Textile, Art, Langage.

Vinken, B. (1999), "Transvesty—Travesty: Fashion and Gender," *Fashion Theory* 3, no. 1: 33–50.

— (2005), *Fashion Zeitgeist. Trends and Cycles in the fashion System*, Oxford: Berg.

Vollmer, J.E. (2010), "Cultural Authentication," in *Berg Encyclopaedia of World Dress and Fashion*, Oxford and New York: Berg.

Von Drehle, D. (2002), *Triangle: The Fire that Changed America*, New York: Grove Press.

Wagner, G. (2002), "Ultrasuede," *Perspecta* 33: 90–103.

Walker, M. (2005), "Cardin, Pierre," in V. Steele (ed.), *Encyclopedia of Clothing and Fashion*, Detroit: Thompson Gale, 224.

Walker, T.J. (2009), "'He outfitted his family in notable decency': Slavery, Honour and Dress in Eighteenth-Century Lima, Peru," *Slavery and Abolition: A Journal of Slave and Post-Slave Studies* 30: 383–402.

Warburton, R. (2007), "'Nothing could be seen whole or read from start to finish': Transvestitism and Imitation in *Orlando* and *Nightwood*," in *Styling Texts: Dress and Fashion in Literature*, eds C. Kuhn and C. Carlson, Youngstown: Cambria University Press, 269–90.

Ward, S. (2005a), "Chemise Dress," in *Encyclopedia of Clothing and Fashion*, ed. V. Steele. Detroit: Thompson Gale.

— (2005b), "Swimwear," in *Encyclopedia of Clothing and Fashion*, ed. V. Steele. Detroit: Thompson Gale.

Warner, P.C. (2005), "The Americanisation of Fashion: Sportswear, the Movies and the 1930s," in *Twentieth Century American Fashion*, eds L. Welters and P. Cunningham, Oxford: Berg.

Weaver, M. (1989), *British Photography in the Nineteenth Century: The Fine Art Tradition*, Cambridge: Cambridge University Press.

Weber, B. (1992), *Hotel Room with a View*, Washington: Smithsonian Institution Press.

Weber, M. (1947), *Max Weber: The Theory of Social and Economic Organization*, Glencoe: Free Press.

Weiner, A. and J. Schneider (1989), *Cloth and the Human Experience*, Washington: Smithsonian Institution Press.

Weinmann, C. (2003), "The Delineator," in *A Theodore Dreiser Encyclopedia*, ed. K. Newlin, Westport: Greenwood Press.

Wharton, E. ([1920] 1968), *The Age of Innocence*, New York: Macmillan.

"What is a Cult?" *The Guardian*, May 29, 2009.

White, N. (2000), *Reconstructing Italian Fashion: America and the Development of the Italian Fashion Industry*, Oxford and New York: Berg.

Whitley, L.D. (2006), "Azzedine Alaïa," in *Fashion Show: Paris Style*, eds P. Parmal, D. Grumbach, S. Ward, and L.D. Whitley, Boston: MFA Publications.

— (2013), *Hippie Chic*, Boston: MFA Publications.

Wilcox, C. (2005), "Alaïa, Azzedine," in *Encyclopedia of Clothing and Fashion*, ed. V. Steele, Detroit: Thompson Gale.

— ed. (2009), *The Golden Age of Couture: Paris and London 1947–57*, London: V&A Publishing.

Williams, B. (1945), *Fashion is Our Business*, New York and Philadelphia: Lippincott.

Williams, R. (1982), *Dream Worlds: Mass Consumption in Late 19th Century France*, Berkeley: University of California Press.

Williams-Mitchell, C. (1982), *Dressed for the Job: Story of Occupational Costume*, London: Blandford Press.

Wilson, E. ([1985] 2003), *Adorned in Dreams: Fashion and Modernity*. London: I.B. Tauris, 2003.

Wingfield, V. (1997), *The Fashion Group International, Records c. 1930–1997*, New York: New York Public Library.

Wolf, N. (1990), *The Beauty Myth*, London: Vintage.

Woodcock, G. and I. Avakumovic (1977), *The Doukhobors*, London: Faber & Faber.

Woodward, S. (2007), *Why Women Wear What They Wear: Materialising Culture*, Oxford: Berg.

— (2009), "The Myth of Street Style," *Fashion Theory: The Journal of Dress, Body and Culture* 13 (1): 83–102.

"The Woolmark brand celebrates 50 years," *Woolmark Company*, March 26, 2014, http://www.woolmark.com/history [accessed June 5, 2014].

Wu, J. (2009), *Chinese Fashion: From Mao to Now*, Oxford: Berg.

Yezierska, A. ([1925] 2003), *Bread Givers*, New York: Persea Books.

Yohannan, K. and N. Nolf (1998), *Claire McCardell: Redefining Modernism*, New York: Abrams.

Zakharova, L. (2011), *S'habiller à la soviétique. La mode et le dégel en URSS*, Paris: CNRS.

Zdatny, S. (1997), "The Boyish Look and the Liberated Woman: The Politics and Aesthetics of Women's Hairstyles," *Fashion Theory: The Journal of Dress, Body and Culture* 1, no. 4: 367–97.

Zhao, J. (2013), *The Chinese Fashion Industry*, London, Delhi, New York, and Sydney: Bloomsbury.

Zubek, J.P. and P.A. Solberg (1952), *Doukhobors at War*, Toronto: The Ryerson Press.

Websites

www.africulture.com
www.modeaparis.com
www.Oeko-tex.com
www.polartec.com
www.religioustolerance.org
www.ultrasuede.com
www.vice.com

NOTES ON CONTRIBUTORS

Rachael Barron-Duncan is an assistant professor in the Department of Art and Design at Central Michigan University. She teaches modern and contemporary art history and her scholarship focuses on fashion history and how avant-garde artists made use of the burgeoning world of mass media in the early twentieth century. She is currently preparing a manuscript on Surrealist advertising in French fashion magazines.

Irene Gammel holds a Canada Research Chair in Modern Literature and Culture at Ryerson University in Toronto, where she is Professor of English and also directs the Modern Literature and Culture Research Centre. She is the author of many articles and books exploring issues of gender, fashion, and identity including *Looking for Anne of Green Gables* (St. Martin's Press) and *Baroness Elsa: Gender, Dada, and Everyday Modernity—A Cultural Biography* (MIT Press). Her current research focuses on the visual culture of the First World War including the intersections of war and fashion. For more, see www.ryerson.ca/mlc<http://www.ryerson.ca/mlc> Follow her on Twitter: MLC_Research

Paul L. Gareau is an assistant professor in the Faculty of Native Studies at the University of Alberta. His main doctoral research has been to investigate the socio-political impact of evangelical Catholic culture on youth identities in Canada. Through his graduate work on the Army of Mary, Gareau is also interested in religious conservatism and gender, and the discursive impact of historiography on shaping identity.

Adam Geczy is an artist and writer who teaches at Sydney College of the Arts, at the University of Sydney. With twenty years of artistic practice, his videos, sculptural installations, and performance-based works have been exhibited throughout Australasia, Asia, and Europe to considerable critical acclaim. He is the author of numerous books including *Art: Histories, Theories and Exceptions* (Berg 2008) which won the Choice Award for best academic title in art in 2009, and *Fashion and Orientalism* (Bloomsbury) was published in 2013. Books with Vicki Karaminas include *Queer Style* (Bloomsbury, 2013) and *Fashion's Double: Fashion and Representation in Painting, Photography and Film* (Bloomsbury, 2015). He is the editor (with Vicki Karaminas) of *The Journal of Asia-Pacific Pop Culture* (Penn State University Press),

Vicki Karaminas is Professor of Fashion and Deputy Director of Doctoral Research at the College of Creative Arts, Massey University, New Zealand. With Adam Geczy she has co-edited *Fashion and Art* (Berg, 2012), co-written *Queer Style* (Bloomsbury, 2013) and *Fashion's Double: Representations of Fashion in Painting, Photography and Film* (Bloomsbury, 2015). She is the author of *Shanghai Street Style* (with Toni Johnson Woods); *Sydney Street Style* (with Toni Johnson Woods and Justine Taylor); and *Fashion in Popular Culture* (with Joseph Hancock and Toni Johnson Woods). Other book projects include, *The Men's Fashion Reader* (Berg, 2009) and *Fashion in Fiction: Text and Clothing in*

Literature, Film and Television (Berg, 2009). She is the editor (with Adam Geczy) of *The Journal of Asia-Pacific Pop Culture* (Penn State University Press).

Karen Mulhallen is Professor Emeritus Ryerson University. She is an editor, critic, and poet. She has published widely on the arts and culture. In addition to numerous articles, she has written or edited more than eighteen books and more than 150 issues of *Descant* magazine. Her most recent book is *Code Orange: An Emblazoned Suite*, translated into French by Nancy Huston (Black Moss Press, 2015). She is now working on a study of William Blake's *Illustrations to Edward Young's Night Thoughts*.

Alexandra Palmer is the Nora E. Vaughan Senior Curator Textiles & Costume, Royal Ontario Museum where she has curated many exhibitions including *Fashion Follows Form: Designs for Sitting*, 2014 Richard Martin Exhibition Award. She is the author/contributor/editor of books and catalogs, including *Les années 50* (Musée Galliera, 2014); *The Chanel Legend* (Draiflesen, 2013); *Dior* (V&A, 2009) winner 2010 Millia Davenport Publication Award; *The Golden Age* (V&A, 2007); *RRRIPP!! Paper Fashion* (Benaki Museum, 2007); *Old Clothes, New Looks* (Berg, 2005); *Fashion: A Canadian Perspective* (University of Toronto, 2004); and *Couture & Commerce* (University of British Columbia and ROM, 2001) Clio Award for Ontario history. She is exhibition editor for *Fashion Theory*. Her current research is funded by the Social Science Humanities Research Council of Canada, http://www.rom.on.ca/en/collections-research/rom-staff/alexandra-palmer.

Susan J. Palmer is a research fellow at McGill University and an affiliate professor in the Religion Department at Concordia University in Montreal. Palmer is the author of over ten books/edited volumes, among them *Moon Sisters, Krishna Mothers, Rajneesh Lovers* (Syracuse, 1994); *The New Heretics of France* (Oxford University Press, 2011); *Aliens Adored: Raël's UFO Religion* (Rutgers, 2004); *Millennium, Messiahs and Mayhem* (Routledge, 1998, with Thomas Robbins); and *Storming Zion: Government Raids on Religious Communities* (Oxford University Press 2016, with Stuart Wright).

Véronique Pouillard is Associate Professor in the History of Modern Europe, University of Oslo. She was previously been affiliated with the Université Libre de Bruxelles, Columbia University, and Harvard University. She is currently preparing a monograph on the transatlantic history of the fashion industry.

Simona Segre Reinach is a cultural anthropologist and Associate Professor of Fashion Studies at Bologna University and teaches in Fashion Curation Studies. She has written on fashion from a global perspective in *Berg Encyclopedia of World Dress and Fashion* (2010), *The Fashion History Reader* (2010), *Fashion Media. Past and Present* (2013), as well as published articles in *Fashion Theory, Fashion Practice, Business and Economic History*, and *Critical Studies in Fashion and Beauty*. She authored: *Mode in Italy. Una lettura antropologica* (Guerini 1999), *La moda. Un'introduzione* (Laterza 2005 and 2010), *Orientalismi. La moda nel mercato globale* (Meltemi 2006), *Un mondo di mode* (Laterza 2011). She is on the Editorial Board of *Fashion Theory* and *The International Journal of Fashion Studies*. She has conducted fieldwork in China on Sino-Italian joint ventures contributing to a collaborative study in Cultural Anthropology. Forthcoming is an edited volume, *Making Fashion in Multiple Chinas* (I.B. Tauris, with Wessie Ling). http://www.unibo.it/docenti/simona.segrereinach.

Jane Tynan is a senior lecturer at Central Saint Martins, University of the Arts London, where she leads the MA Fashion Critical Studies. She has published on fashion and identity, style as resistance, the history of the trench coat and transformations in military and police uniform design. Her recent book, *British Army Uniform and the First World War: Men in Khaki* (2013) traces the social, economic and cultural significance of khaki uniform in the First World War. Her forthcoming book is an edited volume on the global context for the development of modern uniform.

Annamari Vänskä is Adjunct Professor of Fashion at the University of Turku where she is Collegium Researcher at Turku Institute for Advanced Studies. She is also Adjunct Professor of Art History and Gender Studies at the University of Helsinki where she was named Adjunct Professor of the Year 2012. Vänskä has published widely on fashion and visual culture. Her book, *Muodikas lapsuus: Lapset muotikuvissa* (Fashionable Childhood: Children in Fashion Advertising, Gaudeamus, 2012), was awarded an honorary mention as the Best Scientific Book of the Year and is forthcoming in English. She is currently researching fashion consumption and pet dogs. Vänskä is also an independent columnist and curator of *Boutique—Where Art and Fashion Meet* (2012) that opened in Helsinki and traveled to New York, Washington, Tokyo, and Berlin (2016).

Susan Ward is an independent curator and researcher, specializing in textiles, fashion, and design history, with personal interests in twentieth-century modern design, fashion, and retailing. From 1993–2009 she was a Curatorial Research Fellow at Boston's Museum of Fine Arts where she contributed to numerous exhibitions and publications, including *The Look: Photographs by Horst and Hoyningen-Huene* (2001), and *Fashion Show: Paris Collections 2006* (2006). She was later a co-curator (and catalog co-author) for the 2011 exhibition *Knoll Textiles, 1945–2010* at the Bard Graduate Center in NYC. Over the past fifteen years she has worked on a number of research and exhibition projects on the history of Marimekko, the Design Research store, and mid-century modern architecture in the Boston area. She is currently assisting Wanda Corn with research on the wardrobe of artist Georgia O'Keeffe, for the forthcoming exhibition and book *Georgia O'Keeffe: Living Modern* (Brooklyn Museum, 2017).

INDEX

Bold denotes image

A-POC 151 *see* Issey Miyake
Abraham 31
Act Up 126
Adidas 81
Adrover, Miguel 15–18
aerobics 36, 81,
Africa 5, 87, 153, 156, 158, 163, 165,
    166, 168, 169
African wax print 156, **157**
African-American 75, 86–7, 106, 195
After Leaving Mr Mackenzie (1930) *see* Rhys,
    Jean
Age of Innocence, The (1920) *see* Wharton,
    Edith
AIDS 12, 80, 122, 126
Alaïa, Azzedine **3**, 39
Alexander McQueen (firm) 14, 129
Alix 176, 178 *see* Madame Grès
American Psycho (1991) *see* Ellis, Bret Easton
androgynous 63, 75, 81, 105
Andy Warhol's Factory 119
Anne Klein (firm) 206
Anthroposophy 86 *see* Steiner, Rodolf
anti-establishment 119, 188
anti-fashion 5, 119–21, 148, 193
Antwerp 43, 59
Antwerp Six 59
apocalypse 95, 102, 104
Appadurai, Arjun 166
    Modernity at Large: Cultural Dimensions
      of Globalization (1996)
appropriation 15, 18, 65, 143, 163
Arai, Junichi 39 *see* Nuno
Arden, Elizabeth 54
Armani, Giorgio 37, 124 *see* Giorgio Armani
Army of Mary 10, 94–8
Arora, Mannish for Paco Rabanne (2011–12)
    166

artificial 69, 124, 179
    fibers 22, 23, 37 *see* rayon
    gender 13, 119–21
Ashley, Laura 37
Asia 5, 27, 51, 86, 151, 153, 154, 164,
Asian 49, 51, 59, 61, 151, 156
    American designers 165
    interpretation 156
    modernity 162
Atwood, Margaret 206–7
    Dancing Girls and Other Stories (1977)
      206
    Oryx and Crake (2003) 207
Augustabernard 176
Avedon, Richard 179–81, 182, 184

bachelor 9, 19, 72–3, 116–17
Balenciaga, Cristóbal 31, 71
Balmain, Pierre 56
Banjo: A Story Without A Plot (1929) *see*
    McKay, Claude
Barnes, Djuna 200–1, 210
    Book of Repulsive Women (1915) 200
    Ladies Almanack (1928) 200
    Nightwood (1936) 201
Barney, Natalie 107, 200, 206
Barthes, Roland 52, 131, 191, 192
    Système de la mode (1967)
    Fashion System, The (trans. 1990)
    Language of Clothing, The (2006)
bathing suit *see* swimwear
Baudelaire, Charles 171–2
Baudrillard, Jean 122
beat girl 204
Beatles, The 36, 118
beatnik 207–8
Benjamin, Walter 192
Biba 57

bikini 102, 164, 180 *see* swimwear
bikini mania 180
black masculinity 196
Blahnik, Manolo 126
Blass, Bill 78
Blavatsky, Madame 86
bloomers 64, 65 *see* trousers for women
blue jeans *see* jeans
Blumenfeld, Erwin 179
Boateng, Ozwald for Givenchy (2004–7)
    166
body building 4, 78, 80
body stocking *see* bodysuit
bodysuit 34, 124
Bond, James 9, 19, 204, 205, 206 *see*
    Fleming, Ian
Book of Repulsive Women (1915) *see* Barnes,
    Djuna
boots, 75, 197
    Clark's 118
    Doc Marten 122
    Frye 75
    hiking 78
    knee-high 79
    motorcycle boots, 75
Botox 83 *see* cosmetic surgery
boubou 158
Boulet, Denise 64
Bourdieu, Pierre 145, 149
Bourdin, Guy 183
Boussac, Marcel 55
boutique 24, 31, 36, 49, 55, 57, **58**, 65, **116**
    Bazaar 57
    Granny Takes A Trip 36
bowler hat, 138
bra *see* Rudi Gernreich's "No-Bra" 36
bra, *brasserie* 36, 72, 102, 117
brand 4, 37, 48, 49, 81, 125, 126–7, 137,
    144, 146, 156, 158, 164–6, 168, 184,
    186, 192, 206 *see* logo
    affiliation 14
    beauty 69
    ecological 41
    licensing 56
    luxury 5, 56, 59, 145
branded fiber 36
    goods 19
branding in *American Psycho* 206

Brando, Marlon 63, 75, 117
Braveheart (1995) film 12
Brazil 164
Bread Givers (1925) *see* Yerierska, Anzia
Breakfast at Tiffany's (1958) *see* Capote,
    Truman
Breakfast at Tiffany's (1960) *see* Capote,
    Truman
Breward, Christopher 111, 136, 137
Brinkley, Christie *see* model
British Empire 153
British military 140
Brodovitch, Alexy 178
Brooks, Romaine 107, 126, **200**
bulimia 9
Burberry 127, 129, 148
burkini 11
Butler, Judith 107, 125
Butterick patterns 57

C&A 61
caftan 15 *see* kaftan
Callot Soeurs 47, 64, 161, **173**, **177**
Calvin Klein (firm) 37, 63, 78 125, 127,
    185, **187**
    CK One 63, 81
    jeans 34, 63, **125**, 126
    Obsession campaign 1992, 186, **187**
    underwear 18, 63, 81, 126, **185**, 186
Camilleri, Izzy 19, **20** *see* IZ Adaptive
Campbell, Naomi *see* model
Canada 52, 56, 99, 100, 102, 165, 207
Capote, Truman 19, **203**, 204
    Breakfast at Tiffany's (1958) book 203
    Breakfast at Tiffany's (1960) film 203
Cardin, Pierre 31
Cardine 31 see Pierre Cardin
Carlyle, Thomas 88
Carnegie, Hattie
Carnegie, Ladies' Hatter 49
Cashin, Bonnie 30
casino 179
Casino Royale (1953) *see* Fleming, Ian
Catalina 30 *see* swimwear
catsuit *see* bodysuit
Caucasian 125
Celanese 22
celebrity 5, 78, 80–1, 181, 186–7, 207, 210

cellulose 22
Chambre Syndicale de la Couture Parisienne
    53–4, 55
Chanel (firm) 24, 30, 45, 49, 55, 59, 65,
    66, 108, 143, 201, 204, 210 *see* little
    black dress
Chanel suit **25, 109**
Chanel, Gabrielle "Coco" 23, **25**, 49, 113, 153
Chanel, Karl Lagerfeld for (1983–) 59
Chase, Edna Wolman 54
Chelsea Girl 118
Chéruit **175**, 175
child labor 51
childhood 127
children's clothing 14, 137
China 5, 59, 146, 151, 154, 156, 158,
    162, 164
Christian Dior (firm) 5, 28, **29, 116**
Christian Dior *haute couture* 10, 55–6, 59, 63,
    71–2, 113, **114**, 127, 153, **167**, 204,
    206
Christian Motorcyle League 98
Christiansen, Helena *see* model
Civil Rights 75
Claire McCardell (firm) 30, 54 *see* McCardell,
    Claire
Clark, Ossie 57
class, blue-collar 14, 138, **139**
class, white-collar 14, 107, 138, **139**
Colcombet 27
Cole of California 30 *see* swimwear
Cole-Haan 206
colonial 15, 75, 151, 154, 160–1, 162
Coltrane, John 208
Comedy: American Style (1933) *see* Fauset,
    Jessie Redmon
Commes des Garçons *see* Kawakubo, Rei
Comptoir des Cotonnier 61
Connery, Sean **205**
conspicuous consumption 5, 14, 37, 144–5,
    146, 149
consumer capitalism 140, 148
consumer culture 145, 146, 148–50
Cook, the Thief, His Wife & Her Lover, The
    (1989) film 124
copying 47, 53
copyist 52
copyright 4, 47–8

cosmetic surgery 8–9, 63, 70, 80, 83
cotton 4, 22, 23, 24, 26, 28, 30, 34, 36, 37,
    42, 160, 206 *see* T-shirt
Cotton Incorporated 37
Courrèges (firm) **32**, 34, 75, **76**, 117
Courrèges, André 31, 117 *see* Courrèges
Courtaulds 23
Crane, Diana 133–4, 143, 165
Crawford, Cindy *see* model
Crawford, Morris De Camp 44, 55
crimplene 31
cross-dressing 111, 113, 126, 193, 197–201
cross-gender 125, 198, 201
Crying Game, The (1992) film 124
cycling fashion 81

Daché, Lilly 54
Dacron 28
Dahl, Sophie *see* model
Dahl-Wolf, Louise 179
Dancing Girls and Other Stories (1977) *see*
    Atwood, Margaret
Daughters of Bilitis 115
Davis, Fred 131, 143,
de Beauvoir, Simone 114
    Second Sex (1949)
de Meyer, Adolph 172–4, **173**, 179
Dean, James 63, 75, 117
Delon, Alain 63
Delphos 161 *see* Fortuny
Demarchelier, Patrick 186
democratized fashion 56, 119, 191
denim 30, 34, 36, 39, 42, 72 *see* jeans
denim, stonewashed 35
department store 14, 44, 46–7, 54, 56, 113,
    133
Derrida, Jacques 122
Diaghilev, Serge 161
Diane von Fürstenberg (firm) 34 *see* wrap
    dress
digital photography 18, 171, 188,
digital textile printing **17**
Dior, Christian 55, 72, 114, 115, 153, 206
    homosexual 115, 124
disco 4, 34, 36, 78–9
dishdasha 87
djellaba 161
Dolce & Gabanna 126

double knit 37
Doukhobors 99–101
Dovima *see* model
Dow Chemical 27
drag 108, 115, 117, 119
drag king 125
drag queen 119, 122, 125
Dreiser, Theodore, 193, 195, 210
   Sister Carrie (1900) 193
dress paper 34
   sack 31
   vintage 14, 19, 207, 209–10
   wrap 79
   see T-shirt dress
DuPont 23, 27–8, 34, 36, *see* Orlon
Dworkin, Andrea 134

ecosystems 6, 43, 52–3, 59
Ellis, Bret Easton 206
   American Psycho (1991)
Emilio Pucci Emilioform 30
energy crisis 37
ethnic 15, 117, 153–4, 158, 160–3, 168, 195
ethnicity 165
Eurocentric 160
euro-centrism
Eurythmics 86
Evangelista, Linda *see* model
Evans, Caroline 135, 148
Evans, Walker 67
ex-colonial 163
excercise fashion *see* aerobics, cycling, pilates,
   spin, yoga, zumba

fake 47 *see* copyright
Farmer, Frances 207, **208**
Fascism 14, 68–9, 70, 72, 111, 140 *see* Third
   Reich, Nazism
fashion 43, 56, 59, 113
fashion forecast 47, 54
Fashion Group 54
fashion school Antwerp Academy of Fine
   Arts 59
   Central Saint Martins, London 59, 257
   La Cambre, Brussels 59
fashion system 2, 5, 6, 20, 30, 52, 61,
   83, 124, 132–3, 137, 148, 153,
   158

Fashion System, The (1967) *see* Barthes,
   Roland
Fashion Zeitgeist (2005) *see* Vinken, Barbara
fast fashion 5, 14, 41, 52, 61, 144 *see* Uniqlo,
   H&M, Zara
Fath, Jacques 56
Fauset, Jessie Redmon 195, 197
   *The Chinaberry Tree: Novel of American
      Life* (1931) 195
   Comedy: American Style (1933) 195
Fee, Sarah 2
female body 13, 63, 70, 80, 113
Ferragamo, Salvatore 166
Ferretti, Alberta 127
fez 87
Field, Patricia 126
fiber revolution 21, 28, 36
First World War 1, 11, 1, 22, 41, 65, 67, 107,
   108, 172, 191, **198**, 210, 255, 257
fitness movement 4, 34, 63, 69, 80–1
Fitzgerald, F. Scott 197, 198, **199**, 210
flapper 11, 63, 65, 67, 108, 175, 197, 210
fleece 41
   cotton 34
   polyester 41
Fleming, Ian 204, 206
   Casino Royale (1953) 204
Florence, Italy 56
Flügel, J.C. 1, 136, 192
Fonda, Jane 39
Fordism 143–4
Fortuny, Mariano 64, 161
Fox, The (1922) *see* Lawrence, D.H.
Friedan, Betty 134, **135**
   The Feminine Mystique (1963)
Frissell, Toni 179
Futurism 111, 148, 174
futuristic 31, 117

Galeries Lafayette 56
Galliano, John 10, 59, **167**
Galliano, John for Dior (1996–2011) 10,
   59, **167**
Galliano, John for Givenchy (1995–6) 59
Galliano, John for Maison Margiela
   (2014–) 59
Gandapur, Sarah **159**
Gandhi, Mahatma 151

garter belt 34 *see* underwear
Gaultier, Jean Paul 9, 81, 83, 122, 124
Gay and Lesbian Liberation 75, 115, 117
gay men 75, 78, 111, 113–15, 119, 122
   porn 18
   utopia 78
Gay Pride 86, 117
Gell, Wendy for Anne Klein 201
gender bending 13, 120–2, 183, 210
gender equality 102
   roles 75, 85, 111, 115, 120
   stereotypes 68
   neutral 125
   religious 85, 95
genderblending 122
genderfuck 119
genderless 124
geriatric clothing 19
Germaine Lecomte (firm) 177
German Democratic Republic (GDR) 146
Gernreich, Rudi 34, 49 *see* Rudi Gernreich
Gibson, Charles Dana 64
Giguère, Mary-Paul 94–8
Giorgio Armani (firm) **38**, 127 *see* Armani,
   Giorgio
girdle 26, 34, 36, 72 *see* underwear
Givenchy, Alexander McQueen for
   (1996–2001) 59
Givenchy, Hubert de 59, 166
Givenchy, John Galliano for (1995–6) 59
Givenchy, Ozwald Boateng for (2004–7) 166
glam-rocker 117 *see* rocker
global brands 59
global economy 5, 153
global style 15, 34, 146, 154, 160–6, 168
globalization 43, 133, 156–9, 166
Good Morning, Midnight (1939) *see* Rhys,
   Jean
Goodbye to Berlin (1939) *see* Isherwood,
   Christopher
Gore-Tex 41
Great Depression, The 23, 67
Great Gatsby, The (1925) 197–8
great masculine renunciation, the 108,
   136, 154
Greco-Roman 9, 11, 68, 70
Greenaway, Peter 12
Grés, Madam 24, 176 *see* Alix

grunge 19, 124, 188
Gucci 126, 127
Gurley-Brown, Helen 117
   Sex and the Single Girl (1962)
gym 70
gym body 9
gym culture 80, 81

H&M 61 *see* fast fashion
Haight-Ashbury, San Francisco 191
Halberstam, Judith 125
Halston, 34, 36, 78
Hanae Mori (firm) 59
harem pants *see* trousers for women
Harlem 206
Harlem Renaissance 195
Harmon Knitwear 34 *see* Gernreich, Rudi
Harris, Paul 187
Hartnell, Norman 56
hat 131, 137, 138 *see* bowler hat
hat, abandoning 108
hat, marker of class 138
hat, occupational 138
haute couture 10, 45–7, 52, 53–4, 55, 56, 59,
   83, 127, 153, 161
Hawaiian shirt 30 *see* shirt aloha
Hawes, Elizabeth 49
Head, Edith 49, 54, 113
headband 80
headscarf 15, 164 *see* hijab
Hechter, Daniel 56
Heim, Jacques 24
Hellenic body ideal 63, 72
Hemingway, Ernest 201, 204, 210
   Sun Also Rises, The (1926) 201, 204
heroin chic 9, 64, 81, 187
Herzigova, Elvira *see* model
heteronormative masculinity 186
high street fashion 148
High-Performance Microfibers 41
hijab 85, 87, **164**, **169**
Hindu 98
hip-hop 124
hippie 10, 15, 117, 161, **162**, 191, 207
Hitler, Adolf 68, 111
Hollywood 1, **26**, 49, 54, 63, 67, 72, 93,
   113, 207
home-sewing 36, 44

homosexual 13, 111, 115, 122
  consumer 125
  fashion designers 1
  identity 122
homosexuality 111, 115, 125, 126, 209
Horst, Horst P. 176, **178**, 179
hot pants 8, 119
Hoyningen-Huene, George 176, **177**
Hulanicki, Barbara 57

ideal body shape 63, 64–7, 69, 70, 75,
  78–9, 83
Iman *see* model
immigrant 56, 195
inconspicuous consumption 136
India 5, 59, 98, 102, 151, 160, 163, 164
International Raëlian Movement 99, 101–4
  see Raël
Isherwood, Christopher 19, 67, 143, 204
  Goodbye to Berlin (1939) 67, 204
Islam 85, 87
Islamic dress 163
Issey Miyake (firm) *Pleats Please* 39, 40, 161
  see Miyake, Issey
Issey Miyake *A-POC* 151 *see* Miyake, Issey
It girl 63
Italian manufacturers 31
Italy 57, 70
IZ Adaptive 19, **20**

Jacobson, Elie 56
James, Charles 5, **21**
Jantzen Knitting 24 *see* swimwear
Japan 15, 27, 39, 54, 102, **104**, 151, 154,
  162, 166
Japanese revolution 5, 59, 161–2
Jazz (1992) *see* Morrison, Toni
Jean Patou (firm) 65, 108, **202**
Jean Paul Gaultier (firm) 9, **10**, 11, 14, 39, **82**,
  83, **123**
Jeanne Lanvin (firm) 45, 46, 53, 54
Jeanne Paquin (firm) **194**
jeans 2, 14, 31–6, **57**, 65, 72, 75, 78, 117,
  143, 156, 204 *see* denim
  Calvin Klein 63, 125
  clean 118
  designer 39
  gendered 129

Levi's 122
  rebellion 14
jogging suit 34 *see* suit
Jourdan, Charles
jumpsuit 140
jupe-culotte, jupe-pantalon, jupe-sultane see
  trousers for women
Just Kids (2010) *see* Smith, Patti

kaftan 15
Kamali, Norma 34
Kanengeiser, Henrietta *see* Carnegie,
  Hattie
Kawakubo, Rei 39, 124, 162 *see* Rei
  Kawakubo
Kawamura, Yuniya 52
Kenzo, Takada 59
Khanh, Emmanuelle 56
kimono 39, 151, 161
King, Isis *see* model
King, Martin Luther 87
Klein, Calvin 12 *see* Calvin Klein
knickerbockers 110 *see* suits
Knight, Nick 188–9
knit 4, 36, 39, 40, 206
knitting machine 30, 40
knitwear 21, 23–5, 30, 34, 56
Korean dress 152 *see* hanbok
Kramer, Hilton 183

L-85, USA 27 *see* Utility scheme, UK
la garçonne 108
Lacoste, René, 58
Ladies Almanack (1928) *see* Barnes, Djuna
Lady Gaga 81
Lagerfeld, Karl 59 *see* Chanel
Lakota Sioux 98
land girl 197, **198**
Landshoff, Herman 197
Lanvin, Jeanne 45 *see* Jeanne Lanvin
Lastex 26, **26**, 36
Lauren, Ralph 37 *see* Ralph Lauren
Lawrence, D.H. 197, 198
  Women in Love (1920) 197
  Fox, The (1922) 197
LBD *see* little black dress
Le Château 58
Le Coin de Sports 65 *see* Patou, Jean

le smoking see Yves Saint Laurent
leather jacket 14, 19, **20**, 117, 129
leggings 8, 39, 80, 81
leisure suit *see* suit
Lelong, Lucien 49, 54–5 *see* Lucien Lelong
lesbian 13, 75, 78, 107, 111, 113, 115, 117, 118, 122, 124
    chic 126
    culture 200
    designer 124
Levi Strauss & *see* jeans Co. 30
Levi's 122
LGBT 126
little black dress 4, 65, 67, 143, 201–4
logo 14, 48, 144, 184 *see* brand
London 57–8, 144
London Fashion Week, 43
Lopez, Antonio 7
Louboutin, Christian 126
Louis Dell'Ollio (firm) 206
Louis Vuitton 166
Lubovska, Desiree **202**
Lucien Lelong (firm) 45, 47, 54 *see* Lelong, Lucien
Lurex 4, 28, 119
luxury 43, 78, 156, 166, 178, 204, 210
    brand 145, 146
    goods, product 34, 143, 144, 145, 146, 153, 206
    textile 23, 36, 39
    trade 31, 59, 160
Lycra 28, 36–9, 119
Lyotard, Jean-François 122

macho look 122
Madeleine Vionnet (firm) 24, 47, 48, 49, 54, 64, 176 *see* Vionnet, Madeleine
Madonna *Blond Ambition* tour (1990) 124
magazine,
    Dazed & Confused 125, 188
    Esquire 187
    Face, The 125
    Harper's Bazaar 54, 57, 178–9
    Hustler 63
    i-D 125, 188
    Playboy 63, 73, 116
    Purple 188
    Vanity Fair 172, 174

Vogue 9, 54, 143, 172, 174, 176, 179, 183, 201
Maison Margiela (firm) 4, 59 *see* Margiela, Martin
Malden Mills 41, *see* Polartec
Man Ray 179, 210
Mandarom 89–91
man-made fibers 4, 21, 22–3, 26, 27–8, 36, 37, 40, 117
Mansfield, Jayne 63, 72
Mao jackets 161
Mapplethorpe, Robert 207–10, **209**
Margaine-Lacroix (firm) 64
Margiela, Martin 59 *see* Maison Margiela
Marimekko 34
Marlboro Man 9, 63, 72
Marshall Plan 30
Marxist 166
Mattachine Society 115
McCardell, Claire 29, 49 *see* Claire McCardell
McKay, Claude 195–6, **196**
    Banjo: A Story Without A Plot (1929)
McQueen, Alexander 14
McQueen, Alexander for Givenchy (1996–2001) 59
Meisel, Steven **125**, 126, 186
men's dress reform 148
Men's Dress Reform Party 9, 65
metrosexual 64, 81, 126
Middle East 5, 8, 15, 86
Milan 43, 56, 133, **155**
Minagawa, Makiko 39
mini-skirt 8, 11, 34, 75, 79
missionaries 162
Missoni, Ottavio and Rosita (Tai) 34
Miyake, Issey 39, 161–3
model,
    Brooke Shields 78, 84 *see* Calvin Klein
    Christie Brinkely 80
    Cindy Crawford 80
    Claudia Schiffer 63
    Dovima 179
    Elvira Herzigova 80
    Helena Christiansen 80
    Iman 12
    Isis King 64
    Jean Shrimpton 180, 181, **182**

Kate Moss 81, **125**, 126, 186–7, 187
Linda Evangelista 80
Naomi Campbell 80
Sophie Dahl 9
Twiggy 64, 77, 77
Verushka **184**
modernism and fashion 69, 176, 191
*Modernity at Large: Cultural Dimensions of
    Globalization* (1996) *see* Appadurai,
    Arjun
monokini **8**, 49 *see* Rudi Gernreich
Monroe, Marilyn 8, 63, 72
Morrison, Toni 206
    Jazz (1992)
Moss, Kate *see* Calvin Klein, heroin chic,
    model
Mumbai 43
Munkacsi, Martin 179, **180**, 181, 188
Munro, Alice 207
    Who Do You Think You Are? (1978)
muscular body 9, 63, 68, 72, 78, 80, 122,
    184, 204
Musée Albert Khan 153
Mussolini, Benito 70

naked 8, 11, **68**, 70, 88, 99, 100, 101–2,
    104–5, 151, 186 *see* skyclad
    march Dukhobors 11, 99
    policemen 100
Nation of Islam 87
Nation of Yahweh 91–3
natural fibers 22–3, **38**, 36–41 *see* non-natural
    fibers
Nazi, Nazism 55, 69, 70, 111
necktie 79
Nehru collar 97
    jacket 36
Nehru, Pandit Jawaharlal 151
neoprene 39
New Balance 81
New Look 28, 55, 63, 71–2, **71**, 113–15, 179
new man 105, 108, 116, 122, 186
new woman 11, 105, 122,
New York City **12**, 51, **185**, **207**
New York fashion industry 49
Newton, Helmet 18, 126, 181–4, **184**, 186
Nightwood (1936) *see* Barnes, Djuna
Nike 81

Noble Drew Ali's Moorish Temple 87
non-gay men 77
non-heterosexuality 124, 126
non-natural fibers 119
non-Western 151, 153–4, 156, 164, 166
Norman, Ruth E. 93–4 *see* Unarius Academy
    of Science
North America 43, 70, 86
Nuno Corporation 39 *see* Sudo, Reiko
nylon
    clothing **3**, **4**, 22, 27–8, 34, 36 **10**, **29**, **35**,
        77
    Qiana by DuPont **35**
    stockings, 27, 101 *see* tights

Oeko-Tex Association 41
Oriental, Poiret 64
Oriental woman 69
Orientalish appropriation 65
orientalism 160–6
*Orientalism: Western Representations of the
    Orient* (1978) *see* Said, Edward
Orientalist styles 64
Orlando (1992) film 124
Orlon 28 *see* DuPont
Oryx and Crake (2003) *see* Atwood,
    Margaret

Paco Rabanne (firm) 166 *see* Arora, Manish;
    Rabbane, Paco
pants *see* trousers
pantsuit *see* suit
Paquin, Jeanne 65 *see* Jeanne Paquin
Paramount Studios 49
Parrish, Amos 47
Patagonia (firm) 41
Patou, Jean 65, 108, *see* Jean Patou
Paul Poiret (firm) 5, **6**, 8, **44**, 65, 161, 193,
    194
Paul Poiret perfume *Rosine* 47
Paul Stuart (firm) 206
Peacock Revolution 36, 118
Pendleton Woolen Mills 30
Penn, Irving 181
performance textiles
permanent press cotton 28
pet fashion **128**, 129
Philippe et Gaston 55

Pictorialist movement 172
Pierre Cardin (firm) 31, **33**, 34, 36, 56, 117, 181, **182**
pilates fashion, 81
Pill, the 11, 117
playboy 19, 73–4, 115–17
Pleats Please 39, 161 *see* Miyake
Poiret, Paul 47, 64, 153, 161 *see* Paul Poiret, *jupe-culotte*
polaroid
Polartec 41 *see* fleece
poly-centrism 153
Poor Chic 124
Pope, Virginia 54
porn body 9, 81
porno-chic 183
post-colonial 163–4
postfashion 122
postmodermism 122, 191, 197
prison 91, 100, 115
prision uniform *see* uniform
prisoner 10, 100, 140, 151,
Pucci, Emilio 30
punk 10, 119, **121**, 124, 148, **149**, 191
PVC (vinyl) 31, **33**

Quant, Mary 31, 34, 57, 75, 118, **118**
queer 75, 78, 80
Queer Nation 126
queer politics 126
queering 197
queering fashion 124–6

Rabanne, Paco 31 *see* Paco Rabanne
Raël 10, 101–4, 105
Yes to Human Cloning: Immortality Thanks to Science (2001) 102
see International Raëlian Movement
Ralph Lauren (firm) 206 *see* Lauren, Ralph
Rana Plaza 5, 52
Rastafarian 87, **88**, 98
rayon (artificial silk) 21, 22–3, 26–7, 28, 29, 30, 39, 41
Rebel Without a Cause (1955) film 75, 117
regulation clothing *see* uniform
Rei Kawakubo (firm) 5, 59, 60, 161 *see* Kawakubo, Rei

Rhodophane 27
Rhys, Jean 191, 202–3
After Leaving Mr Mackenzie (1930) 202–3
Good Morning, Midnight (1939) 203
Rimala, Annika 34 *see* Marimekko
Ritts, Herb 186
rocker 117 *see* glam rocker
Rodier 23
kasha 23
Rome, Italy 56, 68
Rosenstein, Nettie 49
Rosier, Michèle 56
Rosine, see Paul Poiret
Rubinstein, Helena 54
Rudi Gernreich (frim) 8, 31, 36 *see* Gernreich, Rudi

*sadhu*s 98
Said, Edward 154
Orientalism: Western Representations of the Orient (1978)
sailor 122, 195 *see* uniform sailor
Saint Laurent, Yves 153 *see* Yves Saint Laurent
salsa dancing, 81
Sander, Jil 124
sari 15, 151, 160, 161, **170**
Savile Row *see* suit
Schiaparelli (firm) 54, 111
Schiaparelli, Elsa 24, 27, 55, 111, 113, 210
Schiffer, Claudia *see* model
Second Sex, The (1949) *see* de Beauvoir, Simone
Second World War 13, 27, 30, 54, 55, 65, 67, 70, 86, 97, 113, 138, 165, 179, 191, 206–7
second-hand clothes 14, 15, 19, 156, 207 *see* vintage
sewing machine 45, 49, 134
Sex and the City 126–9 *see* Patricia Field
Sex and the Single Girl (1962) *see* Gurley-Brown, Helen
sexologist 111
shalwar 87
Shaver, Dorothy 54
shawl 15
Shields, Brooke *see* model

shirt 19, 28, 30, 36, 37, 65, 73, 75, 78,
    115, 119, 138, 198, 206, 210 *see* shirt
    dress
  aloha 30
  black Italian Fascist 141
  blue jean 195
  collar 79
  dress 36
  flannel 78
  halter-neck shirt 79
  polo 118
  sports 24, 30
  western 72
  white 209
  with Nehru collar 161
  without, shirtless 122, 183
Shrimpton, Jean see model
Silicon Valley 49
silicone cheekbones 80
Silk Road 160
Simmel, Georg 15, 132, 192
Simpson, Adele 54
Sister Carrie (1900) *see* Dreiser, Theodore
skyclad 99, 104–5 *see* naked
slavery 75
slaves 162–3
Slimane, Hedi 5 *see* Yves Saint Laurent
Smith, Patti 19, 191, 207–10, **209**
  Just Kids (2010) 207–9
Snow, Carmel 54, 178–9
Sonia Rykiel (firm) *see* Rykiel, Sonia
Sorrenti, Mario **187**
South Asian, 163
space age 10, 31, **33**, 36–41
space suit 34, 101
Spandex 8, 28, 36, 79, 80 *see* Lycra
Spanx 9
spin, spinning, 81
sportswear 18, 23–5, 28–30, 39, 49, 54, 64,
    67, 108, 179
Springfield, Dusty 118
status symbol 30, 36, 145, 146
Steele, Valerie 65, 119
Steichen, Edward **48**, **50**, **109**, 174–6,
    175, 179
Steinem, Gloria **135**
Steiner, Rudolf 86
Stock Market Crash 1929 23, 111

stockings *see* nylon stockings
Stonewall riots 75
Straight photography 174
Studio 54 78–9
subcultural style 120, 148
subcultural theory 148
subculture 115, 117, 119, 122, 125, 144
Sudo, Reiko 39 *see* Nuno
suit 19, 23, 36, 113 *see* uniform
  Armani 124
  Chanel 4, **25**, 113
  industry 49
  jogging 34
  leisure suit 30, 36
  men's 29, 30, **38**, **58**, 72, 75, 87, 106, 109,
    110, 111, 113, 115, 118, 138, 193,
    196, 206
  pinstripe 122, **136**
  Savile Row 113
  Teddy Boys 75
  trousersuit/pantsuit 11, **12**, 15, **112**, 119
  women 3, 23, 28, 31, 83, 101, 113, 195
Sun Also Rises, The (1926) *see* Hemingway,
    Ernest
sustainable fashion 2, 20, 37, 41
sweatshirt 81
sweatshirt material (fleece) 34
swimwear 8, 24, 26, 26, 30, 34, 36 *see* bikini,
    burkini, wetsuit

T-shirt **4**, 9, **10**, 14, 34, 37, 75, 78, 117, 125,
    126, 156
  dress 30
  phase 51–2
Techno textiles 37–41
Teddy Boys 75
Teddy-look 117
Temple, Shirley 113
Tencel 41
The Chinaberry Tree: Novel of American Life
    (1931) *see* Fauset, Jessie Redmon
Theosophical Society 86
Thinsulate 41
tights 34, 81 *see* nylon stockings
Tingley, Katherine 86 *see* Theatrical Work of
    the Universal Brotherhood,
    Theosophical Society
Tobé Coller Davis 47

Tom of Finland 78, 122
trademark 4, 28, 37, 48, 174, 184
transgender 64
Triangle Shirtwaist Factory Fire 51
trickle-down model 43
trouser suit *see* suit
trousers 2, 8, 28, 30, 73, 75, 79, 110, 111,
        122, 206 *see* jumpsuit
trousers for women 108–11
    bloomer 64, 65
    harem pants, *jupe-culotte, jupe-pantalon,*
        jupe-sultane 8, 15, 64, 65
    trousersuit/pantsuit 11, **12**, 15, **112**, 119
Twiggy *see* model
Tyvek 34

Ultrasuede 36, 41
Unarius Academy of Science 93–4
underwear 18, 23, 63, 65, 81, 124, 126, 129,
        184, 186, 198, 201 *see* bra, garter belt,
        girdle, Spanx
uniform 2, 14, 36, 57, 78, 113, 122, 136,
        139–42, 143, 149, 156, 163
    Chanel 201
    land girl 197–8 *see* land girl
    military 88, 111
    prison uniform 140
    sailor 78, 109, 139 *see* sailor
    work 108, 138, 142–3 *see* class blue
        collar
uniformed body 111
uniformity 136
Union Carbide Corporation 31
Uniqlo 61 *see* fast fashion
unisex perfume *Le Sien* 65
United States of America 44, 52, 67, 72, 75,
        111, 115, 134, 153, 174
US Rubber Company 26
Utility Scheme, UK 27 *see* L-85
utopia 105, 106, 148, 161
    gay 78
utopian societies 86, 99

veil 15, 96, 97, 163, 203, 210
Versace (firm) 126, 127
Verushka *see* model
Vinken, Barbara 5, 122
    Fashion Zeitgeist (2005)

vintage 207, 209, 210 *see* second-hand clothes
Vionnet, Madeleine 24, 45 *see* Madeleine
        Vionnet
Vivienne Tam (firm) **17**
Vivienne Westwood (firm) 13, 121, 122 *see*
        Westwood, Vivienne
von Fürstenberg, Diane 34, 79, 79 *see* Diane
        von Fürstenberg
Vreeland, Diana 178

Wall Street Crash (1929) 111
Warden, John 58
Warhol, Andy 119
wartime restrictions 22, 27, 55, 56, 113
waste 5, 41, 119, 148 *see* zero waste
Weber, Bruce 184–6
Weinberg, Chester 35
Westwood, Vivienne 124 *see* Vivienne
        Westwood
wet look 31
wetsuit 39
Wharton, Edith 193, 195
    Age of Innocence, The (1920) 193–5
Whistler, James Abbot McNeill 174
Who, The 118
Who Do You Think You Are? (1978) *see*
        Munro, Alice
Wild One, The (1953) film 75
Wilde, Oscar 161
Wilson, Elizabeth 135, 192
Women in Love (1920) *see* Lawrence, D.H.
Women in Revolt (1971) film
Women's Liberation Movement 75, 117
wool 21, 22, 23, 24, 26, 27, 28, 31, 37,
        93, 206
    flannel 108, 111
    jersey 30, 34 201
Woolf, Virginia 201, 210
Woolmark 37, 41
Worth (firm) 46, 54 *see* Worth, Charles
        Frederick
Worth, Charles Frederick 59, 153 see
        Worth

Yahweh ben Yahweh 91, **92**, 93
Yahweh ben Yahweh ben Yahweh 11, 91
Yamamoto, Yohji 5, 39, 59, 162 *see* Yohi
        Yamamoto

Yes to Human Cloning: Immortality Thanks to Science (2001) *see* Raël
Yezierska, Anzia 195
    Bread Givers (1925)
yoga fashion 81
Yohji Yamamoto (firm) 161, 162 *see*
        Yamamoto, Yohji
youth culture 31, 74, 117–19, 148
Yteb, Mme 176

Yves Saint Laurent (firm) 5, **11**, 183 *see*
        Sliamane, Hedi; *le smoking*; Yves Saint
        Laurent
Yves Saint Laurent, Hedi Slimane for
        (2012–16) 5

Zara 61
zero waste 20
zumba fashion 81